Unravel

Rebecca S Lazaro

Unravel

This is a work of fiction. Names, characters, organisations, places, events and incidents are products of the authors imagination.

Text Copyright © 2016 Rebecca S Lazaro

All rights reserved

No part of this book may be reproduced, or stored in a retrieval system, or transmitted in any form or by any means, electronic, mechanical, photocopying, recording, or otherwise, without express written permission of the author and publisher.

Cover art by Lee Fowler 2016

Unravel

Prologue

Maria Calver's gaze swung, loose with codeine, down to the fresh plaster cast enveloping her left forearm, and she exhaled with self-pity and weariness. Her body slumped against the red brick exterior wall of Gloucester Royal Hospital's accident and emergency department with a combination of aching numbness and hollow, dazed confusion resulting from nearly thirty hours without sleep; a night loaded with drama, crisis, and harsh, unrelenting police questions. The fracture would heal, but everything else in Maria's life had broken irreparably.

Her initial arrest, detained at the police station, had developed into a full investigation after Maria stiffly denied the accusations against her. The police, passing smirks and raising eyebrows, had insufficient evidence to charge her and released her on bail; acknowledging they couldn't keep her while her arm required medical attention.

Sheltering from the late morning sunshine, that sweltering July day, Maria waited neither patiently nor impatiently for her ride home: she just stood there, shivering feebly with exhaustion and nerves. She couldn't drive now anyway; along with her splintered arm, the memory of her beloved, smashed-in car returned to her in painful waves.

Clutching around her waist, Maria winced a short groan of discomfort in her throat, embarrassed in front of strangers observing her as they moved through the automatic doors of A&E. She lowered her head, praying no one would recognise her as *that* teacher from *that* school, and as her black hair fell in unkempt, ragged curls beside her face, Maria realised, though the events of last night felt like days ago, it was too soon for all that: she had that delightful notoriety yet to come. Her dishevelled dark suit, that had looked so smart twelve hours previously, was spoiled with dried blood and dirt, and her clinging, white silk shirt was now appallingly torn. She might have wept from shame if she hadn't been in shock.

Something in Maria's mind couldn't even think about what had happened, as if a wall of blissful ignorance arose, any thoughts of last night's confrontations simply bounced off and away before she could grasp them. That her ability to process events had been sodden by heavy painkillers was no surprise to Maria, but she knew the time to face the music was drawing close. Having put into effect a game of dominos, leaving behind her a trail of emotional trauma on the women in her life, Maria had, ultimately, been betrayed by the one female she would - had - fought tooth and nail for, and now she prepared herself to beg for the forgiveness of the only man she really cared for. The one whom she had forgotten was the most important to her: Ben was the one Maria had hurt the most. She needed him now, ironic though, since she had continuously discarded his advice, setting the stability of their relationship on a teetering edge. She had been foolish, and though the disaster had come in the form of heartbreak, and arm-break, Maria felt most ashamed of her stupidity in trying to convince Ben, who knew her too well, that she had everything under control when she didn't.

She had no idea how she was going to explain it all to him. The call she had made to him at six that morning had been sore enough: confessing the trouble she was in; the lies it was clear she had told him over, and over, laid bare. The guilty secret she had been harbouring – Ben had known from the start, but Maria had insisted her denial in ways that seemed now like a sickness, a nine-month long bout of madness. This scandalous affair against which, Benicio, her cousin, her best friend, had warned her. Now, Maria was helpless but to wait with a humble, bruised pride, hugging her sore, shattered body until he turned up to take her home.

Unravel

When the familiar silver Mercedes pulled into the car park to her left, Maria dropped her booted foot that had kept her backside from chilling against the cold wall of the hospital's pick-up point, and she lurched wearily towards Ben's car. He saw her approach and kept the engine running with a dip of his shades, but Maria could barely meet his eye contact, let alone greet him with a smile. She struggled inside the car door and held her plastered forearm as she sat, glancing only briefly at his expectant stare. It was bad enough she had had to wake him up so early, calling him away from what would have been a busy Saturday at his salon, but it was worse that he had to drive all the way from London simply because he was the only person she could call. She didn't need him to tell her what he thought of her, as his disapproving pout screamed it at her through every second of the ringing silence between them.

Ben rolled his car back out of the hospital grounds with a prolonged sigh through his nose, sensing Maria's depletion of energy and assuming his role in taking her home; it was possible Ben may have made the near three-hour journey to Gloucestershire only to be a silent chauffeur to her house. She could have got the bus, she could have got a taxi, but Maria needed him. She knew she couldn't be alone, to go home to the shambles of her life, in isolation, would be unbearable. She couldn't think - didn't want to think; her head would implode if left to stew in its own mess.

She had no other friends who would understand, and that was why she had kept her sordid little secret from everyone but Ben. Her initial admissions to her cousin had come early on when her actions were not reprehensible, but later, when she had knowingly behaved against social and moral codes, Maria had immediately regretted being honest with anyone: she should have kept her mouth shut. However, now it had all come out into the open, and Ben was waiting patiently, Maria knew it was time to start talking.

'So, was it a whole lynch-mob?' Ben asked, turning regularly with the flow of morning traffic out of Gloucester north-east towards Cheltenham. His accent was warmly reassuring, stronger than Maria's; he had moved from Sicily later than her, had been educated in the English schooling system less, and had kept company amongst other Europeans during his ten years in London. His slick hair was just as black, but his skin a tone darker and his eyes a deeper brown. Their mothers had been sisters, and they had bonded ever since Lizabetta, Maria's mother, passed away when she was eight. Maria lost contact with most of her family in Sicily when she moved to England with her father and brothers, except cousin Benicio, who followed her to London when he was old enough. Maria's father had since died in the British army. Her brothers all had families of their own and moved away. Now all she had was Ben.

Unravel

Maria stared out at the fields beyond the highway with a hard, resistant tear welling in her hazel eye. She had, momentarily, forgotten what must have been clear to Ben: that her face had been on the receiving end of last night's violent episode. Her nose and mouth had suffered purpling abrasions, though Maria's tired mood had sunk sufficiently for numbness to envelop her entire body. She caught her reflection in the wing mirror and saw the sharp lines of her eyelids merging with the dark shadows that ringed them; the stripes of her iris shortened by the dilation of her pupil; the thick hair of her brow pinched moodily towards the centre of her broad, Sicilian nose. Maria grimaced, her mouth pressed down in a sulk, her wide lips drained of colour around the ragged slice of angry redness where it had punctured between her own teeth and her colleague's fist. Sighing with heavy thought, Maria looked older than her thirty-two years; she felt older. Turning her cheek towards Ben's strong brown hand relaxed on the gearstick, and the soft material of his rolled up shirtsleeves, Maria steeled her will against the liquid urging from inside her tender eyes.

'Just a few upstanding members of society,' Maria mumbled through her swollen lips. Her voice cracked, tired from dehydration after hours spent defending herself to the police. She'd waited hours more in A&E, having only water to sip; the nurses had given her little else beyond basic treatment: just wrapped her arm, glued her lip, gave her some painkillers, and let her go. Maria didn't want sympathy; she expected nothing. She took full responsibility, although the idea that Nadia had called her bluff from start to finish left her reeling with a confusion that had her blankly reassessing everything she had felt, said and done during the whole school year. She knew it was too much to deal with, she had no idea what had happened. She just felt dead inside.

Ben checked his rear view mirror as his Mercedes pressed forward to overtake a casual Saturday morning driver. 'Was she there too?'

Maria pursed her lips then blinked hard to push out any impending threat of moisture. The question reverberated inside her head, repeating as it sprung away from the stubborn wall protecting her vulnerable core. She knew Nadia had been there, but it had not been the Nadia she had known, whether she was under the influence or not. Nadia's outburst had contradicted everything up to that point, thus destroying everything they ever had, if that was anything at all. Maria scoffed, what did she know? She had behaved like a fool: how could she be surprised Nadia had made a fool of her? Her skin creeping with goose bumps, Maria rubbed above the elbow of the arm she had raised trying to defend her precious car from attack.

'Yeah,' Maria confirmed with a breathy, shameful sigh. 'She fucked me over, Ben. She was just playing with me... all along.'

Creasing his eyes behind his shades failed to hide Ben's obvious wince for his cousin's pain, and Maria knew no pleasure crossed his lips as he grimaced. He needn't act shocked for her benefit: Ben had been the single flashing beacon of her conscience since the fiasco began and any display of self-righteousness would be cruel in the face of her utter embarrassment at ignoring his frequent warning signals.

'So what happens next?' Ben asked.

Maria sighed at length. 'Police want me to be assessed by a professional... you know... a psychologist... to decide whether or not I'm having a breakdown, or something...'

Ben said nothing more for the rest of the ride to Cheltenham and Maria was grateful for his sensitivity. She looked out longingly across to the park near her house, and this time acknowledged the glistening reflections of the sun on the car bonnets; she felt a little warmth on her cheek and tried to look forward to standing under a hot shower while Ben made some tea. However, preparing herself for the absence of her beloved, sweet dog, Leon, and the way he always skipped round in circles welcoming her in the door, made her eyes sting afresh: everything would be harder now, but although love had been lost, and love had been taken away, Maria had a sense it wasn't all over just yet.

Part One

Nine months previously

Chapter One

Maria poured herself a glass of cabernet sauvignon, and took a long sip, before setting the timer on the oven for the vegetarian pasta bake she had made, ready for Lois' arrival. Jazz music played from the stereo in her lounge as she tidied her kitchen. Her little dog, Leon, followed her around on elegant tiptoes, ever hungry for extra morsels, the gentle clipping of his nails on the floor both soothing and mildly irritating.

With some time to spare, Maria took her mini-Doberman-pinscher upstairs to give him the bath she had promised him that morning before she had left for work, and returned the concerned tweak of his eyebrows with a humouring pout as the water ran to his preferred temperature. She shampooed Leon's black and tan coat vigorously to give him as decent an exfoliation as she could with the short nails she had. He soon released prolonged groans of pleasure, his leg twitching as Maria scratched along his skinny back, and then tried to lick her nose when she laughed.

Half an hour later, Maria found herself frowning at the clock, wondering where her girlfriend was. The salad was dressed and wilting in the bowl, a new bottle of wine was uncorked and breathing the scents of the sizzling tomato and cheese dish filling the kitchen. Maria called Lois' mobile.

Lois Vaughan's harassed Australian accent, low and nasal, on a runaway train of flustered excuses, gave no impression of sorrow, and no apology for breaking their plans.

Maria gritted. 'You said you'd leave London two hours ago, you couldn't call me?'

'You know how it is when I'm in the middle of a piece, I can't just leave it!' Lois defended her behaviour as if Maria had no right to question the timing of her artistic endeavours.

Glaring at the dinner plates, so ready, and now so redundant, Maria sighed for her own slowly eroded patience, and suppressed once again her desire to tell Lois exactly what she could do with her *piece*. Lois was no artist; she was more corporate than creative. Over the three years they had been together, Lois had become even more money-oriented and career-obsessed with each success. The "industry", as she called her domain, was hungry for her ideas. Except, none of her work was original, just regurgitated media images that were currently popular, purchased for advertising. Lois only ever made art to sell it; the creative urge would not strike her without the promise of a handsome commission. Maria never had the guts to tell her that her 'art' wasn't actually very good.

'You weren't even going to call me, were you?' Maria asked incredulously.

'I kept meaning to!' Lois whined. 'I literally couldn't walk away from my board.'

Maria imagined Lois working manically over the small tablet she called her board, in front of her computer, clicking and cutting, moving, and pasting image over image, searching for words, fonts, effects, models, taglines, anything to prove her marketing prowess for her clients.

'So, you're not coming at all this weekend?' Maria sighed out.

'Well, I was thinking I'd come tomorrow...'

'Don't bother.'

'Don't be like that, babe!' Lois replied indignantly. 'Can't you appreciate my art is more important to me than, like, even eating? I know you don't have any creative passions so you just have to take my word for it. Seriously... this is *my life*!'

After apologising, insincerely, Maria wished *le artiste* good work and good night, shaking off that sly dig about her lacking any creative hobby as Leon did his bathwater. Lois could be critical, but it wasn't personal, she was like that with everyone.

It was no trouble to freeze the dinner for another night, so Maria ate some leftovers and drank half the bottle of red by herself. She dwelled upon Lois' comment, however: she may not have her idea of an artistic inclination, but to say she wasn't passionate was plain wrong. Maria had grown up with a broad fascination for biology, technology, and geography that had led onto maths, English, and chemistry at college, with a side of history. Further qualifications had earned her a prestigious career as an advanced skills teacher, home-tutoring exam subjects to private students.

Until, the recession forced her to take her full-time job at Gloucester City High school. Those pleasant, middle-class families of fond distant memory chose to tighten their belts around Maria's expertise, and Maria's part-time income could no longer support her expensive lifestyle in London. Her solution had been to move to the West Country two years ago, near to the best-paid permanent work she could find. Pooling her resources, mainly her father's inheritance, Maria bought half of a large Georgian townhouse in the borough of Charlton Kings on the outskirts of Cheltenham in Gloucestershire. It had a garden for her dog, Leon, and plenty of space for her chaotic girlfriend, Lois.

Maria thought about how life had changed since Lois moved out last year. Lois had decided that sleepy Gloucestershire was too slow and quiet for a vibrant, twenty-seven year-old Australian, and she needed to live back in the bitter rush of London town in order to function. She promised she wasn't breaking up with Maria: she just needed "stress and noise to think clearly." Maria had since become well acquainted with solitude, and was grateful for little Leon, who kept her company every evening.

And she could always phone her cousin Benicio for a chat. They tried to speak at least once a week, and she confided in him as if he were her only living blood relative. Ben had encouraged her to become a teacher, believing her broad interests and knowledge could help struggling kids get through the tough exam revision. Maria always listened to Ben: he was her voice of authority in place of the father and brothers who had abandoned her when she had come out all those years ago, aged seventeen.

That mild October night, Maria settled into her deep, brown leather couch, Leon stretching out between her legs, and updated Ben on life in general; her job; Lois, and how amusing it wasn't to realise just how absurdly self-possessed her eccentric girlfriend was.

'She said her art is more important than eating?' Ben scoffed down the phone, his Sicilian accent growling. 'Please let her go mad and cut her ear off next!'

Maria laughed huskily. 'I know! Bless her for taking it seriously, but really, it's awful, the shit she comes up with, you have to see it. She even called it "corpor-art" the other day, it's sickening.' Maria couldn't help lowering her voice; she felt a bit tipsy and she, still, sometimes forgot that Lois didn't live with her anymore, forever mindful of incurring her wrath.

Unravel

Ben sighed thoughtfully and then told Maria how concerning it was that she was so casual towards the way Lois treated her, that he didn't like to hear his cousin was so regularly spoken to with disrespect. He then reminded her that Lois had never made a concerted effort to connect with him, and therefore he had no qualms about encouraging Maria to break up with her and find someone more loving.

Stroking the curve of Leon's tender hip lightly with her toes, Maria pressed her eyes shut, patiently listening. She knew Ben was right about Lois: it was true she had never bothered to bond with anyone who didn't serve her interest, that being, mainly, career progression, and some part of her felt bad for Ben's sense of neglect, but for her own: Maria felt indifferent. She had been with Lois for long enough now to not let it bother her, in fact, it was almost entertaining to observe her ricochet, in the small doses she was prescribed of course, around her hedonistic existence. Maria had taken the role of the dark-eyed, emotionally stable presence in the corner that allowed Lois to bounce, charge and fly back into her life with zeal and confidence. Occasionally it meant she took an elbow in the ribs, but she reconciled that with the pleasure she took from knowing she was helping Lois get where she needed to be; in contrast, if she weren't there, Lois would be a chaotic force upon herself, like a rabid dog chewing its own tail. She would self-combust - Maria was sure. As cruel and contemptuous as Lois could be,

Maria knew Lois needed her; and it wasn't *all* bad, Maria would be a fool if Lois were cruel all of the time.

'I'm not making excuses for her, but you know what she's like, she's just self-engaged, she doesn't mean to be a bitch,' Maria explained to Ben. 'If she were deliberately shit in a personal way I would leave, but just because she's in her own world, doesn't make her a bad person. I'm in my own world too, you know, that's why we've worked together for so long.'

'But it's getting worse, you told me she's getting fucked up all the time!'

'She's an artist, she's allowed to get fucked up!' Maria laughed. 'Look, she's trying to land some big deal that will make her a lot of money, of course she's desperate; anything that gets in her way is getting shot down. I'm not going to get in her way - she can do what she wants.'

'Ria!' Ben groaned, his rolling tongue coiled with defence. 'I wish you could see it from my point of view. That girl is a walking nightmare. You are just too lost in it with her - you don't see it anymore! How about someone who doesn't make you feel like you're in the way? Someone who wants you with them along their journey, not just uses you for their own gain. She'll probably dump you once she's rich and getting attention from others, and it'll probably be a guy too, you know that!'

'How about *you* don't make me feel like I'm a total doormat, because I'm not, okay?' Maria smarted.

'I know exactly what she's like, Ben, I'm not blind or stupid, but I just don't have enough reasons to leave her right now.'

A snort sounded down the line from Ben's nose. 'Baby, when did you turn into a sucker? That is not how I brought you up!'

'Fuck you,' Maria smiled and slugged the last sip of wine from her glass. 'How's Chloe?'

Ben laughed at her change of topic then his voice dropped sensually. 'She's still beautiful... still amazing... nothing else to say.' He laughed again, loosely disguising his utter pleasure for his relationship after lecturing Maria so heavily on hers. Suddenly, from the background, Chloe's distant voice called her husband away and they hung up after Ben promised he would call her again soon.

Maria sat in the silence of her lounge and looked around. Leon looked up at her, his ears pointing expectantly as Maria waited for something too. The call had ended too quickly, she wondered if she had been too argumentative about Lois. She felt a little jealous that Ben was going out for dinner, and didn't like how pathetic it made her feel that she couldn't even get hold of Lois most evenings, let alone arrange something nice. Her wine glass was empty. Maria thought about Lois getting fucked up, and knew that it would be easy and forgivable if she did so too. Thinking about her old friends in London, Maria felt alone and left out. It used to give her some sense of vicarious pleasure being a part of Lois' hectic lifestyle, but now she was not involved, she *did* feel useless and rejected.

Once again, Maria contemplated getting a hobby. Nothing she couldn't do already, she didn't want to have to endure months of being crap at something until she got better - the idea of learning Chinese or taking any amateur class made her cringe. Maria pondered lightly through more ideas as she reached for the wine bottle. She needed a project.

♥

As if the universe answered, Maria was stunned to receive an e-mail from Principal Xavier Woods requesting her attendance at his office on Monday to discuss the transfer of a student from Ireland, whom he had accepted to repeat her final year at the school. The challenge, he warned, was that the student would need to adapt to the UK's entirely different curriculum in order to pass the exams.

Heading into school at the start of the next week, Maria felt a knot of anticipation in her stomach. Gloucester City High was a relatively young building, purpose built for a community keen to evolve up and away from the degenerative stereotypes that had plagued its population throughout the last century. Located north-west of the centre, the freshly funded school boasted excellent sports facilities, newly fitted technology and science departments, as well as a sprawling library with modern booths installed under the long panel of windows for catalogue reference and internet access. The fields surrounding it on three sides, containing tennis and basketball courts, backed onto the grounds of a neighbouring private school with an appropriately distancing patch of woodland in between.

Maria drove into her usual spot in the staff car park and walked in through the main front entrance, which opened out into a widespread foyer: a teal carpeted access to the reception, assembly hall, cafeteria and dining area, as well as staff rooms. Beyond the foyer led a maze of polished pale green flooring, guiding through corridors with notice-board laden walls to the various departments and the library upstairs. The brown banisters of the staircases to upper levels poked around every corner and signage hooked to the ceiling next to them swayed from the constant slapping of palms as they obliged every student's passing with a helplessly friendly high-five.

Beyond, attractively designed courtyards, constructed to join the exterior buildings, the gymnasium and the science block, with sheltered pathways, were of benefit to every student caught in the rain between classes, and of course, to the games and science teachers who found themselves banished to the outskirts of the premises in case of excessive noise, through activity or explosion.

The school housed around sixteen hundred students; thirty full-time teachers; twenty-four part-time teachers; nineteen classroom assistants - including the learning support team, but not including the laboratory and technical support - and seven administration staff. Behind the reception was a separate route through to Principal Wood's office and the general staff room lay along an angled corridor that overlooked the front entrance. The lengthy floor to ceiling windows inside this room enabled the staff to peer outwards through sweeping, weighted blinds that kept the students from peering in, but Maria passed the staff room to make her way to the Principal's office, as summoned.

After knocking on his door, Maria sat in front of the principal's desk with her knees folded over tightly. She felt a chill shiver under the light fabric of her jersey, or perhaps she was nervous to be in his office.

'The girl's name is Nadia Sheridan,' said Mr Woods, 'bit of a trouble-maker apparently,' he frowned downwards to read from a sheet in front of him. '...dropped out of her final year and went on the run from her mother in Dublin, has experienced misuse of alcohol and street drugs...'

The sunlight shone off his smooth skinhead as he creased his sharp blue eyes for emphasis and flapped the end of his tie, allowing the statement to sink in for Maria.

'She has since got cleaned up, is now living with her father somewhere in Stroud, and is ready to complete her education.' He threw the papers down on his desk and leaned casually back, hooking his elbow around the back of his chair. 'Well, seeing as it's October, she's a month behind, but better late than never, and I'm sure with your expertise you can work wonders on her, Maria.'

Maria sat opposite his wide, mahogany desk that was far richer than the one in her office. She decided she didn't like his presumption that she would jump to the click of his fingers, nor did she like the offensive way he cocked his ankle up onto his opposite knee to show he was finished. She stared into him bearing the same serious frown of concern all teachers and carers wore regarding a child in need, and pinched her lower lip between her fingers.

'Xavier, with all due respect, and I appreciate your faith in me, but my expertise is in helping students needing minor tweaks to their comprehension across a couple subjects. What you're talking about is giving complete guidance across all subjects.' Maria appealed.

Woods' face slid into a cool, thin-lipped smile and he nodded, before asking Maria if she could prepare a specific revision guide covering all the girl's subjects. He handed to her the copies detailing what Miss Sheridan had been studying at her last school in Dublin, and which subjects she had chosen for her options at GCH.

'It took a while but I managed to squeeze extra funding for this girl, because she's a special case... I don't want to pressure you, but her success could raise the bar for next year. I have full confidence in you,

Maria.'

It would be pointless to argue or ask further questions; Maria knew she didn't have a choice when it came to the principal's referrals: he acted nonchalant, but Xavier Woods was ruthless when it came to league tables and other such perceived success. Maria left his office trying to rise to the occasion. Her skills were needed to help this girl; she had been missing something like this. Maria never felt so good about herself as when a student passed their exams after taking tuition with her. If this teenager was a drugged-up dropout, well, that made it more of a challenge. Maria knew she would whip her into shape.

Chapter Two

Maria eased down into her sporty steel-grey Audi with a contented sigh, sped out of the school car park, and soon hit the road away from Gloucester. She loved her car, even though it was already four years old, she'd bought it at the peak of her earnings as a treat and not once had she regretted it even though she could have done with the savings had she known the economic downturn was looming. On the route back to Cheltenham, Maria called her dog-sitter, Christian, to say she would swing by to collect Leon on her way home. He was a local boy Maria had tutored when she first joined the school, a decent young man who had done well in his exams. His parents, primary school teacher, Clarissa, and land surveyor, Anthony Webb, had kept in grateful contact via seasonal greetings cards with proud progress reports of Christian's further educational successes: significantly, enrolment onto a music-engineering course that he wouldn't have been able to get onto had Maria not encouraged his experimenting with the latest technology.

After Lois left, Christian offered support by looking after Leon in the afternoons. It was a comfortable agreement, and Maria happily paid her young neighbour a generous rate. He let himself in to Maria's house after his morning seminars at college and walked Leon back to his parent's house to keep the tiny hound company until Maria got home. Leon seemed happy too; he liked the routine activities and Christian was a reliable and responsible guardian, and could be trusted with the keys to Maria's house.

Within thirty minutes, Maria arrived back in Charlton Kings, and drove into the street where Christian lived, just under a mile from her own house. Leon jumped at her knees at the door, and Maria crouched to greet her joyous dog.

Christian lifted a cheerful smile. 'He tried to shag some cute little bitch in the park!'

'Ah, good boy, Leon!' Maria winked. 'He takes after his mum.' She waited for Christian to laugh before she released a toothy grin. She noticed the boy was growing handsome: his brown hair was cut softly, his shoulders were filling out, and his skin was clearing up. 'Same time tomorrow?' She waved, Leon hopping alongside her.

As soon as she got home, Maria thought about the guide she had to create. Using remote access to the school intranet, she worked out what Nadia Sheridan

Unravel

would need from each of her subjects. Maria had tutored foreign students in London, but never with the perspective of approaching the whole curriculum, therefore making notes on which modules the sixteen-year old would be covering in all her options took on a novel dimension. Looking over Nadia's previous school's record sheet to gauge which subjects she would find easiest to digest first, Maria had noticed Nadia had above average grades, across nearly all her subjects.

This was a curiosity and made Maria ponder further upon what events had prompted an intelligent girl to drop out of her final year. But speculating was futile, so Maria shook her head clear, took another swig from her beer bottle and started with the list of all the textbooks Nadia would need for her science options; which chapters related to each topic within each module, which other sources were recommended from the library, and which assignments would be due and when. This was going to be no simple study outline: this was going to be the best exam guide ever designed. Maria felt a tremor of adrenalin run through her.

When the evening came to a slightly fuzzy end, Maria put her work away and let Leon out for a final visit to the garden before getting a good night's sleep. Her mind was still racing as she lay down between her soft cotton sheets, though she couldn't sleep for an hour for making mental notes on how to improve the layout of her guide. She'd never had a project like this before;

it gave her a kick to have something to focus on.

Three more evenings passed before Maria finished the revision guide, and by the time it was all printed out, it had grown to a forty-page handbook. She was happy that it was comprehensive without being overly detailed: she had broken down each subject into its separate modules, clearly defined sections with bold headings, colour-coded directions, hand-drawn diagrams and flowcharts, and a few amusing clip-art pictures to boot. She'd included a contents page as well as an index, and a glossary in case Nadia wasn't familiar with any British terminology. If Miss Sheridan didn't appreciate her efforts, Maria thought about taking it elsewhere: she was sure she could find some publisher who would snap her up if they saw this hot little nugget of educational greatness.

♥

At GCH, Maria had her own office on the school's third floor, overlooking the west-facing playing field, as part of the learning support suite: a team of five who gave varying levels of assistance to special needs pupils, and extra-curricular activities. For her specialist skills, Principal Woods had granted Maria a surprisingly large salary, seemingly desperate to have an advanced skills teacher with her qualifications. Her sparkling reputation as a home tutor, with an eighty-eight percent pass rate on A-C grades would have turned him onto her, Maria was sure, and not that he wanted a handsome, half-Sicilian, thirty-one year-old female on his team. Maria had made him aware of her sexuality, preferring to be open and honest about such things, yet the tall, skin-headed Principal Woods had shrugged and told her to call him Xavier with the slick grin of a politician.

Fellow teachers were somewhat standoffish with her when they learned she was gay, but it was all ignored under the usual heterosexual conspiracy of awkward silence, with excuses of the inappropriateness of promoting homosexual lifestyles in a school environment. Maria couldn't care less for politics: she didn't want to promote anything aside from quality revision, so she kept herself to herself at GCH.

Maria had made a friend, of sorts, in the games teacher, Karen Lenholm. Karen was noticeably short alongside Maria's five foot nine, but she was active for her forty-five years. Under an odd crop of grey hair, she had deep lines around smiling blue eyes and used every facial expression in sharing her most playful temperament with Maria. Karen had made it clear from the outset that she was batting for the same team, something Maria couldn't have guessed: the games teacher lived in her tracksuits, constantly jangling the set of keys to her locker room nervously in her pocket. Acknowledging her physical fitness, Maria did not consider Karen handsome, her eyes had an almost undetectable projection in different directions, and Maria wasn't entirely sure the bold pearls stretching the older woman's pale lips into a broad grin were real teeth.

Maria found Karen to be relatively harmless, and ignored any less-than-subtle hints that she wanted to know her a lot more intimately. That was not going to happen. Maria had made a vital initial assessment of their potential dynamic: Karen, being older, sportier, and certainly more excitable, would try to sexually dominate her, and imagining her lusty advances made Maria feel fifty shades of wrong.

'You look a little blue today,' Karen said lightly as they stood waiting their turn to get refreshments in the main cafeteria, later that week. 'I recommend the *blue*berry muffin, it works, trust me.' She flashed a grin, nodding towards the display of sweet cakes behind the counter.

Maria snapped her eyes away to the hands of the dinner-lady ahead, pouring cardboard cups of tea and coffee, and mumbled. 'I don't eat muffins.'

Karen only had to hold her expression with a poised mouth and sparkling eyes for a second before she broke into laughter. 'Really? That's not what I heard!'

Shaking her head with a wry smile, Maria rolled her eyes at Karen's innuendo, but after some moments felt conscious Karen was watching her, her gaze lingering a little too long for comfort. Maria's mind automatically pushed away any paranoid thoughts about her hair or her clothing, or anything else she felt Karen might be about to comment on.

'You know Marvin *Gaye*?' Karen emphasised, eyes dancing, pocket jangling.

'Don't you ever stop?' Maria groaned.

'*I heard it on the grapevine* that there's going to be a new girl in year eleven.'

'Is there?' Maria asked casually, she didn't care for gossip.

'Come on!' Karen narked. 'I know when you're keeping things from me.'

'I know as much as you do.' Maria sidled away with her cardboard tea.

It was true, in as much as she had barely seen the girl's referral file, but any information beyond that was confidential. Anyway, Karen would undoubtedly find out for herself soon enough.

♥

The following Monday, Maria took a break from her work to eat her lunch, and stood leaning against the window frame in her private office, looking out at the kids playing in the field. Her swivelling desk chair was very comfortable, but after sitting down for hours, Maria felt the need to stand, and even kicked her boot up on the side edge of the chair, stretching her calf muscle out. She glanced around her office fondly, over the years it had grown to resemble her lounge at home:

the bookshelves stacked with teaching magazines, reference books as well as proud displays of certificates and awards, and expensively bound collections of essential readings. Pot plants were also a necessity, Maria needed colour and oxygen within these plain four walls, even though the room was a good size and fitted a couch and coffee table. It could get quite stuffy; being on the third floor, the windows only opened a fraction, for those occasions when a concrete-blurred drop looked more tempting than a towering pile of coursework.

A quiet rap at her door, however, caused Maria to start out of her daydream and bump her forehead lightly against the window. Dropping her foot to the floor, not wishing to be caught in a lunge position, she called her permission to enter, wiping her mouth with the back of her hand and shoving the remainder of her lunch in the top drawer of her desk.

Her office door opened and Maria saw a small head poke hesitantly around it. The door eased open further and a girl with scruffy, long red hair and a green parka jacket stepped forward slowly. The girl didn't smile, she looked very serious.

'Are you Ms Calver? The girl said in a low, trembling southern Irish accent that made her words flow from her lips like autumn leaves.

'Yeah...?'

Maria had a momentary lapse of everything as she stared back at the strange girl. Her eyes, deeply piercing and green, haunted by shades of brown where her curious expression pressed into coves, blinked back at Maria.

'I'm Nadia Sheridan.'

Maria inhaled and felt her stomach squeeze tightly against her lunch. She couldn't believe she had forgotten the transfer student was coming - no, she hadn't forgotten, she couldn't believe this was her. Maria had spent days thinking about this one young person yet she hadn't even recognised when her new girl was standing in front of her.

Feeling stuck suddenly, Maria didn't know if she should go and shake the girl's hand, or bring her in and sit her down.

'Wow, uh... sorry,' Maria remembered to speak, swallowing her blush. Instead of admitting what an idiot she was for not realising, Maria roughed the back of her hair and gestured towards her desk, pretending she had been working. 'I was miles away.'

'I can come back if you're busy,' Nadia said. Her sea-green eyes were earnest yet guarded; they held Maria in a centred gaze that struck as intelligent, yet wary with nerves.

Maria raised her smile and waved her hand dismissively with a standard joke that she was a geek for working through her lunch break. She invited Nadia in and offered the couch.

Nadia slid her bag to the floor and sat down, her knees politely together, her black lace-up Doc Marten boots splayed out. Maria took the seat next to her and presented the guide, briefly explained its contents, and told Nadia that she could find all the listed books in the library on the top floor of the main building.

Nadia frowned over her name in dark-green italics on the front.

'Does everyone get one of these?' She asked, flicking through the pages.

Not being able to help herself taking in the fresh scent from Nadia's hair as it slid forward, tones of red and gold shining under the sunny beam from the midday sun, Maria's words drifted out of her. 'No, this is just... for you.'

As Nadia turned her face up from where she sat only a foot away, Maria became locked into a gaze as her eyes fell over Nadia's oval face. There was an angle of suspicion about her brown eyebrows that arched pointily; her nose was small and straight, with freckles blending across her pale skin. Her lips were slightly bowed towards the centre, as they hung open softly. Her sharp green eyes flickered unsurely at Maria.

'You made this? For me?'

The slight pinch of dimples next to Nadia's smile halted the breath in Maria's chest. She pulled her gaze away: she couldn't allow herself to stare. Maria tried to shrug casually.

'Well, you're gonna need something to help...' She said, standing up and moving away. 'I mean, I'll tutor you as best I can, but you've got a lot of stuff to get through.'

Maria felt strange suddenly. She wondered if the last couple of years spent in school had institutionalised her, and now she had forgotten what it was like to have an unknown pupil turn up on her doorstep like some stray, malnourished kitten. A weirdly pretty kitten. Nadia didn't look like trouble, she looked like she'd seen trouble around her.

'I know!' The girl sighed resentfully. 'The principal told me I won't have any free periods because I have to attend *everything*...'

Stopping to lean against the edge of her desk, Maria folded her arms, realising she hadn't considered after-school tuitions; she huffed, Woods had not told her that part.

'Come back this afternoon then, we'll arrange sessions...'

'I'll check my diary,' Nadia raised her eyebrows sarcastically.

Maria was amused by Nadia's expression. She wanted to see her dimples again, but the only smile came in the slightest curl at the edge of Nadia's lips; she didn't seem ready to smile fully just yet. Maria appreciated that: she wasn't much of a smiler either.

After she said goodbye and left, Maria felt a wave of relief wash over her. So, the girl she would be tutoring, at first impressions, was pleasant enough, in a nervous way, and not too hard on the eye. The information Woods gave her about Nadia being a dropout, a druggie and a runaway must be hearsay: there was no way Maria could see this intuitive young creature running riot.

♥

Fifteen minutes after the final bell sounded that afternoon, Nadia showed up in Maria's office with that same look of suppressed nervousness humming through her concentrated gaze. Gesturing towards the firm couch against the left wall of her office, Maria felt she ought to allow the girl to relax first, so tried some ice-breaking chat before they got down to business. She asked Nadia how she felt about her first day at GCH, but her question drew a puzzled twisting up of Nadia's eyebrows and Maria cringed that she might have sounded patronising.

'I hate being new,' Nadia muttered. 'There were these girls, they wouldn't stop eyeballing me.'

Maria wondered if she meant Samantha Burrows. The sly girl and her friends could be so mean; she tried not to show her distaste, but Maria had a ready dislike for Miss Burrows since her homophobic slur earlier in the term. She bit her tongue on every rising comment, for fear of sounding unprofessional. Instead, Maria marked the start of their tuition, and began by explaining the colour-coded chapters in the handbook.

Nadia seemed to listen, patiently, nodding in appropriate places and mumbling repeated words and phrases to solidify all the information.

After several minutes, however, Maria noticed that Nadia had quietened, a growing frown pressing her eyes into that haunted expression. She began rubbing her forehead under the sweeping, layered curtain of her auburn fringe, exhaling deeply. She couldn't seem to look in Maria's eyes with agreement or comprehension, but the occasional twitch of her mouth revealed her nerves.

It was clear to Maria that something wasn't right, the girl was not responding normally, with the usual wide blinking and frequent nodding of her other students; Maria had lost her.

'Hey, where'd you go?' Maria tried a light smile.

'Sorry,' Nadia said with tense jaws. She held her arms in tight as if she was frightened and was trying to protect herself. 'I keep having flashbacks... this time last year I was so... I...'

Maria's compassion reached out and pressed a hand reassuringly on Nadia's wrist to let her know she was not judging her.

'Look, you should know that I haven't been told anything about you,' Maria said hesitantly. 'I don't know the reasons you left your last school, I don't know what circumstances brought you here to repeat your final year... and you don't have to tell me anything...'

Maria waited for some sign from Nadia, but the girl's face stayed closed.

'I want you to know that as your tutor, my only agenda is getting you through your exams,' Maria made her low voice expressive, 'and I'm very stubborn so I always succeed.'

At this, Nadia did raise a shy glance to meet Maria's eyes and seemed visibly soothed when Maria let her mouth curl with a kind smile.

'Thanks, but I'd rather not talk about it,' Nadia said in a husky Irish tone, then released a frustrated sigh at herself. 'I know I fucked up before, so believe me, I am committed to finishing school.' The pensive frown returned. 'I don't want to make the same mistakes.'

Sensing the gravity of thoughts that plunged around Nadia made it all the easier for Maria to understand how to treat this mature young woman: a student so heavy with unspoken feelings and concerns required a teacher's steady support and consistent kindness, and Maria knew she could do that without a flicker of self-doubt.

'Well, that makes it simple,' Maria offered the palms of her hands. 'You focus on it, I'll focus on it, and we'll make it happen. Then you can put your past behind you.' She noticed she had Nadia's eye contact, a needy expression, wanting perhaps, waiting for more words. Maria thought of what would be best to say at this crucial point.

'I have no preconceptions,' she lied, craving to ask about the girl's prior experiences with drugs. 'You can be yourself, you can be whoever you want to be, I only ask that you trust me and let me help you – that's the only way we are going to get this right.'

'How do I know I can trust you?' Nadia asked, her head tilting sideways warily.

Maria thought, then smiled gently through a shrug. 'I'm still kind of new here... I don't really know anyone in Gloucester,' she whispered conspiratorially, 'and I don't really like anyone in this school.'

Encouraged by Nadia's growing smile, Maria added. 'To be honest, you could do me a big favour to keep me out of trouble by giving me something interesting to do while I'm here.'

Nadia finally smiled, flashing her white teeth and those dimples. 'I can't keep you out of trouble too!'

'Really? I can't trust *you* then, huh?' Maria teased.

Shaking her head, Nadia chuckled and it was pure pleasure to Maria's ears. They smiled at each other, Nadia's eye contact still shy but amused, her nerves waning. Maria felt she had sufficiently broken down the strangeness that had divided the air between them at the start, for the studying to commence at their next session. However, for now, Maria resumed briefing on their project, and then arranged twice weekly after school tuitions.

After Nadia had left, it was nearly four o'clock, and Maria moved back to her desk to work until late as she usually did. Except, this time she found it difficult to concentrate, having just been stimulated by this new student into distracting thoughts of their united mission. Maria considered her and Nadia as a team; their success together would show the principal that he was wrong about young Miss Sheridan. Maria had been shocked at the maturity of this creature, as if Nadia's experiences alone had been enough to evolve her self-awareness - without trying to look or act a year older than the others, it showed in her demeanour. It was intriguing.

Pondering what kind of events had occurred in Nadia's life to make her this way, Maria was sure she would be getting to know Nadia over the next few months, and perhaps by then she would be wishing she rather not know certain things. Who knew what darkness Nadia was suppressing?

Chapter Three

Unspoiled by Lois' abandonment, Maria was still in love with her two-bedroom townhouse. Her spacious kitchen, with a welcoming breakfast bar and a dining table in the corner, connected to the lounge through a pillared alcove. Both colourful and tactile for a minimalist, Maria enjoyed the way her centrally featured solid wood coffee table complimented the rich tones of the warm, thick rug and pine flooring beneath it. The television in the corner that Lois had left behind was mostly unused except for the odd late night documentary or news programme. Tall plants, up-lighters, and bookshelves broke up the high white walls and a long, oak dining table adjacent to the alcove could be pulled out for dinner guests, which Maria hardly ever had occasion to have. Piles of books had accidentally gathered there anyway: Maria liked to read when she ate.

When Lois did finally make it over to Cheltenham, it was mid-week and the only night she could spare before having to attend work socials over the weekend. She had arrived late, as usual, but luckily, Maria had accounted for this and delayed her preparations for their evening meal. Lois appeared slightly wild-eyed and grinning, flushed and tired from her train journeys, and ignored Leon's greeting whinnies, seeking a much-needed glass of wine instead.

'I'm not really that hungry,' Lois's opening words grated as much as her thick Melbourne accent. 'I had a salad sandwich as I left London, I was ravenous, I didn't eat all day, I was so busy, our receptionist Laura called in sick and I had to cover the desk through lunchtime, I was fucking furious, I've got so much work to do, and Jonathan's attitude is totally sexist! You know, like, because I'm the only other woman on the floor, I have to get the fucking phone!'

Lois spilled out with a barrage of swear words aimed at her boss and stopped to take a slurp of wine. She perched on the stool next to Maria's breakfast bar as if it were a cocktail bar, her legs crossed smartly, her painted nails spiking out from her glass.

She hadn't always had a hard yoga body and wear smart vest dresses, bold scarlet lipstick, and black framed spectacles. It was a gimmick. The way she wore her 'look' now made Maria realise that Lois sought little else than to make a name for herself, believing fame and fortune were on her horizon. She spent her days at so-called meetings, more like liquid lunches, where she schmoozed with highbrow arty types;

Unravel

standing around posturing, seductively prodding prospective buyers with her flexible, red-tipped hands; snorting cocaine with them and ranting about marketing concepts for some trendy new brand.

Maria played the tolerant waiter and poised the bottle of wine suggestively. Lois' enthused eyes reared and her glass gravitated towards Maria for a top up. Her verbal flow continued, however, and within fifteen minutes, Maria found her mind quietly seething over the vibration of suppressed, continuous alarms tugging at her patience.

'Well, we got this major contract - this American firm have said they liked my work!' Lois exclaimed proudly in her bright Aussie twang, her teeth gleaming. 'They wanted something alien themed for their latest product, you know, like artificial intelligence and all that. I mean, like, the product itself is super-intelligent so it doesn't need obvious explanations of what it is, it's like, secure in itself, so I gave them simple, bold images to represent what it's about, rather than what it is. Does that make sense?'

Maria turned at the kitchen counter, swaying the knife in her hand over the vegetables on the chopping board. 'You mean like a cut refers to sharpness, to represent a knife.'

Lois pulled a grimace. 'The product is nothing like a knife!'

Maria jerked the knife in her hand, mocking Lois' accent. 'I was using an example?'

'This product is much more sophisticated than that, Maria!' Lois scoffed. 'It is *my* job to show people that this product is so complex, so clever, that they can only comprehend it with really simple images that allow them to get the whole scope.'

Fully aware, given the years of experience and frequency of occurrence, that she should no longer ever really be startled or offended by Lois' curtness, Maria was, nevertheless, annoyed by Lois' insinuation that she didn't understand the subtleties of marketing a product. She held her gaze, her jaw offset, betting Lois didn't even know what the product was.

Lois returned it with the callous, indignant stare of a bitter rival. Maria imagined, shortly, that she did not know this person, and released her grip on the knife, setting it down onto the countertop. Saying nothing was Maria's *modus operandi*. She disliked arguing: confrontation made her eyes prick with tears, her nerves gather and tremble, and heat flare up from her chest; she was sure none of these physiological reactions were a good look for her and so attempted to retain the ability to stay cool and cruise through most of life's tensions.

However, something stung, somewhere inside, and Maria felt a surge of defiance.

'Did I tell you I've been assigned a new student?' She asked, lifting her intonation cheerily. 'She's a transfer so she needs my help to get her through the curriculum in time for exams, Woods referred her to me... she's having to repeat her final year in a different country, different system... I have to get her 'A' grades back... it's going to be hard work for both of us.'

Maria hoped her casual mention of Nadia would somehow poke Lois' jealous streak. Knowingly provoking a reaction from her girlfriend, Maria waited for a string of loaded questions: she prepared herself for them, wanting Lois to know that she, the vastly qualified AST, had valuable qualities other people desired, and yes, she was going to be spending a lot of time with a pretty, clever girl over the next few months.

'Where did she transfer from?' Lois mumbled, picking out the dirt from under her nails.

Surprised by the irrelevance of the question, disappointed by the lack of any noticeable flinch from Lois, Maria's mind went into a strange blankness and she found herself speaking words that were not true: 'She's Welsh... she transferred from Wales.'

She had no intention of lying yet it emerged organically before the guilt of dishonesty struck her. Maria immediately questioned why she had said that, and threw her shame into the pan of frying rice.

'Isn't that part of the UK?' Lois wondered idly.

Her girlfriend's obnoxious disinterest was mind numbing. Maria plucked the kettle off the boil and poured it into the pan, letting the steam scald her flushing face. She was more shocked that she had lied, and could only guess what it meant. Perhaps she was trying to prevent Lois knowing too much; keep select parts of her working relationship with Nadia private, even though she had just told Lois about her in some vain attempt to taunt her.

Her apathy had distracted her, but Maria finally registered the ignorance of Lois' actual query, and frowned over at her.

'They've got a whole different syllabus...' Maria said lightly, absent-minded with guilt; knowing she was not only digging her hole deeper but playing games in the mud while she was there just to prove she was the dirtiest kind of liar.

'Wait, is that off the coast?' Lois rolled her fingers and flicked away some gritty morsel.

Maria winced into her saucepan. 'No, you're thinking of Ireland.' She muttered.

Lois turned her face up behind Maria's back, slid her glasses further up her nose, and raised her nasal voice with an angry smile.

'Actually, I think you'll find that I meant the Isle of Wight... my aunt had a friend who had a boating business out there,' Lois scorned. 'So don't tell me what I'm thinking.'

Maria broke away from her saucepan and turned to seize her glass of wine. She knew better than to push the matter when she couldn't decide who had dished a more foul taste: she could hardly complain that Lois had successfully swept the subject utterly away from

Unravel

her new charge, when she had just randomly lied to her girlfriend's face.

'Darling, if I ever understood your mind, I'd be a much happier person.' Maria drawled sarcastically. She took a long swig of merlot, and ground her heel back around to the hob.

'It would take more than that, sweetheart.' Lois said tightly.

Maria sighed, not caring enough to answer. Raising her eyebrows into the pan, Maria recognised a thought that made her happy when her mind drew towards an instant image from her recent memory, Nadia Sheridan's red hair. It was more auburn than red, and it hung in knotty streaks; the girl seemed to have interesting layers.

Coming to her senses hearing a spiteful laugh behind her, Maria let Lois have the last word, and was grateful for the opportunity to cook and be silent in her thoughts. Her mind bubbled along with the risotto as she tried to process what had made her lie to hide Nadia's identity.

♥

Nadia's pen tapped at her pad of paper, flitting aimlessly over the white blankness, inking mini-comets between the lines. She seemed to be suppressing a hurricane as she fidgeted on the stool next to Maria's desk.

Unravel

As Maria noticed the tension around Nadia's eyes, she took more seriously the robotic blinking she had seen the day before: Nadia was about to overload and she might snap at any minute. Maria stopped her patter and made her voice tender.

'Hey, what's happening?'

'Nothing...'

'Well, I can see something's up,' Maria eased. 'Tell me what's going on.'

Nadia was silent for a few seconds as she tried to gather her words. 'There's so much I have to catch up with, I don't know if I can do this.'

'Don't panic, we'll go through it slowly, okay?'

'I'm not!' Nadia said quickly, but seemed aware of her defensiveness. 'You don't understand, every time I try to focus, my mind keeps running away in the opposite direction,' Nadia's brow pursed deeply as her eyes trembled with a sudden welling of tears. 'I can't stop thinking about everything, and it's stupid because I really want to get it right... I have to!'

Maria lowered her face kindly to meet Nadia's worried expression. 'Nadia, you're putting too much pressure on yourself.'

'Everything's changed so much and I don't know where I am, or even who I am anymore! My head's all over the place, how am I supposed to sit exams? I can't manage everything by myself!' Nadia whined loudly.

Unravel

'Listen,' Maria bristled firmly, she didn't deal with weeping very well. 'You're not by yourself, let me help you. This handbook is only a guide, that's not all the support you're getting.'

'Even if your guidebook gave me all the answers,' Nadia flipped the pages of the tome. 'It couldn't sort out my head for me...'

'Nadia, I'm here to support you, that's *what* I'm here for - that's my job.' Maria said matter-of-fact.

Glancing up at her, Nadia's face pinched. 'Well, good on you for doing your job, Ms Calver, but I'm sure you're not being paid to care!'

Maria stared at the girl beside her, her ego a little bruised that she was right.

'Look, I can't solve all your problems at once,' Maria said hesitantly. 'You're bound to have a hundred questions, but you've got my email, so you can contact me anytime in the evening or weekend, okay? And for Christ's sake, call me Maria, I can't stand formalities.'

Nadia's face fell into silent contemplation; she frowned then. 'Maria?'

'Before you ask, I'm half Sicilian, not Italian, or Spanish... or Mexican!'

Nadia laughed suddenly, revealing those charming dips in her cheeks, and Maria felt a small kick of achievement.

After that, Nadia seemed to relax considerably. Tuition recommenced more appropriately, and Maria sought to introduce Nadia to the school's IT formats, but Nadia gave a guttural groan and a shove to Maria's keyboard, claiming to despise computers no matter what country she was in. Though she was, initially, concerned with allowing Nadia to sit in her chair behind her desk, Maria decided to take it in good humour and after a while wondered if Nadia was playing with her as she seemed to be picking things up easily whilst still complaining. Maria remained a gentle and persistent presence beside her, and encouraged Nadia to relax her thoughts and absorb what was in front of her.

By the end of that first session, Nadia did seem pleased to have learned how to navigate her way around the school Intranet, email and web search engines, the library reference system and the various programmes in word processing for writing up her essays and spreadsheets that she would need for her maths, science and IT coursework requirements. However, by the time they finished, it was a nearly five o'clock; though they had both felt on a roll, it was time to call it a night.

'I've got to run for the bus!' Nadia began hurriedly packing away her things.

Maria wondered about Nadia's home life, who might be waiting for her, and remembered it was just her father. 'So, where do you live?'

'My dad's house in Eastcombe.'

Figuring the buses to that quiet village miles out of the city would be few and far between after six in the evening. Maria felt she had to help. She slipped on her jacket casually. 'Where does your dad work? I mean, is he around Gloucester to pick you up?'

'My dad works nights at the hospital, he'll be asleep now, he takes knock-out pills anyway so I couldn't wake him if I wanted to!'

'So, you're kind of by yourself during the evenings?' Maria frowned.

'Yeah, and it's freezing! He's being a tight bastard with the heating, if I could stay *here* to study all night I would, I hate being there.'

Obviously, it went without saying that it would be out of the question for Nadia to stay by herself in school, so Maria did not even entertain what she hoped was Nadia's casual sarcasm. 'Do you want a lift to the bus stop?'

Nadia gratefully accepted as Maria locked up, and they stalked through the silent halls. Once in the cool evening air, there was a distinct change in Nadia's demeanour as they crossed the car park towards the only vehicle within sight: Maria's silver-rimmed Audi, sleek and slate under the dimming sky.

'Fuck me! This is yours?' Nadia exclaimed.

Maria pressed the keyset remote with a smile and could see by the light of the unlocking orange flashes Nadia's excitement at the prospect of travelling in her zippy sports car. As Nadia threw her canvas bag into the footwell and climbed in, Maria felt a jolt of pride at being able to whisk her young friend out into the night in her hot wheels.

'You're like Batman.' Nadia said cutely from the passenger side.

'Batwoman.' Maria clicked her teeth with a smile.

Reversing out of the parking area, Maria thought to keep the conversation casual.

'So, how are you getting on socially in school? Made any friends?'

'No!' She twisted her spiky little brows as if Maria's suggestion were absurd. 'Everyone's a year younger than me, who am I gonna hang out with?'

'There's some nice girls, they don't all act immature.'

'I don't have time anyway, I need to keep my head down and work. My dad says I'm not here to socialise.' Nadia's words drifted slightly towards the window.

'I like your work ethic, Nadia, but it's good to take time out, have some fun,' Maria told herself along with Nadia. 'It helps replenish your energy.'

Nadia unscrewed a small pot of lip balm and pushed her finger inside.

'My form tutor, Mrs Duncan, asked me to join some of the after school activities, but I can't be bothered.'

'It's worth a try,' Maria reasoned. 'You might find something in common with someone nice and cool.'

Adding some balm to her mouth, Nadia pressed

her lips between her teeth.

'There's just no one I feel like I can identify with - everyone's in groups or paired off already - and the loners are usually freaks. No one's actually spoken to me,' Nadia paused. 'Apart from you.'

Maria shifted gear with a shrug. 'Maybe you have to make the first move, you know... maybe everyone's a bit shy because you're older than them...'

Maria's words fell away as she felt eyes on her from the passenger seat. She wondered what Nadia was thinking. She couldn't take her eyes off the road, but at that moment she felt an energy coming from Nadia that made her ear feel hot.

The moment passed as they reached the bus station, just as Nadia's bus was pulling in. Nadia said her thanks and goodbyes, and Maria waited, ensuring the bus didn't leave without her. Then she found the road back to Cheltenham, feeling deeply pleased with their successful first tuition. The girl was starting to open up with her. It sounded as if Nadia had experienced some traumatic events in the past that were still haunting her. Maria felt as if she were the one who could reach around the veil of Nadia's displacement, and that made her feel as if her job had meaning again.

Chapter Four

Maria recalled odd birthdays from her childhood in Sicily. Always on the edge of poverty, her mother had troubled to provide an experience other than the everyday struggle that had sucked the positivity out of their existence in the country. Mama Lizabetta coped in many ways alone without the support of Maria's father, Lieutenant Richard Calver, for long periods while he was away with the British army, but, on special occasions, dug into the personal savings she had squirrelled in her shoe box on top of her wardrobe.

One day out when Maria was eight, her mother had found a book in the market, and Maria remembered how its cover was torn and stained. Lizabetta believed in fateful meetings, and felt the book had made itself known to her, amongst all the other books on that stall: a book about a young woman seeking to escape her place of birth to find a better life for herself. Lizabetta, a slender, wiry-haired Sicilian seamstress with a sad smile, had bought it and bound the outer cover with a

Unravel

piece of paisley fabric that had belonged to her own mother, and written on the inside that Maria had to make her life somewhere with the promise of prosperity.

It had been the most sacred gift Maria had ever received, made more precious by her mother's handcrafted love, and it was the last gift her mother ever gave her.

Maria had done as her mother wished and travelled abroad to a more wealthy country, unfortunately it was her mother's death that year that prompted her father to take her out of Sicily. Lt. Calver returned to his base in England and Maria and her older brothers had no choice but to follow. Maria became absorbed with her new school studies and never looked back.

Without her mother, Maria's birthdays had passed insignificantly, and subsequently any residual expectation or excitement faded year by year. Even as her affluence had grown, something in Maria's self-worth diminished as soon as her annual day of birth rolled around again. As November grew closer, Maria pushed away thoughts of her upcoming thirty-second birthday, pining over the fact that her mother died just four years older than her.

♥

It was Lois' phonecall, after the school bell had

sounded for the last time that day, that trapped Maria's drifting mood into an intensified corner.

'Why do you have to be so hung up about it?'

'You know I don't like a fuss.' Maria said calmly, clenching her jaws a little.

'Yeah but *I* like making a fuss!' Lois drawled. 'I don't want everyone thinking I haven't done anything for you.'

'What does it matter what other people think?'

'Maria, there are people who care about you who would love to celebrate with you.'

'Lois, I'm not going to send out invites to a party like some ten year old... I'm too old for parties, and no one would make the journey out here, it's depressing!' Maria stared out of her office windows.

'You're depressed *anyway*, sweetheart, why don't you try cheering yourself up?' Lois railed cruelly. 'Stop acting like you're special and do what everyone else does and celebrate their birthday! Why can't you be happy?'

After a few seconds of seething air through gritted teeth, Maria replied. 'You know what will make me happy for my birthday?' She raised her tone. 'How about for one day out of the whole year, *my girlfriend* not give me a hard time, how about that? Can you manage that?'

'What do you mean give you a hard time?' Lois shouted down the line. 'I'm trying to do something for you here, and you keep ruining it! You're so *fucking* selfish.'

'That's a *no* then.' Maria growled and pulled the phone from her ear, unable to listen to Lois' screeching reply. A resentful anger throbbed inside her. She slammed the phone down on her desk and called Lois a word she never thought she'd call any woman. Her senses prickled, and Maria suddenly looked up towards her office door.

Nadia was standing there. Her vibrant, green eyes fully on Maria.

Maria inhaled and held on to her breath, staring back at Nadia. She hadn't heard the girl come in, and had no idea how long she'd been there. Maria gulped. If she had caught the words 'my girlfriend' then Nadia knew her tutor was in a relationship with a woman.

Letting out her breath, Maria felt the heat trapped under her collar, her head rushed with what Nadia might be thinking. 'Hi!' Maria said softly, aware her last swear word was still ringing in the air.

Nadia's eyes were wide and anxious, her lips wavered with tentative expression, searching for words. 'I'm sorry,' Nadia said finally, her voice trembling with nerves. 'I didn't mean to walk in on your call. I knocked and I thought you were speaking to me, but... you weren't...'

Maria's insides ached with awkwardness. 'I'm just having a few problems with my...' The urge to say 'housemate' or 'sister' was tempting, but Maria did not want to lie.

'Your girlfriend.' Nadia finished for her.

Maria felt herself closing up, tense with anger at Lois and cagey about giving away her private information to a student.

'I think she might be my ex now,' Maria joked to lighten the air. Her smile fell quickly, however, and she shook her head. 'You're not due for tuition, are you?'

Nadia looked around the office. 'No, I came to ask you something... but it doesn't matter...'

The way Nadia's eyes were travelling the floor made Maria's throat tighten. 'What is it?'

Nadia blinked and exhaled. 'Forget it... I'll ask you another time... I should go.' She turned back to the door.

'Wait!' Maria called, taking a few steps towards Nadia, clutching at the underside of her hair. 'Look, I'm sorry if what you heard made you feel weird. You know it won't affect anything,' her hand flitted in the air between them. 'It won't change the way I teach you.'

Nadia nodded. 'Yeah of course, it's totally fine,' Her shoulders seemed high with tension. 'So, I was just wondering...' It then took approximately ten seconds for Nadia to twitch and complete a little routine during which she shifted her feet, adjusted the strap of her bag, glanced behind her at the closed door, wiped under her nose with a sniff, and sighed.

Maria's eyes smiled witnessing such a cute performance.

'...if you think it would be okay... just for a couple extra afternoons a week... um... if I could study here, instead of going home,' Nadia's lips pursed tightly with awkwardness. 'I know you gave me your number to call you if I need, but the thing is... I can't work at my dad's house.'

Thumb tucking into the pocket of her jeans, Maria frowned. 'How come?'

Nadia shrugged, looking evasive. 'It's just warmer here.'

'Warmer?' Maria gave a quizzical look. 'You want warmth?'

'He said he doesn't make as much money as he used to when he was a nurse, and that he can't afford to have the heating on all evening... and then he said he "works all the hours God sends" Nadia complained, mocking his harsh Irish accent, 'and hasn't got time to change the settings on the boiler.'

Not wishing to make any comment on Nadia's father's parenting skills, Maria folded her arms and took a slow bite of her lip, considering what Nadia was saying.

'You're asking for somewhere to study, not for extra tuition?'

'Don't get me wrong, I need all the help I can get, but I don't expect you to sit with me. You can carry on with your work, I'd just sit quietly in the corner, you wouldn't even notice me, I promise!'

Maria acknowledged that most of her late

afternoons were spent in her office, so Nadia could stay later than the library was open, and she wouldn't risk being locked in if she was with a teacher. Maria reasoned that it would be no extra work for her and it might even be pleasant to have some company, so long as it wasn't every evening: that would be weird.

'I think I might need to get permission from Principal Woods on that.' Maria stated.

'Why?' Nadia flashed a temperamental frown. 'Because you're gay?'

'No,' Maria replied. 'Because I'm assigned as your teacher, not a guardian.'

She genuinely didn't know if she would be allowed to have Nadia stay extra days after school. She wasn't sure if she should be the one to ask. Perhaps Nadia's father needed to give permission. She wondered if the gay thing would be an issue.

'Hey, when's your birthday?' Nadia asked as she turned to leave.

After letting the air fill with seconds of silence, Maria realised she could not very well lie, and told the truth rather tightly. 'Next Thursday.'

She honestly preferred no one knew, and no one had asked, except Nadia, who exhaled thoughtfully. 'If it's any consolation, I don't like parties either.' Nadia shrugged, opened the door and was gone in seconds.

♥

In all events, Maria's birthday the following week was not unpleasant. Heading to school as normal that Thursday wearing a new fitted waistcoat over a grey shirt, the silky maroon lining kept the underside of her breasts snug all morning even though her office was indeed warm, but she didn't want to take it off: it was her present to herself.

Lois had sent a courier to deliver Maria's present: a new watch, spangling in silver. Except Maria preferred the watch she had already worn for years, having chosen it herself. In her bedroom, she put Lois' gift back in its box with genuine surprise - she had not known Lois would be so generous.

It wasn't entirely true that Maria did not like celebrating her birthday; feeling strongly that expectation in others ultimately led to disappointment, she long ago decided to simply celebrate by herself, please herself with treats, and never risk being upset again. Maria made a special salad for her lunch and brought it from home along with a small flask of rum mixed with ginger ale that she stashed in her compact room fridge. A little tipple now and then kept her smiling all day.

Karen Lenholm always remembered, having memorised the date from Maria's staff file, and in the afternoon patted Maria's new waistcoat, once at the shoulder, once again, as more of a stroke, at her lapel, and then finally, where the waist pinched against the top of her hip, with something of a grip; the older

Unravel

woman grinned from ear to ear creating a smug arrangement of skinny folds. She even licked her lips, just in case.

After the final bell sounded, Nadia Sheridan shifted down onto the couch in Maria's office, opened her bag and slid a cream envelope out of it. 'Happy birthday to you...' She purred.

Resisting the inclination to sit down next to her, Maria stood by the table, her boots steady and wide. She glanced between Nadia and her offering, and frowned with a pursed smile. 'You didn't have to.'

'I know. I wanted to see just how uncomfortable you'd get,' Nadia tested, watching Maria open the envelope, 'and look at you cringing now!'

Like the envelope, the card was handmade: a clean, cream card with a window in the front, framing a simple drawing of fireworks, black sparks and swirls flecked artistically against a light sky. Inside, an italic script with pretty details at the edges; a message of thanks and appreciation. When she flipped the card over, Nadia had designed her own hallmark.

Maria arched her eyebrow, unable to stop a heat rising to her ears and cheeks.

'I made it for you... because you made something for me - yours was a lot bigger but I put my heart and soul into that...' Nadia shushed herself, flapping her canvas bag shut too.

Maria blinked and held her smile back. She felt the rum swaying around her veins and she cleared her throat. 'I don't know what to say...' She couldn't take her eyes off the card. It had been made by a mature, careful hand, and, now that it was sinking in, Maria thought just how much time Nadia must have spent working on it. The inked drawings were painstakingly petite, the card folded and cut delicately, Maria could see no glue or uneven edges, yet it was clear Nadia had made it all herself. There wasn't even any reference to her birthday, just Nadia's message of gratitude, and Maria was reminded of the beloved book her mother had re-bound for her eighth birthday.

'Thank you.' Maria said with breathless sincerity, finally looking up. She wanted to let Nadia know what it meant: the sweetness of the gesture, the time and thoughtfulness put in, the lack of mention of her increasing age, Maria was deeply flattered. Considering that Lois had been not only tactless but cruel about Maria's birthday, and had been generally unloving every other day of the year, Maria felt Nadia's gift, a card and present combined, was more tender and genuine than anything Lois had ever given her.

♥

As soon as she could locate him, Maria beckoned Xavier Woods to one side in a busy corridor and described her situation with Nadia Sheridan, in particular, that she felt she ought to seek some sort of permission in order for Nadia to spend her evenings alone in her company.

Principal Woods leaned his hand against the wall next to Maria, his head leaning in close to hers. 'You know what, Maria, I can't help but wonder what kind of teacher would think of complaining if a student wishes to spend extra time studying?'

'I'm not complaining!' Maria shook her head, shifting back into her own personal space. 'I don't mind, it's just...'

Woods frowned slightly, but his smile persisted, making his stance all the more flippant while his words came blunt, edging towards intimidation. 'I can't allocate any more daytime sessions without knocking someone else off your list, but there's a lot riding on this transfer. We've got to set a precedent, so if you can find the time in your evenings to sort this one out, there'll be a rise in it for you.' He turned to go.

Maria resented his use of the term "this one" referring to Nadia. She called after him. 'Don't I have to ask her father or something?'

'I'm sure she can do that!' He called back as he strutted away.

Watching his bandy-legged, stupid walk, Maria was left feeling confused by his ruthless support. She returned to her office then settled down behind her desk, with a huge mug of tea and a small heater at her feet, a stack of folders growing on one side of her computer, shrinking on another. She felt more focused

Unravel

working there than she did at home, where the lure of wine and comfort food beckoned from the kitchen and overdue household tasks chipped away at her concentration. She thought about Nadia's predicament, understanding her home was tricky in different ways, and rationalised that the girl was hardly eating into her social time.

Immediately after emailing Nadia the good news, Maria had a secondary baulk at the idea of having anyone, let alone a student, disturb her zone of contentment. But after a week or so, towards the end of every other day, she found her mind quietly delighted by the recall that Nadia should be along to join her for a relaxed study session. These sessions differed from Nadia's tuition where, sitting on Maria's office couch, Nadia worked quietly by herself while Maria got on with her own work at her desk computer. She liked thinking about the positive aspects of having an after-school companion. Nadia was emotionally intelligent, both sensitive and humorous, but generally thoughtful and attentive; Maria could think of few other students she would allow to share her space. She could deal with this, and as it turned out, every evening was not so weird.

Sometimes she forgot Nadia was even there, so blissfully silent in turning her pages the girl was, but recently, Maria had felt her own senses prick up and alert her to Nadia's presence. After seeing Nadia was still reading, Maria would frown, wondering what had stimulated her concern. Soon came the feeling that Nadia was indeed looking at her. A sensation close to having a bee hovering towards her ear made Maria's senses vibrate and her neck spike with a rash of nerves. The skin across her chest became hot under her shirt. When she did glance over to Nadia, Nadia looked up at her too.

Maria smiled tightly and looked back to her work, but her mind flew into spirals of confusion: she had thought Nadia was already looking but she hadn't been, and to have looked up at the same moment was almost spooky.

When it happened again, Nadia was the one who looked away first and it left Maria wondering if Nadia was playing some game. Maria kept her position reclined and lifted a casual tone over her desk.

'Is there something you want to ask me?'

Nadia blinked over from the couch, her poker face taught, her lips pouted. 'No.'

'You looked.' Maria shrugged.

'So did you.' Nadia twisted up her eyebrows.

Maria wondered if Nadia was mocking her but then Nadia spoke again, her accent like crackling silk.

'You want to ask *me* something?' Her mouth slid into a wry smile.

Maria smiled down into her lap. The girl could give as good as she got.

The following afternoon they spent next to each other in tuition, Maria leaned into her own space, using her elbow as a barrier between them. Increasingly though, Maria's spider senses zoned in on Nadia's steady gaze on her tingling cheek, and she flushed suddenly, compelled to speak out.

'Why aren't you writing?' Maria frowned.

'I'm listening to you.' Nadia blinked slowly, still gazing.

Maria then force-fed word after word into her mouth like an unchewable toffee, horribly self-conscious of her lips moving. She was used to students staring at her, lots of girls and boys had taken a shine to her and she had enjoyed being able to command their attention: it made her a more successful teacher. But this was different.

♥

In the weekly school assembly that Friday, Maria sat to one side of the hall, in line with other teachers. Her knees swung a little coolly under her crossed arms, but Maria didn't like to sit so uniformly like the others, legs crossed, prim and proper. Until she spotted Nadia amongst the senior year seating, and Maria felt her senses prickle from her jaw to her ears, round her neck and all the way down her shoulders. She felt her sitting posture was suddenly 'too lesbian' and she should pull herself up, but she couldn't move for fear of attracting Nadia's attention. But then she felt her cheek blush, and knew that familiar sensory stroke of

Unravel

nerves down her neck and shoulders was Nadia's eyes on her anyway. She clenched her jaw and tried to focus her thoughts away from Nadia and towards what Principal Woods was saying about how people are like onions: layered and versatile; ultimately an essential basis for a wholesome society. It could have been anyone staring at her, but she couldn't look at Nadia, she mustn't look at her - if they jinxed their eye contact again, Maria felt like she would collapse on the floor.

At the end of that Friday, Maria came back to her office after a chat with her colleague across the other side of the suite, to find Nadia curled up on her couch, evidently sleeping. Maria closed the door and kneeled beside the heavily breathing girl, her hair splayed out over the arm rest, a small silver flask tucked inside her grip.

'Nadia?' She said gently, with a prod to her shoulder. 'Hey!'

Waking with a start, Maria wasn't sure if Nadia had been asleep or just pretending, but her eyes were pinned. She blinked, nearly dropped the flask in her hand as she stirred, then looked up at Maria guiltily.

'I didn't mean to drink it all.' She mumbled, her breath scented of rum and ginger ale.

'You went in my fridge.' Maria stated, unimpressed. The girl was drunk. They could both get in so much trouble.

'I had a really bad day!' Nadia sat up with a whine. 'Stupid Sam Burrows made me look like an idiot in front of everyone!'

'Drinking is not the solution.' Maria answered, snatching the flask back.

'Didn't stop you!' Nadia replied sulkily.

Maria smarted. 'That was my birthday, and it was to celebrate, not escape from my problems.'

'Well, we're not all as perfect as you!' The girl said spitefully.

'Look, if you've got shit you need to deal with, try talking about it, instead of stealing other people's things, and then getting stroppy with them!' Maria's temper flared.

She waited to see Nadia's defences as they rose up, but she was not expecting the flood of information that came out of the girl, relatively unprompted, and was somewhat grateful to the alcohol for loosening Nadia's lips.

'Let me see, what can I tell you?' Nadia pressed her lips sarcastically. 'I left Dublin because my mother hates me, says she doesn't want to see me ever again... It might have had something to do with the fact that I spent most of last year off my tits on a cocktail of recreational drugs, and yes, I was on a self-destruct mission, but...' Nadia flung up her palms high. 'In my defence, my family was breaking apart, what else was I supposed to do? Sit like a good girl through school when my mum was drinking so much she cheated on my dad?'

Maria sighed to expel her intense energy.

'So, my dad moves to the middle of fucking nowhere in England just to escape her, leaving me with her! Is it any surprise I ran away too? I mean, my dad had a nervous breakdown and now he hates me too, because of her. He never wanted me to live with him, so as far as he's concerned I'm just staying there to retake my final year... he thinks he's done enough for me by letting me live there.'

Nadia stopped to take a breath, but seemed shocked at her outpour.

'I'm sorry you're having such a difficult time.' Maria said, her lips tight.

'Don't be sorry for me,' Nadia scowled again. 'No-one else gives a shit. My mum doesn't care and my dad doesn't care and I lost all my friends and I've got no-one else who knows me.'

'Well... I know some things now,' Maria shrugged. She moved back towards Nadia on the couch. 'Look, I want you to call me anytime you feel stressed or alone, and need to talk, not just about schoolwork, about whatever, I said I'm here for you and I meant it, I keep my word.'

In a flash, Nadia leaned over and threw her arms around Maria's shoulders. She laid her head away, pressing the muscles in Maria's back with her thumbs.

Her body seizing, Maria's eyes instinctively darted over Nadia's shoulder to check there was no-one at the door. She felt shocked, like a stray pet had jumped into her arms, she didn't want to encourage it with cuddles, but didn't have the heart to put it down. Maria closed her hands over Nadia's back and patted a few times, then just held them still as Nadia steadied her panting chest.

Chapter Five

Maria was required to attend the monthly meetings held in the learning support suite to discuss students' progress. Principal Woods regularly attended the meeting, but on this occasion, Maria wondered why it was necessary for Victoria Duncan, Nadia's form tutor, to be there.

'How's our newest addition getting on?' Woods asked. He hadn't forgotten their recent conversation - Maria knew he was asking her to play along for the sake of the group. She knew not to mention having Nadia stay behind extra nights, or her impending pay rise, and she definitely, obviously, wouldn't mention the drinking on school premises for fear of incriminating herself as well as Nadia.

'She's trying really hard, she's doing well,' Maria nodded in a circular motion and pressed her lips. 'But I think she's struggling at home... issues with her father or something.'

Unravel

'Well, there's something going on with her, that's for sure,' Victoria spoke up in her placid tones. 'I've found her quite difficult to reach... she's unapologetic when she's late and hardly acknowledges anyone around her, so *good for you* if you can connect with her.' She nodded towards Maria, her carefree greying streaks falling from her loose brown bun.

'Hm, have you been keeping a record of her lateness and absences?' Mr Woods' forehead furrowed, raising his eyebrows at Maria with a feigned concern.

'What absences?'

Both Woods and Mrs Duncan looked drily across at her, and Woods shifted in his chair uncomfortably. 'There have been reports from Nadia's teachers, she's apparently late several times a week and skips many classes-'

'Across all her subjects.' Mrs Duncan finished.

'I didn't know,' Maria raised her own eyebrows with surprise, wondering why Xavier hadn't mentioned this before. 'She always turns up for tuition, and she's never late.'

'Well, that's promising,' Woods acknowledged. 'I knew it would be difficult for her to settle in, given her history, but at least she enjoys her tuition.'

'She can't miss her classes, Xavier, she can't revise what she hasn't learned!' Victoria complained.

One of the learning support team, Tom Berry, with his twenty-something cheer and naivety, piped up. 'It's early days! Give the girl a chance to get her head around all these changes, surely?' He directed this to the group in general, being a bit shy of holding eye contact. 'If she's found a route to learning through Maria's tuition, then she's in good hands!'

Maria offered a grateful smile at Tom for his support, though he was just defending the team. He was young, bless him, Maria thought.

Principal Woods tilted his head. 'Yes, it's early days, but even if Maria is the best AST in the world, Nadia will have to knuckle down in the new term or she'll lose points on attendance, never mind showing for exams.'

'So, maybe it would be better coming from Maria,' Fat Sandra said, folding her arms under her brown bosom. 'She'll probably do a runner if anyone else gives her a warning.'

Maria sensed the agreement around the group. Once again, the onus was on her to take responsibility for this girl, and they hadn't even discussed the issues Maria had raised with Nadia's home and social life.

Leaving that meeting, Maria felt a hint of guilt pressing on the back of her conscience. Maybe Nadia was skipping classes because she had to revise the heavy load of material Maria had set for her. Nadia seemed to prefer the tuition and revision sessions with her one-to-one tutor, to the fresh information and live interaction with her classmates and other teachers, but from behind that reality pushed some pride at the fact she favoured Maria above all others.

Unravel

♥

Something felt different with Nadia at her desk during their next tuition, and try as she might to behave as she did with her other tutees, Maria became conscious of everything, from the state of her own unkempt hair to the painstaking white swirls of corrector fluid adorning Nadia's fingernails, and anything made Maria's mind dance away with involuntary distraction.

Blinking widely, Maria remained sitting awkwardly as they switched subjects and Nadia talked through a French passage she had interpreted. Her understanding of the language wasn't bad at all, but she wasn't making any attempt at the accent and kept her lilting Irish with an amused smile throughout.

'Am I saying it right?' Nadia asked. 'I suppose you're fluent in French, amongst all your other skills, aren't you?'

'Yes... no... I mean,' Maria stuttered. 'I'm not exactly fluent... but you're doing fine...' She faked a cough, pushing her fingers into the hair behind her ear.

'So how would you know if I said something wrong?' Nadia's eyes became serious.

Maria shook her head. 'I know enough to know you're okay... carry on.'

Nadia's lips moved into a smile. 'Don't you think I need to work on my oral?'

'What?' Maria twitched, then felt her upper body seize into her shoulders.

Nadia bit the side of her lip, dimple pressing deliciously. 'It was a joke.' Her voice was low and a little shaky; reflected in her eyes was a gentle nervousness.

Finding every word in her vocabulary had dissolved, Maria tried not to allow her eyes to rear wildly. She had to say something. *Just say something!*

'Actually...' Maria flipped the pages of the textbook between them. 'I'm surprised you are doing so well... because.. uh,' Maria wasn't ever good at disciplining nice students. 'Well, the principal happened to mention that you weren't attending quite a few of your other classes... I guess I'm just worried that you might think that by having revision sessions you can skip the real lessons... because I don't think that's right.'

Nadia looked only momentarily deflated before she lifted her chin and defended herself. 'I make sure I only skip lessons that I know already... I use those hours to get through *your* guide! I sit in the library and revise, it's not like I'm bunking off! Or drinking!'

'Okay, but,' Maria winced. 'If you miss stuff now, you'll have even more to revise come the end of next term...'

'Maria, I'm not stupid,' Nadia said assertively. 'I know exactly how much I've got to learn, but you tell me to concentrate on the important things, and the

Unravel

lessons I skip are the least important parts... like stupid role-playing and group work, they're just to prove we can work together, but I don't need to learn that *shite*, I've done it already.'

Remembering that Nadia was a year older and had suffered bonding sessions in her last school, Maria lowered her eyes and acknowledged Nadia's passionate reasoning. She nodded, for herself as well as Nadia. It flattered her greatly: Nadia was deliberately putting her tuition over and above all else, but it still left questions unanswered.

'So why bother turning up late if you're skipping whole lessons?'

'Sweet Jesus, what else has Mister Principal been saying about me?' Nadia said crossly. 'If you check the facts, I'm sure you'll find that I'm only late for registration, and that's 'cause the bus-wankers give me a hard time, so I get the later one where I get the whole bus to myself and I start my day happy, without being picked on! Same as the bus back into town, there's no way I'm sitting next to those dickheads while they toss segments of orange at my head!'

Maria nearly smiled, but thought better of it. 'Nadia, this isn't college, you can't just rock up when you like. If you miss registration first thing you get marked absent for the whole day.'

'So what?' Nadia scowled. 'I'm here to sit the exams, that's all! Please don't lecture me!'

Losing her patience with arguing, Maria took a breath and let her voice harden a little on its way out. 'If you get marked absent too often, getting one hundred percent on your exams won't count for shit, you'll be failed. I think it's forty percent, that's two mornings a week...' Maria shook her head and jabbed her fingers onto her desktop. 'I'm sorry that you get smushed by satsumas, but the school governers don't see, or care, if you stay behind late to make up for it! You need to get in on time, Nadia, get an earlier bus if you must, but if you carry this on, we may as well quit right now because no amount of tuition from me will be able to save you.'

Nadia's mouth parted, her eyes round and wounded. 'Oh...'

Maria immediately felt bad for being harsh. 'I'm sorry... I don't want to scare you,' she sighed out. 'I can talk to the principal, let him know the reasons you're absent.'

Nadia didn't smile. 'Thanks,' she blinked down somewhere near Maria's knees. 'I'll try and come in extra early so I won't miss registration.' She shot spiky green eyes up at Maria. 'I can't promise I'll go to every class. I need to get in the library when it's quiet or it's pointless.'

Maria nodded and was grateful for Nadia's compromise. The girl kept surprising her with her level of maturity, and getting to know her like this, Maria began to feel they had an understanding that united

Unravel

them. They were in this together and they had to communicate properly, or they would both fail. She didn't let go of Nadia's eye contact as they sat calmly, quietly accepting their mission, and their dependence on each other for its completion.

Then for just a second, a tangible something passed between them. Nadia blinked her eyes, two kisses that Maria felt flutter across on the waves of her lashes.

In the next second, Maria reminded herself of that creeping unease Karen brought out in her occasionally, but shook it off and knew there was no similarity between a sweet-breathed young lady like Nadia and a suggestive old queer like Karen.

Nadia was not gay - she didn't have that look about her.

If Nadia was thinking of Maria in sensitive ways, it was most likely formed out of intrigue since Nadia found out Maria was a lesbian - and Nadia knew her teacher was in a relationship - so there was definately no chance it would ever cross Nadia's mind that Maria might be attracted to her too. Still, Maria contemplated if Nadia did like her, what she should do about it: if it was something she should mention now, while they were being open with each other, or if it was something she should tell Principal Woods.

Resolving that she was going slightly stir crazy being stuck in her stuffy, high-rise office all day, Maria pushed her quickening, paranoid thoughts from her head and told herself it was nothing to worry about. Nadia was no threat and had nothing she couldn't handle.

'Hey, let's call it a night... your French is coming along fine.' Maria said and wondered how she'd come to give Nadia lifts to her bus stop every evening now. She reminded herself it was because it was dark, if the seasons had it sunny at this time of year, Nadia would be walking. Anyway, Maria's brain was tired, she wanted to go home.

At the station, Nadia climbed out of Maria's car, looking around for her bus. It should have been there. Unless it had gone already, some minutes early. She saw Nadia step around the pillars, searching; her mouth open, listening; her hair flying in the wind as she finally gazed up at the departures board. After a minute, Nadia returned to Maria's car with chattering teeth.

'It's gone! The next bus is in, like, forty minutes time!' She called through the lowered passenger window.

Maria immediately clocked the group of middle-Eastern-looking men in leather jackets huddled by the shelter nearby. She couldn't leave Nadia there, where the harsh orange glow of the streetlights cast dark shadows behind the concrete pillars. The coffee shop was closed across the way, and there were few others around.

'Get in,' Maria called. 'I'll take you home.'

Unravel

Nadia's forehead creased up in the strange shadowy light. 'Huh? To my dad's?'

'Or you could wait here with the Addams Family? It's up to you...' Maria shrugged, then waited for Nadia to check out the ugly alternative before re-starting her engine. Nadia stepped back inside and Maria pulled out of the bus station. She didn't know if what she was doing was allowed, but it seemed the only sensible choice.

Once on the stretch of road towards Stroud, Maria thought they might catch up with the bus Nadia had missed, and she could drop her at the stop in front of it. However, they didn't see it, and Nadia informed her the bus took an indirect route through the villages. Maria returned to her silence, doubting herself, wondering what was happening that made her feel so uncomfortable.

Sensing Nadia was watching her from the passenger seat, Maria could feel the tension rising in her. Her mood had changed and she had no patience left tonight. She didn't want to be stared at and if Nadia needed to say something, she'd better spill soon before Maria snapped.

'What?' Maria asked, keeping her teeth from gritting, and glanced briefly over at Nadia, small and folded next to her.

'Can I talk to you about Sam?'

'Sam Burrows?' Maria asked in return, though she knew exactly who Nadia meant.

'Yeah,' Nadia confirmed, then fell quiet for a moment. 'She's gone from being really rude to being really nice in the last week... and I don't know if she's messing around.'

'Look,' Maria said, getting to the point with a tone that reminded herself of her father. 'Sam Burrows is a wind-up, okay, she doesn't take anything seriously or have respect for many things, especially people's feelings. So just be careful you don't get hurt.'

It took thirty-five minutes to get to Eastcombe. Nadia directed Maria down the narrow roads that led to her father's house and Maria noted the route, guessing that she might have to make this journey again one day. When Nadia called to pull over, Maria found herself outside a small, run-down house with a tight evergreen obstructing the view. A tiled pathway snaked from the gate, next to sparse, naked trees that had shed crunchy leaves into muddy, flowerless beds running alongside the gravel which partitioned off the drive. There was no car, perhaps Mr Sheridan was out, though Nadia had said he'd be sleeping around this time; maybe he had no car.

There was no streetlight nearby but a dusty lantern illuminated the porch from under the eaves. It was dull, middle-aged, and Nadia did not look like she belonged there at all. There were hardly any neighbouring houses in the lane, it was secluded and deafeningly quiet. After seeing Nadia safely indoors, Maria wound down her window and breathed in the

Unravel

fresh air as she used her bearings and the occasional road signs to find her way back to Cheltenham.

Nearing Charlton Kings, Maria became aware that she couldn't stop thinking about Nadia. Groaning at her burdened mind, she wished she could teleport home but she had to go to Christian's first and make small chat with him too. Once she collected Leon, Maria tried to play with some energy for her dog's sake, but she had already sunk into an irritable mood. She cared more than she should about what Nadia was doing now, if she was warm enough, if she was lonely, and then, bitter ideas of what Sam Burrows was planning. Maria sighed: Nadia had gotten under her skin and now she felt involved in the girl's life.

♥

Cancelling her afternoon tuition period was a last resort, but Maria had to acknowledge the headache that had been building all day. She had no painkillers on her, so drank some water, and tried to ease the strains from her mind. Standing next to her windows, breathing deeply, Maria noticed the class of girls on the west playing field.

Karen was out there, blowing her whistle and shouting to the bunch of year eleven girls as they ran around in near freezing December temperatures with hockey sticks. They looked cold though clad with gloves, scarves, hats, and outsize hooded jumpers;

appearing older than in their usual girlish attire, Maria considered, with their bitter frowns and ruddy cheeks.

A pinprick of adrenalin alerted her on recognition of the unmistakeable red slash of Nadia's low ponytail under a grey, slouchy woolly hat, but Maria had never seen her in tracksuit trousers and trainers before; she looked boyish pacing the hard ground; her shoulders round, her breath panting out white steam clouds. She ran well, and twisted with impressive agility. Nadia was given a pat on her back as she bent in the stance, and she looked up to see Sam, who held her palm up for a high-five, which Nadia hesitatingly returned.

Deciding her head would benefit from a jet of bracing field air, Maria wrapped her jacket around her and lifted the wool-lined collars under her ears. She didn't like to wear hats, and she was glad for the rushing cold wind through her tresses as they swirled in front of her vision in curly, black streaks. A few of the girls noticed her approach, but Karen didn't see her until Maria muttered a greeting, cutting a dark figure standing tall beside her.

'Christ, I thought you were the grim reaper!' Karen touched her chest with a gasp of relief. 'Give a girl a warning before you sneak up on her.'

Maria huffed a smile though she did not feel like humouring Karen. It was not her intention to bring her bad mood outside, but she knew she wouldn't be able to stop frowning until her headache eased off. She wondered if sitting in her office, being on her computer or reading too much was making her ill: her usually olive skin had become pale this winter; Maria contemplated how fit and well Karen looked for working in the fresh air most of the day.

It wasn't long before some girls started calling over to her, some waving, some saluting with goofy, happy smiles. Maria lifted one hand from her jacket pocket and extended her fingers in a rather feeble gesture, but the chill wind bit at its gloveless skin and she returned it to the warmth of her pocket. In doing so, she saw that Nadia had noticed her, but she couldn't wave again: Maria was not the kind of person to reverse her movement no matter whom it was for. Her hand stayed in her pocket and she nodded instead, an abrupt, cold acknowledgement that Nadia responded to with a prolonged stare and a tug at the strand of hair clinging to her moist, rosy cheek.

'Come on, Lucy, move your ass, you're going to get swiped!' Karen yelled across to the fumbling girls in the middle distance. She stepped back to Maria, shaking her head. 'Amateurs.'

Maria winced at the whistle blow, then Karen shouting at another girl.

'Can you tell me something?' Maria asked quietly. 'Does Nadia ever miss your classes?'

Karen pulled a face and shrugged. 'A couple... mostly indoor sessions, I think... maybe she doesn't like the gym, but she seems to enjoy running around out here... Why? Is she missing tuition? God, she doesn't realise how lucky she is.'

Maria winced again at having to correct Karen. 'Actually, no... Its other classes she's missing because she thinks she can make up for it with tuition.'

Turning to Maria with a smile, Karen chuckled. 'She shows up for you without fail? Eager to please... oh gosh, yes, I bet she loves tuition with you! You realise what that means...'

Inside a deep, cold breath into her lungs, Maria cringed and wished Karen would resist projecting her own desires. 'What?'

Karen hooted. *'Teacher's pet!'*

'Don't be ridiculous.' Maria smarted and glanced over at Nadia.

The girl looked different under the layers of wool and fleece: she looked stronger, athletic like a real sporty type, light on her toes, seriousness pursed about her mouth. Nadia caught Maria looking, and stood upright from her bent hockey stance, patting her stick against the hard ground absent-mindedly, watching Maria with a curious expression.

Perhaps Nadia thought Maria wanted to tell her something. However, Nadia soon pulled her glance away from Maria when Samantha crept up behind her, pinched her ribcage, and made Nadia shriek with shock. Maria despised Sam Burrows. The soon-to-be-sixteen year old compensated for her large breasts and belly rolls with crude makeup around her pretty, blue eyes; a

Unravel

punk parade of studs climbed her ears to a messy array of short, multi-coloured hair. She never wore her uniform or gym clothes properly, having to wear it askew or tie it somewhere just to be alternative. Now, taunting Nadia, she flashed her teeth like a Cheshire cat, her chubby face reddened, and laughed forcibly to disguise her nervousness.

'Look at that!' Karen said out of the corner of her mouth, directing Maria over to where she was already looking. 'Sam's been winding Nadia up for days now... won't leave her alone. Talk about a new plaything!'

Maria cast a fiercely dark, slow glance across at Karen to gage her insinuation, realised Karen meant nothing by it, and slid heavy eyes back to the spectacle of Sam teasing the new girl. As Karen blew her whistle again and shouted instructions to a throng of clashing sticks at one end, Maria observed how Sam was striving for Nadia's attention, throwing her arms out in wide gestures. She pointed towards and then held onto Nadia's shoulders, talking and laughing all the time. Her friends, Kelly, Theresa and Zoe watching her back from a short distance, just where she liked them, and working her wobbling front Sam seduced Nadia under her spell. She plucked at Nadia's ponytail, stroked its length, and then released it with a flick, spinning her solid girth round on her heels on the muddy ground. Maria had only seen Sam dance provocatively for boys before; she was dancing for Nadia though.

Stood watching Sam with bemusement, Nadia turned vibrant eyes back to Maria.

Maria dropped her gaze instantly to the grass and felt the burning rise to her ears. She had to lift it straight away over to where Karen was gesticulating wildly to the outer field positions. Maria couldn't look back now - it would be so obvious. Maria rinsed her mind for what, precisely, would be obvious and had to admit she felt jealous that Sam was making such a fuss of Nadia: *her pet*!

Karen returned to Maria's side. 'So have you told her yet?'

Maria feared to speculate to what Karen might be referring. 'Told who what?'

Creasing her eyes with amusement, Karen whispered loudly. 'Told Nadia her personal tutor is a big fat lezz!'

'Why should I have to announce it? It's got nothing to do with tuition.' Maria scowled.

'She might not want to be your pet once she finds out!' Karen reasoned.

'As it happens, she knows already and she's fine with it, she's secure in herself.'

'Wait, she knows and still comes to all your tuitions!' Karen laughed. 'Well, it's good to know she's gay-friendly... I think Sam's counting on it!'

Feeling her thoughts leap with irritation at Karen's suggestiveness, Maria lost her temper. 'Why are you making judgements about their sexuality? I'd

Unravel

rather not think about students that way, it's perverted! In fact, why do you have to talk about lesbians all the time? You know, just because you and I are gay doesn't mean I have any interest in picking out who else is... Nadia is not a lesbian and you can't turn someone gay by spending time with them!'

Karen threw her arms into the air. 'I never said that!'

Turning away with a moody swish of her jacket, Maria called over her shoulder. 'You were thinking it!' Maria kept going. She stalked all the way back to her office without a second look back at Karen or any of the girls, especially Nadia. She didn't want to be associated with Karen, wished she hadn't been seen standing next to her: two old lesbians eyeing up the girls running around in their sporty outfits. Maria's head throbbed harder. She could no longer bear thinking about Karen, Sam, or Nadia. All she had to do was breathe and calm down until her head was empty of all thoughts.

Chapter Six

Maria's body twitched over images of Nadia sat beside her in deep tuition. Red hair falling over her shoulder, blazing green eyes blinking up at her with curling lashes, her hesitant, then helpless smile, those adorable dimples. Maria felt her blood coursing through her limbs, her mind unable to grasp the whispering torments of Nadia fading one after the other. The shape of her breast, the tilt of her head, the twist of her eyebrow, the pout of her lips, the cross of her legs, Maria touched herself, pressing in circles, over and over. Her body rocked in her bed, her open mouth sucking in her quickening breath as her compulsion brought her to the surface, taking small gasps of air into full lungs before release. Her voice awoke her: a guttural expulsion of her tension, and Maria's eyes flickered open.

She lay very still, thick with her dream, knowing if she moved it would be gone. On her front, zoning down to the warm centre of yearning between her legs, Maria flicked back through the flashes of her waking thoughts, and gulped at her dawning desire.

Leon jumped on her bed. Maria started and then reached to stroke him as he nuzzled into her. She loved him and told him so, but after ten seconds, she was thinking about Nadia again, with a disturbing feeling that sliced open a new channel in her consciousness.

Her phone rang that Saturday morning.

'I got a bonus, baby!' Lois exclaimed with a nasal squeal. 'Jonathan was blown away with my designs, you know, that secured our American contract - he thinks I can get us an even bigger client next time! He said I should add them to my portfolio... then make a push for the Jepson Foundation, they are *massive!*'

'Well done you.' Maria said, faking a happy tone as she slid down into her car.

Driving cross-country in her car with Leon's harness strapped into the passenger seat was always a slight mission, and recently, Maria's mind was heavy with distraction, but the spontaneous, two and a half hour journey to see Ben in London that day was smooth-sailing. Benicio managed a salon called Comb, in Covent Garden, though it specialised in afro-Caribbean hair, Ben had been cutting Maria's spiralling, European hair for years, and she wouldn't go anywhere else.

Maria breezed in the front door of the salon that December day, little Leon in her arms, sending the celebrity hairstyle magazines by the front door flapping.

Maria glanced at the three young, well-dressed Black females laughing amongst themselves on the waiting couches, then nodded to the funky-haired Chinese receptionist as soon as she was acknowledged. Asking for Ben, Maria unzipped her fleece-lined leather jacket now she was warm inside with the heat of the hairdryers, while the girl headed down the staircase to the floor below.

Within two minutes, Ben came bounding up the stairs and threw his arms wide with a broad grin that made Maria's heart pang with pleasure. He took his cousin in his muscular arms, tight and broad under his smart, white shirt, and hugged her, and she felt safe, like she'd come home. If she had not been in a busy salon, a tear might have sprung to her eye, but Ben proceeded to make a loud fuss of Leon too, then called the receptionist, Issy, to bring beer and led them downstairs to his quieter station. In the cooler and slightly calmer basement, sleek reflective surfaces bounced the spotlights haloing from the ceiling; Ben wrapped Maria in a salon gown and lifted her hair from her neck with a dexterous sweep. Leon settled in front of the coat rack and watched the stylists' feet move around the salon floor, shifting through the sprigs of hair falling from other clients' heads.

'Ria, Ria, Ria, what's going on?' Ben shook his head, smiling, his accent powerful.

'My hair's not that bad is it?' Maria chuckled and relaxed as Ben put his fingers through the black curls at her neck.

'It's good to see you... I missed you,' he bent and kissed the top of her head. 'So, tell me everything!' Ben stretched his fingers, then began to dampen Maria's hair with a water spray.

Sipping from the bottle of cold beer Issy brought down for her, Maria began with Lois' recent bonus: she was going up in the world, and she wasn't shy about rubbing it in. 'It's like a constant threat I'm going to be left behind.'

'She has left you behind!' Ben replied. 'She moved out, she's moving on, so should you!'

'I can't just break up with her, what reason do I have?'

'Fuck someone else!' Ben smiled and winked at her.

Maria rolled her eyes, pursing her lips with distaste. 'I don't want to fuck around, Ben, that's not me.'

'Wait,' Ben frowned. 'You're not afraid of being alone, are you?' He exhaled through his nose. 'There are so many women who would love to be with you, you're beautiful.'

Maria looked into the salon reflected in her mirror and saw a few faces in the seats opposite looking blandly back at her through theirs. She had, indeed, been harbouring thoughts of breaking up with Lois, but she had to admit she couldn't stand the idea of the ensuing arguments: Lois' anger and upset, denial and accusations, tears and destruction of property. Maria was always scared to challenge Lois for fear of unleashing that whining wasp of a creature with vicious, flippant jibes and a cutting laugh that sullied Maria down to her bones, yet she knew being a pushover was pathetic.

Ben thankfully changed the subject as he sliced the weight out of her hair, and Maria was happy to hear his news that his wife, Chloe, was pregnant with their second child. Chloe was a gentle, beautiful Carribean woman and Levi a handsome, bright, four-year old boy. Maria listened willingly to Ben talk of Levi, including his preferred activities and first experiences in pre-school; she felt bad she hadn't seen Ben's family in so long.

As her thoughts travelled, however, Maria then felt guilty for not paying full attention to her cousin's stories of family bliss, and wondered if Ben would be able to shed any light on how to deal with her troubling new student. So she broached the subject as something that was playing on her mind, something causing awkwardness at her otherwise pleasantly banal school. Maria told all she knew of Nadia, but heard herself sounding negative about her, when negativity was the last thing she felt in the girl's company.

'She just stares at me a lot, she talks and laughs, then she's quiet and moody, she acts like she's mature then breaks down in tears... it's wigging me out because I don't want some student getting so personal when I'm trying to teach her,' Maria frowned. 'I feel like she wants something, even the staff expect me to give more of my time, but I'm helping her enough as it is... I don't think I can support her in the way she needs, but I feel bad because she hasn't got anyone else.'

'Ria, why did you take up teaching?' Ben pulled some product off his shelf.

''Cause I had a lot of excess knowledge I didn't want to go to waste.'

'No... good try.' Ben looked at his cousin seriously. 'You told me you wanted to provide an easy route towards understanding subjects that needn't be so difficult... That things like emotions, pressure, self-esteem get in the way... therefore if you can get someone to feel relaxed and confident, their learning will boost ten-fold. Is that right?'

'Yeah I guess.' Maria said; she'd forgotten that she used to be so passionate.

'There you go,' Ben shrugged, scrunching the serum through the ends of her hair. 'This girl knows you are the one to come to because you make her feel relaxed and confident, and she's got a lot of catching up to do, no?'

Maria thought for a few seconds, but that didn't reassure her entirely.

'Ben, I swear, she found out I was gay and she looked at me funny, you know... different. Something's changed and I can't figure out what it is. She's not gay, she doesn't flirt or anything... but she's not shy. She

Unravel

just makes herself at home in my office, like she has a right to be there. She attends every one of my tuitions when she skips other classes, like she wants to impress me. My colleague even took the piss that I have a "teacher's pet"!'

'And why is that a bad thing? She wants to work hard for you!' Ben reasoned, starting up the hairdryer. 'She'll pass her exams, and you'll look great.'

'I don't know!' Maria twitched defensively. 'Something's not right.'

What Maria couldn't tell Ben was that she was irrationally attracted to Nadia and had practically climaxed in a dream about her. It seemed uncomfortable and wrong to think about that, now that the feeling had long passed, and it would make her sound like a complete pervert if she confided to him now.

'Look, it sounds like you're doing a great job,' Ben responded. 'You're right to keep professional boundaries though, it's possible she's relying on you for too much. How about you encourage her to make other friends, you know, socialise outside of school?'

'I already suggested that,' Maria shook her head. 'She's as anti-social as I am.'

Ben shrugged. 'What about finding her a boyfriend?'

'A boyfriend?' Maria flashed her eyes. 'How's that keeping professional boundaries?'

'Well... it would take some pressure off you...

might be just what she needs.'

'How am I going to find her a boyfriend?' Maria asked, only to humour him.

'Well, there must be a good-looking, popular boy in her year, tell him that she likes him and get him to ask her out.'

'I can't do that! That's weird!' Maria revolted.

'You have to use your discretion obviously! Is she anything to look at?'

Maria thought softly over Nadia's pretty eyes and skin, and knew she had to be careful of her tone and expression, never mind her words. 'Yeah, she's cute... red hair... but I can't think of any guys in her year she might like.'

'Well, it's in *your* interests to find her someone,' Ben reasoned. 'What kind of thing is she into? I mean, girls like music, so find her a musician!'

There was nothing Maria could recall Nadia saying she liked, in particular, only what she didn't like. She couldn't imagine Nadia with any of the boys at school, then again, *any* boys were impossible for Maria to perceive attractively. She racked her brains hopelessly.

Glancing down at Leon, Maria suddenly thought of one young man who was gentle, could be trusted, and would adore someone like Nadia if the way he adored Leon was anything to go by: Christian. She smiled at Ben and reminded him about her dog-sitter. Ben nodded approvingly and agreed that Maria should introduce the boy to Nadia.

After her hair was finished, Maria embraced him deeply, sent her love to Chloe and little Levi, and promised to call him regarding Christmas.

While returning to her car and settling Leon in the seat next to her, Maria realised she should really make the effort to go to see Lois at work - make a surprise visit or take some flowers at least - but Maria stayed sat in her car, contemplating her options. She knew she did not want to battle through central London, and not even seeing her girlfriend was reward enough to motivate her. Maria looked at her phone, thought about calling Lois, but didn't. She thought about texting a message, but didn't. Maria dropped the phone inside her jacket and drove home.

♥

That weekend, Maria received an email from Nadia Sheridan. She held her glass of wine to her lips in anticipation, but, scanning it, frowned at the content: it was not about tuition, or either of them as individuals. It was about Samantha *fucking* Burrows.

Maria couldn't take her eyes off the white screen as she read it in full, taking in Nadia's writing style, ensuring she read it correctly, imagining Nadia reading it to her in her softly curling accent as if she were sitting right there next to her.

Nadia wrote how she had gone out to a club in

Gloucester with Sam on Friday night, except Sam's friends Kelly, Zoe and Theresa had come too, and they were all laughing at 'in-jokes' and Nadia felt left out. She had spent all her money on getting them drinks, but they didn't buy her any back. She had realised they were using her because she looked older, and the bartenders didn't check her ID. Then some guy had started talking to her and asked her to dance and Nadia said she agreed to because he seemed friendly, but Sam had marched up to her and pulled her away, shouting at her that she couldn't just *fuck off* and leave her friends. Theresa had been sick, according to Sam, because of all the drinks Nadia had given her, and Sam was, apparently, very drunk when she told Nadia she knew all about her past: she had 'contacts' in Dublin who told her what people had said about Nadia in her last school. Nadia had felt paranoid and ran away from them, out of the club and into a taxi. Except she couldn't afford it so she got out at Stroud, telling the driver she was going to get cash out, and escaped through a nearby pub and out the bustling beer garden, tripping over some rubbish, and running for her life down some dark streets. She had stumbled home at one in the morning, some two miles along pitch black roads, upset and terrified.

Maria took a long breath and wiped her face. She felt confused by simultaneous, conflicting feelings of protection over Nadia's vulnerability, and annoyance at her stupidity. Why the girl had accepted Sam's invite out, after she had warned her, Maria couldn't understand. She could see why Nadia had tried to buy friendship and approval through purchasing drinks, but to walk home alone - she was still only sixteen - Maria shivered and felt like writing something suitably reprimanding and teacher-ish in return.

However, Maria's fingers hesitated and she sighed, softening. She had told Nadia she would be there to support her no matter what, and if she cut her down now, Nadia would never open up to her again. After all, girls had to be girls. Maria had learned through her own mistakes and she had to acknowledge Nadia seemed to have enough experience at finding her own way.

Maria sipped her wine, imagining Nadia walking home alone in the dark through that freezing night. She imagined driving along that road, seeing a girl appearing in the near distance, bare legs glowing in the headlights, recognising her, stopping to see if she was okay. Her heart would reach out to any one of her students, trembling, weeping with shame.

But Nadia.

Surely that dream was just a stupid reaction to being driven by concerns for Nadia. Or maybe it was something to do with the brain desiring what it cannot have - the same impulse that motivates petty theft, Maria supposed, the thrill of going against the rules; forbidden fruit. Nadia, with her auburn hair and creamy skin, her orange bow lips and little dimples, Maria thought about the knowing look in the girl's eye, and her stomach fluttered.

Then she was disgusted with herself. Nadia would not be comfortable with a horny teacher: no student would. Maria had to be professional, could never allow her lesbian nature to interfere with their objective, and had to suppress any emotion or desire that arose from spending time in Nadia's company, for Nadia's sake. Maria feared behaving as predatorily perverted as Karen; she couldn't stand it. Maria made a decision right there and then to never indulge Nadia in personal matters of the heart, for fear of her own inability to deal with topics of love, lust, desire and sexuality without bias, and fear of revealing her own sensitive heart. She could never, *ever*, let Nadia see or sense her vulnerability and if that meant lying outright to protect Nadia, and herself, then she would, to the bitter end.

Chapter Seven

Maria listened to the rain drumming down onto the windows of her office, worried: Nadia was late. Waiting beside the radiator, Maria stared out through the fading light, steadily darkening minute by minute, the blinds hanging partway down like sleepy eyelids. The storm hadn't relented all day, now December was turning more bitter by the hour; she hoped Nadia was simply stuck talking to a teacher.

Her tuitions that Monday had been fine, easy in fact, which Maria attributed to the heavy downfall subduing her students. Indeed, the bad weather had not just created a cosy, united feeling in her office; she had seen a moist-headed, wild-eyed look in the kids around school that reminded her of river otters, perky and cheerful; in their element: resurfaced, their coats shaken out. She passed classrooms full of groups closing in to work on exercises, their clothes steaming from their body heat; in the staff room, other teachers had marvelled at the settled atmosphere and briefly quipped that they wished it could always be this way.

But now, the thought crossed Maria's mind that Nadia would not come for her revision session: a worthy punishment for not returning the email about Sam. Perhaps Nadia was sulking, or perhaps, after all, this was the start of her being late for her study hour, too.

Startling Maria out of her sinking mood, the shifting of movement from the office door deposited a faceless, green parka inside her room. There was a dull groan from under the wretched wall of hair, followed by an exaggerated sigh.

'My life is like one everlasting nightmare.' Nadia whined loudly.

'Hey,' Maria dropped her arms from the folded position across her chest and approached Nadia. 'Where have you been? I didn't think you were coming.'

Pushing back her fringe, Nadia scrunched her face, unbuttoning her coat. 'I don't feel very well. I had a nosebleed! In front of everyone at registration, it was so gross!'

As Nadia hung up her coat, Maria saw, with some alarm, residues of dark-red staining around her nostril. She approached, raising her hands, wanting to tend to her, but Nadia pulled away. 'Don't! It's stopped now.'

Recoiling, Maria felt hideous for having reached out to Nadia. The girl did not want to be touched, or else, her nose was too sensitive, and Maria shrivelled in the atmosphere between them as Nadia unlaced her squeaking, wet boots. It set things off badly. Maria didn't know what to do with herself, or what to say, as Nadia silently opened her books and began flicking. She could hear the girl was snivelling and remembered she had said she hadn't felt well.

'Do you want me to make you some tea or anything?' Maria said suddenly.

Without looking up, Nadia murmured. 'Okay.'

It was a definate awkwardness Maria felt, and she wondered what she could do to rectify it as she went to her mini-fridge to re-boil the kettle on top of it. Nadia didn't look ill, but there was something wrong. Had she been telling the truth about the nosebleed? At least if her classmates were witnesses Maria could be assured the girl wasn't trying to seek her attention before pushing her away.

Two mugs of black tea in hand, Maria rested one in front of Nadia's books and turned her back, without saying a word to further annoy or distract Nadia, and returned to her desk. Only then did she hear Nadia's belated 'Thank you,' but she took her own seat with nothing to signal receipt. If Nadia was going to show up late, without a text to let her know; reveal she was bleeding but reject Maria's caring hand, and sit in strange silence drinking tea with no further interaction, then Maria might start letting herself think, for the first time, that Nadia was a typically selfish, ignorant, teenager, with no manners, and no regard for the teacher who was going out of her way to make her student comfortable.

So much for introducing her to Christian. He was a sweet boy whom Nadia would probably chew up and spit out. Maria had serious second thoughts about the reverse of her supposed professional boundaries – it could be unethical to allow her dogsitter to become involved with her vampish student. Never mind fearing Nadia's vulnerability; she obviously knew how to take care of herself and get what she wanted.

In the ten minutes or so that it took for Maria to calm the seething under her skin and forget Nadia's coldness, she had tapped a few items into her internet search engine for Christmas presents, holding her tea against her lips for cooling, regular sips. She could do no productive work while she was angry or upset, Maria had learned that long ago, and looking at wintery warm things and novelty gifts for Ben and his family vaguely cheered her spirit.

Except when she heard a sob escape Nadia's hushed breathing, Maria's alarms set off all over again, shedding every ounce of resentment she had assumed since Nadia's arrival, and she placed down her cup with tentative concern.

'What's wrong?' Maria stood up slowly, looking over to Nadia's shuddering shoulders. The girl was crying, really crying, with genuine trembling of her body and streams flooding from her eyes. Nadia could not speak for strangled sobs and gave futile wipes at her cheeks with her jumper. Maria brought over the tissues from her desk, but held herself back in case Nadia flinched at her close proximity again.

'I'm going to fail!' Nadia wailed finally. 'I'm going to screw up so badly... I can't deal with this, my head is so full of crap, I can't cope, Maria!'

'What crap?' Maria asked patiently.

'Everything!' She sobbed. 'I argued with my dad last night, I was upset about Sam and her stupid friends teasing me, and he said if I can't get on at school then he can't put me up, I'll have to go and live in a hostel with other teenage drop-outs and losers! I'm sick of the way he treats me, I can't cope with all this stress. Maybe I *should* go and live in a hostel, at least then I'd be independant and wouldn't have to answer to anyone!'

'You still have to pay rent in a hostel, so unless you've got a job to pay your way, I'd try to stay in school.' Maria replied reasonably, loitering by her desk.

'Fuck it, Maria!' Nadia slammed her fists on her books, shuddering the mug beside her. 'No one is looking out for me! I feel like I'm doing this to make other people happy, when they don't actually care about me! If I didn't turn up tomorrow, no one would miss me...'

Maria contemplated the gap between them, bemused at the drama of Nadia's self-pity. She wouldn't be able to patronise her like some other students. Maria would have to be genuine, otherwise

Unravel

she would risk losing Nadia's trust.

'I told you I care,' Maria offered. 'I made you tea, didn't I?'

'You made yourself tea as well!' Nadia objected, reaching for the tissue box.

'I cared enough to want to check if your nosebleed was okay, but you didn't let me...'

'I don't need you to stick a tissue up my nose for me, it was finished already!'

'I was trying to show you I *do* give a shit...' Maria shrugged with hopeless shoulders.

Nadia fell quiet then burst into soft sobs. 'I'm sorry.' She whinnied with tender humbleness into the tissue. Her shoulders collapsed into tremors and her elbows retracted tightly against her chest, weeping achingly enough, evidently, to double her into foetal position.

Maria couldn't just stand there and watch.

Stepping hesitantly between the table and couch, Maria placed one hand on the girl's back, between her shoulder blades, so as not to shock her, then quietly sat beside her. Nadia did not flinch away from her this time, which was a good sign. Maria gently guided Nadia towards her and was relieved when the girl leaned into the curve between Maria's jaw and clavicle, hands still pressed against her face with the tissue.

Remembering that Nadia had been weeping the last time they embraced, Maria hoped this wasn't some insidious attention-seeking behaviour, but trusted her instinct that it wasn't. Nadia's tears were sincere: it was neither a sensual cuddle nor an unconvincing act that had led to it. Nadia had not thrown herself against Maria this time, and had not even opened her arms to cuddle back. This was a simple, authentic, caring, teacher-hugging-an-anxious-student moment. There was nothing wrong with that, Maria reconciled. She waited for someone to come in.

Soon, feeling the tension subside, Maria knew she had done the right thing. By keeping Nadia at a distance, it was making the awkwardness between them worse. Nadia desperately needed a friend, and whether she liked it or not, Maria was the only one she had.

'Nadia?' Maria released the girl slightly and looked down at her. 'I think a break is needed, let's take the evening off, go and do something different.'

'Like what?' Nadia asked, the tissue crumbling against her cheeks.

'You like dogs?' Maria asked tenderly.

'Yeah..?' Nadia's interest blinking through spiky, brown lashes.

'Want to meet one?'

'You have a dog?' Nadia asked delicately.

'Yeah... he's called Leon,' Maria tried a light smile. 'My neighbour looks after him while I'm working. He's a rescue, so he just loves company. He'd love to meet you.'

'I'd love to meet him!' Nadia smiled at last, her

mascara pooling under her eyes.

Maria resisted wiping her cheeks for her, and let her arms drop away from holding Nadia with a final, caring rub of her arm. 'Come on then.'

The rain was still pouring, and once in the safe, snug seats of her car, Maria put the radio on so they would not be in silence for the journey that would take a little longer than usual during the rush hour. She was glad as this also gave her time to think more upon what she was doing: Maria couldn't help but feel things were moving out of her control; not that Nadia was controlling things, but things were *happening*, and Maria didn't have time to check whether these things were right for either of them. Something was definately nagging inside; Maria continued the battle in her head with each brake and acceleration.

It felt odd to be taking Nadia north-east out of Gloucester instead of south-east towards Stroud. She was taking Nadia to Cheltenham, to Charlton Kings where she lived - Nadia might find out the street where her house was: it felt like she was doing something immoral; there was that feeling of stealing again. However, Maria again reasoned that she was not taking Nadia to her house, but to Christian's, with a purpose: to meet her dog... *no*... to meet Christian. She was taking Ben's advice and introducing her student to a boy so that she might have a friend outside school - in doing so she might ease the pressure of Nadia's attachment to her. With renewed focus, Maria drove a little faster, and tried not to let her concentration slip just because Nadia was watching her drive.

Nadia leaned over to turn the stereo down slightly. 'Did you cut your hair?'

'Yeah, my cousin's a stylist.' Maria smiled, then felt her cheek blush.

'It looks good...' Nadia fell into a silent stare, seemingly waiting for Maria to acknowledge she wanted to say something else. 'Did you get my email?' Nadia finally asked.

Feeling a heavy need to gulp, Maria let a car turn in front of her, biding her time. 'Yeah, sorry, I was in London at the weekend, I didn't have time to respond.'

There was a few seconds silence during which Maria missed Nadia's expression; she didn't dare look.

'I know it's not your job,' Nadia sniffed. 'But I was hoping you'd be able to give me some advice about Sam.'

Maria frowned. 'Honestly, I don't know Sam, she rarely turns up for her tuition, but I just think she likes to wind people up, you know, test them by pushing them away... she probably really likes you.' Maria immediately regretted saying that.

'You think she was trying to fuck with my head?' Nadia asked, then seemed to have answered her own rhetorical question.

Ignoring the comment, Maria intended to imply Sam would leave her alone if Nadia stuck up for

Unravel

herself: 'Just be firm with her, be yourself, show her you're not a pushover.'

'You think I should just carry on as normal? Pretend nothing happened?'

'Yeah, otherwise things will be weird, you'll get upset and distracted from your studies. It's not a good idea to let these things get in the way. Forget about it, it'll blow over.' Maria heard herself speaking the kind of general advice she would give any student, and was pleased she was able to act, for Nadia's sake, nonchalantly.

After that, Nadia turned the radio back up again, but sat in thoughtful silence.

Maria remembered where she was taking Nadia and had another attack of conscience, questioning her actions. Though for a long time she had considered that Christian would benefit from having a girlfriend, she wasn't sure if introducing these two was particularly clever given that neither of them were aware of the fact that she was trying to set them up, and she hadn't even told Christian she was coming with company. She had not prepared for this at all, and the persistent feeling of edginess about presenting her student to her dog-sitter plagued her all the way to Charlton Kings. Maria eventually sourced one significant concern from the realisation that Nadia's father would most likely not approve of this conduct. Wondering about Nadia's father built up a sudden fear that made her gasp and cut off her train of thought before she swerved into a parked car.

'Nadia, did you say your father works *every* evening?' Maria asked, turning the radio down again.

Turning observant eyes onto her teacher, Nadia spoke seriously. 'Mostly... he says he needs to pay for the house so he works all the shifts he can get,' Nadia pursed her lips. 'But when he has time off, he's just bonkers. He breaks things just so he can put them back together, he collects all these random things and puts them into boxes. It's better when he's working because he sleeps until he has to leave.'

Surprised at Nadia's words, Maria shot a glance across at the girl's sulky profile, turned away, looking through the far side of the windscreen at the world racing by.

Maria reasoned. 'Surely he would know if you weren't there for dinner.'

Nadia snapped with a flaring temper. 'He doesn't make dinner! He doesn't eat, and if he did he wouldn't call me down to join him! I could be dead and he wouldn't know! Sometimes he doesn't even come back for days, he sleeps at work. His house is like a base, and just because I've moved in doesn't make it a home. I'm basically a lodger! Except I don't pay rent, so I clean for him instead!'

'Don't be angry at me,' Maria said firmly, 'I'm just looking out for you. I don't want you to get in trouble for not being where you're supposed to be! Your father might just have a problem with me taking you out of tuition to meet my dog.'

Nadia quietened abruptly and looked back out of the window. 'He doesn't care.'

Maria felt empathy for Nadia's home situation and recalled her own father's absentee attitude. 'Nadia, I know how you feel, it's okay... I hope we can talk openly about things, you know, just... don't get defensive, I'm on your side.' Maria took her eyes off the road once more to seek Nadia's eye contact and waited for her to give a subtle nod of comprehension.

She did, then turned her face back to the window, in which Maria noticed a half-shadowed smile reflecting the orange streetlamps in the glass.

♥

Evidently, Nadia was more interested in meeting the dog than she was in meeting Christian, and Maria was starting to think she had not sold the young chap to her at all judging by the fact that Nadia made no attempt at preening her hair or face in preparation for meeting a human male. Maria didn't know quite what to make of the situation: taking her student to meet her neighbour was so estranged from the reality of her teaching environment. She pulled up outside Christian's house with a dizzy, unsettled feeling of suspense, as if she were waiting for some drug to kick in. She should have warned Christian they were coming; for she would be disturbed if Christian brought a total stranger round to her house.

    Maria tried to reconcile her moral discomfort by simply playing out the part in this innocent act: as far as Christian was concerned, she was coming to collect her dog, as she always did - just with a girl in tow. There was no reason he should mind, and if he didn't, he might invite them in for tea. Maria hoped Christian was smart enough to see she was bringing Nadia round to meet him especially, and really hoped he had showered that day.

    Christian's pleasant features opened with a smile on Maria's arrival, but his light blue eyes flinched as he saw Nadia beside her. Hearing cheery greetings from his owner's voice, Leon came padding down the stairs, tail propelling around, and nosed Christian out of the way to get to Maria with short, ecstatic whinnies. Maria crouched to embrace Leon as Nadia's hands flew to her cheeks with joy.

    'Hey, I hope you don't mind, I brought Nadia, she's one of my students, she really wanted to meet Leon!' Maria said, winking up at Christian.

    Nadia crouched down beside Maria, and Leon nudged his nose against her knees, lifting his paws to hers on her command and licking as much of her wrist as he could reach under her coat.

    'Oh my gosh, he is adorable! He's smaller than I thought!' Nadia exclaimed, her accent thicker than Maria had heard it in a while. Nadia giggled deliriously, and squeezed her face up as the skinny dog licked her chin enthusiastically.

Christian raised his hand in salute. 'Hi, nice to meet you.'

Nadia lifted and creased her eyes for a second to return his welcome, before she continued to coo down at Leon, who rolled over to expose his belly for her to stroke.

Tilting her head towards the lounge inside as a signal to Christian to invite them indoors, Maria let her hands fall into a 'T' shape by her waist, away from Nadia's line of vision.

Christian flinched again, then understood her meaning. 'Do you guys want to come in? I was just going to make some tea.'

Nadia stood up and looked to Maria for her response.

Maria feigned surprise and turned to Nadia. 'Oh well, it's up to you, Nadia, do you feel like staying for a brew?'

'Yeah sure, that would be nice, thanks,' Nadia nodded to Christian, then at Maria. 'We never really finished the last one.'

Christian slapped his hands together and welcomed them in. Maria was relieved to see his t-shirt looked iron-fresh and there were no unsightly stains on his socks.

Maria led Nadia through the hall, after taking her coat, feeling strangely unfamiliar in the house where her dog spent so much of his time. She asked

Christian a few casual questions about Leon, such as what they'd done that day, given the weather was so bad, and listened distractedly to Christian's replies as she made sure Leon was playing nicely with Nadia, crouched on the tiled floor next to her. She enjoyed watching Nadia's smile grow every time Leon pawed her wrist for more attention, but Maria also wanted to make sure Nadia felt included in the conversation.

'So when are your folks back?' Maria asked, not that she cared one iota.

'Oh, next week,' Christian answered, then turned to Nadia to explain. 'They've taken a second honeymoon to renew their vows, rented a villa in Mauritius overlooking Blue Bay.'

Nadia raised her eyebrows to show a little interest, but her mouth twitched sheepishly. 'I actually have no idea where that is.'

Maria liked the fact that Nadia was honest, instead of doing the polite thing and nodding and smiling, pretending she knew her geography. And the fact that Nadia spoke so bluntly and humorously, with her Dublin accent, made Maria consider the girl was different to any of her other students, relaxed in this social scenario. Nadia would probably get on with Christian just fine. It made what she was doing here a little easier to swallow.

'I can show you if you like?' Christian seized an idea excitedly. 'Online!'

'Yeah?' Nadia's interest perked up. 'They sent

you photos?'

'Better than that!' Christian pointed his finger upstairs. 'I'll get my laptop.'

Christian asked if Maria would finish off making the teas and scooted his socks along the polished floor out of the kitchen. Maria figured she didn't have a choice and moved stubbornly over to the kettle once it had popped. She didn't pour water in her cup, it was never her intention to drink the tea she invited her and Nadia in for. When Nadia questioned her, Maria said she changed her mind; she would need to use the bathroom if she drank any more.

When Christian arrived back downstairs with his laptop, he proceeded to show Nadia where Mauritius was on the globe, using the latest internet mapping tool.

'Wow! I've never seen anything like this!' Nadia was vocal in her amazement as Christian showed her how to navigate. He zoomed in to Blue Bay in Mauritius and Nadia continued to gasp as she saw the clarity of the crisp white sands and shallow, sky-blue waters of the bay. 'That is incredible!'

'Yeah my folks are... somewhere around there!' Christian indicated towards a resort of individual villas overlooking the beach.

'Oh, that's looks divine!' Nadia cooed. 'You're one of those technology nerds, aren't you? I'm terrible with computers and things.'

'Yeah?' Christian's blue eyes brightened. 'I

could show you a few tricks.'

'Really? That would be amazing, thanks!' Nadia beamed.

On realising both her young friends had turned their backs against her, Maria looked down at Leon curled on a soft, folded matting; he lifted his eyes and met hers, holding, waiting. Maria knew that if she tipped her head towards the door he would spring up and be ready to go. She thought carefully.

'You guys, I'm just going to go and take Leon back to mine for his dinner,' Maria said and looked at Nadia. 'You'll be okay here?'

A flash of confusion crossed Nadia's eyes at first, but hiding it, she nodded to Maria.

'I'll be back in...' Maria checked her wristwatch, 'half hour or so?'

Maria looked back down at Leon and allowed him the nod he had anticipated since hearing his name. He leapt to his feet and headed straight for the door.

'Bye Leon!' Nadia called.

As she smiled on Leon's behalf, Maria heard Christian explaining to Nadia about some topographical feature, and Nadia's returning query became faint as Maria opened the front door and put it on the latch. She left the house feeling distinctly alone, and the cold, spitting rain hit bitterly against her open, vulnerable neck. She walked Leon toward the park near her house sinking into a sadness she couldn't decipher, she just felt suddenly depressed. In theory, her plan had worked,

Christian had received Nadia well and was being chatty and friendly; Nadia had not resisted spending time in Christian's company and had settled comfortably once they found a mutual interest. That had come about effortlessly. Maria hoped now they would get on famously, and the pressure would be off her if Nadia liked him for a boyfriend.

She should feel happy, not sick and like she were about to cry.

Chapter Eight

An interesting change occurred in the week that passed after Maria had introduced Nadia to Christian: Maria supposed she was pleased they had got on so well and considered it a good thing that Nadia was keen to visit again, but it wasn't clear if it was Christian that she was keen to see, or her dog, Leon. Christian had said Nadia was welcome anytime, suggesting they could walk Leon together, and they had both looked at Maria with wide eyes, seeking her permission as if she were their master as well as Leon's. Maria feigned her choice to acquiesce, and was left reeling that it had been so easy to set Nadia up with a friend, a boy - a trusted, nice boy who she knew would treat Nadia like a princess.

For the last few weeks of the Autumn term, Maria assisted with the hectic press of due coursework for many extra students, so after working through lunches and her regular tuitions, exhausted Maria found herself happy and willing to drive Nadia to Christian's house instead of spending any longer in school.

Besides, since seeing her in this new social light, Maria understood that it wasn't the extra study Nadia needed, it was purely somewhere else to be than her father's house.

Once she had dropped Nadia off in Charlton Kings, Maria went home knowing the girl would be safe with Christian taking Leon for a walk around the park, and she no longer had crises about Nadia's father. It didn't feel wrong to take Nadia to see Christian, in fact, she felt like she was doing a good deed. If anyone at school asked, Maria could hold her head up and say Nadia was simply, and innocently, walking her dog, and had met Christian of her own accord.

Her conscience clearing by the day, Maria was free to get on with checking coursework and writing reports, and she didn't have the yearning loneliness she used to feel when she worked into the evening alone; knowing that Christian and Nadia were just around the corner looking after her dog gave her a deep sense of soothing comfort.

On an afternoon when Christian asked her not to collect Nadia until later, as he was going to make her dinner, Maria felt she had really enabled Nadia a better quality of life and it pleased her greatly. She pictured finishing her work, returning to Christian's and driving Nadia, with Leon on her lap, all the way home, in contentment.

It was worth the extra effort, time and petrol, Nadia looked happier than Maria had ever seen her: an

Unravel

entirely changed creature from the anxious, unsmiling girl who had first walked into her office. She cuddled Leon on those journeys, stroking his ears constantly as she sang along to the songs on the radio in her lilting Irish, full of charm and humour. Maria couldn't help but smile too, pleased for her sweet, young friend. The way Nadia's eyes lit up when she huddled down into Maria's car, Maria wanted to quietly capture that delight and keep it forever. When she dropped Nadia off outside her father's house, Maria wished Lois would look at her that way, sad to see her go, as if she would miss her and Leon over the weekend.

Perhaps she had become too complacent, however, because at the start of the final week of term, Maria had relaxed into her evening alone, having dropped Nadia off at Christian's. Maria knew she had a good hour or so until she had to collect Nadia, had changed into her loose jeans and just poured a small glass of wine, when she had a knock at her front door.

It was Christian, with Nadia just behind him. He was holding Leon by his collar.

'Maria, he ran away from us!' Christian panted, obviously having run a fair way. 'We let him off the lead and he suddenly bolted!'

Nadia's breath was making hot clouds in the cold evening air as she flapped her arms. 'He ran across the road and everything, we were so scared!'

'But he ran right back here, all the way to yours.' Christian looked like he might cry with guilt.

His pale eyes were wide and shaking with shock, Maria pitied him.

'Yeah, he's funny off the lead sometimes: he just tracks a scent and goes...' Maria made a humoured grimace. 'Maybe he could smell me!' Leon had dodged traffic to get back home to her: Maria was deeply flattered and bent to scoop up her loyal pet in her arms. Leon licked her face as she held his slender chest warmly in the palm of her hand.

Nadia wiped her face and leaned against Maria's outside wall, catching her breath as Christian apologised. It was only then Maria realised that Leon had brought the girl directly to her front door. Now, Nadia knew where she lived; Maria's insides seized up. Again, things were developing before she had a chance to stop them. That Nadia had ended up on her doorstep was no one's fault, but if she had any control at all, Maria knew she did not want Nadia inside her house... not tonight, while she was unprepared, so Maria took whatever upper hand she still had, and drove Nadia home.

On the way, Nadia seemed shaken by having lost the dog and was quiet. Maria figured that it was her responsibility to reassure Nadia she did nothing wrong, but knew the 'what-ifs' that were plaguing Nadia's mind would not go away unless Maria changed the subject.

'So, how are you feeling about Christmas?' Maria asked gently.

Unravel

Nadia turned and seemed grateful for Maria's tact, gushing loudly about the school Christmas show at the end of the week, apparently some of the music students had formed a band and were going to perform their own gig. 'I love music!' Nadia enthused. 'I wish I'd taken it instead of drama.'

'Actually, I meant about spending Christmas at home...'

Nadia just shrugged in a prepared sort of way. 'Well, my dad will be working so I'll try and get some food in... watch some films... drink the pain away...'

Worryingly, there had still been no word from, or sighting of Nadia's father, and Maria had a sudden chill that, actually, she only knew of him what Nadia had told her, and maybe the girl had invented some story to get her teacher's sympathy: though Maria didn't like to speculate exactly what secrets Nadia might be hiding.

♥

Later that week Maria realised, perhaps, she should have taken Christian aside and explained to him that she didn't feel comfortable with her students coming to her house, although this felt somewhat contradictory since she had brought Nadia to his.

But, it was too late.

Christian again turned up on Maria's doorstep, with Nadia, having walked Leon back home, which he

Unravel

probably assumed was a considerate move, as it would save Maria the journey to his to collect Nadia and Leon later. Maria smiled awkwardly: she knew it would be ill-mannered of her not to invite them inside for a warm drink, although as Nadia stepped across her threshold, Maria knew a metaphorical boundary had also been crossed. There was no going back now, she thought. After the tense standing in her lounge passed, Maria surrendered an internal shrug; Nadia knew where she lived now anyway, and, surely, with a chaperone, there was no harm in her stopping for tea.

Looking at them together, Maria tried to imagine them as a couple. His chest was filling out, but the hair on his chin was still sparse. If Nadia genuinely liked Christian, then Maria figured that she had nothing to worry about anymore, and she made a mental update to stay focused on encouraging Nadia's new friendship with Christian instead of fretting over her own relationship with the girl.

After that switch in Maria's head, the forty minutes they stayed was actually pleasant: she had nothing to offer in the way of biscuits, but Nadia was too distracted playing with Leon anyway. Christian talked cheerfully about some music he was producing with his exciting new software for a college assignment, laughing that it was nothing but fun, and was ecstatic to be studying a course that he found so fulfilling.

Unravel

    Listening and nodding patiently, Maria kept Nadia in her periphery, checking her demeanour, if she was playing for Maria's attention, or genuinely for Leon's. However, after noticing that Nadia rarely looked up to see if she was looking, Maria reassured herself that she no longer felt the pressure from being one-to-one with Nadia, and found she was actually enjoying the youngsters' company. Her evening would be quiet if it wasn't for this young, vibrant twosome; Maria wasn't expecting any other visitors soon. She liked her time alone, or she thought she did, but now Maria let her mind daydream, as Christian went on, that this is what it might feel like if she had had a family of her own.

♥

There were a series of staff meetings before the end of term, divided by years but united by a small party at the end of the day on Thursday. Though previous tenth and eleventh year teacher's meetings were usually jovial affairs with liqueur chocolates, mince pies and other Christmas treats, all Maria could think about was how much she was dreading seeing Karen after embarrassing herself with a short blast of bad temper on the playing field.
    Maria entered the staff room and was shocked to be welcomed immediately by the friendly faces of colleagues who greeted her cheerfully, obviously high

on sherry. They handed her a glass and clinked theirs against hers, encouraging her to take advantage of the free-flowing tipple, provided by the generous Principal Woods.

When Karen entered, however, she didn't come over to give the light, conspiratorial punch on her arm Maria had become accustomed to as a show of their female solidarity, and she was glad to be surrounded by a chatty group of others. Maria wanted to distance herself from what increasingly felt like a passive-aggressive jostle to remind Maria she had to smile back in order to participate in their pact of sisterhood. Karen sat opposite Maria on the couches and waited, unnervingly, for her eye contact. Maria flicked her dark eyes over at Karen, but chose not to do the cheap smile thing; neither did she move glazed eyes on as if she hadn't seen her. Maria held on to Karen's clever, mischievous eyes and waited to see who would break first.

Just as Maria feared she may have to blink and look away, Karen broke into a broad, joyful grin. Maria finally brought her gaze down, gritting her jaw, realising she hadn't won anything: she'd allowed Karen a long hard look at an expression she'd probably, knowing Karen, interpreted as a lustful longing, and by doing so had impounded Karen's crush on her even deeper. Maria cursed her swarthy, dusky looks: people often thought she was giving them *the eye* when she was really giving them a dirty glare.

Unravel

After some lengthy, monotonous droning from the principal's assistant, Yvonne Pepper, on the autumn term's overall statistics, Woods himself picked up on a mention of the percentage of absent students, and Maria's heart fluttered a little when she heard Nadia's full name. Maria senses became alert as he spoke about the newest student's progress, her habitual truancy, knowing he would soon ask for her insight.

Sure enough, Maria found twelve pairs of eyes on her as Woods gestured to her, addressing the group. 'I'm sure everyone's aware by now that Maria has been working through an intensive tuition programme for Miss Sheridan to catch up on our curricular subjects... Maria, could you enlighten us on our newest addition?'

Without letting her back leave the wall in an effort to appear casual, Maria blinked nervously at Karen and wondered if she should be forthcoming with information, and if she was, whether she should defend Nadia's actions, and explain them to her waiting colleagues.

'Nadia attends all of her tuitions,' Maria began, pacing her words thoughtfully. 'She's coping well with the backlog of revision and is catching up with the coursework. She responds very well to both supervised and unsupervised study, I would say she is highly self-motivated and very capable. It came as a surprise to me when I learned she was not attending all her classes, and after discussing it with her, she told me...' Maria took a deep breath. 'Nadia feels she has sat through the classes already in her last year, and just needs tuition to 'top up' her exams skills. I made her aware her truancy would affect her results, and she appreciated that she had to attend all her classes, which she promises she will endeavour to do next term.'

Woods bowed at the head of the room with a proud smile, bending his arm to gather applause for Maria's efforts, which was politely extracted from the group. 'I believe Nadia will benefit greatly from your guidance, Maria, and you have our faith and support.'

'It's great you're doing our job for us,' Karen quipped, 'teaching her all the stuff we're supposed to teach her and condensing it down to...' Karen twisted her head with a grimace, 'just how much of your time is Ariel taking up?'

Maria lifted her surprise from Karen's taunting smile to address the group. 'She has her scheduled tuition hours, and sometimes, Nadia stays to revise, without my guidance...' Maria panicked slightly, before seizing her defences. 'She's unhappy at home, her father is, apparently, abusive towards her. She has nosebleeds she's so stressed, she's worried she'll have to move into a homeless hostel...' Maria looked back at Karen, 'I'm trying to help her.'

'Don't believe everything she says, Maria,' Woods smirked, rocking back on his chair legs. 'She's got a reputation for lying and turning on the tears when she needs to...'

Unravel

'Yes,' Mrs Westbourne spoke up, the head of humanities freed the arms of her chained spectacles from her blonde crop before resting them over her bosom. 'She told me her father makes her sleep in the attic on a camp bed, and her mother was violent... if either of that's true then anyone who comes from such a dysfunctional family is bound to be damaged.'

'How do you know she's lying?' Maria asked, keeping her voice cool.

'How would you know if she's telling the truth?' Karen shrugged. 'I'm just worried for you, don't get sucked in!'

'I read an article about attachment disorder,' Ali, the purple-headed arts teacher announced. 'If Nadia's suffered breakdowns in her relationships, she's probably looking for another primary carer.'

'No way!' Maria's hand flung itself up with a false defensiveness. 'I'm nobody's carer.'

'Well, that's obvious.' Karen muttered sarcastically.

Maria fell silent as Xavier Woods tactfully moved onto the next subject of mock exams, and the collective gave an audible sigh of tedium, flipping their pads over and underlining the new heading.

Karen held Maria in the tight grip of her stare, her arms folded over her flattened chest. Maria knew she'd had a close shave taking about Nadia and resented that Karen was trying to catch her out. She figured Karen was resentful too, enough to retaliate for

Unravel

being accused of perversion on her playing field, and suggesting Maria was not a caring person was a deliberately spiteful dig. Maria kept her head down and doodled a mermaid on the corner of her pad, her mind distinctly mincing that she didn't care enough about Karen to even play that game.

♥

By Friday, Maria was shattered. From as soon as she woke up, her alarm buzzing from her mobile, her muscles were aching, and even after a shower and breakfast, had to drag her body to school feeling all her energy levels were depleting, draining out of her second by second. She'd had enough for one term and she couldn't even be bothered to dress up for the season, it might be non-uniform day for the kids, but Maria put on a thin tie over her shirt in an effort to combat her lack of Christmas spirit by smartening up. The fact that the students were more concerned about the Christmas show that afternoon than making sure they'd completed their coursework properly, with a contents page and an adequate reference section at the back, irritated Maria; feeling she was alone in caring about these essential academic details made her even more tired with resentment.

After cramming three morning tuitions, with no further teaching responsibility for the afternoon, Maria gave in, and drove to a nearby shop at lunch. She bought a small bottle of rum and a ginger ale, and some peanuts. Locking herself in her office, Maria logged on to a television channel website through her computer, poured herself a drink, slung her boots up on her desk, and entertained herself with a comedy programme. She didn't want to be disturbed, she didn't want to talk to anyone, she just wanted to get tipsy and laugh while the others fussed around the auditorium for the Christmas events.

It worked a treat; Maria knew how to cheer herself up. She chuckled quietly at her screen, occasionally throwing a nut into her mouth between slugs of rum and dry. It wasn't her intention to get royally wasted, but she had to join in with the Christmas celebrations somehow, even if her solution was to get merry through alcoholic means. It took a while for her to relax, being too caught up in her stress, but with continual reminding that her duties were done for the day, Maria allowed a wave of pleasure to wash over her.

That afternoon's end of term shows consisted of a modern take on the nativity by the seventh and eighth years, followed by a gala show featuring a variety of performances from all years including songs, dances, magic tricks and acrobatics. The finale was a rock concert by the tenth and eleventh years: the music students' live bands had been practising in the hall for weeks and had sounded promising - Maria couldn't imagine the pretentiousness of those cool kids would allow them to perform anything under par. Maria didn't have to attend any of it, but she increasingly felt like seeing the concert, especially as she poured herself another drink.

When she finally wandered outside to get some fresh air, Maria walked around the exterior paths to the courtyard, feeling slightly blurry around the edges. She found the grounds, highlighted by random spots of winter sunshine, empty, apart from a couple of red-faced tenth years rummaging out of a bush and around the corner to hide from her. They had nothing to worry about: Maria wasn't going to rat on them for wanting to leave a noisy, busy hall to have a private squeeze out in the freezing cold; rather them than her though. As she looked up to the auditorium, Maria could hear the bellows of male vocals from a microphone, drums beating, amplified and impressively rhythmic. It didn't sound bad at all and Maria smiled down at the path she followed carefully as the song ended and a feisty cheer went up from the crowd of students in there.

Once inside, Maria looked around her, and her tipsiness gave everything a dreamlike quality as the music started up again: a band comprised of several sweaty tenth-years in t-shirts, guitars and drumsticks in hands, long hair flying and spotty necks straining. Beaming, flashing colours of red, green and orange, struck out from the stage, highlighting everyone's smiles. It got darker towards the back until it was practically black where Maria stood beside the sound

Unravel

desk, a nerdy little guy called Watson with headphones on twisting tiny knobs by the shallow light of a fixed lamp.

Only then could Maria see how truly packed it was, like a real gig; the first few years were seated at the front, most of the ninth and tenth years behind them were out of their chairs, dancing, however, and the eleventh years were standing, crowded at the back. The lack of black, uniformed shoulders was refreshing and Maria looked amongst them to see if she could see any faces she recognised in the mass of bodies. There were many: boys and girls who looked so different in their clothes of choice, each dressing to impress friends, and then, feeling the looseness in her neck and eyelids, she wondered if Nadia was somewhere.

Starting a casual crawl along the back wall, Maria stepped, stopped and smiled at the students who greeted her, and pressed on past, through the warm spaces between the dark figures that surrounded her. When she thought she saw Nadia's red hair ahead of her, a couple of metres to her right, she stopped and wedged herself backwards to lean against the wall, at a vantage point where she could see Nadia from behind. She didn't mean to be so covert but she just wanted to see what Nadia was wearing.

Standing next to a handsome boy call Richard, whom Maria had always suspected to be gay, Nadia leaned on him, tiptoeing and then raised her arms with enthusiastic clapping, she whooped, and smiled, the apples of her cheeks lit up by the flashing stage lights. The sleeves of the pale, loose top she wore slipped over her elbows and back again as she pushed her hands back into the pockets of what looked like tight jeans from the curve of her hip, bangles jangling at her wrist. The slashed neck of the pretty, feminine fabric fell over her shoulder simultaneously and Maria saw the creamy skin of her arm against the dark clothing of her year-mates either side of her. Nadia stood out from the others; the colour of her hair was distinctive under the lights – but in this dark it was the way it flicked, messily falling over the naked skin of her clavicle, and swung and slid when she turned to smile.

Feeling the swirl of rum in her veins again, Maria wondered if Nadia had also had a drink to celebrate the last day of term: she would not be surprised if she had. The girl deserved the reward: she had worked hard and survived the difficult first term. Almost wanting Nadia to be in the same state of mind as her, Maria felt she would be able to share a moment of understanding and appreciation if she approached Nadia now.

If Nadia was tipsy too, she might throw her arms open, glad to see her tutor, and embrace her warmly. Maria smiled and imagined Nadia pulling her to stand next to her, closer, linking her arm in hers, but as much as she would like that, enjoy the tingles it would give her, she couldn't chance it.

Unravel

Especially as some boys between her and Nadia were now staring at her and laughing, thinking she was looking at them. Maria realised she had to take her eyes off Nadia or risk them, or anyone else for that matter, realising she was watching a student instead of the show. It wasn't even as if she was keeping an eye on Nadia for misbehaving: Nadia was clearly attractive, and for a lesbian teacher, it was not good to be seen staring. Maria turned her focus back to the show as the band played on, doing surprisingly well, but Maria could not stop thinking about Nadia. She tried for a long time not to look back at her, but the compulsion was terrible and frustrating. With the heat of alcohol flaring her cheeks, she became too warm and wanted to take off the tie pinning her shirt against her, but then she thought of the boys next to her seeing her stripping. Maria kept it on and felt an uncomfortable sweat begin to bead on her skin.

There was no way she could go up to Nadia: it would be wrong. She now imagined herself being weird, staring, perhaps stuttering if she tried to talk to Nadia - if Nadia couldn't hear or didn't care to listen, Maria would have to stand there awkwardly and pretend to be interested in the show. She couldn't move, but she didn't want to leave, either.

Maria suddenly, and fully, realised her deep attraction to Nadia. She felt compelled with every part of her body to place herself directly behind Nadia and put her hands on the girl. Feeling the thick blood of

Unravel

arousal pulse to her thighs and her fingertips, Maria imagined the tight denim over Nadia's bottom pressing backwards against her own thighs. She imagined sliding her hands down either side of Nadia's waist to hold her hips closer; wrapping them around Nadia's waist, feeling her warmth and trembling, twining fingers as Maria brushed aside Nadia's hair and kissed the skin of her shoulder. Maria felt the urge deep inside, and it hurt sincerely.

Her breath became short, it was hot, and there was no oxygen, her mouth and throat tensed as if she might cry, and a sharp pain dug in her stomach. Maria inhaled and exhaled until the pain passed, but her eyes had brimmed with tears. It wasn't the rum, maybe it was the nuts for lunch, but Maria had the dreadful fear that it might be something darkly sick growing inside her that made her need to run back outside. She did just that, before anyone saw her, before Nadia saw her. As she reversed her journey back out of the auditorium, Maria felt the rising nausea come like a wave as soon as she hit the fresh air, and stumbling around the corner, where she was sure no-one could see her, Maria vomited up her rum peanuts into the bush, previously occupied by smooching young lovers.

Unravel

Chapter Nine

A few days before Christmas, Maria's eyes glazed over again as she leaned against her kitchen worktop, clutching her glass of red wine, and blinking back drifting thoughts of desperation. She had to hold it together, but the wine was melting her resolve. She had cooked a substantial amount of vegetable bolognaise, not that she could eat it - her stomach was in knots - and neither was it intended to soften the blow while she broke up with Lois. Maria had simply taken comfort in preparing a meal, doing anything in her kitchen, in her home, to take her mind off the realities that kept grating at her.

She swallowed her nerves with more wine, but her breath seemed to shudder whenever she sighed out. She prepared to take the plunge in following Ben's seemingly sound advice. The food sat waiting, but Lois had called to say she was visiting a friend first, some fellow in Cheltenham she had met during the brief period she lived with Maria. She said she would be

Unravel

along later; she had no idea Maria was planning to serve up a separation notice over dinner.

When Leon came and nudged her leg, Maria realised she had forgotten to feed him, and he looked up with hopeful eyes, his tongue lolling, and he sniffed the air towards the Bolognaise on the hob. Maria broke a smile and leaned to stroke his head, but he pattered away, towards his bowl, leading her in case she didn't know.

Lifting his bowl to the counter, Maria revelled in the opportunity to do something, think about something other than her complicated life, and mixed his dry biscuits with a spoonful of Bolognaise sauce with deliberate and steady co-ordination. After she left him eating, Maria automatically switched on her television, grateful that Lois had left it behind for occasions like this when she did not want to think or feel very much, but skipping through some truly mind-numbing programmes, Maria settled back with the news channel.

And there, blankly watching the world news, Maria's mind was able to erect a thick wall of denial, a blissful break from her own problems: a moment's peace from her misery.

Sometime later, there was a beep from her mobile phone. Maria wondered if she had fallen lightly asleep as Leon had curled up on her feet and the news presenter had changed sex without her noticing. Pulling herself from the warm indents of her couch, Maria returned to her kitchen and reached for her phone, slightly disoriented from the wine and loss of time.

Perching at the stool by her counter, she checked her mobile's inbox, and frowned with a heart-skip of surprise and fearful pleasure to see it was not from Lois, but Nadia.

'Hi! You home? I'm with Chris, wondered if we can take Leon walkies?'

Maria huffed a relieved smile, it was such a simple text, such an innocent, sweet thing to ask, yet her insides gave a stab of anxiety at the prospect of seeing Nadia. She replied, pretending to be casual: 'Yeah at home, come on over.'

Attending to her reflection, Maria had a word with herself to suppress any nerves in front of Nadia; it was silly of her really. She reminded herself how she should be feeling and concentrated on that. It was fine for Nadia to visit, now that she had been over a couple of times already. Maria was especially pleased that Nadia was seeing Christian other than school evenings, more specifically that she had made efforts to find her own way there and not rely on Maria for lifts: that made it more real – Nadia seemed genuinely interested in Christian – and Maria could congratulate herself for playing Cupid and facilitating Nadia with a social existence.

Besides being a convenient distraction from her expected disaster of an evening, it would be good to have her young friends round. Maria wondered if she

Unravel

should think of Nadia as her friend now, just like Christian was more than a neighbour and her dog walker; that boy had no idea just how much of a favour he had done for Maria, and she would never tell him, Nadia was his reward.

When they arrived, Leon leaped at their legs and Nadia chuckled with joy at the welcome from her new favourite dog. Maria keenly invited them in before they took Leon out and Christian groaned loudly, patted his stomach, and groaned for the good scents coming from the kitchen. Nadia stood in the hall and unravelled her scarf as Maria closed the door.

'You okay?' Nadia asked, looking with sharply clear eyes, sparkling from the cold.

Maria feared her eyes were giving away the wild mix of emotions that had sprung back up from within, or that Nadia could smell the wine oozing out of her pores as she realised she had broken out in a hot flush since the doorbell had rung.

'Yeah, course,' Maria smiled and rolled up the sleeves of her smooth knit jumper. Her eyes fell over Nadia's cleavage as the girl opened the neck of her coat, and looked away. 'I was just making some dinner, have you guys eaten?'

Nadia followed her through to the kitchen, where Christian was nosing over the hob. 'No, we were going to grab a pizza on the way back,' she answered lightly.

'Oh, it's Sunday, you've got to have a proper dinner on Sunday!' Maria smiled broadly and swung her arm wide towards the table, looking like silver service waiters had laid it, though she barely recalled doing it.

Observing the table set for two, Nadia blinked back. 'Are you expecting someone?'

Hesitating a moment, Maria rolled her head to the side, wondering if her act of indifference was convincing. 'Well, Lois is... otherwise indisposed.'

'She stood you up again?' Christian asked automatically, but looked sheepish after his cheeky question.

Maria tapped her fingers against the counter edge, then faked a smile. 'I know! What kind of crazy fool goes to a work appointment instead of eating fine homemade food? You guys aren't going to let me down either, are you? You'd better stay, because I'll be doubly insulted if you go for pizza.'

Without glancing at Christian, Nadia's eyes flashed with happiness. 'I'd love to!' She smiled down at Leon and up at Maria again, failing to suppress her grin with a bite to her lip.

'Sweet!' Christian nodded and beamed at Nadia. 'Shall we take Leon out first?' He rubbed his hands together. 'And we'll pop to the shop and get some booze.'

'Would you get some red wine for me?' Maria asked, grabbing her wallet from the counter. 'Here's twenty... get two... Cab Sav, yeah?'

Nadia approached her and reached out for the note, but gripped Maria's hand as she took it and looked up with direct, smiling eyes. 'Why don't you come for a walk with us?'

Refusing, with a gentle smile, Maria said she would get the spaghetti on the go while they were gone. Nadia nodded with a little show of disappointment, pushed the note down into her pocket, and called Leon. They were gone in a minute and Maria exhaled heavily, realising she had been tense through the whole of their visit, quite disbelieving she had invited them back for dinner: in doing so, completely sabotaging her breakup night with Lois.

By the time they returned, Maria had given her bathroom a spruce, changed her jumper to a shirt, tidied her hair, dabbed her perfume, set an extra place at the table, and finally got the water boiling for the pasta. Leon bounded into the kitchen, seemingly delirious to have everyone together in one room, and Maria gave him a chew to take to his bed in the corner.

Nadia took off her coat and shoes and sat up on the stool at the counter opposite Maria, who worked busily preparing some aperitifs. Maria allowed the girl one small glass of wine, and told Nadia that she was only to drink it once they were eating, and that she mustn't tell anyone at school or they would both get into trouble. Christian laughed and slurped his beer, teasing Nadia for still being at school. Nadia mocked his laugh and swiftly kicked at him.

When they sat at the table at last, Maria thanked them for coming and encouraged them to eat as much as they could. They wished each other a merry Christmas but avoided talking of plans for school break, or Christmases of the past, family occasions or holidays; any of these things Maria knew could put a dark edge on the evening if Nadia became upset, and Christian must have known it too for he mentioned nothing at all. The meal, to Maria's significant relief, was jovial and chatty, though Nadia had several top-ups when her back was turned; Maria pretended she hadn't seen Christian pouring it for her, or noticed the depleting line inside the green bottle. Maria felt fine, and continued to feel fine, feel great in fact, until the doorbell rang.

Lois breezed in looking windswept and harassed, talking immediately and marching forthrightly into Maria's hallway where she slung her coat and bag over the banisters, and pulled out a bottle of wine, ignoring Leon bouncing by her feet.

Maria's stomach froze. She couldn't believe Lois had turned up and Nadia was next door in the kitchen. She really hadn't thought this through.

Lois was babbling, explaining she'd had an incredible meeting with her friend, was so excited at their ideas that she had to come round and tell, or rather, ask Maria.

'Ask me what?' Maria pushed down the lump in her throat, it was heavy with wine, and it stuck like a solid bubble of fear that might come back up if Lois asked who Nadia was.

'Oh God, I need a fucking drink first!' Lois said dramatically and strutted out through the lounge. She reached the kitchen and saw Christian and Nadia eating the spaghetti bolognaise meal Maria said she had prepared for her. 'Christian? What are you doing here? And who's this?'

Nadia stared at Lois, her expression one of pure fascination, fork poised with dangling spaghetti.

Christian swallowed his mouthful with a self-conscious flick of his brown hair. 'All right Lois? This is Nadia, she's... uhh...' Christian's description of Nadia fell short as he lost the courage to call her anything prematurely possessive.

Maria scratched the back of her head and muttered to Lois. 'New girlfriend.'

Putting on a patronising smile, Lois squeezed her nose up. 'Aw Chris! About time buddy!' She blinked only briefly at Nadia and pursed her lips into a hastily polite smile before dropping it resentfully down at the plate in front of Nadia. 'So, is there any dinner left?'

Maria didn't appreciate Lois' rudeness, regardless of there being plenty left for her. She ignored

Lois' question and lifted a glass of red wine in front of Lois. 'Didn't you come round to ask me something?'

Lois waved it away. 'I just got my teeth whitened, open the bottle I brought.'

With a sigh, Maria uncorked Lois' bottle of white wine and poured her a fresh glass, noticing that Nadia had not yet taken her eyes off Lois from behind: she was staring at Lois' clothes, her legs, her high boots, and blonde hair.

Tipping a mouthful of white wine, Lois sighed with relief and prepared her speech. 'Okay, check this out,' she drawled with Australian emphasis. 'You remember that guy Tim who ran the gallery in town - I used to help him out occasionally?' Lois didn't wait for Maria's response. 'Well, I saw him tonight and told him about my success getting the American contract, and wanting to put together a portfolio to attract the Jepson Foundation, right? So, Tim reckons I should go one step further than anyone else, set up my portfolio in a gallery to exhibit my work, and invite them over to meet me. What do you think? He's a genius, isn't he?'

Looking around to Christian and Nadia's blank faces, Lois swigged another mouthful and brought her eyes expectantly back to Maria's silence. 'Well, it's only fair to display the pieces in an open space, with good lighting, where they can see what I can do... what I can offer... and then they'll give me the commission!'

'Where do I come into this?' Maria's eyes narrowed.

'Your apartment!' Lois widened her gesture out towards the room beyond the kitchen. 'Don't you think here would be the best place to have an art exhibition? It's much bigger than mine! It's less cluttered, the wall are plainer...'

Not even trying to hide her horror, Maria's lips winched up over her teeth and she shook her head with disbelief. 'You want to *what now*? You want to take over my house to solicit your goods? You want to pimp yourself out from my lounge?'

Nadia snorted a laugh and covered her mouth, but Christian held his face in an O, knowing Lois' temper, and Maria half expected him to make a hasty retreat.

Flipping her hand, Lois dismissed Maria's concern. 'Don't be like that! Hear me out! It won't just be some bigwigs snooping around... I mean, it'll be like a networking event, we could invite other people to make a party of it! I thought you could invite some of your friends, and I'll invite some of mine! We could make some food; have some drinks... It will be fun! Like a post-Christmas party featuring my artwork!'

Her jaw hanging open now, Maria could hardly move to shut it for the terrible scenarios and paranoia rushing though her mind at the idea of a party for pretentious assholes in her house, analysing her, her friends, her decor and her food. They could analyse Lois all they wanted, but Maria did not want them doing it in her *apartment*.

Unravel

'I, literally, have no words.' Maria uttered and lifted her wine, her eyes falling across to Nadia at the table. The girl sat with her fingernail of her thumb pressed against her lips, smiling with wickedly bright eyes. Maria couldn't help smiling back at her, but hid it behind her glass.

Turning an insistent glare round at Christian and Nadia, Lois asked them what they thought. Christian shrugged and looked too nervous of Lois to disagree with Maria. However, Nadia knew no different; maybe she did, Maria reflected, as Nadia nodded with a chuckle. 'I think it's a great idea... I'm sure you'll get lots of interest, this house is perfect.'

She was being mischievous: Maria knew it from the glistening in Nadia's eye as she too lifted her glass to sip with pouting, smiling lips. Maria was embarrassed that Lois was putting her on the spot, and annoyed that Christian failed to fight her corner: his loyalty should lay entirely with her, not Lois just because he was scared of her. Then, he said something that put Maria even more on the spot:

'Can we come?'

Maria did a series of glances back and forth, bouncing off reactions around the kitchen. Lois broke into a broad smile turning to Maria.

Nadia huffed a laugh and nearly spat her wine.

Christian winced and looked sorry, then shrugged.

Lois raised her eyebrows hopefully.

Unravel

Nadia drew her smile down, kicked Christian under the table, shook her head and scolded him.

'Of course you can come!' Lois granted them permission, and Maria felt completely undermined in her own house.

'Wait a minute,' Maria extended her fingers out. 'I don't know if that's a good idea.'

'Why not?' Lois argued in a beat. 'You can have whoever you want here, I'm cool with that! Chris is your good friend and neighbour, let him invite his girlfriend, she's cute!'

At that moment, if Nadia had not been there, Maria could have dragged Lois out into the street and told her that her artwork was fit to be shown there in the gutter. Lois was humiliating her in front of Nadia and it made Maria seethe with powerful yet powerless anger. Yes, her house was lovely; yes, it was spacious; yes, the walls were plain but that was the minimalist look, not the absence of creative couture as Lois made it sound.

'Why would they come all the way out here to Cheltenham?'

'Because I'll give them something to come for, Maria! Some of us know how to put on a show, okay?' Lois hissed.

How Lois managed to be so negative, and presumptuous, and still get her own way, Maria was sure she would never understand, but for now, she had to put it down to Lois' artistic persuasion and give in, or forever hold a silent, fish-faced stutter. She couldn't very well have a tantrum right now, she couldn't be bothered, and Maria reasoned, if she could invite her friends, it might not be so hellish an event. If Christian wanted to invite Nadia, she couldn't say no, or Nadia would be upset at the rejection; and though it felt like she was flying hopelessly over another boundary, Maria couldn't help but think she might quite like to have Nadia come to this so-called party.

After finishing dinner and dessert, two hours later, Maria had sobered, and was fine to drive Nadia home. Lois had departed as soon as she had secured Maria's permission, after the fuss about dinner, she hadn't eaten a thing, and though she tried excusing the nibbles she had earlier with her friend, Tim, Maria knew Lois would have ingested nothing but chemicals for a meeting that egocentric.

However, driving along the quiet, dark roads towards Eastcombe, Nadia had become serious in mood, evidently concerned that Christian had put Maria on the spot, on top of Lois' pressure.

'I don't want to come if you don't want me to come,' Nadia said. Her tone was tipsy, but sincere. Her knees crossed towards Maria, her hands folded in her lap, and her gaze swung between Maria's profile and the passing curves of the hedges outside her passenger window. 'I know you don't like parties at the best of times.'

Maria didn't know what to say. She wasn't sure if it was ethical to have her student at her house, but then Nadia had already been at her house. If Nadia came to the party, she would undoubtedly drink alcohol, but then Maria had already allowed her to drink alcohol in her presence, and if she was worried that would get her into trouble, well, that boat had long left the harbour.

'It's okay,' Maria replied as reassuringly as she could. 'Look, I was only upset at Lois' assumption. I didn't mean to make you feel like I didn't want you there. You should come, if you can stand a dry old arty party... you two will definitely make it more fun.'

Nadia gazed at Maria and whispered. 'We'll make it fun, don't worry.'

Chapter Ten

That Christmas, Maria spent a quiet, pleasant weekend in London staying with her cousin Ben, and Chloe, growing and glowing with child, and little Levi. They all joined in cooking, shared their gifts after dinner, and kept the smiles and drinks flowing. Maria spoke to Paulo, the youngest of her elder brothers, on the phone, only briefly, just for the sake of seasonal goodwill to him and his family. Paulo didn't ask about Lois and Maria said nothing of her either.

Lois did make a flying visit with overly-wrapped presents in huge designer bags. She stayed long enough for a coffee and some brandy pudding, grinning widely as Levi cooed over the gifts, and Chloe softly admonished her generosity. Maria saw Ben notice again that Lois hardly made any eye contact with him at all, and Maria made sure he also noticed that Lois, similarly, made little eye contact with her, to reassure him it really wasn't personal, Lois was just blind like that. The presents Maria and Lois bought for each other were generic and loveless, a presumed favourite style of jumper; some earrings, probably identical to last years. Safe, trusted, thoughtless and empty on both sides. Lois excused herself prematurely, saying she had to get back to sort frames for her exhibition, and when kind-hearted Chloe pleaded with her not to rush off, Lois forced out some conceited explanation of having to bribe the printers to work for her over the holiday. Maria was more than happy for her to go.

Her own preparations for the party began as soon she got back home to Cheltenham, and Maria had a pang of anxiety pinch somewhere in her chest when she realised she would have to rearrange her house as a gallery, as well as cater for the party guests. Maria wondered who amongst her friends would be able to make it at such short notice, as she had already made Ben promise to come purely for moral support.

Having got her prints, Lois busied herself with hanging her artwork whilst talking loudly into her mobile, cocked between her ear and shoulder as she tapped her hammer into Maria's white walls. Maria winced as she saw small chunks of her plaster fall, and continued moving her furniture to the edges of the room. She removed certain personal items, books and gifts that she would rather not be flicked through or examined as if they were part of the exhibition, but kept other ornaments she felt enhanced the artistic environment. The idea of strangers in her house made her more than a little uncomfortable.

The trip to the supermarket was saved until the next day when she wasn't so stressed, and the night before was spent preparing some of the dishes, though Maria had to stop when she got wound up again, hearing that Lois was planning on inviting some people from the office she worked at. She didn't see why they would even want to come to a business party where Lois was trying to get over and above them; believing herself to be destined for the dizzy heights of marketing fame. Maria wondered what kind of colleagues wouldn't mind their noses being rubbed in it.

By Thursday, the house looked impressively decorated with the occasional Christmas touch and a small tree in the fireplace. The walls were adorned with twelve of Lois' pieces, all varying in size and detail, method and meaning. Copies of her professionally bound, sleek portfolio lay spread in half moons around the room, on the coffee table and even in the bathroom upstairs. It was swept and tidy, and looked very attractive, if Maria did say so herself, except she couldn't quite swallow the art work Lois had displayed. Her girlfriend asked her to pretend she were an executive with intentions towards buying some pieces, so she gazed upon each of them with expressions she tried to make look as if she were appreciative.

However, Maria failed to regard Lois' art with any real heart, or perhaps they lacked any real heartfelt qualities and that's the reason they looked like random, alien images. Of course, Lois explained as she talked Maria through her motivations, the pieces were intended to be commercial, and contained some reprinted media images, but Maria felt the obvious representations of women or sex fused with product placement, just made the pieces look too blatent and gaudy when they were trying to be subtle and enigmatic. Maria knew Lois was trying to make a statement somewhere but it felt confused. Maria was certainly confused, but then she supposed she wasn't any kind of art critic and perhaps the Jepson Foundation executives would deem Lois' style to be the big new thing to sell their product.

By the evening, Lois had already polished off most of a bottle of wine whilst Maria ensured the kitchen table was perfectly set with the most colourful dishes of food. Maria smiled over the beautifully arranged plates of sliced meats, cheeses, and crusty bread; bowls of potato salad, sweet and savoury rice, pickles and salsa; alongside crisps, sweet pastries and fruit cocktails: *now this is art*, she thought. Maria even de-frosted the vegetable chilli she had made, in case people wanted to make tacos at some point. By the time the doorbell rang, Maria had moved through her resentment at being used by Lois, and was just looking forward to seeing her friends.

Sadie and Paula, a lesbian couple from Gloucester, whom Maria knew through the school, arrived first with a bottle of vodka and a gift for Maria

Unravel

and Lois: an elegant statue of a nude woman that Maria thought would look lovely in her bathroom. When Maria realised Sadie had sculpted the piece especially for her, she beamed, and vowed to place it in the lounge instead, but not tonight, where it might get knocked. Lois served them drinks while Maria received James and Michelle, some closer neighbours, who brought cake and beer.

Amy, Sarah, Darren and Elizabeth, Lois' work friends turned up next, already drunk, having apparently enjoyed champagne at Sarah's house before they jumped in a taxi. Lois squealed on seeing them and her voice rose several pitches for the rest of the evening whenever she chatted with them. Maria greeted them politely and subtly opened the back door in the kitchen where they should smoke, even though it was freezing outside. Christian's parents Anthony and Clarissa turned up with two bottles, white and red, and Christian followed with a bottle of tequila, and Nadia in tow.

Maria kept her hugs brief and only shook Christian's hand, and touched Nadia's elbow. Nadia looked stunning in a green party dress and Maria could barely let her eyes fall over her figure for longer than a second before she excused herself to go and hang their coats. She wondered if she looked all right in the slender-fitting dark shirt she wore with her tightest jeans and high boots.

At half past seven, she wondered if Ben and Chloe would make it, the executives would be coming

Unravel

to see Lois' exhibition at eight and Maria wanted to know she had her best friend there to talk to while Lois was seducing everyone else. When the doorbell rang again, Leon barked, and Maria's excitement shot through her, but as Leon hushed, sniffing the door enthusiastically, Maria stroked his ears and guided him out of the way as David and Simon, her favourite gay couple, moved through her hall, bearing a gift. Maria was so pleased to see them and delighted at the expensive liqueur she unwrapped before apologising for having bought no presents in return. They laughed and said a good house party was a gift in itself.

Pouring them some drinks, Maria felt more relaxed and more like the hostess she wanted to be. She chatted, gazing up at her handsome friends: Simon, a beardy producer of shows at one of the local arts venues, and David, who used to be her gym buddy and he looked as muscular as always, short and compact, but wide-eyed and clean-shaven, both squeezed her and told her she looked gorgeous.

When two executives from the Jepson Foundation arrived before eight, they seemed like decent fellows and Maria welcomed them in only to have Lois cut in and guide their attention towards the congregation. The lights were kept high as Lois introduced herself and welcomed her special guests, then thanked everyone for coming. She began talking through each of her pieces and was putting on a splendid performance to enthrall her audience. Maria

Unravel

once heard neither her name nor mention of her *apartment*, and decided to leave Lois to it, with everyone hanging off her words. She went to stand outside the front door, pulled out a cigarette, and smoked while she waited for Ben.

Ten minutes later, Ben finally drove by and parked up the road. Maria sighed with heavy relief, she would have been upset if he hadn't come. She had already downed a glass of sparkling wine with the stressful prospect of being so isolated at a party in her own house; she liked her other friends and neighbours, but no one came close to her cousin. He strolled up, beaming, with pregnant Chloe and son Levi bouncing towards her. She greeted them with hushed smiles, and encouraged them in out of the cold.

Inside, she ushered them through to the kitchen to get them refreshments and nibbles. She chatted gleefully with them, then David and Simon drifted away from the group in the lounge, came through and they fussed over Chloe and Levi. Chloe immediately relaxed and sat down with them as they talked eagerly of making arrangements to have their own child. They pawed at Levi, somewhat nervously, roughing his hair and engaging his conversation, joyfully testing their parenting abilities.

As they hadn't had the opportunity to discuss it in their usual frank way at Christmas, Ben took Maria aside and quietly asked her what had developed with Lois since they'd last spoken about it at his salon.

After confessing how she had intended to break up with Lois before Christmas, Maria explained how Lois managed to override those plans with this exhibition party and how things could be different if she got a new job she was happy with.

'Will she ever be happy?' Ben growled in his Sicilian tones.

'She's certainly in her element now.' Maria muttered, looking round the alcove into the converted lounge, it surprised her how well it doubled as a gallery space and having a small gathering of people made her feel a certain, indirect pride at being able to facilitate the event. The festive colours in the room looked stunning, very celebratory; while she did feel a mix of emotions at her changed house, mostly it felt positive.

Catching Maria's eye, Nadia's slim green dress, the poise and angles of her back and arms, the tilt of her head towards the kitchen, disinterested in Lois' art. Maria pulled away her glance and turned back towards Ben.

'Ben? You see the girl in the green dress, side on... red hair?' Maria gestured back through the open door. 'Tell me if she's coming over?'

Shrugging a laugh, Ben flashed a quizzing eyebrow at Maria. 'Why?'

Maria swallowed another deep sip of wine. 'That student I told you about,' Maria hesistated to form the right words, but she had no qualms about confiding in her cousin, 'the one I wanted to back off a bit because she was getting clingy? Well, I set her up with my dog-walker, like you suggested, so I thought she could hang out with Christian while he looks after Leon, right?'

Ben frowned, nodding for her to continue.

'Well, it kind of worked, they seem to get on okay and she's not so clingy anymore, but... he invited her to the party tonight, and she's turned up here with him, and it feels a bit weird.' Maria felt another hot flush steamroll up her chest, then slight disgust at her dishonesty.

'What?' Ben's eyes widened. 'That's her?'

Maria winced but felt a huge weight lifting as Ben humourously leaned back to check with his periphery vision to see if Nadia was still there. His eyes were twinkling with amusement, making Maria smile with nervous energy as they slowly drifted into the lounge and stopped, then became serious as he properly took in the sight of Nadia.

Waiting with baited breath for him to give her some reaction, Maria couldn't help glancing at Nadia to see how Ben perceived her, and made immediate eye contact with the girl, blinking across from Ben's appraisal. Nadia looked away in another blink, and Maria regretted intimidating her with their dual fixation, letting her know she was subject of discussion. It seemed a long time before Ben brought his attention back to her, pursing his lips together with his thumb and index finger. Maria searched his face for feedback:

she couldn't read whether he was about to grin crudely or shake his head with concern.

'She's sixteen?' Ben asked, his forehead creasing with disbelief.

Maria nodded and felt a rush of shame send a flip of queasiness to her stomach. She lowered her eyes to her wine glass and swirled it, afraid Ben would see the truth she was hiding.

'Don't worry about it,' Ben rolled his words gently, 'she's here with Christian and it looks like they're having a nice time, so just relax. Let it go.'

Surprised by his response, Maria said: 'What do you mean "let it go"?' before she realised how defensive it sounded.

'I mean it's your party, you need to chill out and have a good time, too,' Ben said, moving towards her again. He reached out and clutched a strong arm around her waist. 'Ria, you're a great host and everyone is having fun. Relax. Have a drink.' He kissed her cheek. 'Happy New Year!'

Maria's face twitched with an unsure smile, then she felt her eyes prickle with rising tears. Ben was kind. She raised her glass to clink with his. She blinked away her emotions and allowed Ben to lead her back into the lounge.

She did as Ben said and relaxed about Nadia, putting it down to feeling the stress of organising the party. She felt relief that some friends had come, and no doubt the wine was helping ease everyone's flow.

Unravel

Once the exhibition was finished, Lois managed to keep the executives at the party to schmooze some more. Maria knew Lois was good at talking about herself, but observing her closely, Maria began to notice a few tell-tale signs, and realised that Lois had taken some cocaine. Her finger slid under her nose with a quick sniff and a subtle wipe and her tense grin was almost fixed. Irritatingly sensitive to it, Maria could hear nothing but the high-pitched whine of Lois' screechy accent, her false laughter and boasting; trying to sell some of her pieces to Maria's friends, giving away her portfolios as gifts, though they were free anyway. Maria leaned against the door frame to the front hall, it was darker there and she deflated with a sigh, waiting for someone to finish in the bathroom at the top of the stairs.

From where she stood, Maria could see that Nadia did seem to be enjoying chatting and drinking tequila with Christian on the couch; she bent often to pet Leon, who returned to her between regularly milling around the floor, hoping for a stroke and a tasty morsel. Maria watched Leon settle by Nadia's high-heeled boots and regarded her with a similar affection as she felt for her dog: she wanted to stroke Nadia's hair. She was cute. She wanted to go and speak to Nadia, but she knew she couldn't. Not only was Nadia sat with her boyfriend and his parents, but Ben now knew who Nadia was, and she didn't want anyone else to find out Nadia was her student.

Realising how tipsy she was when her eyes blurred down at her empty glass, Maria rolled her body around to the wall of the hallway and blinked her eyes shut, thinking she should eat something. Contemplating getting the chilli tacos going, once she'd been to the bathroom, Maria opened her eyes to find Nadia in front of her.

'You really okay?' Nadia asked, with a hopeful smile and pretty, colourful eyes.

Maria's back straightened as she felt Nadia's presence close. The light from the lamp in the hall bounced off the smooth curve of Nadia's cheek, and chin, and made a shine on her lips like Maria had never seen before, or been that near to see it before, but of course she had, many times, in tuition. It just felt too close in the hallway of her own house, her back against the wall; Maria couldn't move, or speak.

'Are you waiting for the bathroom?' Nadia asked, her gaze lifting up the stairs.

Maria was going to say no, then nodded yes, once she realised she could make a run for it. 'You having a good time?' Maria gulped, her voice cracking.

Knowing the question was forced, sensing that Maria was tense, Nadia must have made a decision to cut through the insincere politeness, but it only made Maria more uncomfortable.

'Would you rather I wasn't here?' Nadia asked. 'It feels like you're embarrassed of me.'

Shaking her head stiffly, Maria replied: 'I'm

Unravel

embarrassed of my girlfriend, sorry.'

'Don't worry about her, talk to me instead,' Nadia shrugged. 'You haven't spoken to me all night.' Her eyes fell over Maria's face with a tilted longing.

Maria couldn't handle Nadia's needy expression; she was waiting for something, wanting something, but Maria couldn't say what was on her mind, couldn't reveal how uptight she was feeling. She had to stay hard, aloof, pretend nothing was wrong, and if there was, it had nothing to do with Nadia. 'I'm kinda stressed, Nadia, I don't really feel like talking.'

Aware at that point, that both hers and Nadia's chests were rising and falling simultaneously, at different heights and rhythms, but heavily and with passion, Maria held her breath until it hurt, felt her face flush with heat and the urge press suddenly upon her bladder. She excused herself and reached out for the banister to climb the stairs. She knocked on her bathroom door and asked the occupant to hurry up.

When Darren and Amy piled out, giggling, Maria frowned, and pushed past them to get inside. She locked the door and hurried to unhook her trousers before she wet herself. Pissing longer and with more pleasure than she could remember in her adult life, Maria slung her head over her knees and breathed steadily to calm her throbbing heart. She vowed she would drink no more that evening or she might lose control in more ways than - Maria checked her knickers - than she had just narrowly escaped.

Standing up to flush, Maria saw the items on top of her cistern had been cleared aside and she ran her fingertip over the space in the centre of the flat surface. An educated guess at the remnants of a white powder and a quick taste test confirmed Maria suspicions that Lois' work friends had brought cocaine with them. Darren was a queer and would have little else to do in the bathroom with Amy, or any girl, other than drugs. Maria thought about asking them to leave, but knew Lois would have a fit if she found out.

Maria returned downstairs and found Lois saying goodbye to her prospective clients, their smiles were tired now and Lois was definately slurring. Maria didn't step in to help her, knowing Lois would have to rummage inside the cupboard for her guests' coats by her stumbling self. Instead, she turned her back and went to the kitchen to find Ben and Chloe. After downing several gulps of water, Maria kept her focus on Levi and encouraged him to try some of every dish on the table. He sat on her lap and wriggled as she piled a cracker high with slices and sauces and held it for him to bite into. Ben and Chloe and some others eating around the table laughed as Levi pulled exaggerated faces of pleasure and distaste, and joined in to create new concoctions to feed the funny little boy.

When Leon, tired of his begging going unnoticed, leapt up to Maria's side, she worried he would snap at the food too near to Levi's mouth or fingers and dismissed him away. The motion seemed to summon her soberness, and Maria suddenly lifted her head clear of the simple world that had revolved around experimenting with one child's love and hate relationship with food for the last half an hour. She recalled that Leon had been keeping Nadia's feet warm, and wondered what Nadia was doing; having lost all sense of her in the vicinity since she went to the toilet - then feared she had frightened Nadia off.

She placed Levi gently back on Ben's lap with a cheerful smile and squeezed through the group that had accumulated in the kitchen to eat. All thoughts of her own hunger had passed as Maria moved through to the lounge, smiling at others but looking for Nadia, everyone was getting tipsy, but the girl was nowhere to be seen. Anthony and Clarissa were talking, chatting contentedly to each other on the couch one second, then calling for Christian to be careful as he stepped back, spilling his father's drink on the floor as he laughed animatedly with James and Michelle, Maria's other neighbours. Christian was drunk on tequila, seemingly oblivious to his girlfriend's absence.

Maria thought to check for her coat in the cupboard, and as it was still there, assumed she was just in the bathroom. Only then did Maria notice that Lois and her friends were also not anywhere downstairs. A slight panic hit her as she realised Nadia could be in the toilet with any one of Lois' pals. She climbed the stairs even quicker than she had when her bladder was about to burst, and though she sort of needed it again, Maria passed the closed door to the toilet and decided to check if anyone was in the bedrooms.

What she saw in the spare bedroom made her stomach churn with an immediate denial, a total unwillingness to accept the situation: Lois' and her friends sitting on and standing around the neat, double bed, watching Nadia, laying front-down on the duvet, leaning on her elbows over an ornate glass mirror, snorting what was obviously a line of cocaine. Everyone's heads turned to Maria.

'What the fuck are you doing?' Maria said with seething disgust. Her eyes tracked between Nadia's wincing recoil from the burning powder in her nose to the rolling eyes of her girlfriend who leaned up from where she sprawled next to Nadia.

'What does it look like?' Lois responded cheerfully. 'This is phase two, work is done, now we party! You want some?'

'You fucking joking?' Maria fumed, her voice a hoarse whisper. 'There are kids here!'

'Oh chill out!' Lois said flippantly. 'There's one kid here and he'll be going home soon.'

Maria stepped into the room and slammed the door behind her. 'There are two kids here and you're giving cocaine to one of them, you dumb fuck, Lois, she's still at school!'

Lois sat upright and the others pulled back to make way for Maria as she went to seize the mirror away from Nadia.

Nadia pushed herself up but did not shift away like the others.

'Don't call me a kid!' Nadia lifted her voice. 'I know what I'm doing, I've done it before! You're not my mother!'

Outraged that Nadia would try and defend her behaviour, Maria was at first shocked but came back with her basic sense of right and wrong. She wasn't about to let Nadia undermine her in her own house.

'I'm fully aware I'm not your mother, so stop rebelling like I am!' Maria yelled. 'You shouldn't even be here! Just because I'm not giving you the same attention I give you in school means you have to resort to this attention-seeking behaviour, does it?'

Nadia looked wounded and slid her legs off the bed, shook the hurtful truth out of her head, and turned to the wall to hide her face as she rubbed her nose.

'All of you are taking the piss, now get the fuck out of here before I call the police!' Maria stormed back to the door and opened it.

'She's your fucking student?!' Lois cried, pointing back at Nadia in horror.

'Yeah, big reveal, Lois! You've been too wrapped up in yourself to see what's going on around you. Nadia is sixteen! Christian invited her, I told you it wasn't a good idea but you insisted they come because it makes you look more popular, doesn't it?!'

All four of Lois' friends folded themselves down and filed out. They were evidently not close enough friends with Lois to fight her corner.

'Well, thank you, sweetheart!' Lois spat sarcastically. 'You've driven my friends away! How could you humiliate me like this? I didn't do anything wrong! How was I supposed to know Christian's girlfriend was underage? I can't believe you've ruined my night! That's it! It's over!' Lois paced past Maria and followed her friends out the door.

Maria was left in the room with Nadia. Her hands gripped her hips as she stood, watching Nadia's body trembling with anxiety. She felt little compassion.

'I thought you were so much smarter than that.' Maria muttered through clenched jaws. She turned on her heel and left Nadia alone in her spare room, to go and face the music downstairs. She could hear Lois screeching but steeled her nerves for one final round.

Chapter Eleven

Maria needn't have prepared for a new battle, Lois did all the work herself. Wailing with hysterical outrage at being thown out of her own event, Lois made a loud, chaotic exit by yanking her artwork off the walls and dragging them out to a taxi cab, as her colleagues grabbed a few remaining bottles of wine from the kitchen table and waved fickle farewells. The sudden upset served only to intimidate the house guests enjoying the otherwise peaceful party.

Following a few sore minutes of head-scratching and apologies, Maria called it a night and escorted her friends to the door, pair by pair. They thanked her for the evening, and wished her well, shrugging with good-natured smiles at the wildness of her artistic girlfriend. Sadie expressed her sympathy for Maria, but Paula tightened at the conflict that wore immediately on her nerves, and seemed more eager to leave than say goodbye. David and Simon made Maria promise to call them if there was further drama that night, or anytime, and they would come to help. Maria thanked them and reassured them she would be fine.

There was much food left on the table, and Ben and Chloe kindly helped condense the dishes down to small plates and squeeze it all into the fridge, and Maria explained to Ben what had happened upstairs as she filled her dishwasher. Separating a few scraps Leon would enjoy, Maria wondered where he was, and had to call him out from behind the curtains where he had probably run to escape Lois' screeching. She soothed him with a cuddle, fed him to cheer him up, and let him outside into the garden.

By the time Maria went to clean up the lounge, and realised Christian hadn't moved from her couch, she saw he had fallen into such a deep, drunken slumber that she could not even stir him. He snored through her shoves to his shoulder, then his arm untucked from under his face and dropped listlessly outwards. She happened to notice it gestured over at someone's handbag, a floppy maroon thing, and Maria recognised it as Nadia's. She turned and looked around her with a slight headache. Though she hadn't seen them leave, Anthony and Clarissa, Christian's parents, had long gone. They had been whispering and giggling to each other all evening; they must have tiptoed out and headed home, long before all the shouting broke out. Maria cursed, Nadia was still upstairs, and she had no way of getting her home.

She locked the door after hugging Ben tightly,

expressing eternal thanks for his presence and help. Then, with a dull sort of resignation dampening any pride at being the last one standing, Maria removed Christian's shoes, covered him with a blanket, and encouraged Leon to stay with him for the night. Taking Nadia's handbag upstairs, Maria leaned into the spare room, and saw Nadia curled up away from her, but she had no sympathy, or pull towards the crying girl.

'Party's over, everyone's gone home,' Maria said, her voice husky with tiredness. 'There's no-one to drive you back, Christian's sleeping and I've had too much. You can stay tonight... your bag's here.' Maria dropped the handbag at the foot of the bed and went to leave.

However, Nadia sat herself up and padded from the bed, across the room towards Maria in just her tights. She bent to pick up her high-heel boots and stumbled putting them on. 'It's okay, I'll get a taxi,' she mumbled.

'What?' Maria asked, feeling her cold control slipping away from her. She reached out thinking Nadia might fall on unsteady heels.

Nadia saw it and pushed Maria's assistance away, pulled on her other boot and stood up with calm balance. She looked up through messy hair and wet, blotchy mascara. 'I'll get myself home, you don't want me here.'

Maria looked down at the hurt she'd caused in Nadia's eyes, still beautifully green, shimmering with blackened tears, her lips trembled and pouted, holding in the flood that swelled inside her. She felt an acute, sick guilt at making Nadia feel so unwelcome, and humiliating her in front of people she was trying to be adult with; she wasn't a kid at all, but Nadia couldn't mess around with adult toys like drugs, not when Maria was, in effect, her guardian for the evening.

'Nadia, stop... Stop!' Seizing Nadia's small, teetering frame as she went to push past her, Maria looked into Nadia's eyes heavily, and whispered as sensitively and meaningfully as she could. 'You don't need to do this.' She meant the drugs; she meant leaving; she meant seeking her attention in general: Nadia had it already.

Nadia stared hard for a minute, before her eyes spilled with shame. 'I'm fucked up.'

Her heart finally pulling back to Nadia's soft accent and sweet-smelling hair, Maria caught Nadia as she leaned toward her and let the girl fall into her arms.

So this was it.

If Nadia wanted her attention, needed a mother-figure, or whatever, Maria had to give it up for her right at this moment. She allowed Nadia to press her nose into her shirt, her fingers curling stiffly into the fabric above her breast as she wept. Unlike the last time she had embraced the girl, Maria felt her own release as she wrapped her arms around Nadia's tense shoulders and held her in closely to her. Hugging her could be simple. The girl needed cuddles, and Maria had been too concerned about showing too much affection to show any.

She had to put her fears aside, all those sensual feelings she'd had recently. Maria held her body firm to be a rock for Nadia, and was flattered the girl obviously needed her support. Suddenly, it didn't feel too much of a hassle to be Nadia's emotional guide as well as her academic one, and Maria supposed she could be like an older sister to Nadia: not that she'd had one herself, but she could imagine it was something similar to this.

Satisfied that she had shown enough disapproval of Nadia doing drugs, Maria felt secure her professional boundaries had not been compromised, and this hug was private between them in this moment; no-one else had to know. Maria was also satisfied that any lustful feelings she'd had towards Nadia must have been extinguished, holding her this close stirred nothing between her thighs and the only urge she felt was to wipe Nadia's tears, prompting her to wonder if it was maternal instincts she felt after all.

She told Nadia she should stay, sleep there in the spare room, and get a good rest. She found a spare toothbrush and some bedclothes for Nadia: an old favourite: a long faded blue 1980's rock band t-shirt, and some baggy pyjama bottoms. She pulled some towels from the airing cupboard in case she wanted to freshen up. The bedsheets were clean and Maria showed Nadia where she could switch the lamp off when she was ready. Nadia thanked her with dark-stained eyes and a stiff purse of her lips. The scruffy-haired girl looked slightly in shock as Maria closed the door from the hallway.

Returning downstairs, Maria drew two pints of water from the tap and checked Christian was still sleeping soundly with Leon watching over him. It was gone midnight and Maria had no idea how it had gotten so late, it still felt early. Back upstairs, she knocked gently on the spare room door and gave Nadia one of the pints of water.

'Hey, I just thought, shouldn't you tell your dad that you're staying here tonight?'

Nadia sipped the water, her sinuses sounded blocked. 'No it's fine, I already told him I'd be staying at Christian's.'

Accepting Nadia's reply, Maria returned to her own room feeling weary, but wired. She took two painkillers to dissolve her headache, brushed her teeth, then put on her vest and boxer shorts for bed, throwing her clothes over the tall, black iron bars at the end of her bed. Maria knew she would struggle to sleep with the knowledge that Nadia was in the next room, probably laying awake too. Except, soon, that feeling made her squirm; a rich, stoned, rolling around state of hot wakefulness; a luxurious minefield of fantasy pressed her imagination with every turn.

For the best part of an hour, Maria tried to link telepathically with Nadia and imagined what she must be feeling. She allowed herself to gage the vibrations through the wall, trying to understand what Nadia was going through, what she must have experienced to do what she did, feel how she felt. Wondering if Nadia was laying there thinking the same about her, Maria had to remind herself that Nadia needed a mentor or someone older to look up to, and she should not project anything onto the girl reflected from her own dubious feelings. Still, the way Nadia looked at her sometimes, the way she stared, almost flirting, made Maria think again what could really be motivating Nadia, or if the girl was just playing with her.

It could have been anything up to a couple of hours later when she was just starting to drift off with surreal re-enactments of the evenings drama; Maria thought she was dreaming when she heard a soft knock on her door. She lifted her head from her pillow and listened, one arm, motionless, tucked under it.

'Maria?'

The gentle curling of Nadia's breathy voice around the door sent a shiver through Maria's stirring alertness. Her breath held tight in her throat, she didn't know if she should answer. She feared Nadia was having a crisis and needed her emotional support, but Maria was too tired for any more mental exertion. Then, Maria supposed it might be something simple Nadia needed, like an extra blanket, and cleared her throat to respond. 'Come in.'

She leaned up on her side to see Nadia's face as she entered. It was dark and all she could catch was

Nadia's silhouette: her hair even more ruffled, the long t-shirt Maria had given her was hanging down over naked legs. Wondering why she had chosen not to wear the pyjama bottoms, Maria's breath caught up with her in a pant, getting the distinct feeling Nadia wanted something more than a blanket. Nadia moved around the door, opening it further with the inside of her knee pressing against the wood. Her voice came out of darkness as Maria's eyes adjusted to the chink of light from the hall outside, bathing the room in deep orange.

'I can't sleep,' Nadia whispered.

Maria rubbed her face and yawned, somehow on command, to let Nadia believe she had disturbed her from blissful unconsciousness. She replied, dryly. 'That'll be the coke.'

Any other student, any other girl of that age in this scenario, Maria would have dismissed, sent away and not engaged, not even humoured out of kindness, but she just couldn't help being glad Nadia had come to her. Apart from the snoozing boys downstairs, Leon and Christian, she was alone with Nadia, and in contrary to the rising panic and nausea she had felt earlier in the evening and at other times during their interactions, it was a strangely relaxing feeling. Maria held herself propped up on her elbow and felt a warm reconnection to Nadia in place of the back-stiffening nervousness she'd come to dread in the girl's presence. This time, this late at night, Nadia wasn't being intense as she could be: her manner was sad, heavy but in a tired, humble way. She was calm as she asked if she could sit with Maria for a while.

Immediately, before her moral reason kicked in, and before her denial even had a chance, Maria knew she would allow Nadia to sit next to her on her bed. Maria sat up and leaned back against the cold iron bars behind her pillows, however, sighing effortfully. She pushed her hair away from her face and squinted to try and make out Nadia's expression from the shadowed blur of her features. The girl was being very casual, like she just wanted to jump in with a friend, nothing meant by it: she wasn't being flirty or cheeky, wasn't being seductive or creepy, she was just like a regular buddy with a sore head.

Perhaps they did know each other well enough to chat in bed, as long as it was just a chat and nothing more. Yet, Maria felt like she had drawn her through somehow, and wondered if Nadia was just pretending to be cool. Either way, Maria wasn't about to be so hard as to refuse the shivering girl, and pulled the edge of her feather duvet back to make a nestlike corner for Nadia to slip into.

Nadia sat small in the deep pocket created between the duvet and the pillows. She pulled her knees up and wrapped her arms around them, too cold to recline; or too nervous to. She remained in breathless silence for an awkward minute, while Maria was accomodating the reality that Nadia was actually sitting in her bed. Maria then realised she should be the one to say something to ease the tension: she was the elder, she had to take responsibility and facilitate Nadia's comfort, but then how much to allow in case she got too comfortable? Maria screwed her eyes closed again, confused by her racing brain. They both sat still for another half minute. Nadia sniffled occasionally, but Maria wasn't sure if that was due to crying or cocaine.

'Sorry for harshing you out,' Maria said quietly. 'I was angry with Lois, I shouldn't have shouted at you.'

Thinking that Nadia might be in an introspective state with enough hindsight to admit she had been foolish to take the substance, Maria hoped for a confession: that Nadia had been seeking Maria's attention, and perhaps it would lead to a weight-off-the-shoulder type of discussion where Maria understood what it was Nadia was looking for in her. But it seemed Nadia wasn't interested in speaking about herself.

'Can I ask you something?' Nadia asked tentatively. 'How you can stand being with her? You're a really good person, and she talks to you like a piece of shit.' Nadia's body trembled every now and then as she spoke, definately more nerves than shivers.

In the silence that followed, Maria wondered what Nadia meant by criticising her relationship, but after remembering it was Lois they were talking about, and justifying that Nadia had a point, she decided against defending Lois, and found herself quite happy to agree with Nadia's statements about the differences:

there were many.

However, thinking it through, Maria didn't want to sound patronising by having to explain why some things worked even though they were opposite, then she remembered her role-model responsibility to let Nadia know that it wasn't very classy to bad-mouth someone; finally she felt she ought not to discuss her relationship issues with a girl she didn't really know, or trust, yet. She came back to her original thought that Nadia might have another agenda for mentioning Lois' poor girlfriend qualities, and settled on saying: 'Every relationship is fraught with difficulties.'

Another bout of silence and Maria felt her eyes heavy with sleepiness. Her mind drifted as she waited for Nadia's response: she prayed Nadia wouldn't say something like 'you deserve better than her' or anything that would cross another line off on her tally of suspicion. Presently, it was comfortable, pleasant and almost no hassle at all to have Nadia sit with her. Except, when Nadia slipped her legs down and turned on her side to curl up, Maria feared the girl was going to start snoozing right there next to her. She opened her eyes with concern.

'Hey, don't even think about falling asleep in my bed.' Maria mumbled.

Nadia tucked her legs up and pulled the duvet up over her ear. 'I'm just going to close my eyes until I feel tired, then I'll go back in the other room, I promise.'

Unravel

Maria thought she should set an alarm for fifteen minutes, but her phone was over on the dressing table; it would require effort to get it, and it was a little too anal even for her. So they'd had a party, Nadia was crashing over: it was no big deal, Maria told herself. She began to soak up the sensation of having Nadia there beside her, as close as they sat in tuition, but this time they were wrapped in a warm duvet together, semi-clothed, in the dark, in silence. She listened for Nadia's breathing and guessed that when it started getting heavier she would wake her and send her back through. Wondering if she'd have to guide her, Maria couldn't expect Nadia to stumble half-asleep down the hall; she resolved if Nadia fell asleep, it would make much more sense, and be far more gracious of her, to go sleep in the spare room herself, and let Nadia rest.

Soon, Maria heard Nadia's breathing becoming steadily deeper and longer, a sweet huffing noise through her swollen lips as her nasal airways were congested. Maria kept telling herself to get up and go to the spare room, but she was actually content for the first time in days and a little voice kept telling her to enjoy every small moment she could from having Nadia safely beside her. But every moment she enjoyed Nadia's gently snoring company was a moment delaying, and delaying, her transfer. Maria fell into a deep, beautifully serene sleep with no regrets or fears.

♥

She seemed to be floating in a soft paradise. Her limbs were suspended in a thick fluid, her body undulating in rhythm to the flow of the slow current. It was blissful, heaven-like, and when she understood the skin of her nudity, Maria bathed in the sensuality of all the feminine power and pleasure of the lesbian.

Following the pulses higher until she arose to the surface, Maria opened the slits of her eyes and looked down on Nadia's head, closer than she had been when they had gone to sleep. In fact, where Nadia's auburn hair spread over the end of Maria's pillow, Maria realised her own arm was tucked underneath, laid out under the feathers that cushioned Nadia's head.

With her body inclined towards her, Nadia's fingers had found their way to the skin of Maria's shoulder, and had folded loosely around the strap of her vest top. Maria gazed down at Nadia's closed eyes, slightly puffy but wiped clean from make-up; in the dull morning light Maria could just see the freckles either side of her nose. Nadia's mouth parted in a soft crescent; her brows in chestnut arches, she looked more at peace than Maria had ever seen her.

Her concern inevitably travelled southward, as Maria recalled the pulsing press on her skin from her erotic dream; she felt Nadia move against her thigh and knew their bodies were connected at other points. Maria's breath halted, she tried moving her leg and soon understood their arrangement after realising Nadia was pinning her down. Their legs had become intertwined. Nadia's naked thigh ground once more against her own, and a sudden, contracting pang of arousal pushed down the length of Maria's body. She couldn't stop the sensation making her insides churn. Evidently, Nadia had rolled towards her at some point during the early hours and Maria had, however unintentionally in her sleep, responded by sliding her own leg further under the girl. Not only that, but her hand had somehow hooked over Nadia's hip, holding her in. Realising this, Maria let go and lifted it clear of Nadia's t-shirt where it had slid upwards over her bottom. They were practically joined at the pelvis, at least it felt like it: their skin had stuck fast with heat and sweat and Maria felt another pang create a swell of moisture inside her shorts.

Nadia was definately asleep, she didn't stir as Maria tried to tug her arm out from under the pillow; she couldn't. She pushed the duvet back a little, feeling her skin prickling with a flush of heat and panic. It would be impossible to move her leg without waking Nadia, and as much as she didn't want Nadia to be witness to this awkward position, Maria didn't have a choice: she would have to get her to move without delay. In terms of appropriate time to wake a student before a teacher took advantage of her sleepfulness, Maria knew it had already been too long: she should have jumped up straight away, repulsed, ashamed. But, regardless of however they had gotten into this embrace, thinking about it wasn't going to save any moral integrity, she had to get out of it right now.

'Nadia,' she said, her voice a hoarse whisper. Nadia breathed on, oblivious.

'Nadia!' Maria repeated, louder, her fear rising with the realisation that Christian could walk in and find them like this. Her heart was beating hard, her skin bristling with sweat and nerves, and all the time an unbearable ache throbbed through the muscles between her legs. She pressed her hand again on Nadia's hip and urged her backwards with a gentle, but firm drive.

Suddenly awakening to the pressure of Maria's touch, Nadia's first instinct was to jolt her knee upwards, her thigh catching Maria's swollen area, making her buckle. Maria bit her lip and eased her hand down Nadia's thigh to guide it in the other direction.

Nadia finally rolled her torso up and out, her bosom, bra-less under the t-shirt, brushed against Maria's, whose nipples vibrated under her vest. Nadia lifted her hand off Maria's body in a tight confusion, her eyes creased with blinks at Maria, then at the tattoo on Maria's shoulder. Nadia breathed in and out through her nose a few times, adjusting to reality from the obviously dirty dream she'd been rudely yanked from. Maria wondered if Nadia was paralysed with awkwardness, or just taking in her scent.

'You have to move,' Maria said in a soft gravel, 'my arms gone dead.'

Nadia silently lifted her head and let Maria slide

her arm out, except, without moving her lower half, Maria couldn't wriggle out from where Nadia had trapped her.

'And your leg?' Maria nudged Nadia's thigh with the muscles in her own, to let Nadia know, in her dazed state, which leg had to shift.

Nadia's breath held suddenly, obviously a little shocked, as she peeled her thigh from Maria's. Sticky in retreat, Maria wondered if the sensation in Nadia's thigh was repulsive to her, if the girl was nauseated by waking in such close proximity to her teacher. Nadia rolled onto her back and blinked at the ceiling, then let her breath go.

Maria sat up, arm tingling. 'I'm really sorry, I don't know how we ended up like that.'

Nadia's head tilted toward her on the pillow, her gaze was back to its usual intensity. Maria could feel Nadia's eyes travelling across the breadth of her shoulders, and her back muscles became tense; she wore nothing but her vest and boxer shorts and she had never intended Nadia to see her in such a state of undress. It made her feel cringingly uncomfortable as her arousal ebbed away.

'Oh God,' Nadia said in a halting, velvety whisper.

Turning gradually, Maria stared down at Nadia's reclined body laying next to her. The girl looked worried, both arms laying open beside her head, stuck in recoil, her eyes blinked up at the ceiling of

Maria's bedroom. She struck Maria as quietly beautiful, there in her old rock t-shirt. They had done nothing, Maria was sure, but it felt like they could have: their hair mussed and limbs aching to stretch.

She had no idea what to make of Nadia's response: it was hard to tell if the girl was as disturbed as Maria had been awakening to the clinging tryst. Nadia could have been having a dirty dream about anyone, Maria reasoned, or maybe there was no dream - Nadia could be pure of mind, an innocent who was thinking nothing of it. If Nadia was that naive, then Maria could only look to herself as some sort of pervert. She realised she could be the only one thinking weird thoughts right now. It made her throat seize up with nausea.

'I'm going to go and make tea,' Maria said, and coughed, remembering she had smoked last night. The dreadful occurances of the party came back to her too, and Maria glanced back at Nadia, recalling the cocaine scenario. She felt disappointed. Angry at Lois. Bitter that her friends had witnessed, or at least overheard, her arguments with her girlfriend. Maria pulled on her jogging bottoms, opened her bedroom door and headed downstairs, knowing it was the wake-up call she needed to finally end things with Lois.

Tipping her head through her lounge door, Maria saw that Christian was still sound asleep, having rolled over a full turn, cocooning himself in the blanket Maria had draped over him, but at least he was deep under and would not know anything of Nadia sleeping in her teacher's bed, unless of course she told him.

Leon jumped down to greet her and Maria let him out into the garden, breathing in the fresh morning air. She made tea and pondered if Nadia would say anything to anyone at school, and what there was to mention. Fairly sure Nadia wouldn't want to speak of her cocaine use, Maria considered Nadia might keep a lid on even turning up to the party, if it risked people finding out she woke up in spoons with her teacher. More like scissors, perhaps, Maria contemplated, and the idea of their hot crotches touching through their underwear sent another squeeze of lust to her clitoris.

She was confused as to how they had become entwined in such a position, and was sure she would not have instigated it even in her sleep. Perhaps she had thought the female body laying next to her was Lois, and embraced her in return: no, realised Maria, that wouldn't happen. Therefore, Nadia must have been the one to climb into Maria's arms. Nadia had obviously reached out for her, maybe it was an innocent rolling over in her sleep, but *if* Nadia was awake when she sought Maria out under the duvet, then why?

As the kettle boiled, Maria hung over the edge of the counter and tried to stop her head swirling with desire, her heart was beating double time. She slipped her fingers down to her shorts, just to check she was right, and felt a mixture of sadness and satisfaction finding the pool of moisture that had gathered there.

Unravel

Chapter Twelve

When Maria took the tray of tea back upstairs, however, she had blanked her mind of all sordid thought, and put on her school face in order to return to teacher mode. She had to view Nadia as a student who had simply crashed over after getting too wasted, and Maria was doing the responsible thing in making her tea before driving her home. It was that simple. Nothing else had happened, and Nadia must never know that Maria was harbouring secret feelings. Setting the tray by the foot end of the iron bedstead, Maria noticed Nadia had not moved to get up and dressed.

'Breakfast in bed?' Nadia looked surprised at the sight of cake.

Maria crossed to the windows. 'Just leftovers.' She said nonchalantly, and opened the curtains a little way. She recalled that she was supposed to have moved to the spare room after Nadia fell asleep, and cursed herself for being fooled: the girl had said she couldn't sleep but promptly fallen under once she'd wormed her

Unravel

way inside. Maria didn't know what Nadia was thinking and hesitantly watched her as she poured two cups from the teapot, but Nadia didn't look at her and Maria wondered if she was reading too much into it - she was the one making it awkward, as if they really did have improper relations.

'Is Christian still here?' Nadia asked lightly. She had plaited her hair scruffily over one shoulder and sat crosslegged under the duvet.

'Yeah, he's dead to the world,' Maria replied and saw a frown grow on Nadia's face. She could hardly take in the fact that she was having a morning-after conversation with Nadia, half-dressed and hungover in her bed. She felt her breath tremble in her lungs. 'Do you like him?' Maria asked randomly, unable to think of what else to say. 'I mean, actually *like* him?'

A long pause passed as Nadia stared with unblinking depth of thought onto the duvet. 'He's a nice guy, but...' She picked at the cake with her fingers. 'He's not the kind of person I'm usually attracted to.'

'Why?' Maria frowned and shrugged with ignorance. Pulling a jumper from her wardrobe, Maria felt too conscious of her chilly breasts in just her vest. 'He's smart, kind, and his parents are well off! What else do you want?'

Nadia's gaze swayed down to her mug. 'He's just not my usual type.'

Maria tilted her head with narrowing eyes,

sensing something in Nadia's evasiveness.

'Well then, what is your type?' Maria asked, with no suggestion or smile behind it. She shut the mirrored wardrobe door.

Nadia's lips pinched, she gulped suddenly and lifted her eyes. 'Can I tell you something? I haven't been completely honest.'

A different chill prickled its way down Maria's spine as a sudden fear of what Nadia might be about to confess struck her. She may have inadvertently opened the emotional connection with Nadia she had been trying so hard to keep closed. 'What about?'

'About why I left Dublin,' Nadia spoke quietly; she looked ashamed.

Maria exhaled a little relief that it wasn't about her. 'I thought your mother...'

Nadia shifted her foot from underneath her and stretched it out along the bed. She lifted her cup to drink, to think, but her words came to her before she could take in a mouthful.

'My mum found out that I got... involved... with someone I shouldn't have, she freaked out... then chucked me out. I had to sleep rough for a while. That's why I dropped out of school.' Nadia looked up at Maria with a direct sincerity.

Sitting at the end of her bed, Maria leaned back against the iron bars, her curiosity turning with temporary disbelief to a hesitant empathy. 'Shit,' she murmured, wondering if she could trust this wasn't

Unravel

another elaboration to Nadia's sob story.

The girl continued, her accent loose with nervousness: 'I got picked up by the police, they took me to my aunt and uncle, but they wouldn't take sides so they called social services and I got sent to my dad's... then when I turned up on his doorstep he was fucking furious with me. Anyway, he let me stay with him as long as I lived by his rules, I'd have to finish school, and I really want to finish school, so I agreed.' Nadia finished and Maria saw moisture in her eyes. Nadia shook her tears away and finally raised her cup to sip the cooling tea.

Maria frowned, trying to work it out. It wasn't that she didn't believe Nadia, but that she didn't know what to say to her claims of homelessness. She struggled to imagine the fine-skinned, sweet-smelling Nadia she knew, roughing it on the streets. Many questions raced through Maria's mind, but as most faded, or were deliberately discarded as unnecessary drudging up of Nadia's painful past memories, one remained: *What could Nadia have done so bad to warrant being chucked out of home?*

'This person...' Maria spoke tenderly. 'They must have been something special for you to get in so much trouble.'

Nadia sustained her eye contact with Maria, and took a breath. 'I wouldn't say she was special... she was just a girl, that was enough.'

There followed a long pause after which Maria

looked down at the crumpled bed sheets. She nodded calmly to herself, although, before she could put a label on her student, as a crucial defining factor of Nadia's history, Maria needed to know if Nadia was a merely a victim of these untimely circumstances, or if she was a knowing participant, even an instigator, of these events.

'Was she the only girl you've been with?' She asked, tapping her mug with her thumb.

Nadia cringed then exhaled sulkily. 'What do you have to ask me that for?'

As Nadia rubbed her forehead with a nervous hand, any instinct Maria had to cheer with joy and pride at receiving a live confession from a teenage gay died like a pre-choking retch in her throat as she realised the gravity of what it meant for her as Nadia's teacher. All the times Maria had found Nadia watching her in tuition, in assembly, in her car; Maria had convinced herself that Nadia looked up to her, respected and admired her, now all of that was in question again.

'You prefer girls.' Maria couldn't believe to whom she was stating those words.

'Please don't tell anyone, I promised my dad,' Nadia begged.

'What? To play by your dad's rules, you have to be straight to stay in school?'

Nadia shrugged, and Maria suddenly resented her calculated, pre-meditated attitude.

'So you're just using Christian,' Maria frowned.

Nadia seemed shocked by Maria's lack of

understanding. 'Please don't say anything! I don't want to hurt him. He is all of those things you said he is, I just-'

But Maria interrupted Nadia's excuses. 'And your dad is more than happy for you to have a boyfriend - that's why you told him you were staying with Chris, oh now I get it!' Maria clicked her fingers to her head with a cool smile.

'Don't say it like that, I didn't lie to him! I thought I *would* be staying with Chris,' Nadia said, her face becoming red, her eyes filling again.

'Hey, look, I don't care if you're deceiving your dad, and I understand why you're deceiving Christian, I really do,' Maria said firmly. 'But don't lie to me.'

'I'm trying to be honest with you now!' Nadia hushed her fearful pitch.

Maria made dark shadows of her eyes. 'Why?'

The tears in Nadia's eyes wobbled. 'Because I think it's important that you know this about me.'

'Know what exactly?' Maria growled quietly, feeling her own eyes stinging.

Nadia's cheeks blushed, she blinked and tears spilled in streams. Her lips pursed together as she struggled to say the words. 'That I'm gay, too'.

Easing back, Maria felt a rush of anxiety shoot into her stomach as she watched Nadia wipe her hot face. Nadia had not just said: 'I'm gay', she had added 'too'. Nadia was coming out to her for being more than a teacher - for being a fellow lesbian. Maria had previously wondered if Nadia had a straight-girl crush on her but now she understood why Nadia had sought her friendship.

'So, you want me to keep your little secret?' Maria asked dully. She glared at Nadia disapprovingly, she wanted to show Nadia she did not care to be involved with a student's personal game-playing regime. It made her feel sick that Nadia would be hanging out with Christian under such false pretences; that he would be falling in love with her and she would be letting him touch her to keep up appearances; and most likely, Nadia would soon come running to Maria to cry at her own self-disgust.

The tears had turned to anger and Nadia's face closed up. 'Forget it! Forget I told you, you obviously don't give a shit! I'm going home!' Nadia put her cup on the side table and scrambled her legs out from the duvet. She stood up, but stopped, and held her head like it hurt; Maria guessed her hangover might be kicking in.

'Wait!' Maria stepped in front of Nadia and lowered her arm. 'Listen, I'm sorry, I didn't mean to be unsympathetic,' Maria said and searched for more words as Nadia gazed up, bridging the several inches between their faces with pulsating emotion. Maria remembered they had woken up this close together, but she had been too distracted to absorb how lovely Nadia was then, as she did now: lovely and cute, even this tearful and grumpy.

Unravel

'I don't want your sympathy,' Nadia said, frowning. Her feelings were hurt. Maria smelled the sweet tea on her breath.

'Well, then tell me honestly...' Maria asked, her fingers touching the skin of Nadia's soft jawbone. She intended the tactile gesture and a soft suggestion to prompt some definitive answer to the question that had been burning on her lips. Surely Nadia wasn't just after her friendship. 'What exactly *do* you want from me?'

A tangible shudder shot through Nadia's body and her eyes dilated as she panted. 'Nothing...' she blinked and stood back from Maria's proximity. 'What do you mean?'

Maria was pleased Nadia had stepped away from her intimation, but thought Nadia looked more frightened than disgusted.

'I just need to know,' Maria said gently, 'if you've got a crush on me.'

Nadia shook her head, her eyebrows twisting up. 'No!'

Maria rested her hands on her hips, relaxing a little. 'You don't?'

'No, I don't!' Nadia said with a stubborn pout of her lower lip, her eyes still wide.

'Not even a little bit?' Maria teased with a pursing smile.

'You're my teacher!' Nadia said, defensively.

'Yeah, and...?' Maria nodded slowly, eyes flashing. 'You wouldn't be the first.'

Nadia puffed herself full of air and took on a less intimidated stance. 'Well, I think that sounds fucking arrogant! And that's certainly not my type!'

'Really?' Maria raised her eyebrows, not expecting this remark, though she took it in good humour and let her smile open to Nadia's criticism. 'Fair enough.'

The connection between them disappeared quickly, and they were left standing awkwardly, each aware of themselves so near to each other. Maria scratched her head with a chuckle.

'Look, I'm sorry... I had to ask,' Maria said, but didn't feel she had anything to apologise for. 'Do you understand why I had to ask?'

Nadia sniffed and pulled a strand from her tousled plait behind her ear, averting her eyes from Maria's. 'Yeah, I get it... still arrogant.' She mumbled.

Maria looked at Nadia's bare legs as she sat down on the edge of the bed with a defeated slump. The bones in her knees protruded but her thighs tapered out to generous curves of pale, soft looking flesh. It had previously crossed Maria's mind that there was little masculinity in Nadia's demeanour; at the most a tomboyish quality could be interpreted from her scruffy hair and temper. However, seeing some new whole-bodied womanliness in the way she sat now, she considered that Nadia had lost some of the girlishness that she had carried with her nervousness. Maria felt her throat was dry, as Nadia looked up at her hopelessly. If

Nadia was really gay, she could possibly turn into one of the most beautiful lesbians Maria had ever seen.

'You should just be yourself, you know?' Maria said in a low, gravely voice that remained at a steady, even tone as words of advice came from her as if on autopilot. 'You can only be you, so you should just be true to yourself. Doesn't matter what other people think or want from you. You can't please everyone. All you can do is make yourself happy. Do what *you* want.'

Nadia gazed up at Maria with something unreadable in her eyes.

Maria shook herself loose and looked down to her feet. She felt a mixture of shyness and guilt, but couldn't tell if either was real; she felt slightly out of control. 'I'm gonna take a shower, then I'll get you home.' She left Nadia sitting in her t-shirt on the edge of her bed; no longer caring to make sure Nadia was okay. She needed to get the hell out of that room.

♥

Since leaving the party, Lois had only texted Maria to say she was returning to Australia to see her family and spend the holidays with loved ones, that she needed to have a break, and she would be back in a few weeks. Therefore, the turn of the New Year passed in dull semi-drunkenness as Maria sunk into a self-pitying funk. Leon kept her company from the moment she awoke, aching with depression, until she drifted to sleep again in front of several seasonal movies. Leon cuddled up with her, loving her warmth and company. She appreciated his loyalty, and acquiesced to his polite nudges for his daily walks outside.

Otherwise reluctant to leave the house and bear witness to the exclusive celebrations of neighbours, even the weather turned to suit Maria's mood by sleeting with cutting ice against her hollow cheek. The wind was rough some days and churned her emotions with it, her eyes streaming, disguising tears; other days it was placid, and her mind remained blank, banal.

Having deliberately perpetuated her intoxicated state of numbness so as not to think directly upon her issues with the girl, in those first dusk-fallen evenings after New Year, once time had cleared the fog of confusion, Maria checked her phone and re-read messages she had received from Nadia. Analysing everything the girl had said to her with this fresh perspective, Maria thought back over her own words, actions and reactions to Nadia, wondering if it was anything she had done to create this situation. The past few months seemed to have been a whirlwind of contradiction now that she knew Nadia was gay.

In all soberness, Maria's heart hurt. She felt a slight betrayal that Nadia had not been straight with her, but Maria simultaneously felt sympathy and understood why Nadia had needed to reveal her secret to someone she could trust, only when she could trust them. Maria figured that waking up in such a compromising position had prompted Nadia's confession, but for what reasons Maria could only guess: and it was the guessing that hurt her head, too. Her rational mind had started spinning whenever she had tried to address it; willingly spun off, zoned out, and frequently hit a bottle.

With a few days to go before the new term started at GCH, Maria knew she had to sort her feelings out before she behaved inappropriately around the girl. Maria chose to drive out to Eastcombe, taking conscious control of the draw towards Nadia's residence. She didn't want to go anywhere near her house, but she did want to follow her feelings: get as close as her desire felt was necessary to have a sense of Nadia. She settled on the snowy hilltop overlooking Nadia's village and let Leon out for a walk in his fleecy coat while she leaned against the bonnet of her car, smoking a cigarette she didn't really enjoy. She thought over what she knew about Nadia, what she could trust, what she believed, and what it meant to her. Knowing Nadia had been in a lesbian relationship, and had suffered for it, changed things.

Maria had believed Nadia was not inclined towards women, but now it seemed impossible to quash those instincts that told her Nadia liked her. Until now Maria thought her own feelings were skewing those impressions she had from Nadia's purring attention; knowing she was not so wrong made her feel stronger in herself. She was glad she had challenged Nadia in her bedroom, even though she had denied it; Maria felt she could once again trust her gut that told her there was something else there, coming from Nadia, not her - and that wasn't her arrogance speaking.

Contemplating upon Christian, Maria wondered if Nadia was just using him to get close to her. After she had allowed the girl to meet her dog, Nadia must have sussed Maria's intentions to set her up with the dog-sitter, but there's no way she could ask Nadia now, and Maria didn't really want to know. In the private silence of her thoughts, Maria knew she didn't mind Nadia walking her dog or visiting her house: it made her secretly happy to see Nadia outside school. She would never be able to tell anyone, especially Nadia, how much pleasure it gave her to have her little friend nearby, and if Nadia was going to deny her feelings, then Maria could play her at her own game.

Chapter Thirteen

Despite having been miserable for the majority of her holiday, by the time the new term started again, Maria felt she'd had a significant break and was actually glad to be back at school. The next few weeks, months even, were booked up with both her regular students referred to her for extra tuition, and several random ones who requested her guidance in preparation for the mock exams due later that term.

Maria expected to see Nadia after school, the first time since the morning-after experience in her bedroom. The memory of the dream, the sensation that awoke her to find Nadia in her arms still caused a prickle of adrenalin; she couldn't help any tingle she felt in her stomach whenever she thought of the girl coming out to her, neither could she stop the hesitant smile that followed. However, time seemed to drag until their reunion and Maria started to lose the spontaneity of her excitement and instead began to feel plain nervousness in her stomach, fearing how Nadia might be with her, and what may be in store.

She didn't mean to keep obsessing about her appearance, but Maria wanted to make sure she presented a cool, collected front for Nadia's arrival, to show that what had happened at the party was as much part of the past as last year. Maria slicked her curls into black tails that spiralled at her neck, and revived her bosoms with a shift and a squeeze. She had received compliments on her maroon blouse earlier in the day and she pepped herself up towards the end of it so as not to look as if she was flagging, but in all honesty, her first day back had been full on. She gazed over her reflection in the staff toilet mirror, counting the minutes after registration until Nadia would be arriving, keeping her thoughts in check, and reminding herself to act normally.

When her office door was knocked upon, Maria's body twitched in her chair behind her desk and she felt a punch of heat encase her at the thrill of seeing Nadia. She breathed deeply, shaking her head clear of the blush that was telling her this felt like a date.

Nadia entered and stood for a moment at the door seeming to check the atmosphere.

'Come in,' Maria said, exhaling her nerves subtly. She was instantly reminded of the first time Nadia arrived in her office, their eyes connecting, Nadia looking wary, Maria taken aback at how aesthetically pleasing this new girl was. The teenager looked well

Unravel

now: her hair was in a neater side plait, and her lips full with some orange gloss. Her lace-up boots were of a different style, but the slightly worried, halting pierce of her green eyes was consistent.

Of course, they knew each other now. Their eyes watched for signals that things would be all right, were the same, and had not changed since the event of their accidental intimacy.

Nadia moved inside and closed the door, lowered her bag in silence and sat on Maria's couch. Assuming their normal positions next to each other, Maria commenced with her best professional behaviour. They got straight down to work, picking up where they had left off last term with mutual focus and deliberately harmonious communication. There was no chatter or banter, and Maria felt her guts unravelling with relief that it wasn't a chore to teach Nadia since their close encounter.

The air between them was light and stress-free, and Maria could hardly believe her luck that Nadia was being so mature, as if their last conversation, where Nadia had denied she had a crush, had never happened. Maria could almost doubt her suspicions now - or Nadia was a very good actor. Although there was a definite quietness about Nadia, an unspoken coolness that Maria knew she was also guilty of, one that united them in their academic endeavours. Maria appreciated it, and felt their bond deepening with forgiveness every minute that passed. She felt she understood what Nadia was feeling, and hoped it was vice versa: in any case, their session continued with ease and fluidity. Even toward the end, Maria was surprised that Nadia didn't want to talk about anything, or if she did, she was stubbornly resisting the urge to raise the subject. It became almost amusing to Maria just how long it would take before one of them cracked and needed to say something; just how long they could draw this out.

At half past four, Nadia stopped writing and put her pen down. She looked up at Maria with a hollow tone. 'Can we stop now? I said I'd go to see Christian.'

'Of course,' Maria said, but felt a curious, sudden judgement flash through her, something resentful that Nadia was still going to continue the pretence of seeing Christian, even though she'd told Maria it was a cover story for her father's sake. She reminded herself that it could just as well be Nadia's cover story to see her and Leon. Maria held Nadia's gaze with wise eyes, saw the girl's open-faced hopefulness, and pushed the criticism from her thoughts, remembering she liked having Nadia's company. 'Do you want me to give you a lift?'

Nadia dropped her glance down to her lap, thinking.

Maria watched for any hint of a smile, unsure what she would do, or what it meant, if she did. Nadia looked back up to Maria in all seriousness. 'If you're sure that's okay?'

'It's just a lift,' Maria shrugged as casually as she could. She wondered if Nadia could tell that she was pretending she didn't care, when her insides were steaming with tension.

As she locked up her office, Maria straightened her blouse under her jacket self-consciously, but grew concerned for her vanity: why she felt the pressure to look good just because Nadia had come out as gay annoyed her. She drove them out of the car park, trying not to drive herself insane attempting to second-guess what Nadia could be thinking about.

Sure enough, though the journey to Cheltenham was relatively short, Maria's jaw clenched whenever she felt Nadia gazing across at her hands, on the wheel, moving the gearstick, and lingering over her clothes. She couldn't even see if Nadia really was or not, but her paranoia ate away at her nerves and she struggled to keep her poker face, wondering what Nadia might be interested in. When Maria glanced into her rear view mirror, she thought she saw Nadia, in her periphery, glance away. Being stared at in general made her itch with frustration, but it was only her own fear of blushing - when she thought longer upon it, she didn't actually want Nadia to stop looking at her.

And so, began a new term of a similar routine. Since they were both reluctant to discuss what happened during the holidays, there existed a stubborn standoff; a willing ignorance regarding their sticky embrace in Maria's bed, this did, in a way, serve to prove that Nadia's sexuality had indeed not changed a thing between them. Maria pursued only her belief that she could play along with denial, in all their one-to-one tuitions, casual revision sessions, and driving her to Christian's house.

Content enough to allow Nadia to spend a few hours each evening with her fake boyfriend if it meant it kept her father off her back, Maria also recognised the importance of Nadia having social time out of school and healthy exercise walking her dog. Nadia seemed thrilled to have a fulfilling schedule, and, reflected in her school work, Maria saw that her specially assigned student was coming on leaps and bounds with so many positive stimulants to keep her buoyant. The girl was as keen as ever to study and worked hard with a breathless force of intelligence in school, but really came alive, in particular, when she got into Maria's car at the end of the week.

While she was sure it would be deemed inappropriate, in anyone's eyes, for her to spend any more time with Nadia, in her car and especially at her house, Maria made sure she slipped Christian an extra fiver to drive Nadia home in his own car after dropping Leon back to her.

One Friday evening, however, when Maria heard the knock on her door, it wasn't just Leon who came bowling in. Christian stumbled, having leaned on the door, and was laughing at his own comedy stunt.

Nadia stood beside him with an entirely unmoved expression.

'He had too much to drink at dinner,' Nadia stated, her arms folded.

Christian began to explain that they had celebrated the official release of their relationship status on their social networking websites, and their announcement had prompted a garrulous response from online friends. He certainly looked pleased with himself, Maria thought. Nadia didn't look as excited, though, and Maria observed her pursed mouth and rolling eyes while Christian slurred through some of the many comments he'd received about Nadia's photo on his profile. Maria wondered why Nadia wasn't drunk too, and then realised the depth of the girl's charade. She had authorised this cyber-engagement as a way of covering her tracks, not because she was into Christian at all. She had allowed Christian to drink and toast to them, but she had not swallowed; now Christian was too drunk to drive, which is why they were here: Maria would have to drive Nadia back.

Without taking her eyes off Nadia, allowing a slow, knowing glare to follow the girl's averted gaze, Maria reached for her keys, bemused to think just what kind of conniving scheming the girl was capable of if she could manifest this scenario. Nadia had gotten what she wanted: more time alone with Maria.

Except, Christian wanted to come. In her car, which suddenly seemed too small to fit a large boy in the back along with Nadia, there was little to say while Christian talked excitedly all the way to Eastcombe, but at least it saved Maria having to do any of the work since Nadia was similarly silent. In her rear view mirror, Maria flicked her eyes to watch as Christian pawed Nadia and tried to kiss her, however, the girl leaned with the sway of the car and swerved out of every wet peck. She, evidently, did not want to be smothered by her over-enthusiastic new puppy of a boyfriend, but it was when Nadia made a full-on grimace, catching Maria's humour that they seemed to share a moment in the mirror that lasted long after Maria had returned her eyes to the road.

There was that unspoken connection again, where they made eye contact at exactly the same moment; that shared appreciation that Maria was beginning to identify as originating from their Sapphic secret. There was no need to say anything, but Maria could tell that Nadia was grateful for her continued support, and all she needed to do was arch an eyebrow at Christian's clinging for Nadia to bite her lip in a smile.

It was fine bidding Nadia farewell in front of Christian, again, all she had to do was watch from the driver's seat as Christian hugged his precious new girlfriend while her eyes nearly popped from her head under the pressure. Outside her father's house, with no signs of life inside, Nadia seemed content to make visible her assumed relationship, however, after turning

Unravel

her car around, Maria wondered if she was the only one watching. She took casual glances over her elbow, resting on the lowered window letting in the cold night air, and noticed Nadia looked at her, every time she was supposed to be kissing Christian goodnight. It was quiet, she heard Nadia tell him: 'No, you're drunk!'

Their separation lingered awkwardly, but Maria was relieved to wave a half-hearted hand to her student as Christian climbed back into her Audi. Maria no longer felt emotional: she would see Nadia next week and felt cool as she drove away, however, she felt a pang of regret hit her as soon as she was back on the winding road home with an irritating, gushing young male beside her, and missed Nadia's feminine grace. Maria's imagination took her back to Nadia's house where, unseen by the bleary-eyed boy, she hopped out of her car, ran back to Nadia, still waiting on her porch, and seized her up in a gentle cuddle.

♥

After that weekend, Nadia returned for her tuition in a sulky mood. Maria could see she needed to talk: her mouth remained in a stiff pout as she laid out her books on the coffee table. Intuition followed that neither of them would be able to concentrate if they didn't clear the air first; Maria put her hand on Nadia's textbook before she flipped it open.

Unravel

'What's happened?' Maria asked directly. She wanted Nadia to know she wasn't going to tolerate any limited response: her patience for Nadia in this mood was slight and any hint it was going to drag out would quickly wear her down.

Nadia swayed her head with pretence at being blasé. 'Sam found out I was dating Christian and has just been shitty with me, that's all... it doesn't matter.'

Maria might have guessed that declaring one's relationship, so prematurely, on a social networking site would have consequences. She pulled her shoulders up straight with a sharp inhale, and looked across at the windows. She remembered seeing Sam pander to Nadia in the hockey game, and smiled.

'You know she's just jealous,' Maria said, trying a gentle humour.

'Why?' Nadia's eyebrows twisted. 'She doesn't know I'm...' She hushed herself.

'Well, not specifically, but she obviously wants your attention in some way, and you having a boyfriend takes it away from her.' Maria reasoned.

'What should I do?' Nadia asked, her mouth becoming soft again.

Maria didn't mind so much, lately, when Nadia asked her advice: it made her feel like a fountain of gay wisdom. 'Try and keep things cool, for the sake of your studies. Try to appease her, maintain some friendship, she's upset now but she'll get over it as long as you don't rub her face in it!'

Unravel

'I wouldn't,' Nadia objected.

'I know, but *you* have to keep up appearances, so don't give her any more reasons to be jealous or she'll start asking questions.' Maria asserted, before settling back.

'I thought you were going to tell me to ignore her or something,' Nadia frowned.

'Well, obviously that isn't working, so you have to try a new tactic.'

Nadia nodded, opening her books, glancing back up to Maria to check the subject was done. The next ninety minutes played out in ways that Maria came to notice was occurring every session she had with Nadia since the new term. Whether they sat side by side or across the room from each other, Nadia seemed fidgety and spirited with humour, in between bouts of intense focus when things were temporarily normal between them. Nadia seemed to have a glint in her eye that Maria deliberately ignored, to all appearances, but inside, her mind was actively trying to look from Nadia's point of view to see the perspective her student had, wanting to understand it without prejudice.

Once, as Maria stopped for a tea break, she had only meant to slip away quietly, but it seemed Nadia did not want to continue working without her. 'It's my birthday next week...'

'Oh yeah?' Maria said casually, flipping the filled kettle on to boil.

'Yep,' Nadia said, with pride in her voice, 'my seventeenth!'

'Mm-hm.' Maria responded lightly, her back turned. She didn't know what Nadia meant by stating how old she'll be, like it mattered. She supposed all young people did that, and pride in announcing one's age stopped by the late twenties. Still, Maria realised it did matter to Nadia, and if she let herself think that way, it mattered a whole lot to her too, it was certainly different to sixteen. It was nearly eighteen, in fact... *and then what?* Maria thought.

'Chris wants me to have a party,' Nadia lifted her voice, 'but you and Christian are my only friends. So, I was thinkin' maybe we could all have dinner or something?'

Nadia caused Maria to turn around with this suggestion; she stared back at the girl. She remembered she had woken up very close to Nadia, they had been close in many ways and discussed intimate things, and Nadia looked up to her. Maria knew she had the power to crush Nadia's youthful hope in her professional, uncompromising, humourless fist, however, she couldn't accept a dinner date with the girl - she just couldn't.

'I'm sure Christian would rather have you all to himself for your birthday,' Maria said at last and prayed that didn't sound too sarcastic given they both knew Christian was a stooge.

Unravel

There was a long wait before Nadia spoke again, and by that time Maria was on her way back to the couch with mugs of tea.

'Maria, what happened at your house... when I stayed over...?'

Maria felt a kick of excitement that Nadia had caved first in bringing up that subject, but it swiftly followed with dread. She stood above Nadia's nervous fingernail picking.

'I know you don't want to talk about it, but you haven't been the same since, and I just want to forget about it so we can be friends,' Nadia shrugged. 'It was no one's fault, it just happened. We were just sleeping.'

'So why did you come out, like, straight away afterwards?' Maria asked.

'I wanted to be honest with you,' Nadia's eyes creased. 'I didn't want you to think I was just some kid cuddling up to her mother.'

Maria frowned. 'Are you saying it *was* sexual?'

'No!' Nadia shook her head. 'Not intentionally. I just like sleeping close to... females,' Nadia glanced over to the door to check it was shut, 'I can't help it.'

'You really could have told me that before you got into bed with me,' Maria said, never taking her hardened gaze from Nadia, safe in the knowledge she had definitely shut the door.

'I just wanted to be friends,' Nadia appealed.

'I'm your teacher,' Maria replied without missing a beat.

Nadia looked upwards, her eyes glowing in the reflected overhead lighting. 'But I *want* you to be my friend... you're the only lesbian I know in this town.'

Maria lifted her hot cup to her lips, feeling her senses tingle up and down the back of her neck and across her shoulders. 'I can't exactly introduce you to some of my friends.'

Nadia smirked a little. 'Well maybe you should take me out to a gay club.'

With a slow shake of her head, Maria held back her smile and let her eyes answer for her. There was no way she could be seen out with such a youngster, whether Nadia was recognised as her student or not, but she knew Nadia was just playing around. The girl was surely more interested in keeping her teacher to herself.

Maria realised she was flattered by more than Nadia's attentions, it was her cleverness, her foresight, her subtlety, even her game-playing was intriguing. If Nadia had come right out and said it, Maria would have cut it short right there. But the thrill of not knowing kept Maria baited, she felt Nadia was keeping her tagging along, involved in this secret game with each other, and she liked it. She wondered if Nadia knew she had her teacher eating out of her palm. Either way, Maria could no longer be concerned of getting too close: she had already gotten too close with Nadia.

Unravel

Chapter Fourteen

She didn't have many free periods lately, but once she found herself with an hour to spare, Maria took herself for a walk around the school, for a change of scenery, to stretch her legs, and absorb the quiet halls whilst everyone sat snug in heated classrooms. Slanting eyes through small windows, Maria did not envy her colleagues, teaching the same topic four or five times a day. At least with exam guidance, she covered all the subjects, the weighting of which depended on the needs of individual students, and that allowed sufficient variety to keep one's sanity. She much preferred her privileged position.

Maria strolled out of the main building, and through the courtyard, enjoying the pointlessness of her journey and not thinking about anything in particular. She had work to get on with, of course, but Maria felt compelled to take the opportunity for a break. She did not bring her jacket, anticipating the stimulation of the refreshing January chill outside. Moving around the exterior pathways, Maria turned a corner, catching the open breeze from the north field and felt her muscles tense against the cold. She put her hands in the pockets of her smart trousers and hunched her shoulders up to her ears; still, she was grateful for the bite against her senses and smiled as she felt a surge of appreciation for the school at peace during this pre-lunch hour.

The peace was broken, however, by a slamming door at the end of the long north-west wall, echoing in the distance. As Maria squinted ahead, a hundred metres or more, she made out the small figure of Nadia, instantly recognisable to her, heading quickly across the field. Nadia was looking down, walking away from the school, with her bag clutched tightly against her. She was moving fast, and did not look to have seen Maria behind her.

Maria wondered where Nadia was going, and what she was thinking going anywhere in the middle of third period. Then, as Nadia rapidly cut a path towards the woods, Maria saw Paul Dawson, Nadia's science teacher, appear at the same door, looking left and right for his student, his tie flapping in the wind.

She realised Nadia had absconded.

As it happened, Maria was intending to enter this door, and when she reached it, she greeted her colleague who immediately despaired at having lost control of a row in his class. Paul stared out to the diminishing girl on the field with a shrug.

Unravel

'I tried to get them to stop, but they kept goading, I've given them detention already, but I doubt it even registers with that lot.' Paul put his hands on his long, shirted hips and sighed.

Maria enquired, 'Which lot?' and heard Sam's name, and her usual cohorts, Kelly, Theresa and Zoe. 'Sam's been giving her trouble over some boy.' Maria frowned, careful of her words.

'I can't leave my class, could you talk to her if you're free?' Paul pleaded, glancing at her shirt; he must have noticed how cold she was. 'She'll listen to you.'

Folding her arms across her chest, Maria nodded. 'Sure.' She walked in Nadia's direction and then scooted into a light jog some way past caring if Paul was still watching.

She had meant to return to her office after a brisk walk, but now Maria found herself chasing after Nadia into some woods at the far end of the field, an area unknown to her beside the fact that it divided GCH property from the private land of St. Helena's girls school the other side. This was typical. How fate had thrown her into this situation, Maria had no idea, but she couldn't very well turn around and go back, for the sake of her own comfort, and leave the girl wandering upset by herself.

On entering the woods, Nadia was nowhere in sight, and Maria stood for a brief moment, listening to the crackles of creatures and wind in the trees. Maria

Unravel

could feel her heartbeat and the breeze caressing her hair against her neck. Her ears and eyes open, Maria adjusted to the darker light and shadowy contours of the woodland, and felt a pinch of humour dare her to be afraid. She had certainly not bargained for this sort of change of scenery, but Maria took a deep breath, summoned her internal warmth, and embraced the elements.

She didn't want to call out, but she saw no movement and was worried about Nadia. Surely, Nadia would step out into her periphery once she recognised Maria's voice, but something told Maria to try to find the girl without making her aware of her presence. Maria pressed on, quietly, stalking along the dirt path worn of wood chips. Within minutes, relief flooded her as she saw Nadia's auburn hair, spilling around her neck, her back bent over as she sat on the stump of an old tree, her shoulders were shuddering, and she was doing something with her hands.

'Hey,' Maria said casually as she approached.

Nadia jumped, fumbled hurriedly, and glanced around with an indignant, accusatory expression, seemingly shocked and annoyed at being disturbed. When she realised it was Maria, she wiped her tears and said, 'What are you doing here?'

'I saw you leaving the building. I was a way behind you, too far to catch you up,' Maria crept closer but stopped several feet away, where she could see

Nadia's face, 'looked like you were determined to get out of there.'

'I just need to be alone!' Nadia sobbed. 'I didn't want anyone to follow me.'

'I know,' Maria soothed, 'but I don't want you to be alone.'

'What about what I want?' Nadia cried out suddenly. 'Doesn't anyone care about that?'

Maria crossed into Nadia's space and crouched beside the girl, whose arms recoiled inside their sleeves. Maria saw fresh dots of blood on her cuff, and frowned. 'What's happened here?' She slipped her hand inside Nadia's and turned it over, easing the white cotton of her shirt back. Nadia didn't resist. When Maria saw blood seeping lightly from a half inch-long cut, she knew it was self-inflicted.

'What made you do this?' Maria stiffened, folding and holding the shirtsleeve over the shallow wound to apply pressure. 'Talk to me.'

Looking down at Maria with reddened, moist eyes, Nadia sucked in a breath between sobs. 'People are being so nasty, just because I want to mind my own business! They hate me now and they're giving me shit every day! It's like accepting their friendship on 'fakebook' gives them licence to spy on you and spread shit about you, I can't stand it!'

'Is it Sam again?' Maria asked, feeling her anger bubbling.

Unravel

'Sam is always rude - but it's the others who laugh along with her! Her stupid friends are total bitches and they hate me, they try every way to humiliate me!' Nadia moaned.

Maria tried explaining that the other girls were probably all nervous of Sam, and they weren't laughing to be mean, but she knew Sam and her pals were every bit as smart-mouthed and cruel as Nadia confirmed.

'I just hate being at school surrounded by stupid kids who act like assholes!'

'How do you think I feel?' Maria huffed a laugh, her hand still pressed with a tender firmness on Nadia's sleeve. 'Present company excluded.'

Nadia continued her tirade. 'I don't want people to know my business, I don't want any of them to know anything about me, I don't want to answer their questions!'

'Look, have you considered that a pretty girl who acts so elusive is seen as something of a mystery? Of course they're going to be curious about you.'

At this, Nadia seemed to stop and listen. 'You think I'm pretty?'

The urge to laugh and dismiss it came and passed, and as she crouched in front of her, Maria held Nadia's eyes steadily. 'I think you're beautiful, inside and out.'

After a smile dabbled on her lips, it was Nadia who laughed it off with a wince and a shake of her head. 'Shut up!'

Maria seized the moment to stand and hold her hand out to Nadia. 'Come on, it's freezing out here.'

On the way back, Nadia walked loosely, and veered into Maria, leaning against her teacher for support. Maria put her arm around Nadia's shoulders and held her in place, with reassurance and protection from the cold, nothing else. Nadia admitted to have used a piece of glass she found in the woods; she insisted she'd never done it before, but seen other girls doing it. She agreed to visit the school nurse to get her wound cleaned and dressed properly.

'Don't make me go back to class,' Nadia gazed up in appeal.

Maria accepted this, but intended to go to speak with Paul Dawson so that he could have a word with his class on bullying. They walked in stride for thirty more yards, until it became unnatural to be so close, re-approaching school, and Maria dropped her arm before anyone could really see their embrace from the windows of the building.

♥

As Nadia's seventeenth birthday arrived, Maria took herself into town at lunchtime, and feeling disoriented amongst the Gloucester shoppers, she spun on her heels, frustrated at not knowing what to get, and not knowing *if*, indeed, she should get anything at all. She passed every window in the mall: wincing at jewellery towers, lingerie mannequins and all the overbearingly saccharine premature hype of upcoming Valentine's Day; cards and pre-wrapped gift sets. Maria dabbed the gathering beads of sweat from her temple and checked her watch.

Eventually, she found a section in a craft shop displaying plain, bound writing papers, and inspired by Nadia's carefully hand-made card, Maria decided to get her something similar, knowing she would like it, at least, and a book was not only harmless, but most appropriate. Picking one attractive leather bound book with an opal sewn into the centre design from a display table, Maria found a young assistant beside her: she was older than Nadia but bouncy on her toes. She had glasses, mousy hair tied back and a substantial breast, and her face blossomed when she smiled up at Maria. 'Is there anything I can help you with?'

Appreciating the girl's kindly, gentle Welsh tones, Maria instantly recalled that she had lied to Lois, saying that her new student was Welsh. Horrified to have a lie come back to haunt her, Maria wondered why she had done such a foolish thing, then considered she might have gotten away with it, seeing as Lois hadn't mentioned the girl's definite Irish-ness at the party. However, having left for a home visit, Lois may have had time to think upon the reasons why Maria hadn't introduced Nadia as her student.

'Well,' the girl raised her eyebrows, 'let me know if you need something.'

Unravel

Maria realised the assistant was walking away and came to her senses. 'Oh sorry, how much is this?'

The girl reached for the book in Maria's hands, then mouthed the code towards a chart on display. 'That one is more expensive, but it's for someone special, right?'

'What?' Maria stared at the girl. She didn't know how to answer. Yes, Nadia was special, but no, not like *that*. 'Is this the kind of present you'd give to...?' She asked, with a good impression of confusion.

'Oh no, I do apologise, I just thought I saw a certain look in your eye, that's all!'

Maria smiled awkwardly, beginning to fear her facade was futile.

Feeling compelled to buy the book, Maria rapidly asked the girl not to gift-wrap it so that she could write something on the inside. On her drive back to school, Maria's head was jammed with numb ideas turning over, and over, like the pages in the heavy blank book she'd just purchased. She didn't know when would be the best time to give it to Nadia, in or out of school. During tuition? Or behind even more private doors at home?

Nadia had mentioned the dinner Christian was cooking for her on the evening of her birthday, but had not spoken of any other plans. It seemed unlikely that Nadia's elusive father would do anything for her, if she even let him, Maria supposed.

Unravel

She returned to school to sit behind her desk and forced her indecisive mind to place some poetic words down on the inside page of Nadia's gift. She couldn't be too sentimental; she couldn't be too stiff. Emotional expression was never her strong point. Maria felt nauseous. She didn't want to patronise Nadia, but neither could she treat her with all the maturity of an adult, yet. Underneath the drama and the drugs, Nadia's default demeanour seemed to be a quiet, self-assured presence, thirsty to learn: those green eyes looked out and took in with razor-sharp clarity. She was, like all teenage girls, clouded by hormones, peer-pressure, family issues, and life challenges but once she was through all that, Maria felt Nadia Sheridan would be a force to reckon with in her adult life.

Maria had to shake her daydreaming out of her light-headed brain. Imagining Nadia in the future went against all her beliefs in not projecting hopes and expectations on to anyone. Nadia might turn out to be a crack-addicted prostitute, but in the here and now, Maria had a chance to help her. Looking at Nadia at seventeen, a year older than her classmates, Maria saw that the girl's isolation had made her too serious, almost listless with the lack of hearty cheer. This clearly contributed to her aloofness and made her seem even older. The times Maria had made her laugh, Nadia's smile was slow and mistrustful at first, now it was ready and willing. Maria knew in her heart she was doing something right for the girl; her own feelings aside, Nadia needed her.

Writing suddenly in the inside cover of Nadia's book, Maria wanted her to know that if there was anything Nadia couldn't talk to her about, then she could write it all down, right there in her new journal: Maria's gift to her.

But that afternoon, Nadia only popped by Maria's office to say she couldn't stay for tuition. Her face was a little flushed as she made her excuse: that she had to go home to get ready for dinner with Christian.

Even though she had declined Nadia's invitation to her birthday dinner with Christian, Maria felt an itch of jealousy she knew she had no right to scratch in front of her. It felt like Nadia was forgetting that seeing him was an act, a cover for her secret identity, and it angered Maria that she was allowing Christian to believe she really liked him.

'Of course...' Maria smiled breezily. 'You have a great time.'

Nadia squeezed her eyes in a kiss of a pleading blink. 'Maria, I...' She faltered, but persisted with renewed breath. 'He's picking me up from mine, but I was wondering... if you wouldn't mind taking me home afterwards? He always drinks too much... and I wanted to spend some time with you.'

She had to admit a small pinch of pleasure that went straight to her heart, compressing and expanding without a flicker of stirring on her face. Maria pretended to be inconvenienced. 'As long as it's not too late.'

'It won't be, I promise,' Nadia smiled, and then said she had to go catch her bus.

Checking her watch, Maria remembered the orange segments. 'You'll be okay?'

'Yeah, I'll stand next to the driver or something,' Nadia shrugged and smiled tightly.

After she left, Maria stood beside her window and pressed her forehead against the glass. She sighed, and exhaled again, still feeling the stress of nerves juddering in her body. Maria felt torn. She wanted to run after Nadia, wish her happy birthday because she'd forgotten to, amid the twist of jealousy and excitement, but she knew she couldn't. She wanted to turn up at the bus stop and give Nadia a ride home as she'd done before, sweeping her into the evening in her fast car, but she knew she couldn't. Maria turned and looked at her desk, her computer with working files open and needing completion, then at Nadia's gift, wrapped and waiting. She rubbed her head and groaned: she would have to be patient, for another few hours at least.

Chapter Fifteen

Christian had dropped Leon back already by the time Maria got home, in order to go and collect Nadia from Eastcombe. It had begun to snow on her journey back and Maria wasn't sure if it would settle or not, but she would have to be careful on the small country roads later. As those hours at home rolled by, Maria resisted the bottle on her kitchen counter, and instead busied herself with cleaning jobs; a brief but hard workout with her weights, a hot shower and a bowl of rice, vegetables and tofu for dinner. She imagined Nadia showing Christian around her father's house, proudly talking to her boyfriend within earshot of her sleeping father. It annoyed her that Nadia was so thorough in her deception, but Maria rationalised that Nadia was doing what she had to for the sake of her education.

As she waited for Nadia's call to let her know her birthday dinner with Christian was over, Maria stared at the gift she had bought Nadia and tried with all her might not to imagine Christian making a move with his feeble paws. The longer it took for Nadia to call, the more intolerable her frustration. She didn't feel resentment for Nadia; she just wished she could stop checking her phone every two minutes. She just wanted to give Nadia her birthday present and have that moment over and done with: she couldn't stand this build-up.

Eventually, over an hour later than Maria expected, Nadia texted to say she was ready to be collected. Maria slipped Nadia's book into her glove compartment and drove through the light blanket of snow to Christian's, feeling strangely light, almost empty with blind anticipation. She didn't know at what stage of the journey to Eastcombe she would tell Nadia to open the small hatch under the dashboard; she wanted to see how Nadia was before she committed to giving it to her. If Nadia was too drunk Maria would seriously reconsider giving the gift to her, thinking Nadia could potentially see the gift as meaning more than it should if her emotions were overly heightened.

Sliding into the passenger seat, however, Nadia was perfectly composed and elegant, though more than a little tipsy, shivering in a small leather jacket and jeans. She greeted Maria with a broad smile, her dimpled cheeks warmed by the interior lights, then tugged at the cream woollen scarf from around her neck. 'It's snowing on my birthday!'

'How was your dinner?' Maria asked casually.

'It was nice... thanks for asking,' Nadia replied with a luxurious huskiness in her voice, as if she'd been talking a lot, or laughing a lot. 'He made me eat steak, sorry.'

Maria gave a quizzical look. 'Why are you apologising?'

'Because... well you know...' Nadia mumbled shyly.

Maria ignored it and headed south out of Charlton Kings to drive along the main carriageway towards Stroud. Nadia tuned into the late night dance music on the radio, her bright eyes moist with happiness and her flushed cheeks seemed permanently bunched into apples. Grateful that Nadia, drunk or sober, had the sense to spare them awkward silence, or, even more awkward conversation, Maria used the time to plan how she should act when she gave Nadia her present.

Suddenly, an impulse seized her; she indicated right, onto a road she hadn't been along in a while. Nadia gasped and held onto her passenger side handle as Maria's car swerved around the corner, sliding in the snow, and delved into the blackness of trees abandoned by the streetlights of the main road. Maria slowed and eased around another gentle bend, glancing at Nadia, whose eyes were wide open with seemingly excited alarm.

'Where are we going?' Nadia asked with a tremble in her voice.

Deliberately not responding, so that Nadia stared in her direction and waited for an answer instead of looking out of her passenger window, Maria drove through the gate to a car parking area. With only reflective strips on wooden poles to warn drivers of the edge, no other lights bore down on their private clearing, and no other cars interrupted their quiet turn left to face the view from the top of the beacon.

Maria turned off the engine as Nadia gasped. All at once, her eyes filled with the sight of the city of Gloucester, sprawling into the vast beyond, the giant blanket of orange lights dotting and blinking like a sleeping sea monster.

Falling into a laugh, Nadia sat in the silence and awed at the view of the horizon from the hill's edge, far left to far right, half of the whole sky, so much life and buzzing activity underneath it, still, at this time of night.

'Oh, it's so beautiful!' Nadia sighed.

'Gloucester's only pretty from this distance,' Maria smirked.

After a minute, Nadia turned to her, smiling, and Maria saw the glisten of a tear forming. 'Thanks for bringing me here. It's a sweet birthday treat.'

'Actually, I...' Maria paused and thought twice about leaning across Nadia's lap. 'I got you something else: it's in the glove compartment.'

Twitching her brow, Nadia smiled and opened the latched door in front of her knees. She pulled out

Unravel

the wrapped gift and held it up by the hazy interior lights to see it better.

Automatically, Maria hit the overhead lamp so Nadia could see her present, and was relieved for the brightness, feeling instinctively that Nadia was about to unwrap a whole lot more than the paper.

As she unravelled the book, Nadia turned it over, and over, examining the rich detail of the cover. 'Oh!'

Maria watched the smile growing on Nadia's face as she ran her fingertips over the brown leather, the patterns along its edge, and the taut binding that held the pages in. Slowly she untied the leather laces that held its outer cover securely over the mass of creamy empty pages inside, Nadia lifted the inner page and read Maria's inscription breathlessly.

'It's a journal,' Maria explained seriously. 'So you can write all your secrets in.'

Looking up with sparkling eyes, Nadia gazed in awe. 'All the secrets I can't tell you?'

Thinking of frowning to discourage Nadia's romantic notions, Maria instead decided to be kind, and smiled, ever so slightly, and nodded gently. A part of her knew she was treading over the line by allowing Nadia to have this moment with her, but more important was that Maria wanted her to feel special: she deserved it, regardless of what anyone else thought.

She hadn't planned what would happen afterwards though, and Maria's breath stopped in her lungs as Nadia leaned over towards her. Maria's first impulse was to pull away, but she didn't want to have to do that: reject Nadia on her birthday, and leave her upset. However, when Nadia reached her left arm up and around her shoulder, Maria was not just relieved, but filled with joyful warmth. A cuddle would be fine. Maria felt the fingers of Nadia's hand stroke the curls of hair at the back of her neck, and she liked the tingle of her skin springing up.

Lifting a hand to the overhead light blinding her, Maria switched it off and lowered it to Nadia's back, though it slipped down to the dip of her hip as she bent her head to nestle against the girl. Nadia smelled lovely, her hair was soft against her cheek and their upper bodies fit together neatly, locked in just as easily as when they had awoken in bed.

The memory of it had drifted Maria's eyelids closed, and a gentle, happy sigh escaped her, knowing this time they were both awake and their tenderness was real, intentional: irresistible. Maria felt utterly absorbed, relaxed, warm, almost sleepy with pleasure, but, seconds later, the sensation of Nadia kissing her neck jolted her eyes open again. She gasped, then, with a twitch, pulled away, although the clench in her clitoris compelled to keep her there.

It was, really, only a peck, but Nadia's lips had been full, soft, warming, and ever so slightly moist: Maria could tell, from the cool air that rushed to the erogenous part of her neck as Nadia slowly drew away.

Guiding Nadia's arm down, Maria stuttered before she found her words. 'You... you don't have to thank me like that...'

'I wanted to...' She whispered. Her dimples formed as her lips tried to stay pursed with seriousness.

Maria's heart fluttered at this subtle smile. Her neck still prickled from the impression of Nadia's lips on them, and every second that she allowed Nadia to remain sitting so close to her crumbled Maria's pretence that she had minded even slightly.

The air in the car with them felt intimately close, and stiflingly heavy with the absence of any noise or light. Maria stared hard to see Nadia's expression then looked away, back to the view they had forgotten. She questioned herself harshly, why had she brought Nadia here? What did she expect would happen? There was no one to blame for any of this, other than herself.

'I should get you back.' She gritted.

Maria reversed her car out of the parking area, and found the road to Stroud again, taking Nadia home as quickly as possible, before anything else happened - before Nadia could see her edges were fraying.

♥

Evidently, Lois arrived back from Australia early, as she turned up, unannounced, on Maria's doorstep to surprise her, acting as if nothing had happened and her weeks of absence had been nothing but a weekend break. She modelled her newest purchase, her January coat, which was 'all the rage' in Melbourne, apparently: a bright yellow plastic trench coat with pointed collars and a hood that reflected luminously against the snow, and, though it made her blonde hair look ashy and dull, Maria said it suited her.

Lois had bought Maria a present too: a scarf made from bamboo, which was surprisingly soft, and it pleased Maria enough to temporarily forgive and forget the circumstances of their brief separation. She hadn't missed Lois while she was gone, had hardly thought of her at all, but now she was back, Maria felt as if she had missed her, in a way. However, as soon as she came inside, Lois demonstrated just how much she had missed Maria by pulling her clothes off and dragging her upstairs.

Tripping on their discarded shoes and falling down into each other's grasps, Maria let herself be devoured by her hungry, estranged girlfriend, all the while observing the acts remotely, detached, as if from some voyeur's point of view. Even though her body was involved, physically stimulated, Maria's mind regarded it all with a cynical smugness that Lois wasn't able to stimulate her heart and soul: these she kept precious for the exclusive enjoyment of Nadia. Their sex was more passionate than ever, yet Maria had to stop herself almost cruelly laughing at Lois, wanting to punish her for being too stupid to realise it was all an act by fucking her harder.

Nothing could touch the secret lust she felt towards Nadia, and Maria deliberately used Lois' body to satisfy her carnal cravings, unable to stop flashes of Nadia spurring her desire. Though as soon as Lois, hissing through her teeth, reached her peak, Maria's dream-spell was broken, and she faked her own orgasm, just so Lois would stop.

Falling away with exhaustion, Lois asked Maria to fix her a drink, and Maria happily obliged, going downstairs to bring herself off passionately behind her kitchen counter, thinking only of Nadia kissing her neck. Returning upstairs, it both annoyed and thrilled Maria that Lois couldn't see Maria's heart wasn't in it anymore, and the fact that Lois assumed she could come back and pick up where she left off was a significant insult.

When Lois began droning on about her relatives, Maria feigned interest, however, when Lois mentioned she'd met a man on the flight home who had shown enthusiasm over her artwork, something clicked inside Maria, and she wondered why her interest had not risen with Lois' tale. Noticing she couldn't muster even a vague hint of jealousy, Maria knew the extent to which her own enthusiasm for Lois and her artwork had long gone. She felt massive relief: getting over Lois wasn't going to be a problem, now all the screechy egoist had to do was leave for good.

Unravel

'So what do you think?' Lois called from the bathroom.

Frowning, having been lost in her thoughts, Maria called back. 'What?'

'Shall I call him or wait for him to call me?'

Maria shrugged with careless eyes. 'Call him.'

♥

It had been playing on Maria's mind that she hadn't engaged much with Karen in the last few weeks, even though the games teacher had made efforts to renew their communication. First, Karen had included Maria in a group email to all staff containing a selection of amusing pictures of animals dressed in human outfits, then, she had forwarded another email, just to Maria, with an anecdotal story that she 'thought Maria would enjoy'. Sitting at her office desk, Maria deleted this second email without reading it, although she kept the first as the animal pictures had made her chuckle.

At first, Karen's attempts at regaining her friendship seemed fickle since their last real interaction in the staff meeting before the holidays was evidently Karen's jealousy flaring that Maria was spending more time with Nadia than with her. Maria regretted calling the games teacher *perverted* out on the field, especially when it dawned on her what a complete hypocrite she was. Understanding that being hard on Karen because she didn't want to be like that was pointless - Maria already *was* like that, it was too late. She was the one who fancied her student and she was taking it out on Karen, who was relatively innocent by comparison. Her defensiveness would be spotted soon enough by eagle-eyed Karen, if she wasn't careful, and it struck Maria that she should not make an enemy of her if she could help it. She resolved to call a truce with her closest colleague. She did have some things she needed to confide, but she would have to choose her words carefully. Therefore, Maria was the one who suggested they catch up at lunchtime, knowing she would have to swallow her pride before she could digest any food. They met in the cafeteria and took their usual seats in the teacher's booths.

'What's been happening then?' Karen asked as she sipped coffee, her eyes wide and penetrating over the rim, demanding Maria's honesty.

Knowing she wouldn't be able to fob her off with any excuse, Maria gave Karen a small portion of the truth, on a subject she knew would seize Karen's immediate intrigue and send her bloodhound-like sniffing way off track.

'It's Lois.' Maria sighed with resignation and pretended she didn't notice the twitching of Karen's mouth behind her mug, although, gazing out across the cafeteria, she could see it in her periphery. 'We had a... trial separation,' she paused for dramatic effect, 'but, now she's back. Nothing's changed for her but things are different for me and I don't know what to do.'

Unravel

'Oh damn, I'm sorry to hear that!' Karen stated, lowering her mug with a startling bang. Maria wondered which part Karen was sorry for, their separation or Lois' return.

The games teacher continued with her brows set in a stern expression of seriousness. 'I wondered why you'd been so edgy, I was about to suggest you get yourself medicated for your hormone problems!'

Forcing a smile to pacify Karen's remedial tone, Maria bit inside her cheek, insulted by her patronising colleague. Karen had no right to assume her body had control over her emotions, but the cringe that followed, realising again she had fooled herself, made Maria's stomach flip with anxiety: when it came to Nadia, Maria's hormones went into over-drive, and her emotions went haywire. She exhaled and felt a crawling unease that Karen would dig too close for comfort. She didn't want to say anything further about Lois. As miserable as she was, she didn't like spilling her guts about her relationship or bad-mouthing anyone. Especially not to someone like Karen who seemed a little too eager to find out more.

'Look, why don't you and I have a good, long chat over a bottle? I know this fabulous new bar, its gay friendly, so we can talk in depth about what you're going through,' Karen said, reaching her hand over to Maria's forearm with a firm press. 'You know I'm here for you.'

Maria glanced down at the vein-woven hand against the navy-blue fabric of her jumper. She wanted it off, away from her, and feared her elbow may jolt up suddenly to send it flying. If she did, at least Maria could blame her 'out of control' body, however, instead, she patted her hand on Karen's lightly, patronising in return. 'I'd love to, but I have so much to get on with, I really need to stay focused on work, you know?'

Tilting her head with apparent carefree dismissal, Karen returned her mug to her lips and muttered something about waiting until Maria was 'done'. Unsure whether that meant done with her schoolwork or done with Lois, Maria, again, pretended she didn't hear it, instead realising that her distracted mind was on anything but Karen.

The games teacher was the last female she could consider, and though Karen Lenholm wouldn't be a hideous choice for some brave lady, Maria knew that she would never be able to be more than friends with her colleague. Feeling vaguely bad for Karen, and sympathising how hard it was to find a woman who stimulated all aspects of one's mind, body and soul, Maria could only reject thoughts of attraction to Karen and graduated towards her steadily-establishing concern that she was the one with the irrational crush on her student.

Unravel

'Can I ask you something? It's about Nadia Sheridan.' Maria asked, carefully constructing her sentences in her head.

'Ariel?' Karen raised her eyebrows. 'Go on.'

Maria lowered her voice conspiratorially. 'I know last time you, rightfully, warned me about not getting sucked in, but I don't think she's lying... Nadia's mentioned her home life is miserable. Her father hardly sees her, she's alone for hours in the evening, often without heating,' Maria checked Karen was imagining it along with her. 'When I realised how lonely she is, I introduced her to my dog-sitter, he's a nice kid in my village. Thing is, they hang out now and I end up playing taxi, and I'm not sure I should be doing that. Do I have to ask someone's permission? Should I tell Xavier?'

Maria's head spun with self-criticisms and became overwhelmed by the depth of her conniving. What version of the truth was she peddling to protect herself?

'So you've found her a boyfriend?' Karen asked contemplatively. 'Doesn't he drive?'

'Yeah, but he says he doesn't have money for petrol,' Maria excused.

'Well, you know where I stand,' Karen shrugged. 'As long as it's not putting you out, just don't be letting Nadia take advantage of you.'

'What do you mean take advantage?' Maria asked, a little shocked.

'I mean taking up your precious time, sounds like she's using you, getting you to ferry her about, I hope she appreciates how generous you are,' Karen asserted.

Shaking her head with confusion, Maria wasn't sure what advice Karen was giving her. 'Do you think I need to have it authorised, officially I mean?'

'It's not like you can claim travel expenses out of petty cash, Maria!' Karen laughed. 'If you're so keen to socialise that little madam then I'm afraid you're on your own! And I wouldn't bother Woods about it - I don't like the idea of that twat thinking his female staff aren't capable of making decisions with their own sound judgement.'

Maria sighed with quiet disappointment. She had almost wanted Karen to chide her, tell her that her actions were inappropriate, to tell the principal - but at least she knew now that Karen didn't suspect anything of her closeness with Nadia. Things had become so complicated and Maria tried to see clearly the path of the righteous professional to lead her to do the right thing. Ultimately, she was relieved for Karen's response; she wouldn't have to go to see Woods with tricky excuses. If he forbade her driving Nadia to and from her village in her car - that meant not seeing Nadia outside of school anymore. Everything in Maria's system exhaled with a need for simplicity - Nadia wanted her friendship and Maria enjoyed Nadia's company. They had a connection, and perhaps in time it would pass, but for now, there was no reason Maria could not have her cake and eat it.

Chapter Sixteen

The next time she saw Nadia, a few days later, things had changed. Maria had missed her and felt estranged from their usual close contact, but the last time she had seen her, driving her home on her birthday, Nadia had kissed her neck, and the memory made Maria both flush with desire and cringe at her own stupidity. She hadn't known that would happen, but she felt she had allowed it, invited it, even. Now she was confused as to whether Nadia was expressing deeper feelings towards her after all, and what it meant that the girl had not turned up for Monday's tuition.

She had spent at least half an hour attempting to compose a text to Nadia asking if she was all right and where she had been, but she had received no response all night. Maria's concerns had plagued her, she hadn't gone to bed until at least two in the morning, and now her shoulders ached from restless sleep. All day Tuesday and still no reply, but the hope of just seeing the girl after school would reassure Maria that she was fine - and then she could ask Nadia if she enjoyed the rest of her birthday, and if she had christened her journal yet.

However, when Nadia showed up at her office at the end of the school day, her demeanour was low, avoidant, and Maria knew something was wrong. The wall of auburn hair swept down over her face, hiding her expression, as Nadia sat on Maria's couch, opening her books weirdly hunched over.

'Nadia?'

'Can we just get on with it?' The girl's voice tightened with emotion.

Leaning against the edge of her desk, Maria folded her arms and thought intensely. She couldn't very well begin tuition when the atmosphere in the room was tangibly disturbed. She wondered if what had happened between them in her car at the beacon had upset the girl, or perhaps if she had said the wrong thing, or been too flippant in her text messages regarding Nadia's absence. Maria wasn't sure what to say, but her instincts told her that she shouldn't approach Nadia at this time: her aura was volatile.

'What's happened?' Maria asked plainly, shrugging to herself.

'I don't want to talk about it,' Nadia seethed, her jaw sounding rigid.

'Well, I think it's best to clear the air before we get down to work, so I'd appreciate it if you'd tell me what's going on,' Maria said casually, pretending to lose patience.

'I can't tell *you* about it!' Nadia snapped, then hushed herself, folding her hand over her mouth.

The silence that followed was powerful.

'What do you mean you can't tell me about it? You talk to me about everything,' Maria scratched the back of her hair. 'I thought you told me I was the only one who understood you.'

'I can't tell you about this,' Nadia whispered hoarsely.

Steadying herself on the desk behind her, Maria felt her heart beating double-time. The air was thick with their unspoken tension and she felt locked helplessly into this moment.

'Why?' Maria said, lowering her gravelly tone to hide her fear, 'because it's about me?'

There was no movement from Nadia, her head neither nodded nor shook. Her hair trembled as she exhaled haltingly. She might have been crying.

She'd had to take the plunge: it was the only way to know, to stop this endless cycle of pretence and denial. Though Nadia was not responding to confirm either way, her resistance spoke volumes.

Stepping closer to Nadia, Maria braved the move towards the girl by sitting on the other end of the couch, keeping a more professional distance than on previous occasions. She turned her knees inwards to Nadia and leaned her arm back to present as the cool,

Unravel

calm teacher she should have been from the start. 'Nadia... look at me?'

The girl sat frozen, turned away, refusing to bring her body around.

Maria knew she had to nip this in the bud. She couldn't allow Nadia to ruin their study time together because of whatever personal dramas she was probably manifesting to sabotage her exams. If her instincts were right, and Nadia had feelings, it was Maria's job to stop them developing further. Right now. This was the time. It was dangerous territory, but she could not be seen to ignore it.

She made her voice firm. 'Look at me.'

Nadia took a minute to compose herself before shifting her lower half on the couch, her torso followed and last, her head. As she lifted it to bring her eyes up to Maria's, her hair fell back from her face, revealing a reddened bruise that surrounded the side of her mouth.

Maria stopped, her breath caught in her throat. 'Oh shit.' Her posturing weakened as she leaned toward Nadia, everything she had been thinking temporarily forgotten in this new light. This was the reason the girl had been absent, this was the reason she had been withdrawn.

'What happened?' Maria demanded, defiantly this time.

Nadia winced and squirmed as if she wanted the earth to swallow her.

Unravel

'I don't want to talk about it.' Nadia said, shaking her head, her eyes cast down.

Maria could see the bruise around her mouth, it was more purple than red: a couple of days old. There was a cut to the lower lip Maria could see now, close up, and that was very red, deep bloodied red, the whole lip swollen and sore.

'Did someone hit you?' Maria asked firmly, keeping the emotion from her voice. 'You didn't do this to yourself?!'

'No!' Nadia's eyes blazed back up at Maria. 'It was an accident, I wasn't attacked!'

'Someone *has* hurt you though...' Maria gritted her teeth. 'Tell me who did it? Was it Sam?' She felt her anger rising, making her overreact; she could feel it. 'Was it your dad?'

'Don't!' Nadia appealed.

Maria grimaced with her frustration. 'Why are you so upset if it was an accident?'

'Please!' Nadia's mouth tightened. 'Just leave it!'

Knowing she was upsetting Nadia didn't stop her wanting to push her until she snapped - Maria wanted an answer out of her. 'No, tell me what happened!' Maria insisted. 'Did you say something that someone didn't like? And they hit you?'

Blinking up with incredulous, quivering eyes, Nadia's lips gaped open and closed several times, but she failed to utter her words before she lost her composure and spilled with tears. 'I'm sorry!' Her face flushed bright crimson. 'I'm sorry, okay? I never meant...'

Pulling her brow into a deep frown, Maria's head jerked back with fresh confusion. 'Why are you apologising?' Staring hard at the fear in Nadia's expression, Maria slid a quick look to the door to make sure they didn't have silent company. They were definitely alone, and her mind began reeling, working it out.

'What does this have to do with me?' Maria leaned in closer to Nadia. 'Did you write something in your journal about me?'

Nadia was pressing her fingers under her eyes with dismay, and Maria took it as a sign that something was truly wrong here. She spoke aloud her mind's processing.

'I can't imagine you'd say anything bad about me...' Maria paused, honing in with the dawning of her awful suspicion. Her voice became a slow growl as she stared through the coffee table. 'I think you said something nice... and someone got jealous, that's what I think... Am I wrong?'

Wiping her tears, Nadia lowered her fingers from her cheeks and gazed at Maria with yearning, her eyes shining with pleading sorrow. 'Please don't be mad at me,' she begged; her poor mouth ugly with the bloodied laceration.

She couldn't be mad, but Maria wasn't happy about not getting the answers she needed. She needed to know if she could trust her protégé, or if Nadia would lie to her face again. Asking her straight out if Nadia had a crush would only bring the same reply as before, Maria felt - she needed another, indirect way to show her acknowledgement.

'Tell me something, Nadia, this female in Dublin you got in trouble over, was she a teacher by any chance?' Maria asked, then leaned back and searched Nadia's face; the girl's response would let Maria know just what kind of creature she was dealing with.

'No!' Nadia said after a few seconds of horrified speechlessness. 'No...' She whimpered again, and shook her hair, blinking out fresh tears.

She looked sincere enough, but Maria felt her instinct warning her away from the girl. She wanted Nadia to exclaim: *'I don't have a crush on you!'* but she didn't. Now was Nadia's opportunity to make it clear that Maria was not somehow involved in her crisis.

Except, Nadia just cringed, with intense meaning in her eyes, and Maria stared back, feeling more serious than she had ever felt in her life. What was this moment they were having? Nadia was neither confessing nor denying doing or saying something about Maria that had resulted in her split lip. The urge to reach over and shake the girl was quite strong, and just as Nadia looked as though she wanted to collapse into her arms, Maria stood up and walked to her desk.

Knowing she had to break their eye contact, her chest heaving and cheeks burning, Maria recalled every single time she'd previously suspected Nadia had feelings but convinced herself out of believing it. After admitting she was gay, Nadia had denied any attraction to Maria; even if that were true at the time, when had it changed? What had happened to make Nadia develop desires towards her teacher? Maria had strived to retain normality in her behaviour since the new term had started, but now she grew concerned that her failure was being too easy-going after their tryst. She should have pulled back - instead she had allowed Nadia to think it was acceptable to be so intimate with her teacher.

Maria swallowed a heavy, stubborn lump in her throat and felt a cold sweat come over her. She had done this. She had caused this. She had brought this about. Nadia really did like her, stealing one last look back at her, now it was plain to see. Nadia wanted Maria to know it too; she was neither hiding it nor flushing with mounting horror: the girl bounced back her look of fearful, nervous longing, their understanding mutual and undeniable.

'I think you should go now,' Maria said, her eyes glassing over, her mouth stiff. She felt her heart thumping as she finally dropped her eyes to the ground,

Unravel

letting Nadia know she was no longer welcome. Maria needed time alone to think.

Sensing Nadia's desperate shame at the dismissal, Maria stood firm but turned away so she didn't have to watch Nadia slide away in any more agony than she was already in with her sore lip. She knew turning her back was a cruel move, but she had to let Nadia feel her disappointment, and righteous anger at being lied to.

Nadia *did* like her. Nadia really did *like her*! Maria had thought it, now she knew it for sure: *of course* Nadia liked her.

Hearing movement, Maria closed her eyes to stop the rush of tears from reaching any further than her eyelashes. When she opened them again, Nadia had collected her books and was leaving. Immediately, Maria felt sick inside. The connection she had cruelly broken from Nadia now felt like it was trailing out of the door, bleeding like a severed vein in the shadow of Nadia's path. The way they had gazed at each other, however painful with meaning, floated across Maria's eyes like blots of sunlight with every stinging blink. Nadia had given her the look of love, and it had caused Maria's heart to flutter and fall.

Wondering, fleetingly, if she had been able to hide her own feelings, Maria could only sink down into her desk chair and despair at the prospect of no longer being able to disguise feelings once they were recognised as mutual. Now that Nadia had let her teacher know, surely, it wouldn't take long for the girl to figure out that Maria didn't mind, and then she would start questioning why.

Chapter Seventeen

Maria drove home in a daze. She felt miserable and longed for a drink, but feared it would take a whole bottle of wine before the pain from these latest events began to dull. She felt as if she were losing control, and had no idea what she was doing. Everything was a mess. Her relationship with Lois was hanging ridiculously in limbo, seemingly unable to end; neither of them were happy, Maria was sure, but the thought of discussing it felt more detrimental than simply continuing in unspoken insanity, and Maria didn't need extra grief right now.

Her job at the school was mind-numbingly hectic. She was grateful to be kept busy, but troubled over the prospect that her life would revolve around the same academic calendar, year in, year out, until she was as flaky and tired as some of the other teachers. She wanted more than that. Her life needed to change every now and then or she would become old before her time.

Unravel

Even her social life was embarrassingly poor. She lacked the motivation or the energy to contact her old friends from London; since Lois had moved back there, the only person she confided in was her cousin, Ben. In fact, the closest friend she had was her dog, Leon.

And the female she thought about the most was her student.

Maria felt pathetic.

On her way to collect Leon, Maria walked with her hands in her pockets, braced against the cold. She half contemplated asking Christian out for a drink but realised she had nothing to say, nothing she could really talk to him about anyway.

Ringing his doorbell, Maria heard Leon's small bark and smiled. She smoothed her hair and waited for her dog-sitter to come to the door. His parent's cars were in the drive, but Christian would know it was her calling at this time. When he opened it, it was not with his usual cheery greeting. 'All right?' he mumbled.

In the light from the porch, Maria saw a short cut, high on his forehead, where his grown-out, brown hair parted and hung, unwashed. Maria frowned.

'Hi,' she said, hesitantly. Her nerves suddenly jangled, seeing his expression.

Leon bumped against her leg. She bent to scoop him up, but knew she was stuck.

'You okay?' She asked, holding Leon high like a distractingly cute shield.

Unravel

Christian lifted his eyes to hers and held them in a wary glare. 'Not really.'

She didn't want to ask, but she had to pretend ignorance of everything. She nodded to his injury. 'What's that?'

'I had an accident,' he muttered self-consciously.

Maria hoped he didn't want to talk about it, and she wouldn't push as she had with Nadia. She could shrug and walk away from Christian, shoot home as fast as she could.

'Have you seen Nadia?' he asked, closing the door behind him.

Sighing, Maria shifted her feet. 'Yeah,' she replied, lightly, having to answer confused questions in her mind about preconceptions of violence. She had spent the afternoon thinking that Sam or Nadia's father had inflicted her wound, but she knew in her heart that Christian could not hurt a fly, not deliberately. 'She didn't tell me what happened though.'

'No, I don't suppose she would,' Christian said sharply. 'Seeing as it's your fault.'

'What?' Maria goggled in genuine surprise at his tone.

'Well, the way you treat her!' he hooked his hands on his jeans in an aggressive stance. 'Give her all this special treatment - letting her think you two are best buddies!'

'Chris, in case you forgot, I introduced her to you!' Maria appealed.

'Yeah, but I can't get a word in edgeways because she's always going on about how brilliant you are, and how much you're doing for her!' Christian glanced behind him to make sure the door was shut, then lowered his voice so his parents couldn't hear. 'She knows you're a lesbian and I can't help but think you're somehow *turning her* because she doesn't even want to have sex with me.'

'Dude, she's only just turned seventeen, maybe she's not ready for sex with you.'

'Well, maybe she's ready for sex with you!' Christian spat, 'because when I went down on her, it wasn't my name she was saying – it was yours!'

The yank in Maria's stomach nearly floored her. She felt her skin flush cold and stared back at Christian's death-glare with horrified guilt.

'That's how *this* happened!' he jabbed his fingers towards his head. 'She said *your name* and we both sat up at the same time, and I head-butted her face. It was a fucking accident!' Christian shook his head. 'It wasn't just her lip that got busted - I've still got her tooth imprinted in my skull!'

Feeling too strange to even speak, Maria turned away and held her stomach in, trying to breathe deeply so she didn't vomit after swallowing a rising bolt of sick in her throat.

Nadia had said her name during sex.

'What are you going to do about it?' Christian demanded. 'When are you going to stop letting her hang out with you? When are you going to stop driving her everywhere? She can get here by herself, she's not stupid, she can get the bus, or I'll pick her up!'

'Look, I didn't know, okay?' Maria flustered, feeling heated with the interrogation. Leon wriggled under her grip, concerned at the terse voices.

'Well, now you do!' Christian smarted. 'She fucking fancies you! Maybe you should get with the programme, and set her straight!'

'All right! Jesus!' Maria scowled. 'I'll talk to her, okay?' She flipped her palm in the air to signify enough. She couldn't deal with any more criticism. She needed to go and think.

'Aren't you forgetting something?' Christian held out his hand for his usual payment.

Maria averted her eyes, fishing in her back pocket for notes. She only had twenty.

'That'll do fine, thanks,' Christian took the note from her fingertips. 'Think of it as compensation.'

After he shut the door, Maria hurried away from the house, lest Anthony or Clarissa hear of their confrontation and charge out to find her, either their sympathy or accusation would be unbearable.

Maria stalked home, the sudden pain of her new, dreadful comprehension gnawing at her. *That's* why Nadia had apologised to her, in advance of Maria finding out this awful, humiliating occurrence. Maria pictured the scene: Nadia letting Christian go down on her, imagining her teacher there instead; climaxing suddenly, saying Maria's name by accident; being shocked at her slip of the tongue as she realised Chris had heard her whilst making his own. Their heads colliding as they sought to retrieve a moment lost to a mistake; Chris urgent for clarification, Nadia hurrying to make amends. Maria cringed deeply imagining the bang of Chris' head against Nadia's mouth; the terrible minutes after when blood, tears, and anger spilled forth.

♥

As soon as she got home, Maria fed Leon, desperately thinking of what to do next. She stared at the fridge, feeling her appetite dissolve with her fear. She emptied a glass of red wine into her stomach, and called Nadia's mobile.

'So that's what you couldn't tell me?' Maria railed.

'You don't understand!' Nadia sobbed down the line. 'We were having a drink and he wanted to have sex, but I didn't. So, we watched a movie on his bed and I fell asleep... the next thing I know, he was going down on me, I mean, it felt kind of nice, but I must have been dreaming still... ' Nadia paused and sighed. 'He said I said your name, but I don't remember! I promise I wasn't thinking of you like that!'

Unravel

At first, she didn't know what to think; she couldn't believe she was having this conversation, but listening to the feeling in her gut, and trusting it more than she had before, Maria knew, for sure, that Nadia was lying. She decided to stop playing and brought her mouth close to the phone, whispering intensely.

'I think that's bullshit. You've been making eyes at me for months. I think you lied when you said you didn't have a crush,' Maria gritted. 'I demand the truth *now*!'

'I am telling the truth!' Nadia cried, breathing hard. 'Of course I *like* you, Maria! You're amazing, but I would never make a pass at you...'

'Really?' Maria sucked her lip. 'So what would you call that? In my car last weekend?'

The silence lingered for a few seconds. 'It was just a thank you for my present.'

Nadia's claim she had not been thinking of Maria sexually made no sense, and it infuriated her that Nadia wasn't going to drop the act. She decided to ignore her pretences and cut out the crap. She couldn't keep playing this game with her, even if Nadia had convinced herself this wasn't happening.

'I've been working so hard for you,' Maria started with a heavy, dark tone. 'I've been going out of my way to make sure you have all the help you need. I've given up my lunchtimes, my afternoons, and lately my evenings to make sure you're supported and happy. I've introduced you to my friends, let you spend time with my dog, allowed you to stay for dinner and sleep at my house. I just wanted to help you, Nadia, but all the time you've been getting your rocks off!' She ended in a bitter growl.

'I haven't! I swear!' Nadia appealed, her voice hollowing with shame. 'I value everything you do for me, I don't think of you with any disrespect at all. I can't help that I like you.'

'You know I can't keep teaching you if you have feelings for me,' Maria said plainly.

'No, no, please!' Nadia broke into a desperate plea. 'I'm just going through a weird phase, I'll get over it, I swear! Please don't stop seeing me, I need you! You're more than a teacher to me, I'm just in awe of you or something, but I promise whatever it is will pass, you know?'

Maria slid with a disheartened slump onto her sofa, feeling the severity of the situation: had she caused this? Had she made Nadia spin out like this? Had she really been secretly toying with Nadia's attentions? Her own selfish feelings driving her onward, deeper into the subtle role-play they were acting out?

She knew it wouldn't be fair of her to punish Nadia by stopping her tuition sessions, that could potentially ruin the girl's school career and any chance of her ever passing her exams would most likely be lost forever. Maria couldn't break Nadia's heart, she couldn't; that, and she didn't want to stop seeing her.

Sitting forward, rubbing her forehead, Maria sighed again and creased her eyes shut. She imagined Nadia waiting, breathless, poised on the other end of the phone, like a puppy with both ears up, waiting for the ball to drop.

Maria decided to pick it up and throw it again. This game wasn't over.

'I can't punish you for having feelings,' Maria said as sincerely as she could muster, 'but, Nadia, you've got to promise me... whatever feelings you have for me, you have to get over them so we can continue with tuition. I don't want to hear any more about this - otherwise I'll have to tell the principal.' She thought she sounded fair and reasonable, but suitably threatening, then hoped Nadia didn't find her authoritative voice sexy.

With a sniff, Nadia made the promise, and hung up the phone.

Maria flung herself onto her couch, then called Leon up for reassurance, thinking hard.

As the confusion and fear eased off, Maria noticed the strangely light feeling of warmth emanating from within. When she lifted her head and looked at things as objectively as she could, she recognised a relief that Nadia really did like her, enough to cry her name out during orgasm. Mistake or not: Nadia had done only what Maria had done many times by herself, and deliberately, with Lois.

Unravel

The idea that they liked each other with equal measure filled Maria's heart with sudden, overpowering happiness. Nadia was strong and independent enough to keep up this artful pretence, and once again, Maria felt charged with belief that if Nadia could manage to keep her emotions hidden even from her, then Maria would beat her at her own game. The idea that she and Nadia had their own secret world of love and denial made Maria's mouth twitch. She allowed herself a small, private smile, but the only thought that threatened to change it was the idea of Nadia finding out. Nadia must never find out.

Chapter Eighteen

As with every previous year at GCH, the month of February prompted a near impossible increase in Maria's workload. Aware that the mock exams were around the corner, her daily tuitions were interrupted by constant knocks at her office door by students sporting frowns and lost expressions. Those seeking her expertise on any given subject across the syllabus tapped her arm in the corridor, during morning break, as well as in the library, at lunch. Maria did her best to answer the requests for revision tips, potential exam questions, and whole module overviews from random students who were not her regular tutees.

This year, more than ever, Maria appreciated being so busy, taking the opportunity to throw herself into work meant she had less time to think upon her own issues - until she went home at night and, by that point, she was usually so exhausted her brain could only manage half a crossword before she fell asleep. She went straight into work mode from the moment she woke again the next morning, and charged through showering and walking Leon before making her way to school.

    Even if she did have time, Maria didn't want to think. Thinking would inevitably lead to Nadia and if she allowed herself to dwell on her thoughts about the girl, then her feelings would start to swell in her heart and loins. When these stirrings did slip in, Maria's emotions tangled with a conflicting mix of annoyance and arousal, guilt and secret delight. Finding herself lingering on daydreams of Nadia rapidly resulted in her heat rising, her stomach flipping with butterflies, a rash suddenly upon her cheek. Or worse, Maria found her skin crawling hot and cold, a sticky nausea washing over her as she realised she was in the most inappropriate place to be lusting after a student: in a school, beside a pupil staring at her expectantly, bemused by her blushes.

    Nadia, herself, had been keeping a very low profile and Maria had not spoken to her since she had phoned her after Christian's revelation. She had seen her around school but a week away from each other had been undoubtedly needed. Maria felt she had done the right thing in spurning the girl, however, she couldn't say how well it had worked. Their eye contact was fleeting, and in assembly, Nadia averted hers with rapid, stunned blinks when she was caught looking. Maria decided it was best if she pretend nothing was wrong: making silent signals with her expressions would only be asking for deeper, personal reactions, and they were precisely the encouraging behaviours Maria simply had to withdraw from Nadia.

Then, a text from Nadia to ask if it was safe to come to tuition made Maria's stomach flutter. If it was *safe*? She knew she couldn't respond with anything other than direct language and just replied, 'Of course.'

When Nadia arrived after the final bell, she stepped gingerly into her office and sat down haltingly, waiting for her teacher's communication, but Maria felt quiet, even shy.

'How's your lip?' She asked stiffly.

Nadia opened her bag and eased out her books onto Maria's coffee table, blinking up thoughtfully. 'It's okay... healing.'

Nodding, and stuck for what to do with herself, Maria remained standing by her desk and shuffled with some papers. She should sit down, next to Nadia, as she always did, but she couldn't. She knew she should act normally, but if she sat down she was afraid Nadia would hear her breath shivering or smell some nervous pheromones oozing out of her skin.

Glancing up, Nadia noticed Maria's shifting delay tactics. 'Are you okay?'

'Yep,' Maria buttoned her lip and made herself sit down on the couch. 'Where are we up to?' She asked, reaching for the guidebook that Nadia had bookmarked with a piece of fabric.

Unravel

Holding her elbows, Nadia shrugged. 'I've fallen behind a fair bit, I haven't been in the right head space.'

Letting the painfully obvious atmosphere linger for a few seconds, Maria winced. 'You know you have mock exams after half-term.'

'I know, I know,' Nadia inhaled and sighed out, her eyes cast down. 'I just don't want to be...' She paused, thinking.

'You don't want to be here?' Maria suggested.

'No, I *do* want to be here,' Nadia replied. 'I just don't want to be thinking about all this stuff.'

'You're here to study, Nadia,' Maria said tersely, 'nothing else.' She sensed a hurt, sideways glance from Nadia as she gestured to her guidebook. 'Where do you want to start?'

Beside her, Nadia fell quiet, she had tightened her folded arms, and she seemed to be exercising the holding-breath technique of someone trying not to cry.

Clenching her jaw, Maria ignored it. She sat forward, leaning over the coffee table, and bore her eyes into the books in front of her. She felt riddled with guilt but unable to stop this cruel streak flooding the gap between them in cold, hard lashes. Here she was - sat next to the one she thought about constantly, who was evidently humiliated and probably desperate to ease the tension with discussion, but Maria could not go soft: she could not show her emotions. Her insides ached with restraint; she felt torn between remaining professional in discouraging Nadia's feelings, and allowing her tender side to reassure Nadia it wasn't her fault. But, Maria could not be seen to encourage the girl, and she could not risk revealing her own feelings.

Bracing herself, Maria turned her head and hooked her glare over her left shoulder to where Nadia sat, chin trembling, beside her. She turned back round to the table with a heavy sigh. 'Okay, let's forget it.'

'What?' Nadia asked, crackling with confusion.

'I can't do this, Nadia,' Maria answered, getting up from the couch to put some distance between them. 'I can't teach you if you're being like this.'

'Being like what?' Nadia appealed, sitting up straight.

'Being weird!' Maria complained. 'I can't concentrate!'

'I'm not being weird!' Nadia sat up defensively, but hushed her voice from rising too. 'I was fine when I came here - *you're* the one being weird!'

Maria huffed, but knew Nadia was right, she *was* being weird but she couldn't stop. 'Look, I told you I wouldn't be able to teach you while you still had feelings.'

'You said you wouldn't punish me,' Nadia interrupted, tears welling in her eyes.

Recalling her own words, Maria faltered and swore, rubbing her head. 'I know, but I *cannot* deal with this drama in school!'

Unravel

'Well then, let's talk about it outside of school,' Nadia pleaded.

'Are you joking?' Maria gave a bitter laugh. 'Now that Christian knows, I'm not going to be able to drive you home anymore...' She said, that cruel streak lashing again. She turned toward Nadia with a quieter growl. 'Or let you hang out with my dog, or at my house. It's not right I let any student spend so much private time with me, let alone one who fancies me.'

'Christian won't say anything,' Nadia whispered, wiping her tears.

'How do you know?' Maria frowned angrily. 'His parents know me, they put him through this school, one word from them could ruin my reputation.'

'He's not going to tell them, Maria!' Nadia exclaimed. 'He's too embarrassed!'

'As he should be! He molested you whilst you were sleeping, that's non-consensual, you know that,' Maria seethed.

'He didn't molest me...' Nadia said quietly, 'he thought I was awake.'

Maria sighed out heavily at the change in story. 'I don't want to know the details! What matters is what you feel, because if it doesn't change soon, I'm going to have to stop seeing you altogether.'

'Why?' Nadia muttered. 'Because you're so scared you'll get in trouble?'

'Yes, actually,' Maria jerked. 'If anyone finds out that I've been tolerating your crush, encouraging you with *alone time*, I'll get in trouble, not you.'

Nadia screwed up her face and glared through her blurry tears. 'So you thought you'd punish me anyway, just *in case* someone finds out *something* to tarnish your fucking halo!'

As Nadia stood up and began scooping her books into her bag, Maria felt her pounding heart hurting inside her ribcage. 'Where are you going?'

'The fuck you care?' Nadia trembled with anger. 'If you want me to get over you, Maria, you're doing a damn fine job of making me.'

The door snatched open and Nadia was gone, leaving Maria in ringing silence, mind reeling, her breath trapped in her chest, a painful lump of regretful guilt blocking her emotion from leaking out of her.

♥

That evening, and for most of the following days during that half-term week, Maria lay curled up around her cushions on her couch, staring through the television, unable to cry, unable to eat, her mind a numb depression. As if to rub it in, Valentine's Day coincided with a particularly painful period, and dosing herself up to the eyeballs with pharmaceuticals, Maria couldn't touch the bottle of red wine she'd bought to ease the pain of knowing she'd rejected Nadia. She felt stupid

Unravel

for having been the one to stop their tuition to talk about their personal matters when she was the one who had told Nadia to get over her feelings. Maria knew she'd behaved in an unacceptably contradictory way, and now she'd upset Nadia even further, which hurt more than anything. She didn't want Nadia to hate her: Maria had just been so scared of Nadia figuring out that she wasn't the only one with feelings.

    Maria squeezed together her sore, dry eyes, her guilt and sadness weighing her down into the couch so much she didn't think she could even move to use the bathroom. Her brain ached as soon as she awoke from trying to process what was happening, trying to work out what she should do next to make it look like she didn't care so much; she ended up returning to sleep throughout the day, waking groggier than ever and desperate to fall back into the numb, black, peaceful sea. She took consolation in Leon's company, as he slept at her feet, and was relieved for the opportunity to avoid seeing Christian for the whole week.

    In bouts of clarity, Maria tried to think as a teacher with every right to be angry that her student had lied to her about having feelings. Then she tried to think as a teacher with compassion for a student, who, *of course* had feelings, after all, it was no-one's fault but her own that she had allowed Nadia to get so close to her. Wondering if she had given Nadia any clues towards her own desires, Maria rolled over, and over, trying to think back upon all the times she had smiled at, or encouraged Nadia. However, being able to remember things objectively was proving difficult, Maria felt utterly swamped by her miserably confused brain.

When her home phone rang, Maria's first thought was that it might be Nadia and she sprang from the couch with surprising energy considering she had nearly succeeded in sinking into the deep, body shaped dent in the soft leather. She collected the handset, her heart beginning to thud, but within a second of seeing it was Ben calling, Maria's spirit sank again, realising that Nadia was the last person who would be calling her.

She answered the phone to Ben, but her words came out monotone and stopped mid-sentence, as if the wind had fallen out of her sails. She knew Ben was just phoning to see how she was, but she couldn't risk him finding out she was involved in a tangled affair with her student, especially as he'd seen Nadia at Lois' exhibition party after Christmas.

'What's wrong with you?' Ben asked with a vaguely irritated scoff. 'Are you drunk?'

'It's nothing,' Maria said dully. She didn't feel like talking, or joking, though some part of her wanted to wail to her cousin that *everything* was fucked up, *everything* was bad and wrong. On the contrary, there was no way he would understand what she was going through, and there was certainly no way she could confide in him of her deepest, most private pleasure that Nadia shared her feelings. The idea of admitting all this to Ben made Maria's stomach turn again. She swallowed her secret and tried to form comprehensible words. 'I've just got a major workload on at the moment and I've lost all sense of joy and purpose.'

'How're things with Lois? I can't believe you took her back!' Ben grumbled like an old man. He was sounding more and more parental these days, even with Maria.

'Lois is Lois,' Maria replied, but didn't want to have to explain why she took her back. Ben had been through it all between her and Lois and Maria was fairly sure he didn't really want to know, he was just being polite and trying to make conversation. 'She's fired up by some bloke she met on the plane and reckons she's closer to getting a commissioned series.'

'Yeah?' Ben sounded unimpressed. 'Maybe once she's made something of herself she'll treat you with a bit more respect.'

The word 'respect' brought back Nadia's last desperate bid for Maria's forgiveness when she swore she had never considered her teacher with any disrespect. Thinking upon it now, Maria had to acknowledge that the girl's behaviour had always been consistently respectful. Nadia had never flirted overtly, never made Maria feel uncomfortable, never done anything tacky or crude like some of the other girls, over-licking their lips in parody of her sexuality, uncrossing and re-crossing their spindly legs; Nadia had never even done anything suggestive such as opening her blouse button to show off her cleavage. Maria supposed that's why she was able to convince herself that Nadia didn't have a crush: the girl never showed it. The idea that Nadia didn't want her teacher to know she had a crush sent a warm wave of genuine reassurance throughout Maria's body, and she smiled for the first time that evening.

'And what about that girl?' Ben asked, his voice strangely close, almost soothing with tenderness, the same as he might use to lull little Levi to sleep.

'Who?' Maria's voice sounded light and girlish by comparison. She knew exactly who and Ben did too, and she felt the hairs at her neck prickle as she spoke the name. 'Nadia?'

'Yeah, what happened with her?' Ben fell quiet, listening, waiting.

The silence was deafening to Maria. All she could hear was her throat gulping, trying to push down her noisy heartbeat. She wondered if he could hear it too, pulsing up through her ear, transferring all the way along the line.

'She's all right, getting on with her studies...' Maria's words drifted, eyes rigid on the floor. She knew she had to say something else as she had stupidly told Ben that Nadia was still clingy even after dating her dog-walker. 'She's settled down now, still seeing Christian...'

Unravel

'Aw that's good,' Ben seemed happy with that. 'I'm glad things are cool there... as long as you're okay.'

Unsure if Ben meant with regard to Nadia, or in general, Maria brushed over it and assured her cousin that she was well, just tired and not very talkative. He let her go after he had made her promise to call him should anything get too much to deal with. She promised.

As soon as she was off the phone, Maria used the bathroom then made some tea. She stirred the teabag with glassy eyes, growing paranoid that Ben knew more than she had thought. She had refrained from telling him that Nadia had come out as gay, but he always was intuitive, especially with her, and it had sounded like he was fishing for information, trying to gather insight to her feelings. That was Ben's way, a subtle challenge without any harsh confrontation: he could well be testing the water. Maria wondered if she would be able to tell him the truth about Nadia after all, then swiftly shook the concept from her head: no one could ever find out her shocking secret. She would tell no one, even if Ben, her closest relative, asked her outright - Maria made a decision, there and then, to deny it all.

Preferring to imagine that Ben was rightly concerned for her relationship with Lois, and, knowing that he had her best interests at heart, Maria convinced herself that he was only hinting towards significantly less subtle signs that she should break up with Lois. Maria acknowledged that she thought little of Lois anymore, and when she did it was with a general indifference, but that was only because she preferred not to think of Lois at all. If she did allow herself, Maria felt a less intense version of the resentment she had previously, which traced back to how self-centred Lois had become about her art projects. Lois had always been career-driven, but lately, Maria knew Lois had taken her for granted more than normal for a partner.

Left to her own devices, Maria had not divulged any information to Lois about her own life, discussion of daily experiences were kept to a minimum, and there was no time or room alongside Lois' inflated ego for Maria to talk about anything that was important in her small teacher's existence, and besides, Lois never asked. In letting Lois carry on oblivious, Maria was retreating, half-intentionally, but knowingly, into a thickening, solitary darkness.

♥

It was towards the end of the half term break that Maria had a call from Karen who persuaded her to come out for a drink and by the end of that tortured, sober week, Maria never felt more like a drink to drown her sorrows. Making Karen one very happy games teacher,

Unravel

Maria met her at a local bar and ordered a large rum and ginger ale.

'It's great to see you outside of school at last,' Karen smiled and raised her glass of dry white wine, then puckered up her forehead. 'Although I'm worried about you to be honest, I've noticed you've been more than a little withdrawn lately, and you've lost weight!'

Maria tilted her head with distinct annoyance, but remembered she had to keep her colleague on side. 'I thought you liked the skeletal look – you're always trying to jump my bones.'

Karen opened her mouth wide and laughed a little too heartily.

'You cheeky...!' She chortled and slapped Maria's shoulder non-offensively. 'Well, it's bloody good to see you've still got a sense of humour,' Karen raised her eyebrows over the rim of her wine glass, sipped and smiled. 'You're entirely right, of course.'

What Karen had said chimed with truth, also. Maria had been bordering on depression and couldn't remember the last time she had been humorous, or found something funny. She hadn't been eating properly and, indeed, she had noticed she'd lost several pounds, she could tell by the slenderness of the muscles in her arms where they had once been round and the grazing of her thumbs against her hipbones every time she removed her trousers. Maria feared it would blow her reserves putting out continuous jovial, smart-witted energy for Karen, but she was pleased that she had achieved several goals in one fell swoop: to reassure Karen she was fine, to divert attention from the real reasons for her lonely misery and to play with Karen's obvious attraction to her as part of that diversion. With a tired sigh, Maria took a lengthy, thirsty swig.

'I gotta tell you,' Karen let her hand drop to the table with a heavy slap. 'I've been hanging to ask you what the hell is going on with Nadia!'

Maria choked and sprayed her mouthful of rum and ginger accidentally over Karen's hand on the table.

Karen lifted her hand, grimaced, and wiped it on her thigh. 'Maria, I like you and all, but I don't know if I'm ready to exchange bodily fluids just yet!'

'Sorry!' Maria wiped her chin, then jumped up to get a cloth from the bar. It was a hasty move to prevent Karen seeing any further sign of her shock and Maria planned her mode of response as she waited for the bartender. Karen couldn't know – there was no way she could know otherwise she wouldn't have sat and laughed with her over drinks. Maria relaxed the stress out of her brow and returned with an apologetic smile and the cloth.

'What were you saying?' She asked as she mopped up.

Karen shrugged. 'Oh, just wondered if you had any insider gossip on Nadia. She's making shockwaves, you know. Her habit of staying quiet is only making people speculate about her, and now there are rumours flying around.'

Unravel

'What rumours?' Maria interrupted, sitting down. 'I haven't heard any.'

'Really?' Karen pulled her chin back into the rings of wrinkles at her neck. 'Well, that doesn't surprise me with you being such a workaholic! You're just as elusive you know! That's probably why you get on so well together.'

'What rumours!' Maria snapped, then tried to quell her impatience with another swig.

'About her and Sam!' Karen replied. 'Apparently they've been seen together, holding hands, getting cosy, whispering in each other's ears, giggling... I know what you'll say – that's regular girly friendship – but I've always thought that about Sam. I reckon they've started up a little something there, even Sam's buddy's are giving them a wide berth... there's no smoke without fire! I thought Ariel might have talked to you at least, I wanted to know if it's true she's *joined the team*!'

Maria shook her head with a weak act of disbelief. 'No, it's not true, it can't be. She never told me anything... she would have told me,' Maria lied, and then realised with a flushing heat that she had told a proper lie. Hypothetically, if Nadia ever told Karen, or anyone, that she had confessed her sexuality first to Maria, then Karen would know she had lied. She felt the sugary liquid burn deep in her throat again and Maria knew now wasn't the time to be sick. 'Anyway, she and Sam can't stand each other.'

'I beg to differ!' Karen smirked knowingly. 'If they fell out then it must have been a lover's tiff, because my sources would say they were making up by *making out.*'

'Your *sources* have seen them kissing?' Maria frowned patronisingly, despising Karen's excitable emphasis. 'Who are your sources? We've been away for a week!'

'Who do you think?' Karen flipped her hand with self-importance. 'Sam's neglected gaggle of girls. They emailed me because they knew I was the best council for all things gay, and of course they couldn't talk to you because Nadia's your darling pet.'

'She's not my pet!' Maria growled.

'Ooh-hoo!' Karen teased. 'Not anymore she's not, hey? Sounds like you're going to be having words with a certain little madam. Quite a thing to be hiding from you, and you had no idea she was one of us? Really, Maria, time to pull your head out of Lois' backside and smell the coffee!'

'Look, Nadia doesn't have to tell me anything, okay? In fact, it's probably better she doesn't, it could potentially...' Maria searched for her rightful indignation, 'compromise our working relationship!'

'Oh don't be ridiculous!' Karen said dismissively. 'You're such a stickler! Why do you get so defensive? *So what* if a student comes out to you? That means they trust you and you've done your job well. Nadia obviously respects you, so relax a bit and she might be able to talk to you about it, but she's not going to if you insist on these sky-high boundaries between you!'

'I can't imagine she'll respect either of us for sitting here gossiping about her, if those girls came to you in confidence then you're the one spreading rumours,' Maria quipped.

'Well, those girls will tell the world when they're back at school,' Karen nodded assuredly, 'and if it's based on fact - this is going to be massive!'

Maria did relax with Karen's advice, not because she knew she was being too strict on Nadia, no, Maria felt she had every reason to be unremitting in her discipline of Nadia, as private as those reasons were. Maria relaxed because she understood just how little Karen knew about the situation, and having projected the scenario that had already occurred, Karen's perception of the sexual boundary issues between student and teacher was nothing to cause her further concern. Karen was not only too blind to see it, but too dumb to imagine it. Karen hadn't even questioned what Nadia might be doing with Christian, so keen she was to hear that more young females were signing up to her crew.

Taking their glasses for a refill, Karen left Maria at the table with a reassuring pat on her arm. With a kick back in her chair, Maria's thoughts, of course, turned to Nadia and Sam. She didn't want to believe those rumours were true, but if they had come from

Sam's friends, now made resentful by their auburn-haired replacement, then there must be something occurring. Maria had not seen Nadia for a whole week, and thinking overly upon how much she missed her and wallowing in self-pity, Maria had not given a moment's thought to what else Nadia might be getting up to.

Perhaps Nadia, fleeing from her teacher's rejection, had fallen right into the arms of the person against which Maria had tried to warn her. No, surely the real reason Nadia was playing this game with Sam was to get back at Maria. Of course, it was simple. Nadia was the fickle one. Lesbian or not, the girl liked to mess with people's heads. Karen was right - Nadia was a scheming attention-seeker after all.

Chapter Nineteen

The next day, having had no contact from Nadia and figuring she would not be receiving a visit from her during the lunch hour, Maria took the short journey across the third floor to the glass-fronted library, spanning the whole east side of the building. She'd had the smallest hope of seeing Nadia there, though it wasn't likely: Nadia couldn't stand the busy comings and goings of the warm school hub, Maria recalled with pained fondness. In the eventuality of Nadia actually being there, however, Maria prepared to keep her eyes down, deliberately not look around, in case Nadia had noticed her first.

Knowing the extent of her obsession had become tiresome, Maria completed her tasks in the library with a partially flushed cheek, paranoid she was being watched from a slit in the bookcases, and was hyper-aware of her own movements. It bothered her that she couldn't drop her anxieties by choice, she felt helplessly controlled by her feelings, and as she left the library, Maria contemplated throwing herself down the stairs in hope of knocking herself unconscious, just for a minute or two's blissful break from the incessant, manic fixations of her mind.

She planned to pop quickly to the cafeteria to get a snack, however, waiting in the slow-moving stairwell, Maria happened to glance out the window to the north playing fields, and noticed a group of students swelling against the wall of the gymnasium. She turned to step out of the passing flow of bodies and stood by the window to see properly. Wondering what was causing this grouping, Maria narrowed her eyes against the glassy light of the midday sunshine, fearing it was a fight. Focusing on the centre, to where the crowd seemed to be directing their attentions, Maria spotted the over-familiar sight of Nadia's hair, unlike any one else's around her with that recognisable red. She was leaning against the wall, and beside her was Sam Burrows, one leg cocked up on the wall behind her. They were leaning in closely to each other, and talking, Sam was laughing, and it looked like Nadia was chewing her fingernail. No, she was smoking.

The crowd, many of them boys, were just standing around, staring at them, then jostling with their friends and laughing, before looking back at the girls. Then, as Sam stood away from the wall, pulling Nadia to come away with her, Maria saw they were holding hands. Nadia lifted herself from the wall, passed the smokes to Sam, and waved flirtatiously to the

Unravel

bystanders unable to peel their eyes away from the clutching fingers of the two girls.

Maria pushed the immediate rise of affronted anger back down her throat. It disgusted her to see them parading around together; Sam was acting bizarrely proud in displaying her new girlfriend: smiling with a bravado sort of confidence, delighting in her shocking statement to everyone that she and Nadia were an item. They passed the smokes back and forth, smiling, swinging their gripped hands as if they were inseparable. Maria was even more disturbed to see Nadia putting on such a convincing act of laughing and feigning affection. She twirled into Sam's shoulder and out again, bumping and doubling over with the thrill of receiving so much attention, but knowing the girl's previous reservation, Maria could tell Nadia was self-conscious.

She knew Nadia's body language better than anyone, and just as she had seen with Christian, Nadia wasn't letting Sam get too close. Nadia was making a show of it: it was a masquerade. In fact, now she saw it, Maria grew entranced - exactly like with Christian, Nadia wasn't letting Sam actually kiss her, but turned her cheek, smiling all the while, her eyes open to check who was watching.

The girls walked slowly, teasingly, past a group of girls and their boyfriends eye-balling them from the courtyard. Sam hollered something out to them, throwing a horsey, defiant laugh, and in a dismissive motion to an apparently negative response, she lifted her hand to gesticulate the sentiment of her words. Nadia copied her, then put her arm around Sam's shoulders. They walked on, receiving more comments that were offensive, it seemed, from the ugly faces of their spectators, though Nadia and Sam cruised through the onslaughts as insignificant as small islands of litter in their otherwise pure, freshwater stream.

Maria didn't like this sight: Nadia and Sam united. She wasn't convinced it was real.

'This week just keeps getting better and better!' A purring voice said from her shoulder. Maria glanced beside her at Karen's smiling, lined face gazing beyond the glass to the courtyard below, and relaxed the heavy frown from her own, stressed brow before Karen spotted that too.

'You don't need to tell me you were right,' Maria grumbled, standing back before her close breath made a patch of steam against the window, 'even if my eyes weren't burning after witnessing that car crash in full motion, I could tell it from the smug look on your face.'

Karen snorted her laugh through her nostrils and smiled with twinkling satisfaction down upon the new young lesbians. 'Don't you think it's fantastic? Look at them, so out and proud!'

'Seriously? Samantha Burrows was homophobic until about a week ago!' Maria grimaced, then considered that to be a consistent point to back up her account. 'I guess that's why Nadia didn't tell me, she knew I wouldn't approve,' she said airily.

'Approve?' Karen sniped. 'What are you - her mother? I thought you wanted Ariel off your back - you should be happy. Anyway, it's obvious now "Sam the homophobe" had some pent up frustration from latent gayness!'

'What?' Maria scowled down at Karen's newly cut hair, even more grey than before. 'Don't try and pull that one, Karen, I don't think this is what it looks like.'

'Oh, come on, what's your problem? Let them have some fun. Leave the negativity to the other teachers trying to criticise the happy couple for distracting the other kids. I think *you and I* should be fighting their corner! Encourage their show of openness – I think it's a positive distraction, a lesson for the kids about real life, their friends in real relationships... and I think having such gorgeous, feminine young members of our species will prove a lot of people wrong in their assumptions of us all being butch.'

'Jesus, Karen, if *you* weren't so distracted you might be able to see it's bullshit,' Maria pulled her eyes away from the courtyard. 'They're just kids, they're not in it to fight for *the cause* - they're just experimenting! They're not members of our *species*, they're attention seeking little brats! I can see right through them, and there's no way I'm going to encourage their contrived affections when the rest of our hard-working, honest kids have enough to deal with!'

Maria took to her heels and paced down the stairs to the ground floor, eager to hurry away before Karen had a chance to yell something after her about taking things too seriously. This was serious, and Karen knew nothing; Maria had to leave to make sure it stayed that way.

Feeling her insides burning, Maria felt compelled to stalk outside past the courtyard, deliberately ignoring Nadia and Sam, but her feet tapped at the edge of the sensor mat that pulled the automatic doors apart. It didn't suit Maria to feel inhibited in her actions, but her better sense knew that crossing paths with Nadia and Sam would allow them to gage her reaction, and Maria wasn't sure her reactions were under protective guard at that moment. She wasn't ready to advance to the next stage of these mentally taxing, complex developments - her head hurt with all the second-guessing: if Nadia saw that she had seen them, then Nadia would know that she knew. This was all happening too fast.

Maria turned back and walked along the ground floor corridor, pushing through the masses of pupils gathered outside lockers and toilets, her jaw set with determination to not be caught in an expression of vulnerability. She didn't want to be seen, even if it meant delaying the inevitable. Maria just managed to

Unravel

locate a solitary toilet cubicle before hot, furious tears spilled down her face.

♥

Maria sat staring at her mobile, waiting for Nadia's response. The bell for registration had rung and Maria had texted Nadia to ask her to come see her after the final bell. Maria didn't expect her to come for tuition, but she had to see her, she had to talk to her. All afternoon, since she had wept in the toilet, and during her post-lunchtime tuitions, Maria had worked over in her head everything she wanted to say, collected all her arguments and made sure she was calm enough to say them coherently. She didn't want to send Nadia fleeing again, but Maria desperately wanted Nadia to know that she could see what she was doing and she thought it was pathetic.

However, Nadia's text didn't come through for the entire fifteen minutes of registration, and Maria grew even more frustrated at the idea that Nadia was ignoring her; she always texted back straight away, always keen to engage in communication with her favourite teacher. Nadia was playing games, and while Maria clutched her phone, staring out of her window as the trickles of children rolled away from the school grounds, she deliberated between calling her and texting again.

She began to punch on the buttons, trying to bring up Nadia's number; she stared at it, feeling her pulse racing, knowing she had become obsessed. She couldn't let it go, she had to see Nadia, she couldn't let the girl leave without an explanation of why she was doing this to her, why she was messing with her head like this.

Then her mobile sounded. It was from Nadia. Maria's heart thumped.

`'I'm going home to study, sorry.'`

Maria knew it was a lie. Nadia wasn't going home, she was going out with Sam, or going round to Sam's, or maybe Sam was going round to hers. Seeing as Nadia's reckless behaviour indicated she no longer cared to have her sexuality hidden at school, there was no reason why she wouldn't flaunt her new girlfriend in front of her own father, from whom until recently she had been so desperate to keep the truth. Maria was concerned: perhaps Nadia had flipped and was really going off the rails.

Perhaps, Maria feared, she had caused this by giving the girl such mixed messages. Nadia might be about to spiral into the same pattern of destruction that had resulted in her dropping out of her exams and her mother chucking her out of home.

Tapping passionately into her mobile, Maria texted back that it was really important she see her. This girl needed guidance like no one had ever given her before. If someone had stepped in and helped her in

Dublin, Nadia might not have ended up on the streets. Maria knew she was that person. Nadia was her responsibility. She was more than her teacher - she was Nadia's friend, her confidant, her guardian.

When Nadia failed to arrive, or return the text, for ten minutes, Maria figured she wasn't coming and, with slightly shaky breath and nerves making her hand tremble, she called instead.

'Has someone died or something?' Nadia asked straight away on answering.

Maria focused and tried to keep her voice steady. 'No, but I really need to speak to you.'

'Well, I'm on the bus already...' Nadia sounded blasé.

'Where are you going?'

'I already told you I'm going home... I've got loads to catch up on.'

'Yeah, I heard, sounds like you've been having a lot of fun.'

'What are you talking about?'

'Well, I wanted to tell you but you're on the fucking bus!' Maria hissed.

'Look, I can't talk now, it's too noisy on here, I'll call you later okay?' Nadia hung up.

Maria released an angry growl at the dead tone on her phone. She thought quickly then snatched up her things and locked her office. She felt overpowered by her sudden compulsion to get to Nadia, to have it out with her as soon as possible. There was no way she could stop herself now.

Suddenly, she was driving into town, hurriedly swerving, steering dangerously around dawdling vehicles. Pausing to assess her actions at this moment in time was not an option; Maria didn't care for yelling road-users or the police, she had one goal she had set her mind on, though some observing part inside her was amazed to see herself like this. She was usually so controlled, at her worst she could survive on autopilot while she privately contemplated, but this was nothing she'd ever experienced before. This was reckless, ruthless determination driving her onwards with focused yet blind passion; her all-seeing eye taking care of the roads, lights and cars while the only vision that filled her windshield like a vast angel as high as the sky, was Nadia at the bus station.

It may well have been a vision, as Maria's insightful projection placed Nadia exactly as she had imagined her: waiting by the granite pillar under the pigeon-infested roof of the station. Maria's heart filled with melting relief that Nadia's bus home had not yet swept her away; it felt as if Nadia would be gone from her forever if that had happened.

However, her adrenalin spiked again on seeing the multi-coloured hair and hunched shoulders of Sam Burrows standing next to Nadia at the bus stop. Maria had second thoughts of what she was about to do, but

Unravel

knew she didn't care what Sam thought: she had to get Nadia out of there.

Maria followed the route round to the bus lane, zipped into the area unauthorized for cars and screech-stopped right next to Nadia. Her passenger window flew down at the firm press of her thumb and she glared across at Nadia. 'Get in!'

Nadia bent down, staring in at Maria's stress with wide eyes. 'What are you doing?'

'For fuck's sake, Nadia!' Maria exclaimed with frustration. 'Can't you tell this is urgent? I drove here in four minutes to catch you, now get in!'

Nadia stood upright and shrugged at Sam. 'Sorry.'

'Oh fine, fucking leave me then!' Sam sulked. Maria could only hear her voice and see the bulk of her tummy pushing her jumper out, and was glad she couldn't see her face.

Nadia jumped forward off the kerb to open Maria's passenger door. She slid in and settled her bag down in the foot-well with a concerned, slightly alarmed expression that she didn't take off Maria's profile for the next part of the journey out of town.

'Where are we going?' Nadia asked, her voice small against the loud revs pumping Maria's engine.

'I don't know... somewhere.' Maria replied, but could make no decision until she calmed down. She had Nadia - now the question was - what to do with her.

Unravel

Chapter Twenty

Speeding out of the town centre, Maria headed in the vague direction of Nadia's home, but found herself veering off the main streets down roads unknown. She wanted to take the girl somewhere private they could talk, undisturbed, away from the prying eyes of anyone they knew, and strangers alike.

'Please tell me what's happening!' Nadia's voice shook. 'Are you kidnapping me?'

'Oh, you're a kid now!' Maria smarted and pushed up a gear, the buzzing revs providing ample emphasis for her escalating mood. She couldn't slow down, she felt enraged.

'You're scaring me!' Nadia cried out and gripped on to the door handle.

Maria had to admit, she wanted Nadia to be scared. Glancing at Nadia's pale white hand on her car's black interior made her feel the abductor, being powerful and back in control. She thought of the girl's hand clutching Sam's, stroking Sam, rubbing Sam, and it scalded her mind. She wanted Nadia to come out of her idiotic bubble, stop playing games, take this seriously. Realise she couldn't go around being false. Realise who was being true to her.

'I'm just sick of you winding me up!' Maria said bitterly, her teeth on edge. 'I want to know what the fuck you think you're doing! You're supposed to be focusing on your work not parading around with straight girls! I saw you putting on that show at lunch – what the hell are you doing with Sam?'

Nadia only gaped in shock for a moment before she defended herself. 'Excuse me! It's none of your business what I do!'

'It *is* my business, Nadia!' Maria argued. 'I'm the one who teaches and supports you and tries to guide you on the right path.' She had to keep her eyes on the road, but she wanted to meet Nadia's electric direction she could sense was fully on her.

'Right path for who?' Nadia objected. 'You couldn't deal with seeing me just because I had a crush on you – emphasis on *had*! You lost your right to help me when you pushed me away over one, stupid moment when I forgot where I was...'

'It wasn't just one moment, Nadia, that wasn't the reason I told you that you couldn't come round my house anymore and I couldn't drive you home!'

Nadia laughed spitefully and gestured within the car at Maria's contradiction. 'So what's changed?'

'You've changed!' Maria raised her voice, slamming her steering wheel with her palm. 'I thought you didn't want people to know about you, and now you're rubbing it in everyone's faces! You told me you were afraid your dad would find out, and that's why you were happy to date Christian – well, what's he going to say about all this?'

'I don't give a flying fuck about my dad!' Nadia buckled. 'He sure as hell doesn't give a fuck about me. He hasn't a clue where I am or what I'm doing, I could be dead in the attic for a week before he'd notice! So what difference does it make if I come out at school?'

'It makes a big difference to me!' Maria said passionately. 'Don't you see? People *do* notice you - and now you've *come out at school* - they are going to start looking directly at me because I'm the lesbian teacher who sits with you alone for hours!'

Nadia rubbed her forehead with nervous fingers and pushed her hair back behind her ears. 'You don't get it.'

'No, I don't, Nadia, that's why I wanted to ask you what you're playing at, because I'm sick of messing around now. I just want to get back to the way things were before we started acting like lunatics.'

Sensing Nadia's silence, Maria took the opportunity to scan the quiet road ahead for a turning, or a clearing, or anywhere she could pull over and calm down. Soon, there seemed to be a private track alongside a field, the gate was open at least, and Maria

Unravel

turned in, guiding her car under the balcony of trees, the last of the afternoon sunlight bouncing off her car bonnet, dappled through the leaves. There were no other cars in sight as they followed a dirt road up and over a hill, and Maria's insides sighed with relief at finally being able to speak privately.

In the ticking noise of the engine settling, they sat facing forward: Nadia glaring out across the bland field surrounding them, Maria tilting her head back on the rest.

'Don't do this,' Maria whispered to herself.

'I've been trying!' Nadia moaned in response. 'I know it's awkward for you, but it's difficult for me too. I've been trying my best to sort my head out! I'm sorry if, in the meantime, I've upset you by distracting myself with other people, but I've had to do that to leave you alone, I thought that's what you wanted!'

'But why Sam?' Maria shook her head with revulsion. 'You know she's not right.'

'I know she's not, but I needed someone to take my mind off you!'

'So it *is* all a facade!' Maria felt a futile smugness emerge and sink away again. 'You're using Sam – just like you've been using Christian!'

Creasing up her face in exasperation, Nadia repelled. 'Of course it's a fucking facade, I don't have feelings for her, I don't even like her!'

'So what - you're trying to make me jealous?'

'God, you don't even know!' Nadia shook her head.

'Then, tell me everything, Nadia, because now's the time before I start thinking you're completely mental!'

'Okay!' Exhaling, Nadia wiped her face and fidgeted with her coat. 'I was thinking, after what you said... I was worried Christian might say something... I thought if I pre-empted – is that the word?' Nadia blinked at Maria.

'I don't know...' Maria shrugged with an impatient grimace.

Nadia continued. 'I thought if I pre-empted anything Christian could say about me by coming out first, then I could divert attention away from you...' Nadia made a small dance with her fingers, 'by causing a scandal with someone completely... opposite.'

Maria blinked heavy eyelids. 'You did this to *protect me*?'

Staring back down at her buttons, Nadia's eyes sprung tears. 'Just because I'm stupid enough to fall in love with you doesn't mean you have to suffer for it.'

Her throat tightening, Maria felt her blood flush with ice. 'What did you say?'

Nadia steadied her voice from wobbling. 'I'm sorry... I can't help it.'

The physiological sensations that arose in Maria's heart and stomach were unbearable and uncontainable within her car. She popped the seat belt release and opened her car door. She stood to breathe in the cool breeze that swept across the angled field, her mind reeling from these new revelations. It was too much to deal with. She felt glad to be wrong about Nadia's behaviour but terrified to be right about the girl's emotions. She leaned against the driver's door and wrapped her black jacket around her, clutching her arms over her swirling insides.

Hearing the car door slam from the passenger side, Maria sensed Nadia moving around the front of the Audi and walking out in front of her. 'Did you hear me? I said I can't help it!' Nadia cried into the wind. 'But it's not *all* my fault!'

'What do you mean?' Maria called back; unsure she wanted the answer.

'I'm trying my best to get over you, but you won't let me!' Nadia kept at a safe distance but almost toppled on her feet with exclamation. 'You keep being nice to me and I don't know why – no one else is nice to me! Everyone thinks I'm some sort of fuck-up but you go out of your way to make me feel relaxed and happy, it confuses me!'

'I never meant to encourage you... like that.' Maria cringed.

'You haven't!' Nadia's Irish accent grated with her shout. 'I just mean that any other teacher would have stopped seeing me, would have run straight to the principal to cover their ass, but you didn't. You listened to me and you did what was best for me...' Nadia pulled her hair back from whipping around her face. 'So how am I supposed to get over you? Even now, you've driven me out here though you said you couldn't drive me around anymore. You told me you couldn't see me out of school, so what are you doing to me? Because you're right, I can't do this to you, I can't ruin everything because of my stupid feelings. But that means you have to leave me alone! Because I have to get over you, right?'

Maria shook her head with confusion before she realised she should have nodded.

'Oh god!' Nadia appealed. 'Stop looking at me like that! You've got to stop looking at me! Don't be nice to me! Don't pay any attention to me! And don't criticise what I do or who I see if you don't want me to keep feeling this way, because it's hard, Maria, it's really hard to stop feeling this way!' Nadia broke with tears and she wept into the sleeves of her coat.

'I can't...' Maria said in a low, shaky voice, feeling a sea within her swell. 'I can't do it.'

The wind had calmed. Nadia lowered her sleeves and shook her head, her lips retreating from her teeth, and her eyes creased with confusion. 'Do what?'

Looking upon the dimples that had first arrested her attention, Maria wondered if she wanted to say this. She had to say something, and all she knew was she couldn't push Nadia away. Maria wanted her near, to keep her near.

Say it right, Maria told herself, *say it right.*

She exhaled her nerves. 'I don't want to stop seeing you.'

A painful ten seconds passed during which Nadia held her grimace, her disbelief obvious, and her anger too stubborn to see. Throwing her hands in the air, she laughed finally. 'That is the exact kind of fucked up, mixed message I can't deal with, Maria! You want to keep seeing me? What, now it's okay that I've got feelings for you? You don't mind?!' Nadia stepped in a frustrated circle. 'I think you just like having a student fancy you, don't you? How many other girls have you done this to, huh?' Nadia flew forward and kicked Maria's wheel as hard as her foot could manage. 'You couldn't stand it as soon as I took my attention away from you and now you want it back, don't you? You really *are* jealous!'

Flinching at Nadia's attack on her precious car, Maria stood firm and tried to repress her nervous shivers. She couldn't tell Nadia that indeed she had been jealous. Nadia was too upset to realise she was right. Maria couldn't speak; she was so close to revealing her feelings that she was scared to say anything at all.

'You don't want to stop seeing me?' Nadia shook her head, wiping her tears away in black streaks. 'What does that mean? We'll just *carry on* in tuition acting like none of this happened? You'll pretend I'm not in love with you and I'm supposed to sit next to you, dying every minute I want to touch you... you

Unravel

might be fine with that Maria, but I'm not! I can't pretend anymore, not with you.'

Nadia turned and faced away, her green parka and flicking auburn hair silhouetted against the setting sun. She was crying hard, her black-clad leg jutting out defensively.

Taking a careful look around, down the lane behind and in front of her car, Maria knew they were alone. Her trembles seemed to dissipate as she called Nadia's name softly.

When she half turned, Nadia's eyes were dark and full, her brow puckered together with concern for Maria's intention.

'Come here,' Maria extended her arm forward and held her hand open.

Nadia looked at it contemplatively, and then frowned harder, back up at Maria.

Gesturing with her fingers, Maria offered herself for a warm hug: one that she never had the chance to give around school, and was too nervous to anywhere else.

Appearing hesitant at first, Nadia pursed her mouth against her tears, but wiped her face and inched closer. She was unsure, evidently, but Maria saw a change overcome her, and it was the same proximity-driven, chemically-reactive draw that had lured their knees together on countless occasions in tuition. As if entranced, Nadia stepped towards her slowly, staring at

Unravel

the magnet of Maria's hand, her mind having deserted her craving body.

She took Nadia's hand, and guided her gently in, raising her other arm around Nadia's back.

Nadia gazed stiffly over Maria's shoulder with a drowsy kind of surrender then relaxed into the embrace. 'Maria...' She whispered before she clutched her cold hands inside her teacher's coat.

Maria felt them slide around her waist against the fabric of her shirt as she wrapped Nadia in her coat and held her in. The cool rush of open-country breeze circled around them now they had closed the gap, and Maria's eyes shut with the gloriously warm feeling of Nadia's body against hers.

With Nadia's head tilted into her neck, Maria could feel her tingling hot breath spreading through the spirals of her black hair, but the feeling was different to the last time when Nadia had kissed her there. This time Nadia was weeping; the soft shudders of her shoulders grazing against Maria's arms.

Lowering her hand around Nadia's hips, and rubbing her back a little, Maria gave a caring cuddle; she wanted to show her that she cared, like a friend, a close, loving friend.

'It's so good to hold you...' Nadia mumbled. 'I wish I could hug you more.'

Bending her head close to Nadia's ear, Maria whispered back. 'Me too'.

However, after a few seconds, Nadia pulled her body away slightly. She pressed her forehead against Maria's clavicle, and her hands moved to Maria's stomach, her fingers running down the front buttons of her shirt. Maria held her breath, wondering if Nadia could feel the triple-time beat of her heart. She feared her game was up. She loosened her hands from Nadia's coat and let them fall quietly to her side as the girl looked up with her beautifully shimmering eyes, a deep green, wavering sea.

'Maria?' Nadia gulped her tears away. 'Seeing as you don't mind me being in love with you an' all... would you mind if I kissed you?' Nadia asked with sweet, trembling breath. 'Just once... just while we're here and the sun is setting, I'll remember it forever... and I won't tell anyone.'

Feeling locked into this connection with Nadia, and thinking about kissing her, Maria knew it could happen, right now. She could simply let Nadia kiss her. She knew it would make Nadia feel special, and she wanted her to have this moment. It would be like a charity kiss, Nadia's once in a lifetime chance to kiss her teacher. Maria cast her eyes down in thought, weighing her options, checking her liabilities. Nadia would be grateful and would never have to know how much Maria had dreamed of it too.

Of course, Maria's stomach began fluttering with sudden adrenalin, her clitoris gave a twinge, and she knew she wanted to kiss. Nadia lips were so close, and gazing at them, Maria liked the soft, moist appeal of them, their succulent orange bow-shape. She nodded dreamily, and tilted her head down and to the side, just enough to let her lips linger beside Nadia's.

This is it, Maria thought. She took in Nadia's scent, having a fleeting thought that the kiss might be awful then both their problems would be over.

Yes, Maria decided, it was better to find out if there was real reason for all this fuss.

Nadia's mouth moved in slowly, just before her eyes closed, and Maria watched as they pressed lips, the cold tips of their noses touching each other's warm cheeks. Maria's eyes closed too, pleased that the difference in their height was perfect for kissing, she knew it would be. The sensation of Nadia's hot, tear-moistened lips undulating nervously against her own seemed to fall into slow-motion as Maria tried to remind herself not to get swept up and away. This wasn't Lois; this wasn't anyone else she could let go with normally. Maria couldn't let herself French kiss and confuse the poor girl - she had to keep her lips shut and just let Nadia kiss her.

But, this was Nadia, actually Nadia, live and in the flesh, and even without tongues, it was sensual. Maria, drawn in by the rhythmic press and suck of Nadia's breathing, knew at once the girl was a good kisser. Nadia gasped lightly, taking in a panting breath with a shot of cold air, and enclosed her half open mouth onto Maria's, pursing them shut and opening again, rubbing moistness between them, then trembling her exhale. Nadia's hands moved up to Maria's cheek, her chilled fingers clutching at the dark hair blowing around them and smoothing it back, then holding Maria's jaw, Nadia licked the inside of Maria's lips, with a light flicker of her tongue, sending shivers down to Maria's clitoris.

Gasping herself now, Maria enveloped a sort of daze as she tried to concentrate on resisting kissing back. However, she couldn't seem to stop her mouth stirring with Nadia's hungry, circular sucking. Every time Nadia's tongue pushed between her lips, Maria felt her will and control shudder out of her. She became conscious of sucking back, gripping Nadia's lips with hers, swaying with the motion, breathing with her, but she was unable to pull away or stop the throaty noises of pleasure that came from her now as well as Nadia. The slowness oozed with luscious sensuality.

One of Nadia's hands moved up to her shoulder, gripped the muscle, slid over her neck and down again to the inside of Maria's coat, where it joined the other clutching around her belt. Maria became aware of her torso, rising and falling, her breath deepening under Nadia's touch; she feared she was going too far, letting this kiss develop, but she couldn't stop it. Some part of her figured Nadia must know already, and she let her tongue roll over Nadia's lips, just once, but then again and it met Nadia's tongue and they both lingered at that point of slow, wet, mutual licking that felt like a climax with their breath in their mouths. Maria felt her internal muscles squeeze and release a rush of moisture between her legs.

Nadia's hand returned to the front of Maria's shirt and rested over her breast where it stroked down and caressed upwards, cupping Maria's erect nipple between thumb and forefinger through her bra. Maria gasped and Nadia pulled her hand away with surprise.

The kiss broke.

Their eyes opening onto the sight of each other's swollen lips, Maria breathed hard, unable to believe their kiss had felt so good. Nadia was still close, panting, drunk with arousal. The air between their lips stung with cold, the promise of warmth lured Maria back in, and as she lifted eyes heavy with lust to Nadia's, she felt utterly compelled.

Feeling as if a rope had lassoed her, Maria pulled Nadia beside her and leaned her against her car, covering her body protectively from the wind. Taking the back of Nadia's neck in her hand, tipping her face up to meet hers, Maria gazed intentionally into the girl's eyes, and felt no fear. With renewed vigour, Maria wanted to give Nadia the sexiest kiss she would ever have, wanted to make her melt. Under Maria's direction, the second half of their kiss, soft and wet from the first, became deeper and hungrier.

Pushing her hips against Nadia's, Maria found power she had been missing for months. She kissed Nadia's mouth with passion, with strength from her jaw and from the muscles in her neck. She felt her hands charge with energy as she gripped Nadia's cheek and neck. Her heartbeat pounded through every cell in her body as Nadia caressed her breast. Again, all Maria could think about was savouring this delicious warm, sensation of Nadia's mouth, for all those months of longing, now it was hers, at last. She couldn't believe how aroused she had become, so quickly, that addictive throbbing between her legs beginning to burn.

The sudden, nearby barking of a hound made Maria snatch away from their kiss, her glare shooting down the dirt track where an elderly couple of ramblers walked their dog. They had emerged from the bushes Maria now saw hid a turnstile to a footpath; they would have seen them, and chosen to walk in the other direction hopefully from politeness instead of disapproval. The beagle gave one last bark toward Maria before leaping after his owners.

When Maria turned back to face Nadia, something - everything - had changed.

Maria stared at the shock reflected in Nadia's eyes, and realised what she had done. Everything she shouldn't have; everything she knew she mustn't do. She had brought this girl out here in a jealous rage, shouted at her, demanded honesty from her, and then not only encouraged the girl by permitting one innocent kiss by sunset, but turned into a horny dyke and given her mind-blowing mouth-to-mouth. They could have gone for hours if they hadn't been disturbed.

The sun had nearly reached the horizon and it was turning cold, the wind bitter without the heat of daylight. Nadia looked overwhelmed, confused, and gazed back, speechless. Her eyes were round: almost scared. Bleary with mascara and dried tears, her lips swollen from their clinch, Nadia seemed as if a dawning horror was rising inside her. Her fingers touched her trembling lips. 'I'm sorry!'

The girl never looked more like a child. Maria was suddenly disgusted, appalled at herself. She looked upon Nadia with dark shame, her guilt soaking down her.

'Fuuuck!' She cried into the wind with frustration, her teeth gritted. It was no helpful release. Averting her eyes from Nadia, Maria's chest hurt as she panted. She knew that it wasn't Nadia's fault, it was her own; Nadia had no way of knowing she was going to kiss her back like that. She glared back over at Nadia, knowing she should reassure her, or be kind, or something, but she couldn't make this mistake again.

'We have to go.' Maria said mechanically, stepping back towards her car, glad it was getting dark enough to disguise her expressions. She thought she might cry; her emotions wrought. She never felt more conflicted: the kiss with Nadia had been incredible but now she couldn't stand the idea she'd lost control and let that happen. Maria had done the worst thing possible, all for a moment of desire.

'Maria, I'm so sorry!' Nadia wailed as she jumped in the passenger side and slammed the door. 'I didn't mean for that to happen!'

Starting the engine, the headlights bright against the grey-blue evening, Maria reversed quickly back up the dirt track. She didn't want Nadia to stare at her; Maria felt nauseous. Until only a minute ago, they had been enraptured in a glorious embrace, their tongues winding and folding, their hands grasping and clutching with desperate yearning for deeper, longer passion, more pleasure, more satisfaction. *Where would it have stopped?* Maria wondered, they had been entirely elsewhere, in their own world. She shook her head with awe and deep fear.

'Are you mad at me?' Nadia asked, biting her fingernails.

'No.' Maria replied firmly, pulling back onto the main road towards Stroud.

Nadia watched Maria's profile, waiting for some reaction. 'But you're upset...'

'Not at you.' Maria held her eyes on the road; she couldn't look at Nadia.

'It's not your fault!' Nadia insisted. 'I was the one who kissed you!'

'I shouldn't have kissed you back!' Maria smarted and pushed the gas down. She wanted no further discussion, just wanted to get Nadia home as soon as possible. Maria knew she had fucked up, really fucked up bad this time. She could try to keep Nadia on side, make her promise to tell no one, but Maria was already beyond her own levels of self-loathing and no amount of persuading her student to keep quiet was going to reassure her.

Her paranoia going into overdrive, Maria felt the awful dread of something else bad happening now. If she had a crash or got caught speeding, she would have to explain the presence of her student in her car. Maria imagined Nadia's father would be at home to witness the state his daughter was in, spilling out of an angry, weird silence in her teacher's car. Disgraceful. Maria despised herself more than she could ever remember. She felt like a dirty lesbian, a perverted teacher, an uncontrolled predator.

'Are you not going to talk to me now?' Nadia blurted across at Maria. 'After you gave me the best kiss of my whole life, you're going to ignore me?'

Maria gulped down the sickening lump in her throat. 'I just need some time to work this out, okay?' She replied through a tense, clenching jaw.

'Can't we talk about it?' Nadia began to cry softly as she spoke. 'Please take me back to yours and we can talk about it there.'

'God, no.' Maria said coldly. She really couldn't give out any energy at this time, Maria could only think of going home, alone, to implode.

Chapter Twenty-One

Maria hadn't been able to stop thinking about Nadia since she'd left her standing outside her father's raggedy house in Eastcombe, looking mortified that Maria had dropped her off so heartlessly. It was a sorry thing to do, but Maria had no choice by that point, she'd already lost her control and it was never an option to drive Nadia to an even more private place to discuss what they'd just done. Maria wasn't sure if she could ever allow them to be alone again.

Laying in her bath later that evening, Maria tried to focus on the drift of classical music from the digital radio that she propped against the folded towels on the rustic shelves in her bathroom. The tall candle she had lit cast a murky light against the tawny brickwork and the cream and brandy walls, and was far from soothing. A relaxing candlelit bath usually helped ease her long day out through her pores, yet that night, Maria felt drained of any ability to take pleasure from the calm white milk water in which she immersed herself. She did not feel dirty after her clinch with Nadia. She felt dead.

Staring across, dully, at the taps over the water, Maria couldn't even close her eyes for fear of the reoccurring images of Nadia's nose and mouth next to hers: the tear-strewn eyes and her swollen, puckered lips. Instead, her mind raced with anxieties, dragging its regrets, towards a wasteland of hopelessness.

The thrill of their kiss had come back in regular, pulsing shockwaves during the journey back to Charlton Kings, however, painstakingly knocking on Christian's door to collect Leon, Maria had suffered a terrifically awkward exchange as the young man asked after his estranged girlfriend.

'She won't answer my calls,' he moaned, shoving his hands in his jeans pockets.

Stumbling on what to say, Maria shifted her feet on the porch, desperate to leave.

'Maybe she just needs some time?' She knew it sounded lame; she was too busy wondering if her eyes were giving anything away.

Waiting too many excruciating seconds, Christian seemed to be thinking. 'How has she been with you?' he asked.

'I haven't seen her!' Maria lied, all too quickly. 'I think she's... trying really hard to focus on her studies right now. She hasn't even come for tuition.'

'Oh,' Christian said, looking down at his socks. 'Maybe she's embarrassed.'

'Yeah,' Maria agreed and began to make a move. Leon responded with a dip of his head and a waggle when his master looped his lead tighter. 'She'll get over it though,' Maria paused to cringe. 'I mean, she'll get over this... phase.'

With a sorrowful nod, Christian accepted Maria's payment for dog-sitting and closed the door in silence.

After that, Maria's guilt had set in fast. Her ability to lie was disturbing. Her loyalty to the one young man she trusted to look after her beloved dog had been overturned, at the flick of some auburn hair, because he now posed some loose threat to her personal and professional security. She had to maintain an appearance of casualness, or Christian may see something was up. Maria had to do her best to deter him from saying anything to anyone about his girlfriend and her 'crush.' Lying, she could evidently do, but she didn't like it, and Maria felt miserable.

Text messages from Nadia had inevitably come through, asking Maria to call her; apologising, and asking what Maria was thinking.

Maria spent an hour in her bath until it went lukewarm, thinking all right. She was thinking through what Nadia must be thinking - what it must look like to her now that they had kissed. The girl had requested to kiss her, but Nadia hadn't expected one in return. Maria had only wanted to make her feel special in kissing her back, but how could Nadia have interpreted that intense oral exchange?

Closing her eyes, Maria felt the stirring once more between her naked thighs. There was Nadia, trembling against her body, the taste of her breath, a bite from her teeth, Maria's pelvis tilted against the water and back again with contraction. There was no denying it had felt incredible - Nadia had obviously felt it, and Maria couldn't pretend she hadn't felt it too.

Blinking her eyes open again, Maria winced at the memory of being witnessed by the elderly walkers. If anyone else had seen them, someone they knew, Maria would be shot. She realised how reckless she had been in driving Nadia to an isolated area - of course something was going to happen. She had felt so mindless with desire; she had even felt a kick from scaring Nadia, although her jealousy of Sam seemed so long ago now.

From anyone else's perspective, this situation was scandalous. Maria: a highly respected advanced skills tutor, supposed to be helping a vulnerable transfer student after a difficult year, seduces the poor girl with kindness and generosity. Along with the company of her dog, rides in her car, dinner, and parties, she fails to report alcohol on school premises or even drugs in her own house; fails to reject the girl's affections, then kisses her passionately. It didn't look good. It would ruin her reputation, colleagues wouldn't talk to her, students would mock her, parents wouldn't trust her and she would never get teaching work again. Maria wondered what Ben would say. She knew he would be devastated and disappointed in her, and that made Maria sore in her heart; she cared more for Ben's opinion than anyone else's.

A new text message arrived from Nadia with a vibration.

It read: 'Please don't ignore me, I can't handle this alone. There are some things I need to tell you, please call me... x'

Maria knew she had to plan her excuses properly in order to discourage Nadia.

Suddenly, her phone began ringing in her hand and Maria jumped with surprise, nearly dropping it in the bath. As she looked upon the caller's identity, a rancid sickish taste arose in her gullet. It was Lois. She swallowed and tried to breathe calmly.

She had automatically thought Lois knew something, but once Lois, as usual, began talking about herself, Maria felt relieved and almost grateful for Lois' egotism.

'You remember I met a guy on the plane back over here?' Lois asked in a voice thick with the kind of rapid, self-important bragging that accompanies cocaine. 'He's asked me out to dinner to talk over ideas I've got, he is seriously interested in my conceptual work.'

'Are you asking my permission to go to dinner with some guy?' Maria asked dryly.

'No, I'm already going, he's picking me up in a minute,' Lois replied and could be heard clacking around on high heels. 'I just wanted to say thanks for ruining my exhibition.'

'What?' Maria scowled.

'Well, think about it, I would never have gone back to Melbourne and would never have met Rupert on the plane back, so I wouldn't be about to get a big fat commission!'

With outrage peaking and dispersing in a second, Maria couldn't be bothered to think of anything to say, her mind was on more important things. 'Then I wish you all the best of luck.'

'Don't need it! But thanks anyway. Catch ya later!' Lois hung up the phone.

Maria hung up too, and stared at her mobile, wondering what was happening to her life.

Leon eventually wandered into the bathroom, drawn by the sound of her silence after the call, and nosed Maria's hand hanging off the edge of the bath. She cooed down to him and he licked the milk water from her pruning fingers. She smiled sadly. Taking the sign to get up and out, Maria felt the dead weight of the water dragging her down and she towelled herself slowly, aching, her muscles strangely tense as if she had overdone it at the gym. She went through to her bedroom and lay on her bed, her hair wrapped turban style, her phone in her hand.

Reading Nadia's texts again, they seemed to have swung between sorrow, pleading, and indignation. Maria didn't know what to reply that couldn't possibly incriminate her. There were no words coming forth as excuses and she couldn't say anything near the truth. Neither could she reassure Nadia everything was going to be okay, it wasn't. With pain in every push of her thumb, Maria texted:

`'Please Nadia, I just need some time to think.'`

Maria threw her mobile on her bed and crumpled into her duvet, curling foetus-like against her pillows. Her eyes leaked thick tears at the realisation that she had gone too far to go back now. Her desire for Nadia had taken her over and she worried she had shown herself, revealed her lustful inclination towards her student. Surely, Nadia knew, if not now then it would dawn on her soon.

It frustrated Maria that she was not being as strong as she should be, she felt Nadia had somehow taken the position of puppeteer, and she was the one dancing to the girl's tune. She hated that her feelings were overpowering - had overpowered her - and now the consequences were inescapable. She wished she could hold it together, but Maria felt as if she was the schoolchild with the big, scary crush. Her mind played havoc with her nerves anticipating detention, suspension, expulsion. Maria folded tightly, and put herself on the naughty chair in the corner, for the worst possible behaviour.

♥

Driving into school the next day, Maria already felt like a criminal and prepared for the paranoid scenarios of her nightmares to become premonitions. She dreaded the eye contact of her colleagues and couldn't face the staff room: the guilt on her face alone would let them know everything they may have heard was true. Although it was unlikely, Maria felt compelled to scare herself.

Mostly, she dreaded seeing Nadia. Her heart and mind had been too confused to plan a suitable statement to put to Nadia that didn't cause her to stutter and blush. Maria hoped Nadia would be gracious enough to give her a day's break in response to her request for time, but she knew Nadia would not leave her alone until she had reassurance.

Once in her office, Maria began to feel slightly more in control. Over the morning tuitions with her regular students, it occurred to her that her colleagues might not be so judgemental, particularly recalling Karen's view that any number of students was likely to develop crushes on their teachers, gay or straight: it was natural. Maria even had the idea of pre-empting Nadia's potential spilling with her own account of things - she could present it as if Nadia was simply confused since discovering her sexuality and made a pass at Maria. That was enough of the truth to provide herself with a back up. In fact, Maria could go straight to Principal Woods - have a quiet word, get him on side - just in case anything was said, or any rumours started.

Maria suddenly stopped in her tracks, wondering if she *was* being manipulated by this flame-haired creature, and if she should actually talk to someone. Maria soon shook the thought from her head: there was no way she could risk anyone looking into the way she had allowed her personal relationship with Nadia to develop. They would soon understand that Maria had not only failed to discourage Nadia's feelings, but had taken her own pleasure from the girl's company; and, *of course* they would be judgemental.

That lunchtime, Maria had a steady string of visitors: students traumatised by the countdown to mock exams. They were coming and going so regularly, Maria considered keeping her door open, but the fear of Nadia hanging across the hall, watching her like a ghoul, would knock her concentration, and she couldn't have that. She received a text from Nadia on her phone, which she didn't read, as she was with a student. Sometime later that lunch, a student opened her door to leave and held it open for the next in the queue, and Maria just happened to glance up to see the vision of Nadia, leaning against the wall, waiting for a chance.

Maria froze, and didn't know whether to smile or frown. In the seconds that she thought about it,

Unravel

admiring Nadia's sultry stare, the door closed and it was too late. The new student started talking and Maria keenly listened, focusing very hard on what the boy was saying.

Between her afternoon tuitions, Maria checked her phone, and read Nadia's text:

`'I'm outside, I need to talk to you, can't you get rid of this lot?'`

Maria wrote back:

`'Don't wait around, I'll call you when I'm free.'`

She thought that sounded suitably professional, at least, there was nothing in it that anyone else could find suspicious. It was also a firm attempt to discourage Nadia's behaviour: she was not an exception. Even if she was, Maria couldn't let her think she was.

Yet, that night, Nadia would not relent. She called over and over, but Maria let it ring, staring at it vibrating on the coffee table. Clutching her glass of wine, Maria couldn't speak to her, couldn't discuss it yet, and couldn't even think straight; it was too much.

Nadia texted: `'I'm going nuts here, how can you do this to me?'`

Considering what to reply, Maria knew there was no way she could allow any reference to their unorthodox relationship in case someone found their texts. She wrote:

`'Nadia, I can't talk to you about this.'`

Unravel

Maria became aware of a growing kick of adrenalin every minute that passed while she awaited Nadia's next message. When it came, seeing Nadia's name, the adrenalin that jerked through her veins let her know what kind of a dangerous thrill she felt to be involved in this intense interaction with her special student.

Nadia texted back: `If you can't talk or write, can't we meet up?'

Taking her time, Maria sipped on her wine and contemplated being alone with the girl. There was a resolute mindset she had entered, which had pulled up a drawbridge behind her.

`No. No more mistakes.'

Nadia didn't respond straight away, but left it a few poignant minutes:

`Obviously it won't happen again... but I need to tell you things.'

At this, Maria was struck. The girl had suggested it was obvious they wouldn't kiss again, when Maria thought it was obvious they would. Taking a long time to wonder what Nadia was thinking, Maria came to the conclusion that this was the exact reason they could not indulge in a conversation about it: she would drop herself in it for sure.

`I don't want to discuss it.'

Rapidly, Nadia's response came:

`Don't shut me out! You can't ignore me.'

At that, Maria did, cruelly, ignore her. She turned her phone off and drank another glass of wine before going for a workout. She could imagine Nadia scowling now, in her father's cold house in Eastcombe, and it made Maria's dark side ache with deep unrest. Although she knew she had to drive Nadia away again, as she had been trying to - before she made the mistake of kissing her, drawing her back in - Maria craved to console Nadia, meet with her and tell her she was sorry. However, Maria's resilience had set up camp, her ignorance fuelled by the heavy weight-lifting of booze and guilt.

Chapter Twenty-Two

The season was turning warmer, but wetter, and Maria could have felt the rain on its way in her bones if they weren't aching already from lack of sleep. The bad dreams of many previous nights had put her mind into such overdrive that the stress and paranoia enveloped her within a waking state of exhaustion through the wee small hours and far into the morning light. Between five and seven, she had managed to get some rest, however, on hearing her alarm, every cell, every sense comprising her physical and emotional being surged with dread at the coming day.

She felt ill; perhaps it was more than just a hangover. It had hardly ever occurred to Maria to take days off work, as she was hardly ever sick, and the few times she had been over the years, she could never take respite comfortably knowing she had let others down. Confident she could function doing most things in life even if she were struck deaf, dumb or blind, Maria resolved to dose herself up with vitamins and nutritional supplements, which her body had felt starved of for the last few months, alongside some painkillers.

It was only when stepping outside for the morning walk around the green with Leon that Maria registered it was raining. However, instead of the dull, draining mood that soaked the landscape of Charlton Kings, Maria lifted her hood and felt a strange kind of bliss as she walked out under the fat drops that fell straight down in wide, heavy splashes. At first, she attributed it to the influx of quality chemicals she'd just imbibed, making her head roll, vaguely numb on her stiff shoulders, and her heart tingle with lightness. After a dozy reminder of what day it was, though, Maria realised it was the prospect of seeing Nadia later in tuition that was making her insides flutter. She took Leon back home early to dry him off, set him some food, then stood in her kitchen and forced herself to eat a rather brown-skinned banana for breakfast, although it made her gag she was so nervous.

It rained on and off all morning; in between, brief bursts of adrenalin kept Maria's body zapped with reinvigorating pulses like electricity. It felt as if the air charged with energy, the atmosphere felt springy, the grass on the fields and the leaves on the trees seemed to bounce back up and reach for the stormy clouds overhead, and Maria even felt her students enter with static in their clothes and hair. There was something tangible about the elements that afternoon, and it made

Unravel

Maria fear what might build up by the time Nadia arrived at the end of the day.

The absolute last thing Maria needed was a session with Samantha Burrows, although she hadn't been in weeks, so Maria released one weary prayer for another absence. The bitter conclusion that Sam would probably rather spend the time with her new bosom buddy Nadia, both stirred then calmed her; Maria would rather deal with her own helpless jealousy than Sam's hateful company for an hour.

Her headache had lingered, and more painkillers had maintained a zombie-like sullenness; a steady expression of a persistent mood stiffened her jaw and brow. The idea that Nadia could have told Sam about their kiss kept rocking the sanctuary of her denial; what might Sam bring to her office? Maria didn't know if she could trust Nadia. Preparing her defence in case Sam threatened to get her in serious trouble, Maria let no fear or surprise cross her features as Sam knocked and entered her office.

The change in Sam's demeanour was incredible. She sat opposite Maria at her desk with a humble sort of quiet, her eyes lowered with respect, quite unlike the knife-like glare with which she usually regarded everyone. Her lashes were still surrounded by black kohl but they had a softness to them Maria had never witnessed before. Her mouth didn't curl into that slippery, glossy grin, instead she pouted and held her chin with a hint of stubbornness: that Maria had seen many times on many students but this one was shrouded by a cloud of apparent remorse.

'I owe you an apology,' Sam began, blinking fully at Maria's desktop.

'What for?' Maria asked tentatively, her hands felt twitchy in her lap.

Sam rolled her eyes slightly, seemingly pained to have to list her reasons. 'For all the things I've said to you... all the times I've been rude.'

'Ok-ay...' Maria said in a halting, accepting tone. 'What's prompted this?'

Turning wide eyes to the windows, Sam sighed and reflected with something sounding suspiciously like genuine regret. 'I guess I realised that it's not right to be mean to people because they are different... it's good to be different... but I think I was rude about you being a lesbian because... I didn't know how else to talk about it.'

Maria pushed down a difficult gulp, and cleared her throat. 'If you wanted to talk about it, there's nicer ways to provoke a conversation.'

'I know... I know that now,' Sam grimaced. 'Nadia's helped me understand a few things.'

'Nadia?' The name sounded limp coming from her mouth; Maria cringed internally.

'I thought I didn't like her,' Sam continued. 'She was being all stuck-up and not talking to us... and then we had a proper deep and meaningful, just me and her, and I realised she wasn't afraid to be unpopular, and that made me really think.'

'About what?' Maria asked hesitantly.

'Well, the thing that made her different was the thing that scared me... when she told me she used to have a girlfriend... I realised I liked her a lot more than I'd ever liked anyone.' Sam looked uncomfortable and dug her thumbnail into the arm of her chair. 'So we talked about it and she made me realise I had been defensive... in my attitude to a lot of things... and my behaviour towards you.'

Maria smarted a little, thinking about Nadia's grand scheme. 'Wow, she's turned a homophobe into a homosexual, that girl works wonders.'

Sam flashed an irritated glance at Maria. 'Look, I don't know if I'm a lesbian, I just know I like her, that's all.'

'Right.' Maria said, somewhat satisfied that Sam was still the mean, fickle creature she knew would make a comeback after this 'phase' with Nadia was over for her.

'Miss Calver, I said I'm sorry.' Sam changed back to her authentic-looking plea.

Maria was reminded of the fact that only Nadia called her by her first name, and that was another one of many things she hadn't yet given away to Sam. Looking upon Sam's seemingly rueful state, Maria found her forgiveness in feeling suddenly sorry for the girl. However temporary they might be - Sam's feelings were real, but she had no idea that Nadia was using her and would trample on her heart one day, just as she had Christian's.

'Okay, well... apology accepted,' Maria lightened her voice. 'Do you still want to use the time for tuition?'

'No thanks,' Sam shook herself down. 'I think I'll go to the library, there's some stuff I need to look up.'

'Fine,' Maria squeezed out a tired smile, then stood and went to escort Sam out of her office door. 'Let's make a fresh start next week.'

Sam nodded and smiled graciously, it was a sight to see.

As Maria opened her door, letting Sam out, she noticed another student waiting outside. It was Nadia.

Sam smiled at Nadia and Nadia nodded to Sam. 'I'll meet you in there, okay?'

Sam nodded and ducked her head down as she staggered away, pulling her shirt and jumper down where they had risen up over her backside. She must have known Nadia was outside waiting the whole time.

Wondering if Nadia had put her up to that apology, Maria stared down at the auburn haired girl in front of her now, and knew she had no choice but to let her in to her office. The wiry weather outside seemed to come inside with her, and the change in the atmosphere felt as if it could induce schizophrenia; Maria knew something intense was about to occur.

Unravel

Closing the door behind them in silence, Maria felt her heartbeat rising; having Nadia stand in her private room. The static in her hair lifted up the strands across Nadia's shoulders; it was no longer raining, but Nadia looked damp, her face covered in a light mist, her cheeks rose-coloured. Her breath lifted her bosom under her shirt as she stared back at Maria seeming to have grown in stature, with defiance or lust, maybe both.

Yet her power seemed to diminish as the seconds passed when she failed to say what she had probably planned to once in Maria's presence. She gaped and fluttered, her stance shifting ever downwards as she summoned her bravery.

'What did you do to Sam?' Maria spoke gently and moved to her desk.

'Huh?' Nadia looked flushed.

Maria tried to be humorous. 'She's different... she's nice,' but it just sounded sarcastic.

'I told her to have more respect,' Nadia sighed impatiently.

'Was that part of your plan?' Maria raised her eyebrows.

'Yes,' Nadia gushed, stepping forward. 'It's working... no one knows *anything*... and I want to keep it that way.'

Maria folded her arms and leaned against her desk. 'You haven't told anyone?'

'No! And I know you must be worried, that's what I wanted to talk to you about!'

Rubbing her brow, Maria lowered her voice. 'We can't have this discussion in school.'

Nadia moved closer to Maria and whispered. 'But you won't talk to me outside school... I need you to know you can trust me.'

It felt too much, too close, too quiet, too weird, and Maria stepped away towards the windows, yet she felt the pull from Nadia as she would a net that had caught them both.

'I can't ask you to keep this secret for me!' Maria seethed through her jaw that ached with tension. 'I can't ask you not to tell anyone because it makes me feel like I'm some sort of fucking paedophile, Nadia, so I have to tell you to talk to someone, okay?'

'You want me to tell someone? Anyone in particular?' Nadia scorned.

'Listen,' Maria turned, emotion pricking her eyes. 'The sheer fact that I feel relieved that you haven't told anyone what happened makes me feel sick! We can't be colluding on this, do you understand? So even if it gets me in trouble, I'm telling you to talk to someone, because *what happened* was wrong.'

'*What happened* was my fault...' Nadia approached Maria, whispering. 'I kissed you!'

'And I kissed you back...' Maria tightened her whisper. 'I shouldn't have!'

Nadia appealed. 'I'm not going to tell anyone.'

Creasing her eyes, Maria felt her tears brimming. 'I don't need you to protect me.'

Nadia touched Maria's arm desperately. 'I promise you it won't happen again.'

'How can you say that?' Maria hissed. 'You don't know what will happen, you have no control.' Maria blinked shocked droplets, knowing too well she was the one with no control.

'Why are you crying?' Nadia gazed up at Maria, her eyes dancing with fascination.

Maria's resentment flared. 'You're not the only one with feelings, Nadia,' she spun to the windows to hide her emotion. 'I think you should go.'

With her back to Nadia, she couldn't tell if the girl had even registered her confession until Nadia spoke, and Maria realised she had interpreted her words differently.

'If you're so fucking scared, why don't *you* tell someone?' Nadia scorned.

'What?' Maria turned around to face her again.

'Go on! Run to the principal and tell him how awful it was, how you couldn't stop it! How I told you I loved you and then jumped on you, make me sound like some sort of animal, because I'm *so* out of control, and you're *such* a victim. Tell him you hated every second of it, especially the bit where you pinned me against your car-'

Maria switched. Her hands flew to clamp over Nadia's mouth and the back of her head and she pushed

Unravel

the girl back against her desk. Nadia sprawled and gripped the desk edge for support, a high, muffled scream escaping as Maria loomed over her, pressing her legs apart.

Standing there, her fingers hushing Nadia's loud words, Maria's eyes spilled angry tears close to Nadia's face. 'Maybe I *should* go to the principal,' Maria spat, her lips curling up, 'before I do something I really regret.'

Blinking back at Maria, Nadia's cheeks rushed with colour, her body quivered under Maria's close contact and her legs twitched a contraction Maria felt emanating from the girl's hips. Nadia lifted her hand to grasp Maria's arm and groped up along her forearm, squeezing the muscle under the fabric of her shirt, before her fingers tugged at Maria's hand over her mouth.

With no choice but to release her, Maria let Nadia guide her hand away and watched as Nadia panted her breath back. The girl sucked her lips, looking closely at Maria's. She had surrendered to Maria's powerful advance and her eyes had dilated, she trembled and held herself open.

Maria felt a shockwave as she knew Nadia wanted to kiss her again. Her own lips were wet with tears and it would be so good, so deep and so right, just like last time.

But she couldn't. They were in school - anyone could come in. Maria shuddered and pulled her body aside, stepping away, tearing herself back from Nadia's temptation. She averted her eyes and shut down her emotion, observing her periphery silently and painfully as Nadia quickly retrieved her bag and left her office, still panting, and shocked.

Chapter Twenty-Three

Getting home without losing her mind was the hardest, most dangerous trial Maria had endured yet. Suppressed howls of agony built up in her as she drove out of town, trying to keep her face straight and the blurring wobble of tears from disturbing her vision. She had nearly revealed everything to Nadia, at the very least she had shown further weakness in her professionalism.

More frightened than she could remember being in all her adult life, Maria climbed into her house at three o'clock, doubled over with anxiety twisting her insides. She was grateful to have a few hours before she needed to collect Leon from Christian's house: she needed to collapse, overwhelmed by the paranoid thoughts and crippling, self-directed anger at letting this perverted fantasy get so out of hand. Her stomach panged with angst when she thought of how close she had come to letting slip to Nadia. Chronically embarrassed, shocked and ashamed, Maria lay on her couch and heaved with disgrace - and it could all get so much worse if Nadia didn't leave her alone.

If Nadia had learned her feelings were reciprocated, Maria wondered who would be next to hear of their sordid affair, as it felt inevitable that people would. Word that this teacher, renowned for her excellence, desired her same-sex student seemed to be one of those irresistible nuggets of gossip that would get passed on for years to come, becoming part of GCH's school legend. Maria could see herself becoming *that* teacher with the tainted mark against her name: it seemed already a new identity, written out in her destiny.

Pouring a glass of whisky felt like the only thing Maria could do without doubting if she could manage it all or fearing the repercussions of drinking it. It went down easily and Maria gasped with a small, dry choke from the strong alcohol. It burned her throat pleasantly, though the surge in her veins made her eyes sting with fresh tears, and she felt sorry for herself again. She sat at her breakfast bar, reminding herself of her little old Sicilian grandfather, Popa, hunched on a stool, staring into a glass, rubbing his head, having spent the last of his savings in the bar. There, with her head in her hands, up to an hour could have passed - Maria could no longer keep track of time in her state of near-breakdown; her thoughts spiralling out, her feelings simultaneously imploding like a black hole.

When she heard a knock at her front door, everything sucked, very suddenly, back into reality; her heart started again. Sitting up straight, Maria became alert and horrified all at once; she wasn't expecting anyone. Christian would have called first if he'd needed to drop off her dog, and any other neighbour wouldn't just show up without a good reason. Her pulse fed hard; there was only one person who might turn up unannounced on her doorstep: Nadia.

Nadia was the one person who meant so much she could destroy everything. The idea that she was outside, wanting to come in, filled Maria with the pure dread of facing her darkest, most fantastic dream. She didn't know if she could let Nadia in. It felt as if allowing her in would make everything all right, yet might subsequently lead to the end of the world. However, after a swift mental slap, Maria realised she was winding herself up again: it might not be Nadia. Obeying some inherent religious duty to welcome a potential intervention in her time of need, Maria figured she should answer the door before whoever it was went away. In the unlikelihood that it was a Jehovah's Witness, Maria knew she would welcome them in anyway; she needed all the help she could get.

The rap came again from the door. Maria slid off her stool, feeling sodden with whisky and torment. Checking her tired face in the lounge mirror, she sighed and wiped away the creases from around her eyes, then went to the door. Opening it, she settled weary eyes on

Unravel

Nadia, standing anxiously in her doorway, the ends of her hair wet where the hood of her army parka had failed to shelter all of her from the rain. She had removed her school tie, and the top buttons of her white shirt were undone.

'You shouldn't have come here,' Maria said with a heavy heart.

'Well, I'm here now,' Nadia crackled impatiently. 'I don't care if you don't want to talk, I need to sort this out.'

Rubbing her brow, Maria shook her head and stepped aside with resignation to the inevitable. Nadia moved through into the lounge, sliding her coat off whilst heading to the kitchen. She hung it on the back of a chair, and Maria marvelled at how comfortably Nadia then took a glass from her cupboard and poured herself some whisky. She topped up Maria's glass, and passed it to Maria, who had to unfold her arms from the tight, guilty clutch around her ribs to receive it in silent surprise.

'I had time to think on the bus over here,' Nadia headed assertively back through to Maria's lounge and sat on the deep leather couch, tucking her tight black leggings under the coffee table. 'There I was, too busy worrying about ruining our friendship... not letting anyone find out what we did... but when you were upset earlier, I started wondering why.'

Remaining stood in the alcove by her kitchen Maria awkwardly held her glass and hooked a thumb in her pocket. 'I wasn't upset, I was just tired.'

'You were crying!' Nadia exclaimed, 'and I got to thinking about...' Nadia softened her tone, 'our kiss... maybe you didn't hate it so much, and that's why you were so scared.'

'I don't know what you're talking about,' Maria grumbled her willing ignorance.

'Maria, I *felt something*!' Nadia's Irish sounded emphasised. 'From you! Today, when you tried to shut me up by *pouncing* on me,' Nadia's eyes flickered with bemusement, 'it felt like you wanted to kiss me – and it made me think over the way we kissed before, like you wanted to... like you wanted *me*.'

'I just got carried away!' Maria dismissed, letting her head roll on her neck.

'I don't believe that!' Nadia stared. 'I think you liked it as much as I did.'

'I think you're fantasising,' Maria slurred and took another swig.

'Maria, it's okay!' Nadia appealed. 'I'm still not going to tell anyone, but I need to know.'

'What do you need to know?' Maria blurted, waving her glass indignantly.

'That it meant something!' Nadia pleaded. 'I told you I was in love with you and you let me kiss you! I know I asked, but it didn't feel like you were doing me a favour...'

'That's all it was, I felt sorry for you.'

'I don't think you're that cold.'

'You don't know me.'

'I think I do! I think you liked it and it's freaked you out!'

'Who's arrogant now?' Maria smarted.

'You could have gone to the principal, but you didn't, why? You could have sat me down and done the "professional teacher" speech, but you didn't, you avoided me, you ignored me, why?' Nadia demanded. 'Because until I came to your office today, I never thought it would happen again... now I'm not so sure.'

'You want me to admit I liked it?' Maria flipped her palm in the air. 'Sure, I liked it! There – you happy?'

Nadia lifted her chin higher. 'And do you like me being in love with you?'

The tension in her body broke as Maria realised she had to stop Nadia's line of questioning. She moved towards her, seating herself on the coffee table opposite her and placing her drink down gently, trying to calm her nerves.

'Nadia, you're not in love with me, you just think you are because I'm a lesbian and you look up to me,' she said sympathetically. 'If you had someone else, you wouldn't idolise me.'

'Don't tell me how I feel!' Nadia snapped, her accent harsher than before. 'It might have started out like a silly crush, and I denied it because I thought it would pass – but this is more than that – you know this is real, don't you?'

'No, I don't.' Maria sat back again, averting her eyes from Nadia's pretty passion.

'Yes you do!' Nadia urged. 'You *know* you're the first thing I think about when I wake up in the morning, you're the only reason I come to school!' She half laughed. 'When I think about seeing you, I get so nervous, I tremble, but when I'm with you everything feels right, and my insides feel warm... and when I'm not with you I ache, Maria, I ache because being apart from you feels so wrong.'

The girl's romantic words made Maria's insides melt too, but she couldn't let Nadia see her softening before her. She hardened herself, bristling with whisky.

'You want to be with me, Nadia? You want to be my girlfriend?' Maria opened her arms mockingly. 'Can't you hear how delusional that sounds?'

Nadia sat forward, incensed. 'I never thought we could be together, I'm not that stupid! I know you care about being a teacher and professional boundaries and all that shit - but I want to know why you let me kiss you! And before that, when I told you I loved you, you said you didn't want to stop seeing me! What the fuck does that mean? The only times you've ever warned me away was when you were worried about what others will say - how it looks to others around us. I mean, if no one else existed, what would happen then?

Would you mind us hanging out? Would you mind if we got closer? Would you mind if we kissed again?'

'Would you stop it?' Maria snarled. 'Stop reading into things!'

'Yeah, I think I'm onto something, that's why you're so afraid of talking to me, because I've figured it out. You said I'm not the only one with feelings, I didn't get it at the time, I would never have believed it, but you like me too,' Nadia asserted, 'don't you?'

'What do you want me to say, Nadia?' Maria shrugged defensively. 'Okay, so I kissed you when I shouldn't have... I got sucked in because I like you - I didn't realise it would feel so good. I messed with your feelings and made everything more difficult, and I'm sorry, I'm really fucking sorry! I never meant this to happen! I'm supposed to be your teacher and I let you down because my feelings got wrapped up in yours - I couldn't be less professional! I mean, you come in and you're cute and... troubled and... then you tell me you're a lesbian... and everything I held up about myself goes flying out of the window. I like spending time with you, sweetheart, I genuinely enjoy your company, but we crossed a line, we got too close and we went too far... now it has to stop!'

Nadia had slowly deflated into a slump, as Maria's words appeared to have overwhelmed her. She blinked widely and giant splashes of tears hit her hands holding her glass.

The guilt in Maria's heart doubled seeing the reality of her rejection hitting Nadia. She wished she could reach out and console the girl, but Maria could not let her guard down any further. She sat stiffly, reflecting on her words, wondering if she said the right thing, or if she said too much. It felt good to tell the truth at least, even if it was the drink talking; she could feel the sway of whisky in her brain as she tilted it to the ceiling and exhaled her relief.

When she looked back down, Nadia had fixed her eyes on her again. They were sharply angled and swirling with moisture, two green pools fizzing with electricity. The girl sat up straight and brought her glass to her lips. Maria watched her sip, swallow, and lick her lips.

'How long?' Nadia asked, her voice catching.

'What?' Maria murmured, staring back, hard.

'How long have you liked me? Since we kissed? Since seeing me with Sam made you jealous? Since Christian told you I came saying your name? Since my birthday when I kissed your neck? Since I came out to you after we woke up in your bed? Before that?' Nadia's mind was working terribly hard. 'All the times you accused me of having feelings? All the times you made me feel like shit for liking you when I couldn't help it? Did you like me that whole time? When did you know?'

'I don't know!' Maria's eyes widened with surprise.

'That's bullshit!' Nadia slammed her glass down. 'You're a fucking hypocrite!' Nadia stood up and went to the kitchen to get her things.

'Where are you going?' Maria stood desperately.

'Anywhere! I can't deal with this!' Nadia clutched her coat and bag, heading for the door. 'Maybe I'll go and see Sam!' She said spitefully.

Banging her shin on her coffee table, Maria reached out in a panic. 'Nadia, don't go!'

'Fuck you!' Nadia switched direction and lashed out at Maria, pushing her backwards away from her. 'How could you make me feel so fucking stupid, when you're just as bad?'

'I couldn't tell you! I couldn't tell anyone!' Maria begged. 'I'm not supposed to feel this way, you're my student - I had to discourage you, you know that!' Maria lowered her voice. 'Believe me, it hurt me as much to hurt you, but I couldn't risk you finding out. This has never happened to me before, I have never fallen for a student, I don't know what to do...' Maria felt her words slipping out of her mouth before she could stop them: it felt too good to say them out loud. 'Do you have any idea how much trouble I could get in for even having these feelings? I keep making mistakes because I've lost control and all perspective of what I should be doing - what any other teacher would do.' She staggered backwards, rubbing her head. 'I didn't report it when I first found out you had feelings for me,

I should have, but I was afraid they'd stop our tuition and I didn't want that. And when I tried to tell the principal and some others that we were getting too close, they told me I was doing a great job and to carry on – I was the one who was alone and confused!'

'You were never going to tell me?' Nadia asked, still accusing with disbelief. 'You wanted to keep this secret?'

'I thought it would freak you out,' Maria winced.

'It has!' Nadia grimaced.

Maria folded with a dizzy wave of sorrow and nausea. She sat against the armrest of the couch and wiped her face.

'Please don't think I'm some perverted teacher, you know I'm not like that... All the things you were saying... I felt... I feel them, too.'

Nadia softened, her hands slipping from her hips. 'You do?'

Maria looked up at her sincerely, feeling her heart open for the first time and it consumed her with emotion.

'I miss you when we're not together, I think about you all the time... Nadia, I had to push you away to do what's best for you – but I didn't want to lose you... I tried to hide this, but I can't, not from you... you're the only one who understands how I feel.'

After precious moments of absorption and comprehension, Nadia replied.

'You're in love with me?' she asked breathlessly.

Maria nodded, and let her tears fall freely. 'And I've never been more scared.'

Moving closer, Nadia stepped between Maria's legs, and raised her hands to her shoulders. 'It's okay,' she soothed.

Shaking her head, Maria felt lost in her despair. 'It's not okay,' she wept, unable to rest in the swell and scent of Nadia's breast.

Rubbing the back of Maria's neck in the same way Maria often did, Nadia used reassuring tones to help ease Maria's fears. '*We'll* be okay,' Nadia whispered into her hair. 'We'll just have to keep it *our* secret.'

Lifting her forehead away from Nadia's chest, Maria gazed into her eyes, searching for signs that Nadia knew what she was saying, what it meant.

Nadia cupped Maria's face in her hands and wiped her tears with her thumbs, smiling with disbelief at the opportunity to touch her teacher so intimately at last. She gazed back into Maria's eyes. 'You have to trust me that I won't tell anyone, because I want to keep this...' Nadia breathed sensually on Maria's lips, 'for us.'

'Us?' Maria whispered in awe. She closed her eyes a second later when Nadia leaned in and enveloped her mouth in a warm kiss. A tingling shot of pleasure went straight down between her thighs, the same as the first time. Maria knew this was real.

Standing, Maria took Nadia in her arms and felt the girl weaken in her embrace. Their kiss deepened shortly before Maria felt her own body shaking down to her feet. She guided Nadia around the side of the couch, to sit more comfortably. There, with their knees pressing together and whisky infusing their united breath, Maria held her protectively and carefully let her hand slide down over Nadia's thigh. She couldn't believe she was doing it; couldn't believe she had Nadia in her arms. She felt the girl becoming lustful as she moaned and grasped Maria's shoulders.

Their bodies automatically fell into recline and they cuddled side by side on the couch, kissing slowly and hungrily, trembling and gasping to catch their breath. The heat between them rose quickly, making their skin sticky and flushed. Nadia kicked off her boots, lifting her leg to allow Maria's thigh to press between hers, and huffing gently with arousal, she writhed against it and kissed Maria's neck, right on the spot that made her teacher lose control.

Maria struggled to co-ordinate her hands as her mind reeled with the reality of what was happening. She held Nadia close and wanted to open her blouse, caress her breasts, and peel her tight trousers down; she felt the hot urges spreading her wetness and knew they could do it all right here - that Nadia wanted her to and would let her do anything. However, Maria knew she

Unravel

could not get carried away, it pained her to stop it but she had to.

'Please don't stop...' Nadia moaned, pulling Maria back into her steamy corner of the couch, but Maria squirmed away, and held Nadia's hands from grabbing.

'We mustn't,' she explained, her voice rocky with desire. 'We can't go further.

'No one will find out, I swear,' Nadia begged.

Maria leaned on her elbow and gazed down at Nadia's small earring, glinting in the lamp light. 'Look, it's one thing to have feelings for each other, but something else to act on them, that would be wrong.'

'What?' Nadia turned quickly upset with frustration. She sat up, pouting and frowning.

'We just have to take a step back and think about this, we can't just jump in with both feet,' Maria reasoned, sitting up, too. She gulped and adjusted herself, smoothing her hair and clothes. She felt herself going into teacher mode and she struggled to contain the dismay she knew would inevitably come for unleashing her lust demon so prematurely. 'We have to be patient, wait until the time is right.'

'How long do we have to wait?' Nadia slouched, her lips full and eyes darkly dilated.

Maria shrugged. 'Legally... until you're eighteen, I guess.'

Scowling, Nadia shifted to the edge of the couch. 'I can't wait that long!'

Catching her before she bolted again, Maria held Nadia's hand. 'If this is real then it's worth waiting for... at least until the end of school.'

As she sighed away her glare, Nadia looked more kindly down at Maria's hand on hers; she took a moment then smiled to acknowledge the sentiment. 'You're like a gentleman...'

'Excuse me?' Maria mocked a frown.

Nadia chuckled. 'A gentle-lesbian?'

Letting herself laugh, Maria shook her head. 'That's two strikes...'

'Okay!' Nadia wiped her face afresh, smiling happily. 'I can wait... I'll wait for you.'

'That's better.'

Everything inside Maria seemed to sigh all at once. She smiled humbly and rubbed Nadia's hand in hers, then pulled her towards her for a tender kiss. They gripped each other after a few moments, for dear life, it felt. Maria sensed Nadia's sadness and desperation that they might never see the day when they could make love properly without fear of judgement and punishment; Maria felt that too. But it was one exciting prospect.

'Can I stay with you tonight?' Nadia asked as she pulled back. 'I won't try anything I swear.'

Maria gazed back at Nadia, entranced by the bow shape of her engorged lips and piercingly attentive eyes. She pursed her own lips, trying not to smile, but she couldn't help it.

This girl.

This is the girl, Maria thought, *who has my heart. This is the girl who has the rest of my life in her hands.*

Chapter Twenty-Four

Though Nadia had insisted her father wouldn't notice, Maria couldn't allow Nadia to stay over that night. It wouldn't have been right: it was too soon and it was a dangerous practice to get into - having agreed to wait, the temptation of removal of clothes might bear too much. Maria empathised with Nadia's urge to bond, but that small niggle of doubt straining to balance her overwhelmingly biased judgment pressed upon her that she only knew of Peter Sheridan what Nadia told her, and she didn't yet fully know if she could trust what Nadia had revealed about her father, on the basis that it was very little. Maria had still not met this single parent - this ex-nurse, this workaholic - and something about it disturbed her. Not that she wanted to meet him, especially not to ask for permission for his daughter to sleep with her, but the fact that he remained a passively threatening influence from the shadows only added to the darkness of Maria's paranoia.

After taking Nadia back, driving slowly through the rain and alcohol in her system, Maria returned home to find a hungry Leon there waiting for her; Christian must have brought him back in her absence. She looked at her watch, it was gone seven o'clock, and though it was disorienting to think she had spent so long with Nadia, Maria felt remarkably changed. She felt better: her heart felt lighter, her brain was dazed, pleasantly surreal. Her thoughts were not so constantly clouded with Nadia but drifted with a heady swirling sensation every time she remembered what had occurred between them. Their confrontation had been exhausting and epic, and Maria held her pillow that night as if it were Nadia, and slept more soundly than she had done, so far that year.

The beautiful dreaminess of her waking state, on recalling their emotional union, stayed with Maria throughout the next day, through her travels, her tuitions, and her meetings. She clung joyously to the contented feeling within her that Nadia was hers; their pact was a thrilling and troubling secret that kept her insides skipping and her breath trembling with excitement.

Maria attended the weekly staff meeting with her learning support team. However, on anticipating mention of Nadia Sheridan, Maria prepared her outward reactions so they would not be observable, though every muscle in her body warned her that hearing the girl's name could make her involuntarily buckle out of her seat. She would have to suppress every little flinch or else get busted for her obvious affections. No doubt, they had either witnessed or heard of Nadia's relations with Sam Burrows and they must have all been wondering how Maria was dealing with Nadia in tuition, probably dying to ask out of curiosity how she was coping with the new lesbian dynamic.

Victoria Duncan, there yet again, raised her concerns as soon as Nadia's turn arrived.

'I'm really worried that Nadia and Sam are going to drag each other down with all this business,' the form tutor said, flipping her hand dismissively. 'I'm not sure what is going on and I don't want to know, but I can't help feeling it will have negative results.'

'It's hardly serious, Vicky, they're just having fun,' Tom Berry chimed with a shrug. 'Let kids be kids I say!'

'Neither of them are gay, they are just doing it for attention.' Fat Sandra nodded at Tom, her dark brown cleavage wobbling.

'I think they secretly hate each other and this is the only way they can stop arguing,' smiled Ruth, the member of the learning support team Maria liked the least, an irritating rat-faced creature; but on this issue she made an interesting point. 'Make love not war an' all that!' Ruth chuckled, looking around for support.

Maria felt her nerves shudder. She was amazed, listening to the others mocking, chiding and dismissing Nadia and Sam's relationship, but as she bit the inside

Unravel

of her cheek to remind herself to keep quiet, Principal Woods asked her opinion.

'What are your thoughts on this, Maria?'

Scratching the back of her hair, Maria cleared her throat with a grumble. 'Nadia's definitely distracted... but I'm working on it.'

Principal Woods pouted, his arms folded as he kicked the table nervously with one foot.

'I know there have been some discussions around whether Miss Burrows and Miss Sheridan are genuine or not, but regardless of that, we need to ensure the other students are not disturbed from their studies.'

'Excuse me?' Karen Lenholm interrupted from the other side of the staff room. 'Why would students be disturbed if two of their classmates became involved? And why the assumption that it's not genuine?'

Mr Woods smarted and twisted around, seemingly disgruntled by Karen's political correctness as well as her intrusion from the tea station. 'When I said disturbed, I meant distracted, but let's not be naive here,' Xavier Woods turned back round to address the team, ignoring Karen. '*Any* new relationship is bound to cause some degree of excitement amongst the pupils, but a *lesbian* relationship is certain to create stirrings of a kind not appropriate, or welcome, during this period of concentrated exam revision.' He went to cross his legs, but stopped himself.

Victoria Duncan piped up in his defence. 'I agree! As Maria explained, Miss Sheridan herself is distracted, I just don't want to hear any complaints from parents that their children are pre-occupied by thoughts of these kind.'

'Of what? Homosexual relationships?' Karen blurted out defensively. 'So now it's inappropriate to even contemplate sexuality? Christ, this is worse than a catholic school!'

Joining the other teachers in a general squirm, Maria wondered if she could back Karen up on this one. But her head felt too crowded with thoughts of self-preservation to put together a coherent argument to support the gay cause.

'What are you even doing here?' Karen yelled directly at Victoria. 'You're not in learning support!'

'Nadia and Sam are both in my form and have issues with learning,' Victoria fired back. 'What are you doing here? This is a meeting!'

'I can make myself a drink, can't I?' Karen retorted. 'Talk about human rights.'

'Ladies, please!' Woods intervened. 'I'm sure we could continue this inspiring debate another time, but for now we have an agenda to keep to.'

'Like there's any time for the gays,' Karen muttered, determined to have the last word, and turned her attention to the kettle to finish making her coffee.

Bemused by the direction the conversation had taken, Maria kept her calm and checked that she had not said or done anything to antagonise that situation, now the air was suitably uncomfortable, and a swift topic change brought in. Happy that she hadn't contributed to the awkwardness, Maria relaxed and felt she had spoken appropriately; more importantly, she had not lied. With Karen now replacing her as the difficult lesbian, Maria sat back with her fingers to her chin, and wondered how they could all be so blind. She couldn't even sense a vague inkling that they might see through Nadia's behavioural intentions, but if they did, they were not saying anything in front of her. Maria was incredulous that no-one had talked about her relationship with Nadia, they were too distracted by talk of Nadia with Sam. That understanding led to the realisation that Nadia's plan had indeed worked.

When Karen found her afterwards in the dining hall, she cornered Maria in their regular booth, sitting too closely for Maria's comfort.

'So what do you make of that crock of shit?' Karen moaned. 'Do you agree with him? You still believe those girls aren't for real when they're still hanging off each other?'

'He didn't say it wasn't real,' Maria replied with a sigh, 'he just knows they're both attention seekers and he's rightfully worried the others will lose focus from their studies.'

'You *do* agree with him!' Karen prodded her elbow with an accusing glare. 'Let me ask you one thing – why in the world would they fake it? When it's so hard for gay boys and baby dykes to come out at school; when they have to suffer the prejudice and intolerance of ignorant bastards everywhere – why would they dream of pretending?'

Wincing at her foolish mistake, Maria realised again she was not helping her own situation by insinuating Nadia was even partially responsible in fabricating the pairing. She needed to shut her mouth and let Karen think it was real, what she wanted to believe, so she didn't ask any more questions. Hoping she hadn't already planted a seed of doubt into Karen's mind, Maria shrugged as casually as she could.

'Who knows what's really going on in their heads?' she said, and forced herself to eat her roasted pepper and hummus wrap though it stuck in her throat like insoluble bricks of guilt.

♥

Several hours later, Maria found herself at home, smiling at the intonation of Nadia's text messages; she got a kick out of the generous series of full stops that dotted along after her lingering sentiments, and especially the kiss. That small 'x' meant so much. It reassured her that Nadia was sincere, though she struggled to permit herself to return such evidence of her declaration. If anyone read Nadia's phone inbox, Maria wanted to ensure they would find nothing incriminating from her. Still, warmed by the affirmation, Maria gave Leon his evening meal and went to her bedroom to change into her gym clothes. Allowing herself to feel joyfully content for the first in a long time, she felt enough motivation to head down to her local gym for a work out. However, as soon as she pulled her trainers on, Maria heard her phone ring. She felt a buzz of excitement, wondering if it was Nadia. It wasn't though, Maria saw as soon as she scooped up her mobile: it was Lois.

'Hi...' Maria said tentatively, knowing something was going to be wrong.

'Hi? That's it?' Lois replied sharply, mocking Maria's voice in her cutting Melbourne accent. 'I was hoping you'd say: *Sorry baby, I've been meaning to call you all day, but I didn't get a chance, let me take you out to dinner.*'

'Why would I do that?' Maria grimaced, not appreciating Lois' tone.

'Oh my god, you really have forgotten!' Lois exclaimed and audibly stamped her heels. 'How could you be so fucking retarded? It's my birthday, Maria, I can't believe you've forgotten!'

Maria pulled her mobile away from her ear and cursed silently. The date came back to her and she realised it was true. The months had passed so quickly while her mind had been so preoccupied with Nadia that she had not given even one thought to celebrating Lois' twenty-eighth, and now that she was taking too long to think of an excuse, Maria knew pretending to have forgotten was out of the door. She couldn't feign an act for Lois anyway. She couldn't be bothered and it wasn't her style.

'Jesus, I'm sorry,' Maria began, 'I had no idea what the date was, my whole calendar is focused around work... I didn't even-'

'You didn't even think about me!' Lois shouted down the phone, 'and after I spent so much on that watch I got you for your birthday - the one you never wear! Fuck, you're ungrateful!'

'I said I'm sorry, Lo!' Maria appealed. 'You should have reminded me!'

'Why the fuck should I remind you when you can't spare a second to do something nice for me, any time of the year, let alone my birthday? You're so wrapped up in your stupid job at that school, you're forgetting you're supposed to be in a relationship!' Lois snarled.

'Hey, you've been working on your own thing too. In fact, you're always doing your own thing, you never have time for me,' Maria said, defensively, and immediately regretted it.

Dangling a few seconds of painful silence over the phone, Lois' tight mouth gave a bitter response. 'Are you criticising me on my birthday?'

'What do you want me to say, Lois?' Maria asked, rubbing her head. Her eyes felt suddenly sore, her temples pulsed with blood and she felt a fake, angry

Unravel

smile leap from the depth of her sarcasm. 'Happy birthday... Sweetheart!'

Lois made her tone light with a testing cruelty. 'I want you to treat me to dinner, then take me out to a cocktail bar, then take me home and fuck me... really hard!' She ended with a cold fury. 'Can you do that, darling? Can you do any of those things for me?'

'Can we do it another time?' Maria made her voice gruff. 'I have a migraine coming on.'

'Like fuck you have!' Lois spat, the disgust in her voice undisguised. 'You can't pull a stunt like that to get out of this - since when do you get migraines?'

'Pretty much any time someone phones me up screeching,' Maria growled.

'Oh really? I'll give you screeching!' Lois screamed down the line, her nasal pitch shooting up, piercing Maria's ear. Her hand automatically jerked her phone away from her head but Maria could still hear Lois continue to yell from the mobile in her hand. She couldn't help but listen – it was about her – and though it was harshly negative, it was all accurate. It felt like a worthy punishment for her infidelity to hear Lois spitting and raging at her, and Maria could only imagine the reaction if Lois ever found out the real reasons she was neglecting her.

Sitting on her couch, her head genuinely pummelling, Maria knew she would not make it to the gym and put her head in her hands. Placing the phone on her coffee table in front of her, she left Lois screaming her tinny, rasping tirade, and after a minute, it became a blur of words. Maria could only listen to so much before her natural defences kicked in; she didn't deserve that level of abuse. She stuffed her phone under the cushion to hide the noise – she couldn't incur Lois' wrath even more by hanging up on her birthday, but hopefully Lois would hang up after her fury was spent and she realised Maria had left her to it. That often worked with Lois: to allow her to tire herself so that she felt better, and then sorry for losing her temper. Long-suffering Maria could not summon the energy to fight her girlfriend anymore; their relationship had ended and this was just the start of their ugly separation.

It occurred to Maria that Lois had been drinking, hence her ready anger and unfiltered choice of words. Now seemed as good a time as any to drink, given that the opportunity to share it with Lois for her birthday had long gone, and that in itself was something to celebrate.

♥

Two hours later, Maria's drunken guilt overwhelmed her and she dialled Ben's number, squeezing balls of tears from her sore eyes. Why drinking had seemed a good idea she could not fathom, but having forgotten about her headache, Maria was left with the terrible remorse from forgetting Lois' birthday; the shameful reality that signified her lack of loving care, and the inevitable slipping of her control when it was Nadia who occupied her every consideration.

Finishing the bottle of whisky facilitated her depression, and as Ben answered, Maria couldn't speak for a minute, trying to control her breath so she didn't sob and break down.

'Ria?' Ben excused himself from his noisy quarters and moved to a quieter room, responding immediately to her uncharacteristic hesitance. 'What's going on?'

Just hearing his deep, soothing voice made Maria weep even more, and she folded her knees up under her chin and hugged herself, rocking softly to calm her emotional crisis.

'Everything's fucked,' her voice emerged as a whisper, then blurted as she coughed through a whisky-infused globule in her throat. 'I'm a thirty-two year old fuck-up and there's nothing I can do about it. I'm screwing everything up but I can't stop... I can't stop it...'

'Hang on, what the fuck is this about?' Ben said firmly, cutting straight to the point. Appreciating that he wasn't one to fuss over such claims with: 'It's not true', or: 'No, you're wrong', Maria couldn't tell him the truth of what was plaguing her, tormenting her deeply, but she had to tell him something.

Gulping hard and sniffing up the excess fluid congesting her head, Maria felt dizzy as she closed her eyes and gathered the more acceptable reasons.

'I forgot Lois' birthday. She went nuts... told me I'm a shit girlfriend, that I don't care about anyone but myself, that I'm cold and unloving... and the worst thing is, she's right about that - I don't love her anymore. I don't care about the things she does, or the shit she talks about,' Maria heard herself slurring and tried to pick up her words, 'but it's not true that I don't care about anyone but myself. I have a lot of love to give to someone who needs me, who is sweet and loving and doesn't...' Maria lifted her head and her brain swayed wave-like after it, 'doesn't make me feel fucking useless...'

'Ria, please,' Ben said, and hearing the steadfastness in his voice made her nerves tremble through her body. 'I'm glad you've finally decided to break up with that hell-cunt, you are better off without her. Just don't be losing your confidence 'cause of her, someone perfect will come along.'

'Perfect?' Maria half-laughed sorely. 'What if Miss Perfect comes along when you're having a mid-life crisis?'

Ben was quiet for a few seconds longer than Maria would have liked. It sobered her up somewhat as she listened for his continued presence on the other end, briefly thinking it typical that she received the same treatment she had given Lois mere hours earlier.

'So how are things with Nadia?' Ben asked directly. He sighed through his nose gently and Maria imagined he'd just pressed his fingers against his chest with his bicep, as he always did when he was listening intently on the phone. 'Last time we spoke you said she was seeing Christian. Is everything still cool?'

Maria's couldn't breathe for fear that the suck of air would give her away. However, it was obviously too late: Ben knew.

He knew something was going on with Nadia. Damn his intuition.

'Look,' Maria tried to explain. 'Nadia's sweet, she's just... She came out to me and it's kind of changed things... made things kind of awkward.' Wiping fresh tears, Maria felt sudden release at actually talking to Ben about it, however restrained their discussion was about to become.

'Ria, listen,' Ben responded with an even deeper, quieter lull in his voice. 'Just because Lois makes you feel bad, doesn't mean you should be flattered by just any fresh interest. Nadia is a beautiful young woman, and intriguing I'm sure, but don't get confused, okay? You need to stay focused on your job and keep your distance, yeah?'

Her face falling, Maria wept into her knees. Partially with the humiliation that her cousin knew of her strange relationship with her student, but mostly because she wished that she could explain to him how happy it made her that Nadia had agreed to wait until things were right. There was no way she could reveal that now; Ben expected her to heed his advice, and he wouldn't want to hear any more drunken excuses. She had called him for a reason – to ask for his help – now she had to acknowledge that from an outsider's perspective, it sounded ungrateful to refuse it. Thanking Ben for his support, Maria replaced her phone and collapsed sideways onto her couch, where she let Leon lick the salt from her cheeks and nose.

She tried to imagine she were someone else - another teacher in her situation. She would be horrified to hear of a secret, sordid pact between a trusted tutor and their assigned student, on the promise of a relationship at some future point. The idea made her feel sick. The reality that she *was* that perverted tutor resulted in a rush of saliva coating the inside of her mouth, which was just enough notice to allow her to bolt towards her kitchen sink before she vomited surges of whisky water.

Maria clung on to the edge, heaving deeply with the realisation that her affair with Nadia was entirely wrong and, indeed, sickening. She knew she must be having that mid-life crisis she spoke of to Ben. There was no way things could end in any way other than badly with Miss Perfect. She had a duty to stop this before it really started.

Unravel

Chapter Twenty-Five

The morning after was spent with a rancid hangover and bilious self-disgust, and Maria felt some part of her soul, as well as her body, was truly poisoned. She could still smell the whisky-sick on her skin even though she had leaned under a hot shower for fifteen minutes. Creeping downstairs to an anxious Leon that morning, Maria let him out into the garden after apologising for worrying him, with cuddles and whispers.

She had slept off her nausea but her tiredness was dragging her bones and muscles into the ground, and teaching in this state would be a foul struggle with her usually good nature. Even in her car, Maria felt the dizzy sway of her cerebral liquid when she looked over her shoulder, and her eyeballs scratched against their sockets like peeled grapes every time she looked up at the traffic lights. Maria took her morning tuitions with slow blinks and dark flashes under heavy frowns; her eyes were not attractive today, she was sure of it, and she was dreading seeing Nadia later in the afternoon.

Making sure she kept herself dosed up on painkillers, with plenty of water and chewing gum, Maria gradually started to feel better after eating a hot, filling lunch from the cafeteria. She reflected that it had been necessary to punish herself so grievously with alcohol, as there had been some level of enlightenment reached in her pit of gloom last night. After her bitter row with Lois, it was the added shame of Ben *knowing* that helped Maria realise that what she was doing with Nadia was fundamentally wrong. Whether or not Nadia appeared to know her own mind and was able to vocalise her desires eloquently and passionately, Maria knew the responsibility in persuading the girl to trust, to come close, to form a private bond: an inner circle with no one else but them, ended with her.

She knew she had to undo this; she just didn't know how, and she didn't really want to. She wanted to keep Nadia for herself, but that wouldn't be fair on the spirited teen. Maria's eyes prickled at the lovelorn, romantic notion that she had to set Nadia free.

She saw Nadia sitting next to Sam in assembly.

Though she strived to remain as professional as she always was, Maria found herself beset with a seriousness that teetered on the verge of tears. The hollows of her cheeks ached with a sense of loss, and when she swallowed, her jaw clenched with such tender cramps, she thought she might retch again. Knowing that Nadia was sat there looking at her, Maria felt so different this time; having last discussed their mutual

Unravel

feelings and struck some harmony, her mind had turned with the tide, and it felt as if an astral cycle had passed between them now. She couldn't bring herself to look at Nadia. It was worse than before. Now she was guilty: she had it written all over her face, and if she looked at Nadia, Sam would see it too.

All through her lunch and afternoon free sessions, she had concerned students arriving asking for help, each with all the varied, usual fears for their exam revision. However, when Nadia returned after her classes for tuition, Maria found Sam had tagged along: evidently keen on sitting in on their one-to-one. Her office was stuffy from frequent stressed visitors; her desk messy with textbooks and scrap paper she had used for visual aids. As she opened the windows to the fresh breeze and tidied up, Maria cast her glance under a dark frown.

'What's going on?' She asked, cracking a bone in her neck with a taut twist.

Looking over at Sam with tender trauma, Nadia bit her lip. 'Is it alright if Sam stays?'

Maria joined Nadia's turn across to Sam and raised her eyebrow. 'Why?'

'I'm curious to know what you two talk about.' Sam smiled with false ease.

'We talk about the modules she's missed and how to revise them quickly,' Maria said impatiently, shoving books back on her shelves. 'All the stuff that bored you first time round.'

'I thought repetition helps drum it home!' Sam replied, without missing a beat.

Inside, Maria's soul screamed for her to be as casual as she could - Sam was on to them. Releasing an irritated sigh, she looked over to Nadia. 'Do you want her to stay?'

Shaking her head slowly, nervously or apologetically, Nadia spoke calmly to Sam.

'Maybe you should go, you'll only distract me,' she gave a light curl of a smile.

Sliding another clever little glare towards Maria, Sam leaned into Nadia to give a very deliberate kiss, one to confirm who had possession of which dynamic when it came to Nadia's time. Nadia offered her cheek and received it, embarrassed, with a series of blinks. Sam left with no further challenge and Maria wondered what she was playing at.

'Why'd you let her come in here?' she asked with quick temper.

'I couldn't stop her, she insisted,' Nadia whispered, 'she doesn't know anything!'

'How do you know what she knows?' Maria gritted her jaw, 'she's sly... you might not have to tell her anything for her to figure it out.'

Nadia made a move toward Maria but stopped herself, she twisted her hair unsurely, staring after her, yearning to connect. 'Maria, I think there's something you should know,' Nadia offered nervously, then retreated to the couch to pull out her books.

Unravel

'Can it wait? I'm not in the mood,' Maria said, stalking resentfully behind her desk. 'I'd rather we didn't talk about this stuff in school.' She spat her gum into her wastepaper basket and reached into her mini-fridge to get a bottle of water. Maria failed to calm her agitation, realising just how much Sam's intrusion had gotten to her. She drank a long, cold glug of water and wiped her mouth, moving behind the short table to Nadia's side with a gruff cough and an assertive posture.

Although she tried her utmost to focus on Nadia's tuition, the icy press of fear kept on waging war with her conscience, and Maria's usually steely nerve was reduced to the shakes. Hearing her own words coming out of her mouth felt distant, but entirely unlike the times she had been previously self-conscious around Nadia. This time, her own voice caused flashbacks to her over-emotional confession; the humiliating outpour of her heart: her raw sensitivity exposed. It sickened her now that she had shown everything to Nadia, and since Ben had revealed what he knew of her and her situation, Maria wished she could take it all back. She wished she could zip it all back in, compact it down into her heart, from where her dark secret should never have spilled out. Now, sullied by her toxic bloodstream, and nauseous from Sam's demonic smile, Maria felt a million miles away from the desire for Nadia's mouth on hers, and she couldn't help holding her resentment over Nadia's head.

Evidently sensing the sore atmosphere between them, Nadia's eyes searched Maria's. 'What's wrong?'

Sighing out through her nose, Maria shook her head. 'Nothing! I'm just tired.'

'Are you sleeping okay?' the girl asked carefully.

'Not really!' Maria answered with bittersweet sarcasm. 'I've had a lot on my mind.'

'Well, so have I!' Nadia jerked her head defiantly.

'Yeah, you've got a heap of plates to balance, haven't you?' Maria smarted.

'What's that supposed to mean?' Nadia turned a mortified glance to the door, and brought it swiftly back again. 'Listen, you know what I'm doing with Sam.'

Maria couldn't stop herself sounding pathetic. 'Yeah, you're doing Sam alright.'

Slapping her palm on her book, Nadia's brows turned up, and she looked hurt, genuinely so. 'Maria, don't twist my words, you can't be jealous!'

Unable to cope with Nadia's emotion, Maria clapped her own hands onto her thighs with a similarly audible effect to signify her equal air of indifference. 'Nadia, I told you, I can't deal with this personal shit in my office.'

'But, I thought we sorted things out,' Nadia appealed in her tender Dublin tones, 'what are we doing here?'

'Apparently not tuition.' Maria remarked, her dark eyes flashing.

Nadia shook her head with frustration. 'I mean arguing!' She then relaxed her frown. 'Look,' she reached down for Maria's hand between her open knees, 'can we start again?' Her fingers entwined with Maria's, but even though they were alone, Maria pulled her hand away in a terrible, rejecting flinch.

'What the fuck are you doing?' Maria gasped, her shoulders high with tension.

Devastated at the repelling effect of her touch, Nadia reigned in her hands with horror.

'What the fuck am *I* doing?' Nadia scorned. 'What are *you* doing, more like? Why are you being like this?'

Maria turned away and pressed her elbows into her knees with her hands over her eyes. It stung to close them but the water she felt gather between her lashes felt soothing. 'Nadia, I know we made an agreement but... I don't know how to be around you in school, I'm on edge! I don't know if I can do this.'

'Don't know if you can do what?' Nadia asked witheringly.

'This!' Maria snapped, dropping her hands and looking at the wounded expression on Nadia's face. 'It doesn't feel right. What we said... what we did... outside school, it might have felt good at the time, maybe we made the best out of a bad situation... but I don't think we can carry this on through school. I shouldn't have asked you to wait, it's not right. We still have work to do and that's more important than holding promises of something that might not be there at the end,' Maria paused to see just how much she was breaking Nadia's heart.

'Who says it won't be there at the end?' Nadia whined, holding back tears.

Lowering her voice to a gentle gravel, Maria told the truth. 'I have to be your teacher, I have to get you through your exams - but if I fail at that because I'm distracted and you're distracted, then I'll be failing you, and you won't want to be with me afterwards!'

Nadia's eyes quickly darkened and brimmed with tears. 'Don't you think I'm more likely to fail my exams if the person I'm in love with keeps messing me around? I'm sick of this!' Nadia's cheeks flooded with colour and water as she began to scoop up her books. 'You're the one who's going to ruin things for us, before we've even begun! You're gutless!'

Feeling her nerves jangling, Maria became desperate for Nadia to accept her reasoning, as a professional, as an adult, as a gentleman, or whatever, Maria had to do the right thing.

'We have to go back to being just teacher and student for a few more months, then we'll see where we stand,' Maria appealed.

'Nice to know your job is more important than my feelings,' Nadia said miserably. She looked devastated as she stood and headed to the door.

'Nadia, I'm sorry!' Maria called out.

As the door slammed shut behind her, Maria felt a deep remorse at Nadia's leaving on such bad terms, but more importantly, her headache had come back with vengeance, and, she had to admit, the urge to lock the door in silence and crawl under her desk was more appealing than Nadia's return.

It took her the full evening to recover, and curling up in her bed that night, Maria went back over her regrettable last conversation with Nadia and realised it had all happened because she had drunk too much last night. She had not only bawled like a child on the phone to Ben, and been vulnerable to his deciphering her big secret, but she had been cruel and impatient to the one person she was going through this dilemma for. She shouldn't have taken it out on Nadia. She shouldn't have let her own head and heartache interfere with providing the girl's tuition period. Saying that, Maria felt her irritation at Sam's assumption she could swan in and eye-ball her through a session was justified.

Overall, Maria knew she didn't want to upset Nadia further, no matter how much she was seeking to do the right thing, in all soberness she could not and did not want to retract her pledge of love. The girl certainly had to prioritise her exams and keep an eagle-eyed Sam Burrows at bay; they both had to be clever about this. Maria went to sleep working out how to maintain a professional distance, not too close and not too far, in order to provide Nadia with enough hope to keep working, and enough deterrence to avoid risking another awkward rejection.

♥

Later that week in March came a heat wave that caused everyone to slide into various states of arousal, and given that the mock exams were beginning, Maria observed how the sweat and stickiness provided ample ground for both extremes of positive and negative energies. Standing amongst the few other learning support team members to watch over the eighty, or so, students taking the intermediate level maths exam, Maria kept to the side of the corridor, closely surrounded by the humming, nervous crowd and shushed them when they became too noisy.

 The principal's deputy, Mrs Yvonne Pepper, and her assistant were checking everyone's names off their list and it was taking an age for everyone to filter through to the gymnasium. Maria hated having to quieten them when she was just as impatient, but that was the whole point of her presence. Noticing how the bright-eyed boys and girls, with shiny cheeks and wide smiles, seemed to be taking up the challenge and enjoying the prospect of their imminent test, Maria saw others whose faces were blotchy with anxiety, they stood listless and quiet, unsmiling even to their friends, and wiping their hot brows. Maria looked for Nadia.

When she saw her, Nadia kept her usual, cool pose: one hip jutting out, her arm folded over the other, her chin high and her eyebrows turned up with beautiful concern. Her mouth seemed to have fallen into a crescent, in a sub-conscious sort of way, and Maria knew Nadia had not seen her yet. Sam was beside her, talking away, as usual. As they approached, however, Maria wondered why Nadia was not looking for her as she gazed ahead to the front of the line, whilst Sam was the one with eyes all over the place. Maria tried not to stare; she shouldn't seek Nadia's eye contact, especially when Sam had clocked her.

'Wish us luck, Miss Calver!' Sam called to her across the hallway with a direct, expectant pause for the standard response. She had dyed her hair different colours again.

Maria tilted her head as she tightened her folded arms. 'It's not about luck really, is it? More, to do with how much attention you paid in class instead of talking.'

While Sam over-curled her lip with a good-humoured roll of her eyes, Maria saw that Nadia looked down to her shuffling feet and realised the girl was avoiding her eye contact after all. She had to do something; she couldn't let Nadia go into her first exam without her support. In the queue, Sam was also noticing that Nadia was ignoring her tutor, and Maria knew she had to break those crucial few seconds of awkwardness before it was too late.

Unravel

'Nadia?' Maria called out, and gestured when the girl looked up. 'Come here a sec?'

Leaving Sam's side, Nadia stepped across the corridor towards her, but didn't lift her worried eyes until Maria put her hand upon her shoulder.

'Are you okay?'

Shaking her head slowly, Nadia seemed aware that Sam was keeping her eyes peeled. She blinked nervously and cast her eyes down to her feet again.

'Are you worried about the exam?' Maria asked tenderly, but when Nadia failed to nod, just slid her eyes down to the side, it occurred to Maria that she was trying to hide her expression from Sam. Maria tried again. 'Are you pretending to be worried about the exam?'

That Nadia caught herself from a brief chuckle was promising, and when the girl nodded, Maria exhaled with relief that she hadn't lost her loyal, sweet companion.

'Look, just get through this one and we'll talk after, okay?'

'Tonight?' Nadia whispered.

'Yeah,' Maria replied and saw Nadia smile as she eased the girl in for a somewhat tense sideways hug. 'Everything will be fine, I promise,' Maria spoke proudly, unafraid to reassure her audibly when the double meaning was their secret. She felt Nadia's fingers clinch around her waist, hidden against the wall behind them, and Maria had to lift her smile along the queue instead of allowing it to fall over Nadia's tender features.

'Can I have a hug too, Miss Calver?' Sam said as she left the queue and joined them. Her face was one of genuine hope and Maria knew to shoot down her openness would be too cruel. Releasing her hand from Nadia on one side, Maria opened her arm on the other and let Sam climb under, though she wrapped both arms around Maria's waist and squeezed her torso. Maria patted Sam's shoulder robotically, more as a signal that her time was up. Glancing at Nadia, and seeing the girl sigh as she turned away, Maria felt pained at having let Sam near her and rolled her body away from Sam's grip. Sam went away grinning, seemingly happy she had received an equal share to Nadia, and returned to the queue. Maria watched and sighed as Nadia kept her back to her, and Sam returned to chatting.

♥

The mock exam went ahead smoothly, everyone's nerves were enough to keep them focused, and though the weather made the hall stuffy, Maria did her job in observing the students to the best of her ability. She had to stay behind to help collect the papers and file them in the right order with the deputy, so by the time she had returned to her office, she had several texts on her phone from Nadia asking where she was, and when they could talk, as Maria had said. Maria texted back to apologise and made her excuses. Although she wanted to see her, the battle to do the right thing and remain on professional terms until Nadia had finished school, raged on inside her.

The conversations she had had that poignant night, with Lois and then, drunkenly with Ben, causing her subsequent guilt, seemed to have faded away. She had spoken to neither of them since, though Ben had left voicemails to check she was okay, and now her interest in connecting with Nadia seemed to have resumed its former drive. Maria sat at her desk, her legs tired from standing up in the gymnasium. As a sweat trickled down between her shoulder blades, she plotted thoughtfully.

She tried to remind herself that the situation she had been, until this point, trying to avoid, had happened – and had gone better than she could have imagined. Nadia had stood in her lounge and listened to the spilling of her stricken heart, and had not run to tell everyone she could that her tutor had confessed her love. Nadia could have laughed in her face or screamed 'I knew it' or 'Gotcha!' but she had clung to Maria, after her initial shock, and wept with relief. Their two bodies embraced as if they were magnets; one soul wrongly separated. It had felt good and natural to communicate with Nadia in that way and their pact to wait until their duties to each other were over to consummate their relationship had felt powerful and righteous. Maria had never assumed it would get anywhere near this point, and now she struggled over how to deal with her feelings for the girl both in and out of school.

Nevertheless, the new worst-case scenario would be that others found out about her feelings, and it was now Maria's main priority to protect her love for Nadia from the misunderstanding, unforgiving outside world. She would be a fool to invite prying interest by continuously seeing Nadia socially. To have Nadia in her home during mock exams could be offensive enough to the education system to warrant complaints from other parents. Maria knew she was skating on thin ice, but she wanted to see and speak to Nadia so much: just to hold her and reassure her that they were going to be all right, as she had promised. Nadia seemed miserable without her contact, as defiant as she was trying to act; Maria knew she was making Nadia more vulnerable than ever, and the last thing she wanted to do was mess up the girl's exams because of her own indecision.

♥

The plan was that Nadia would go to Christian's house under the pretence of making up for her indiscretion by spending some quality time with him as a friend. She owed him that much, even if saying Maria's name during sex had effectively ruined their budding relationship. Christian had often messaged Nadia, asking how she was – she said she had avoided contacting him for over a month, but knew he would jump at the chance of having her over for tea. She told Maria she would offer to bring Leon back home after six o'clock, and then they could spend the evening together, just talking, nothing else.

Looking forward to having Nadia's company, the stress of their secrecy nonetheless took constant toll on Maria's nerves, and she was unable to concentrate on her work for the rest of the afternoon. By five o'clock, Maria resigned to going home to shower, considering a little food shopping on the way.

She wondered how wrong it was to make Nadia dinner, and whether that would look as if she were trying to seduce the girl. Maria considered it as objectively as she could, and reconciled that it wasn't grooming if Nadia was fully aware that her teacher's intentions were determinedly *not* to bed her.

Locking her office and heading out to her car, Maria shook her head at her naivety: *of course* it was seductive to make Nadia dinner. It was different at the start of the year, when Christian would come too, and Nadia didn't know – but now they knew – it *would* be like a date. Resolving not to make a special dinner, Maria drove home, and freshened up whilst preparing her greeting for when Nadia brought Leon back.

Around half past six, the knock on her door lifted Maria to her feet again, effortlessly this time. The ache of the long day spent waiting and hushing for silence in the corridor had washed away with her shower and Maria answered the door with a kick of adrenalin in her stomach to be able to have Nadia to herself for a few hours.

However, it was only Christian bringing Leon back, and as Maria's face dropped, she looked over his shoulder with a sinking feeling in her gut.

'She's not here then?' he asked, letting Leon off his lead.

'Who, Nadia?' Maria tightened her smile. 'No, I thought she was with you.'

'We had an argument... over *you*,' Christian flicked his eyebrows.

'Me?' Maria scrunched her hands behind Leon's soft ears and pretended to be casual.

'I thought she was sorry and wanted to get back with me,' Christian said, obviously put out, 'but she still couldn't stop talking about you.'

Her attempt at seeming unfazed by it made Maria feel deceitful, but it's what she had to do. 'It's not me, Chris, it's her revision, you know... she's just started her mock exams.'

'She didn't mention her exams once,' Christian stated bitterly. He pushed his lips out with a suspicious glimmer across his eyes. 'Just how forgiving you've been about her little crush.'

Maria calmed her defence. 'Nadia hasn't got a crush on me,' she sighed through her nose, knowing in her heart that his ex-girlfriend's feelings towards her were much deeper than Christian could ever know or hope to understand. 'I'm just the tutor giving her a second chance at her finals, so I'm like, on a fucking pedestal right now, that's all.'

Maria pressed her knuckles against Christian's shoulder and gave him a supportive nod as he blinked, unconvinced, back at her. She turned to reach into the cabinet drawer and pulled out a twenty-pound note, and pushed it into his hand.

'Twenty?' he asked, surprised.

'For bringing Leon home,' she shrugged. Closing the door on her dog-sitter, Maria felt her heart pounding and an itchy sweat climbing up her spine. She took Leon through to the kitchen for his dinner and made herself some tea to calm down and process her thoughts. Fearing that Christian believed her to have some strange influence over Nadia, Maria was angered that the girl was talking too much about her, revealing too much about her feelings. It all made Maria look stupid, firstly, for apparently not realising Nadia had feelings for her, and secondly, by highlighting that she wasn't doing anything about it. Maria wondered if Nadia thought it okay to talk to Christian because he wasn't in school, but then she wondered if Nadia was playing another game – one that she was being too slow catching up on.

Maria wiped her face, perhaps she should trust that Nadia knew what she was doing with Christian:

however peeved Christian had seemed, he undoubtedly didn't for one minute believe that anything real was happening between his ex-girlfriend and her teacher.

Chapter Twenty-Six

The following day, checking her emails on her office computer, Maria found one from Lois, sent the previous evening. At first, every instinct inside her repelled away, fearing Lois' harsh criticism would carve a path of bad energy throughout her day if she read it, but she couldn't help scanning it for swear words. Once Maria saw it was relatively harmless, she returned to the beginning and read it properly. Lois firstly dismissed their argument, not that she had forgiven her for letting her down, but she was willing to allow Maria to make it up to her. Lois then explained that she wanted Maria to take her out for dinner, not for a belated birthday, she was 'over that', but to celebrate her success, as she had finally earned a commission to produce a series of designs for the marketing department of an exclusive London advertising company, Red Light Ltd.

Blah, blah, blah, Maria sighed. Then, with dismay, she re-read the part where Lois was insisting that Maria pay for their dinner, and she expected champagne, of course. She closed the message without replying: she had mock exams to stand in on all day, so that would give her ample time to consider whether or not she was prepared to cough up for bubbles *and* endure Lois' smug self-congratulation.

Her morning mock exams were leg-achingly monotonous, but Maria could only moan internally as she paced slowly up and down the aisles, subtly stretching out her tightening calf muscles with each step.

Grabbing a chilled iced tea from the cafeteria, Maria returned to her office at lunchtime and tried to hide her pleasure at finding Nadia waiting for her. It felt so long since their last doomed tuition, though they'd seen each other every day in school, and while it seemed fate kept intervening to stop them having moments alone, Maria couldn't help wanting to.

'By yourself this time?' Maria said dryly with a half-smile as she unlocked the door.

Nadia kept her smile closed as she eased away from the wall. 'Not now you're here.'

Opening the door, Maria felt a swirl of power and cool control at having Nadia follow her inside. She threw her keys on her desk and hit the air-conditioning unit button. Turning back to Nadia, who propped her bag on the coffee table and opened it, digging around, Maria kept hold of her drink and leaned casually against the edge of her desk.

'Have you come for revision?'

Shaking her head quickly, Nadia looked sincere. 'I just wanted to see you.'

Maria nodded, lifting her iced tea to hold it against the rising temperature of her cheek.

'What happened last night?' Maria asked, but she knew already. She came clean: 'Christian told me you... wouldn't stop talking about me... that's not exactly subtle.'

'No, you don't understand, you weren't there,' Nadia shifted, a frown forming between her worried brows. 'He was trying to talk about sex! It was all I could do to avoid throwing up, so I kept talking the whole time and you were the subject that seemed to put him off!'

'Oh, great!' Maria rolled her eyes. 'That's nice.'

'I wanted to come straight to you but I knew he would come over with Leon,' Nadia explained and approached Maria beside her desk. 'You know when you said we'll be okay, does that mean we're still on?' she asked hopefully, 'because I thought you changed your mind.'

Biting her lip, Maria sent a glance over her shoulder to the windows behind her looking down on the playing field. There were boys running, absorbed in their football, and girls resting by the side of the pitch, absorbed in their magazines and music players; the likelihood that someone would look up to the third floor from outside and spot them was minimal – still, Maria felt too exposed.

Unravel

She breathed out her tension, the delay in her response was excruciating for her and she imagined how it must feel for Nadia. Eventually she said: 'I haven't changed my mind.'

Nadia's lips twitched with a relieved smile and her hands drew in close to Maria's belt. 'Do you think you could prove it?' her eyes lifted to Maria's, flashing her flirtation.

The girl sounded as if she was craving the hit of a drug, and Maria realised she was the drug. Weighing up what was worse: Maria considered either taking Nadia into the corner for a hot, brief kiss that could easily get carried away, or leaving her to stew in her own juices which could result in her blowing her top at some point during her afternoon exam. Maria decided and snatched Nadia's hand, pulling her towards the wall next to the bookcase, where forgotten winter coats hanging on pegs behind the door provided a padded, private corner.

There, gasping at the way Maria held her against the wall, Nadia wrapped her arms around Maria's back and hugged her closely. The warm spread of pleasure soaked into their clothes and sent Maria's muscles tingling. With Nadia against her chest, she could feel their heartbeats as one. The nerves in her body compelled her to pull away at any second, afraid of conducting such sordid affairs in her office, but her desire, stronger, compelled her further in, the risk of being caught driving her heart and loins. Lowering her face to Nadia's, their mouths found each other's and locked into an urgent suck, silent and lengthy.

She broke away with a firm press of her lips against Nadia's head. Breathing in the scent of Nadia's hair, Maria exhaled her yearning, trembling passion. She rubbed Nadia's shoulder down to the small of her back, heavily and sensually, and up again slowly.

Nadia gazed up and whispered. 'Tell me you love me?'

A chill ran across Maria's nerves; her muscles seized in her jaw. 'Tonight.'

♥

The afternoon mock exam was for English Literature, and Nadia had struggled hardest to catch up on reading the books the others had had two years to learn. Maria watched her from a distance - staring at her paper, screwing up her eyes, flicking her pen the way she did, pushing her fringe across her forehead, swapping her ankles. All signs, she knew, that Nadia was having trouble, and becoming frustrated with herself. Maria wondered if she, as her tutor, was able to go to her side, and whisper a few words of reassurance, but she guessed it would be frowned upon for her to give assistance unless Nadia raised her hand - and she daren't ask.

Contemplating ahead to later that evening, Maria wondered what she was thinking of doing with

Nadia and how she was going to manage taking the girl somewhere they could be alone to talk without risking any physical interaction. It made sense for Nadia to visit her house, but then, without the convenience of seeing Christian first, the organisation it would require to co-ordinate times and meeting places with Nadia felt too much like a surreptitious affair. Something inside Maria repelled the idea of lying and sneaking around when they were in fact trying to do the decent thing and not engage in inappropriate activity. However, something else inside Maria strongly urged her to make sure she kept Nadia as close to her chest as she would keep her hand at a poker table. She had to allow Nadia to meet her in private, to keep that promise, at her request, to keep her happy and quiet until the end of her schooling. Maria resented having to resort to closing doors, turning the lights out, looking over her shoulder: they were not actually doing anything wrong, she reasoned. They were really trying.

At the end of the day, Nadia returned to Maria's office for her usual tuition, and as if nothing had ever changed between them, Nadia sat down and turned the pages of her books whilst Maria covered the last few sections of her revision guide. It felt a relief that they could still be teacher and student without the inescapable, unspoken air of awkward attraction that had plagued them for months. It was still there, but it had settled to a calm, genuine bond where they could smile without nerves and if their hands or knees brushed by accident, it wasn't followed by a jerk away or a swivel in the other direction. Nadia was lovely, and gentle, and Maria felt for her more tenderly than ever before - now that she knew Nadia was committed to going on the long haul with her, and was ready to do whatever it took to protect their secret.

It wouldn't have been right to hold hands in the office. Not only would it have sent Maria's nerves on edge if anyone should dare walk in without knocking, but it would have felt unnatural, given that their working relationship during tuition had long been established as one of focus and seriousness. To rub Nadia's back or push her hair behind her ear during these intense hours, Maria felt it would disturb their dynamic, and assumed Nadia felt that too, as she tried nothing of the sort.

All that changed, however, when it was five o'clock and tuition time was over. Maria shook off her teacher mode as she strutted around her office, closing down her computer and the windows. She felt the cooler evening breeze move her into a different, easier gear, and she returned her concerns to getting Nadia out of there without raising suspicion.

'Fuck it, let's just walk to your car,' Nadia shrugged. 'There's hardly anyone around except the cleaners and if anyone does see us, they'll just think you're giving me a lift after tuition, that's what you usually do.'

Unravel

'I only ever gave you a lift before because it was dark over the winter months, doesn't it look weird if I take you when it's still light outside?' Maria queried. 'Next thing they'll see us riding off into the sunset with the roof down.'

Nadia chuckled happily. 'Your roof comes down?'

Maria didn't smile, but stared at Nadia, thinking. 'Okay,' she nodded. 'I'm just giving you a lift home: we're not doing anything wrong,' she reminded herself sombrely.

Joining Maria's seriousness, Nadia relaxed her excitement, left the office ahead of her teacher, and waited for her to lock up. They walked down the stairs and out the fire exit towards the car park, separated by a generous few paces, not smiling but not sneaking. There were only a few other cars remaining in the enclosure: Maria recognised one of them as the librarian's, and figured she would not be the type to stare out of the window at this time of the evening; the other one belonged to one the rugby coach. She then clocked him with the group of boys on the field. They had re-commenced after-school games some weeks back with the warmer weather, but they did not seem to show any interest now as Nadia stepped down into Maria's car, with a flick of her red hair.

Rolling out of the school grounds with Nadia silently tuning through the radio stations on her car's dashboard, Maria buzzed with the thrill of their casual getaway. Once on the road to Cheltenham, Maria allowed herself a smile and sat back in her seat to rest her shoulders back. Now she felt her old self again, and the past few months' internalised agonies were ebbing away sensually like the morning dew after so many cold winter nights. Recalling with a cringe the route she had taken out of Gloucester when she had driven Nadia maniacally to an off-road clearing, Maria decided to redress the balance and take Nadia elsewhere; somewhere nicer and better, with less harsh memories of jealousy, anger, and loss of control associated with it, even if that was the place they first kissed.

Her little Audi sped along the winding lane that took them towards the beacon, the trees bowing down over them cutting off the sunlight. As the view spread forth to the horizon, Maria did not need to remind Nadia this was the place she had given her birthday gift, and they sat in the car as before, revelling its sights and beauty. There was one other vehicle at the apex, a large van painted deep green with cartoonish flowers twisting around the windows. It was smoking from a short pipe at its top, and Maria figured it must be some old hippy cooking up a treat on his stove, built in to his converted home. There were two dogs tied to the end ladder with ropes, one stood up and barked.

It was different seeing it all shining under the late afternoon sun. Maria opened her car door and stepped out. It was windy on top of the beacon, but Nadia didn't seem to care. After following her out the car, Nadia walked beside Maria until the gap between them felt wider than the valley beneath them. Nadia had wrapped her summer coat tightly and battled through the wind, though her hair caught in her eyelashes and she soon tripped over a hump of grass. Maria turned, stood beside her loyal companion, and blocked the wind for a moment's respite. Nadia looked up and smiled cheerfully as Maria tucked the auburn hair behind her ear, the girl's eyelashes fluttering, and a trace amount of moisture gathering at the outer corners ready to stream.

Putting her arms inside Maria's coat, Nadia clung against the warmth of Maria's body and there they stayed for a few minutes, staring out across the shimmering landscape. Maria felt an overwhelming contentment and purpose: doing her duty in protecting her girl from the elements, and casting a brooding eye around them, checking for any unwanted attention. She felt a squeeze from Nadia's arms to signify she should let go, and Maria felt a rush of cold air hurry to replace Nadia as she moved away.

'Can I stay with you tonight?' Nadia asked directly, her eyes suddenly pleading.

Maria stepped back on the hill, putting her hands in her pockets. 'Why?'

Flicking her hair aside, Nadia pursed her lips tightly. 'I don't want to go home.'

With a rub to her brow, Maria shook her head. 'I can't let you stay over just because you don't want to be at home.'

Nadia dropped her gaze to the grass, seemingly quitting her efforts by sitting down resolutely in a quick collapse. Her eyes had faded to as dull a green-grey as the scenery reflected in them, and Maria joined Nadia's side on a patch of grass.

'I just want to talk to you, that's all, I promise,' Nadia complained.

'We can talk here,' Maria said with a taunting smile, her eyes travelling over Nadia's skin and the shape of her mouth. It wasn't that she didn't want to have Nadia all to herself in her room – she did – but she felt she should try to teach Nadia some measure of patience, however much she was failing at this moment to discourage her.

She must have sensed the twinkle in Maria's eye, because Nadia's pout melted into a curly smile that slipped upwards forming those dimples that made Maria's belly tingle.

'Well,' Nadia's magnetic eyes held onto Maria's, 'what if I don't want to talk here?'

The girl's hand emerged from her coat pocket and found its way to Maria's neck as if pulled there by an unseen twine. Her fingers were warm against Maria's exposed skin and the draw in towards Nadia's lips felt beyond her control, like the mindless drive of a thirsty child towards a gulp of water. Yet, Maria held

Unravel

back. She took Nadia's hand with hers, lowered it to her lap, and wrapped her fingers inside, rubbing with her thumb for assurance.

As Nadia's eyes returned swiftly into confused, worrisome pools, Maria needed a moment. She wanted to kiss Nadia but she felt her heart skipping and the anxiety rising: she didn't want to feel out of control. She didn't want Nadia to feel her nervousness. Especially when Nadia seemed so sure, so willing and ready.

Maria shifted her leg up and around Nadia's back to straddle either side of her, and shifted in to embrace the girl from behind. Nadia immediately giggled and nestled back into Maria's warm arms. She tucked wind-swept, escaping strands back behind her ear; the last of the sunlight was oozing a deep orange against her hair. Maria sighed, her heart helplessly pounding against her chest.

'Well, we got our sunset,' Maria smiled. 'Not exactly roof down but it's as good as...'

Nadia lifted her face towards Maria's neck. 'This way you can close your eyes and still drive.'

There was no one else around. The wind locked them in, and all of Maria's senses vibrated in tune with Nadia's; the girl's eyes dilated, she gasped ever so gently as her lust took her breath. Maria closed her mouth upon Nadia's and, once again, for those timeless, tingling, melting moments, Maria felt like she was flying.

Unravel

♥

They had left the beacon when the sun had dropped and it was decisively too cold to stay up there. They had driven to Charlton Kings to collect Leon, who was delirious to jump in the car with them and sat pertly on Nadia's lap. On the darkening, winding back roads into Stroud towards Eastcombe, still with a distracting swell of moisture between her thighs from lengthy kissing, and Nadia chatting happily beside her stroking Leon's small body, Maria steered loosely around the dimly lit corners musing vaguely how her dreamy arousal was affecting her driving. As she glanced in her rear view mirror to check there were no cars behind them, Nadia suddenly screamed at a figure walking in the road a few metres ahead. Maria swerved away just in time to avoid knocking the person down, then pulled an emergency stop and swore loudly.

Checking Nadia and Leon were okay first, and after receiving an alarmed, shaken glance from Nadia holding Leon safely in her arms, Maria felt a pain in her hand and rubbed her sprained wrist. The pedestrian had been way out in the middle of the dusky road and had been so close to being run over, Maria had to get out and say something.

'Maria, wait!' Nadia called as Maria threw open her door and climbed out.

She just wanted to check the man was all right, and as she saw him stumble onwards without hesitation, wearing loose, dark clothes and clutching a dirty rucksack, Maria realised he was drunk and she snarled.

'Hey! Didn't you hear me coming? I could have killed you!'

The man's face shot up directly at Maria with hardened, cold eyes that reflected huge red circles in her rear lights. The image of the man looming out of the insidious dark was frightening, like something from a zombie movie. His face was pale, shadowed with deep, skeletal ridges above the pinched skin of his cheeks, and his brow became fiercely focused as his methodical stepping forward headed straight toward her.

'I heard you coming! You wreckless cunt!' The tortured bum hollered. 'You're driving on *my* road with your fancy car! Why don't you watch where you're going instead of-?'

Maria's heart had chilled at the sound of the man's voice: his Irish accent cut through her more than his abusive tone, but now he had stopped, staring with fury down at Nadia in the passenger seat.

'What the fuck is this?' he bellowed, banging his fist against the window sheltering Nadia. 'What are you doing in there?' he shouted to his daughter.

Leon began barking at the noises, and crying out with urgent desperation, Nadia called to Maria. 'Please just get in and drive!'

With a gulp, Maria tried to process this strange reality. 'You're shitting me.'

Peter Sheridan raised hateful eyes directly back up at Maria. 'Who *the fuck* are you?'

Shuddering with intimidation, Maria registered Nadia's pleas and Leon's barks distantly; she stammered. 'I'm Nadia's teacher, I was just giving her a lift home!'

'Like hell you are!' The irate parent boomed. '*You*, get out! Now!' he yelled at Nadia, tugging the door handle, but she had locked it from the inside. He thumped again on the window aggressively, swearing despicably.

'Mr Sheridan, calm down, I'll get Nadia home safely,' Maria floundered. 'I could give you a lift if you like?'

'As if I'd get in your poncy car, you stupid bitch! The way you drive, you'll have us all killed!' He lowered his threatening face to Nadia's passenger window and Maria saw flecks of spit shoot from his mouth onto the glass as she bent to witness the ugly scenario. 'Nadia, you get out right now or I'll give you a beating you won't forget!'

Nadia immediately put Leon on Maria's seat and opened her door, getting out wasn't a move Maria was sure was aimed at obeying or fighting off her father, but as soon as she saw the old man strike his daughter, something in Maria flipped. What happened next was a blur. Maria shot around her car to intervene, to placate, to prevent such violence, but, in retrospect, she should have held back and thought it through. As Peter turned on Maria, pushing her back against the car with his elbow in her neck, Leon launched himself off Nadia's seat to attack the stranger harming his owner.

Leon bit at Peter's legs, growling with deceptively strong aggression, he may have been slight in frame but his Doberman nature was rearing its dangerous head, and Peter yelled and swore, releasing Maria and stumbling back. He looked down, bewildered at the little dog hanging on to his flailing leg with vicious teeth, and then, with a terrifying swing of his foot, Peter slammed Leon into the wheel arch.

Maria heard the crippling thud of metal breaking bone, and Leon's agonised cry. The little dog fell to the ground having let go of Peter's leg, he slumped against the wheel and tried to stand on his legs but before she could stop him, Peter came again with his booted foot and kicked Leon's ribs, pinning him to the wheel with brutal intention.

Leon gave another pained yelp and Maria threw her fists blindly out through the air at Mr Sheridan, howling herself, enraged and horrified. She pushed him away, as far away from her and Leon, away from Nadia, summoning her fury and her desire for vengeance. But somewhere behind her, Maria heard her name, and Nadia crying Leon's name, and then her focus snapped back to saving her loved ones. She turned and helped Nadia back into the car with Leon on

Unravel

her lap, and leaped back into the driver's seat, blocking out the inane rants of the psychotic father sprawling himself against the window as she spun her wheels to get away.

Taking a turning back to Stroud, Maria wiped her eyes clear and desperately focused on getting to the emergency vets. Her little man was laying limp across Nadia's lap, whimpering pitifully, and Nadia stroked him tenderly, weeping and pleading him to be okay. He wasn't responding, but Maria couldn't look at him now, not while she was speeding towards traffic on the darkened roads home, and trying to blink her tears away.

Once on the carriageway, Nadia suddenly screamed that Leon was having a seizure. Her hands elevated in horror as the crumpled black and tan body convulsed in an ongoing fit. Maria saw the traffic congesting ahead and pulled over into the hard shoulder, stopping under a streetlight. She jumped out and ran around to Nadia's side, opening the door wide so she could squat down by Leon's face to see what was happening. She could see blood coming from his ears, his tongue was hanging out, and his eyes were rolling.

'Leon!' Maria wept and she lifted his head in her hands. His lovely, scared brown eyes locked onto hers and then his fit seemed to stop. Maria's breath suspended as she waited for Leon to blink, or breathe. But his misshapen ribs did not rise again, and his breath

Unravel

did not pant again long after Maria had left it until the last possible moment she could gasp for air and release a tortured moan of sorrow.

She wrapped her arms around his small body and lay her face against his, her tears rolling onto his snout. His eyes were still open and fixed on her and she couldn't bear to move knowing she would leave his sight. It was too late to take him to the vets. He was gone. Nadia's father had killed him.

Nadia sobbed uncontrollably, she held one hand over Leon and stroked Maria's hair with the other. She kept saying she was sorry, that it was her fault for opening the door, but Maria couldn't blame her. When she found her strength, Maria closed Leon's eyes and kissed his nose, and drove back to Charlton Kings where she wished she'd kept him, instead of taking him for a drive.

Home at last, Maria put Leon's body in his bed and covered him with his favourite blanket, surrounded by his favourite toys. She even placed a fresh bowl of water just in case his spirit was thirsty. She did all those things to look after Nadia too, who couldn't seem to shake her sadness washing the blood from her hands, and sobbed weakly even as she curled up in Maria's bed.

Easing her body around Nadia's, Maria tucked her legs under to spoon the girl and wrapped her shoulders with her arms. Nadia snuggled back against her warmth and took Maria's hand to kiss her fingers.

'He loved you so much!' she mumbled through her tears.

Maria kissed Nadia's shoulder, and whispered. 'I love you.'

Nadia's body trembled with fresh, happy sobs, and she squeezed Maria's fingers against her wet lips. Settling her head back, Maria knew she would be awake a while, but wanted to hold Nadia while she cried herself to sleep.

She blinked in the darkness of her room. Peter Sheridan's face, like a demon with hollow cheeks, and dark-circled, cruel eyes, possessed her closing images. She couldn't believe Nadia had been born from that hideous creature. Reminiscing over all the times she had doubted Nadia, and worried the girl was reeling her in with sob stories, Maria now knew that everything Nadia had said was true, and it meant that she could trust the girl. Though it felt broken from the loss of her closest friend, Maria's heart filled with swells of protectiveness over her newest. The girl's father was a monster; it was now her duty to take on a role as Nadia's guardian and carer as well as mentor, teacher and later... lover.

Part 2

Three Months Later

Chapter Twenty-Seven

My name is Dr Evelyn Richmond. I am a fifty-five year old, forensic psychologist living and working in Gloucestershire. I have been referred a new case through Gloucestershire police on behalf of Gloucester City High school to assist with an independent investigation. A member of their staff, Ms Maria Calver, a single, thirty-two year old advanced skills tutor, stands accused of conducting a sexual relationship with her seventeen-year old, Irish transfer student, Miss Nadia Sheridan.

After being arrested ten days ago, the twentieth of July, Maria Calver was released pending further enquiries. Ms Calver is firmly denying all accusations and - I have been informed – Miss Sheridan is also denying any physical relationship with her teacher. Therefore, as the school board wishes to pursue the investigation, I have been assigned with the task of assisting the police by interviewing all witnesses involved and compiling a report for a disciplinary hearing. The principal of GCH School, Mr Xavier Woods, is the main accusing party in this case, and it is he who I must first visit to gather all the facts and accounts that I can in order to see if the matter needs to go further, and be dealt with in a criminal court of law.

    I arranged to meet Xavier Woods in a quiet office room in Gloucester Council's building, adjacent to the conference rooms used for general meetings.
    It was the height of summer, and Xavier Woods appeared uncomfortably hot in his suit and tie. He smiled briefly at the colourful silk scarf atop my standard grey skirt suit before his face flattened, hopefully sensing my seriousness. I have spent years building a reputation for being no nonsense, intolerant of hysterics, and my technique of waiting until someone has exhausted their nervous patter before asking them another question, works just fine for me.
    'Dr Richmond, I am relieved to have you looking into this,' Woods announced with an indignant bluster. 'I trust that you will do a great, thorough job, and I can only pray that you regard my long years of service, and agree that I am within every one of my rights to flag up this situation to the board.'
    I nodded in acknowledgment that Mr Woods had a respectable career spanning nearly two decades. I didn't know him but he produced impressive results so I had no reason to distrust the man, yet I had to remain unbiased whilst he told me what he knew. As it stood,

there was not enough evidence to take this to court, and if it was just his word against hers, then it was down to my independent decision as to what, if any, disciplinary action could be taken against Ms Calver.

It soon became clear why Xavier Woods had such a bee in his bonnet.

'Maria Calver has personally offended me!' he sighed, a sweat already spreading across his bald head, 'she lied to me repeatedly, and deceived me about the nature of her relationship with Miss Sheridan after I asked her to nurture the girl's wellbeing for the sake of her exams, I feel like a fool! She made a mockery of me, right behind my back!'

'Surely, it must be more than pride that's driving you to press charges against the teacher you apparently fought so hard to employ onto your team?' I reasoned with him. 'I can see you're upset, but you must provide me with details I can qualify.'

'Details?' Xavier exploded. 'I don't want to think about the details! The idea of a teacher being sexual with a student disgusts me! The concept of an adult in charge, engaging in acts of physical intimacy with a young person in their care makes me so outraged, I *have* to stand up and demand she be punished!'

'I appreciate that, Mr Woods, I feel the same,' I replied, 'but my hands are tied unless you can report specific events or show me the proof these things actually happened between them.'

'You want proof?' Xavier said, his mouth mincing as he dug in his satchel. He pulled out an artefact that seemed to be a leather-bound book, with a large, opal stone sewn into the centre of the cover. He slid it across to me, and I picked it up to flick through the wad of cream-coloured, high quality paper within. It was a journal: every page filled with a girl's handwriting, exclamation marks, ink-filled love hearts and, to my revelling surprise, one name repeated frequently at the head of every dated entry: *Maria*.

'Where did you get this?' I asked, my voice sounded robotic; my brain processing.

'Peter Sheridan, Nadia's father, brought it in to me,' Xavier folded his arms, 'he found it in her room, suspicious - rightly so - after he found Maria in his house, with Nadia!'

I winced and closed the journal. The pages were filled with more than enough detail, all the detail I could have hoped for, except, the explicit descriptions of their sexual adventures made me flush suddenly, and I had to compose myself in front of Principal Woods.

'Well,' I started, swallowing a gulp. 'Thank you for handing that over, however, I will need to study it in depth to discern whether or not accounts can be traced to actual events.'

'Come on, Dr Richmond, what more do you need?' Xavier held out his palms toward the journal, his eyes reared wildly as he spoke. 'I understand my word is not enough as evidence, but with Nadia's own father pressing charges, as well as this - documented proof - of an inappropriate affair, surely that's enough for you to recommend this case gets taken to court!'

'Do you want it to go to court?' I frowned, concerned for his motivation. 'The papers will have a field day with a sordid case like this and Gloucester City High will acquire a terrific prejudice, an awful association with sexed-up teachers, no matter what a court decides.'

'I *want* the press to find out! I *want* her hung, drawn, and quartered under society's good, moral code for what she has done! She was supposed to be a professional! I want her fired, and charged with anything that will deem her unfit to teach young women again, she might as well be put on the Sex Offender's Register!' The man railed, his colour rising steadily under the moistness of his forehead. 'Maria Calver is a liar and a pervert, and I will fight for this case to go to court! Even if the justice system fails, I want the press to know the school had no knowledge of the affair, and will not tolerate inappropriate relationships, including homosexual ones. We have standards to maintain for the sake of our reputation!'

I waited until Xavier had dropped his voice and calmed down. I stared at him coolly. He was very passionate, and if he was right about Maria Calver, he had every reason to be furious. However, I could only sense his defensiveness at being deceived by his employee, or his perception of being deceived. I wondered what real evidence he had to suddenly revile her so much, and if he was aggressive towards her as a duplicitous female, or simply because she was a lesbian.

'Let's put things into perspective here, Xavier, Ms Calver is not a paedophile, Nadia is over the age of consent, and she has not only claimed her responsibility, but vindicated her teacher of any wrongdoing. Please, let's not be so alarmist,' I said, extending my fingers gently. 'We must proceed mindfully, and with caution, that this could all be a series of misunderstandings, so let's go back to the beginning.'

Ignoring his mutterings, I glanced at the file photo of Maria Calver, a clear, colour, headshot paper-clipped to the inside of my manila folder. It had been taken from the notice board in the school's reception area, so I could get an idea of who I was dealing with. The woman who looked back at me was not smiling, but held a relaxed stare through the camera to the person beyond, and while her expression gave nothing away, Maria's dark, swarthy, Mediterranean features emitted knowledge, confidence, warmth, and sensitivity all at once. She was a handsome woman, but she appeared strong-minded and I might have liked her, (if I wasn't currently pillaging her employer for her lecherous secrets), so I could easily imagine students wanting to be close to her.

'Okay, without opinion or emotion,' I paused to pick up my pen before sweeping the edge of my hand

Unravel

over a fresh sheet of my notepad, 'tell me when you first had suspicions of Maria's behaviour with Nadia.'

Principal Woods admitted he never saw or felt any strange intimacies between Maria and Nadia. If anything, he was proud of Maria for doing such a good job with a 'trouble-maker'. He recalled how Maria helped settle in the transfer with ease, and when Nadia started missing classes - or turning up disrespectfully late for other teachers - she always showed up for Maria's tuitions. Woods scoffed: 'Now we know why!'

'She once mentioned Nadia was relying too heavily on her for support, and I advised her to continue as best she could manage!' Xavier shook his head, dismayed that he had actually encouraged Maria, but he quickly pointed out that was why he felt so personally betrayed, because Maria was deviously fooling him the whole time. 'She had ample opportunity to report Nadia's attentions, and chose not to - that implies her guilt! She was keeping Nadia's affections secret because she enjoyed them and plotted to mislead me so that she could return them in private.'

I implored Mr Woods to put his bitterness aside for the moment and concentrate on telling me when he first learned of Maria's alleged affair with Nadia.

'Were you aware of any rumours about them around school?' I suggested.

After re-folding his arms in a sulk, Xavier shrugged. 'None that made it to my office... maybe the staff kept them from me,' he said, pulling his mouth down. 'Maybe they thought that I wouldn't hear a word against Maria! However, there were quite a few issues circulating... talk of...' Xavier exaggerated his voice: '*les*-bians.'

'Go on...' I urged, growing impatient.

'Well, there was disturbance among the eleventh years because Miss Sheridan was making waves, behaving overly affectionate towards another girl in her year, Samantha Burrows,' Xavier shifted his shoulders uncomfortably. 'No one could stop talking about them, whether positively or negatively, mainly because they were both attractive girls and didn't seem to have expressed any *inclinations* until that point... everyone got up in arms about them either faking it for attention, or getting excited by them being new role models... I found myself resenting the disruption it caused amongst a year group that should have been focusing on exam revision. I felt quite irritated that *certain colleagues* seemed to be promoting the flaunting of sexuality in a school environment... accusing me of homophobic repression.'

'Who do you mean exactly? Maria?' I queried.

'No, it was Karen Lenholm, being pedantic,' Xavier's face jumped with annoyance. 'Maria was, in retrospect, quiet on the matter, evidently she had her own reasons for being distracted by Nadia!'

'So when Nadia came out, albeit with another girl, did you not make any association with Maria's sexuality? Did you not question Maria on what she made of it?' I was incredulous at his ignorance.

He fell silent, and I heard his breathing furious through a slight whistling from his nostrils. 'Call me naive,' he said, 'but I never assumed a student's sexuality would at all affect Maria's professional conduct. There are boundaries in place for tutors and I had no reason to doubt Maria's refined status. She was a highly reputed AST before we found her!'

'But did you not suspect that Nadia might have been responding to Maria's sexuality by trying to get her attention?' I asked; it seemed a simple question.

The principal switched his response. 'I never thought *Maria* would respond to *Nadia*.'

Woods went on to divulge the circumstances when he first learned of this alleged relationship between Ms Calver and her private tutee. He remembered well the call to his office from Peter Sheridan, but admitted he didn't believe the man, at that stage. Xavier thought the father sounded like an Irish lunatic, and, naturally, was still protecting Maria, his star tutor, who had already mentioned the man's mental issues a few months previously. Therefore, hearing Mr Sheridan rant about Maria being in his house led Xavier to leap, out of fear and weakness, to Maria's defence, justifying that his AST was only looking out for his daughter by making sure she got home safely after tuition, and literally gave the enraged father the

Unravel

principal's very-own authorisation for Maria to keep doing so.

'I feel foolish for believing her and not listening to the poor man,' Xavier said with remorse. 'I presumed he was paranoid, I mean, he told me that Maria had tried to run him over in the street, and I just dismissed it.'

As Xavier's brows furrowed together at the sore memory, I sat back to rest my hand from the tension of its furious scribbling. I also took the moment to think upon how clever a teacher would have to be to sow subtle seeds, in the principal's mind, of a father's mental disarray, so that she may rely on his support once that father inevitably awakened to her sly seduction of his daughter. Unless Maria genuinely believed Peter Sheridan was mad.

Mr Woods then described when Mr Sheridan turned up at the school, some weeks later in June, and demanded to see him. Throwing a book on his desk, the blotchy faced, wiry man explained he had found it in his attic where Nadia slept. At first disturbed by a father's invasion, Xavier revealed that after having a flick he was shocked at the content.

'It was so graphic, I was speechless!' he grimaced, glancing towards the same journal on the desk between us. 'Such filth, I was mortified, I didn't know what to say! I tried to placate Mr Sheridan by reasoning that his daughter writing down her feelings was a positive thing, but he started shouting that I should read it properly,' Xavier twisted his brows. 'Obviously I couldn't, so I said that I believed Maria to be of sound character and I could not hold her responsible for what Nadia wrote in her private journal about her teacher... well, he got madder after that!' Flipping his strong hand against the air as if channelling God, Xavier looked anxious for an intervention. 'I felt like I needed another opinion so I went next door and called Karen from my secretary's desk. I had to show someone else, I was desperately hoping it was just a mix-up, that it wasn't Nadia's journal at all, but Maria's name was written everywhere - I wanted to know if it was Nadia's handwriting.'

'So you asked the games teacher?' I almost scoffed. 'Why didn't you ask her English teacher? Come to think of it, why didn't you just call Maria?'

Irritated by my questioning, the principal wrestled against his chair again. 'Because I didn't want to disturb Maria when I honestly felt this journal had nothing to do with her. I asked Karen because she had verbalised, previously, how scheming Nadia Sheridan could be!'

'And what did Karen say about it?' I asked, smiling, sensing precisely that his inability to cope with lesbian material led him to call the second-most qualified person he knew.

'Well, she laughed at first, she seemed to think it was a hoot!' Xavier scorned.

'I take it this wasn't in front of Mr Sheridan?' I clarified.

'No, I sent him away. I told him we'd look into it, that we'd have to keep the journal as evidence - he seemed to accept that.'

'So Karen came, laughed at first, then what?' I continued.

He explained that Karen said it was racy stuff, but that she believed it was fiction. There was no way Maria would be involved with any student on this kind of level, and Nadia was certainly smart enough to have dreamed it all up, but the question was why. Why each entry was addressed to Maria - as if it had been intended to be presented to Maria as a leaving gift. They realised its premature discovery might have saved Maria a terrible embarrassment later. They resolved to keep it under wraps; they agreed not to concern Maria with it - she had enough on her plate tutoring such a 'promiscuous little madam' as Nadia. The senior year, in the middle of exams, needed to stay focused and a revelation like that would tilt everyone askew.

'Karen said she would keep an eye on Maria,' Xavier finished, 'and we left it at that - she would get back to me if any she had any reason to be suspicious, but assured me her priority was not to raise unnecessary alarm.'

I nodded with grave interest. 'You were content to leave the matter with another teacher? Who, as a lesbian - and a person you have already mentioned was protective of gay rights - may have had her own agenda in reporting issues between Maria and Nadia? What if Karen disliked Maria and wanted to get her fired? She could have imagined up anything, and told you something awful had happened - she could lie and you would have trusted her. Or, say, Karen was in love with Maria, and her reports came back biased and untruthful in the opposite way. Did you not think Karen could be the least reliable witness, because she was a lesbian?'

'Now who's being homophobic?' Xavier smarted. 'No, I didn't! I've known Karen for years and trust her implicitly, we don't always get on, but in general, she is a highly credible, honest, loyal colleague! She never came to me with any reports and I was reassured that she had seen no evidence of wrong-doing; I assumed we could forget all about it now that exams were over and it was the end of term.'

I stretched my back upright, not letting my temper reach my face. 'So tell me, when did you next hear from Karen regarding this matter? My records show that something happened at the prom - end of the final week?'

Xavier Woods played it out for me, as he had observed it. He had been enjoying the end of year celebration from the staff lounge, with most of the older staff, relaxing with a sherry or three, whilst the younger teachers watched over the kids in the hall dancing dreadfully to dreadful dance music. Having heard nothing back from Karen following the 'Sheridan leak',

Xavier had taken the liberty of showing a few other colleagues Nadia's journal to see what they thought. It seemed a safe enough thing to do, seeing as the term was over now, but just as they were taking turns tittering, passing it along, flicking the pages and reading aloud some excerpts, Karen burst into the lounge announcing that everything was true, she had evidence.

'She said she had not seen it exactly, but felt it, in the hall, talking to Maria, when Nadia was there. She saw the look in Maria's eyes when she mentioned the journal,' Xavier related gustily. 'Karen was so overwhelmed, she could hardly explain herself. She insisted I follow her, but I thought she was joking - I half hoped I was being dragged out to a surprise thank you announcement - I wasn't prepared at all,' Xavier shook his head at his own vanity.

Karen had apparently led him through to the auditorium where the prom was in full swing, flanked by all the staff members who, having their curiosity piqued reading up on Maria's scandalous relations with young Nadia, were scurrying along whispering, drunk on sherry. A frustrating, lengthy scan of the hall resulted in Karen swearing loudly that they were gone, and leading the group first to the ground floor toilets, a spacious area off the main corridor, where they failed to locate them, they then moved back out of the lobby entrance and round to the car park. They all followed, working themselves up to a frenzy speculating on where Maria might have taken Nadia. Xavier recounted the scenario through the liqueur-infused confusion.

'There were others with them in the car park, I couldn't see who in the dark exactly, but as we got closer, I recognised Nadia's hair and it was Maria holding her tightly, quite possessively, away from the others. Well, my first thoughts were that Maria was trying to abduct Nadia, the way she was holding her arm out for them to stay back, as if she was taking the girl hostage. I realised I'd had a little too much to drink, and was just working out what to say when Karen stormed straight up to her, pulled Maria round and punched her in the face!' Xavier adjusted himself in his chair, seemingly regretful at such violence.

'I'm not saying I thought Karen was right to do that, but it sobered me up when Maria dropped to the ground. Nadia looked shaken and was being comforted by her friend Samantha. There was another woman, Australian, by the sound of her, she began shouting at Karen, I didn't know who she was, but she was shouting at everyone,' Xavier's words faded then.

I asked him to complete his statement for me, I had to know if he challenged Maria, what she said - what happened next - I was intrigued.

'Maria said nothing, she was on the gravel, wiping the blood from her face, everyone was shouting, everyone had an opinion. There was a lot of questions from all sides, everyone was arguing, then Nadia spoke up suddenly, I think she might have been drinking, she had a loud drunken slur... actually, she sounded quite like her father.'

'What did she say!' I demanded.

Xavier gazed at me coolly. 'She said: "None of this is real", of course, everyone stopped and looked at her. She was trembling - she wasn't wearing much! She said she had been making it all up, that she had been playing a game with Maria, that she had made a bet with Sam that she could seduce Maria, to get good grades, that it had worked - and she had won.'

I listened carefully as Xavier mentioned how everyone was outraged at Nadia for doing such a thing; how Samantha had agreed, begrudgingly, that they had indeed made a bet, though she looked shocked at the reality of Nadia winning, that she really had seduced their teacher.

'How upset did Maria look when Nadia announced she had been manipulating her?' I asked slowly for emphasis.

Xavier replied genuinely. 'Very upset.'

I nodded, ready to conclude the interview. I already knew that Xavier Woods went ahead that night and called the police. He wanted Maria arrested for what he felt was her participation in improper conduct and failure to report a student's attentions, which indicated some level of responsibility he believed warranted investigation.

So here I am, backtracking through these events.

Unravel

I probably shouldn't admit this, but hunting and plucking out the debris of the aftermath makes me as happy as a pig in shit.

Unravel

April 12th

Maria,

I've been afraid to put pen to paper in this journal, but now I know what to write. I have something to write about - at long last – you. Four months... it's been too special to touch, like you were before our bodies touched for the first time and now I need to express every detail in these pages.

    We'd been so good, trying not to, and we were doing fine until that night. Watching that movie with you was bliss, curled up on your couch, drinking a little wine, we only kissed every now and then, but we were in tune. Our souls were connected, and we laughed together, and breathed together. We never took off our clothes, you were shy to even stroke any part of my skin as you held me in your arms.

    Until we had a visitor. Someone you knew, who knew, who accused us, but you defended yourself, you defended me. You told him the truth but you had to lie to him to make him go away. It was hard on you and you wanted me to go, but I wouldn't.

Unravel

I told you I wasn't leaving you, we hadn't done anything wrong. You went to your bedroom to put on your jeans, you said you were driving me home, and I didn't know what else to do so I took off my clothes. You stared at me, asked me what I was doing, asking me if I was crazy, that we'd nearly been caught, but I felt hot and the shame took me over. In just my knickers I wedged myself in the corner by the door and dared you to move me.

    You didn't know what to do. I saw your jaw grit with anger, or something. Suddenly you leapt forward and grasped my body, pulling me from the corner, but I clung to you, wrapping my limbs around you, and kissed you. You picked me up and held me, carrying me to the bed where you laid me down but I wouldn't let you go. We were half wrestling, half frantically kissing. You begged me to stop as you couldn't, but I said I never want you to stop. Your hand led your mouth all the way from my neck to my nipple, and back again, stopping midway to lift my hands over my head. I had no control over myself, I was delirious. It felt incredible and I wanted everything at once, I pulled off your jumper and squeezed your breasts through your vest. You licked my skin all the way down to my stomach, breathing in my scent. I lifted my leg over your shoulder and held your head as you kissed along the inside of my thigh and over the fabric of my knickers. You held off and I could feel your hot breath against my openness. I trembled and wrapped my other leg around your back, pulling you in. You kissed on top of where my clitoris was, but soon I felt your tongue massaging through the lace-edged cotton. All of a sudden I came, at least in part. I apologised as you moved up to my face, you looked shocked but I told you it was okay, it didn't count as my knickers were still on.

    I knew you were helpless to stop kissing all over my body again, going between my neck and my nipples, pushing your pelvis in between my spread legs, before going back down to kiss over my knickers. This time I was swollen and my knickers were soaked, and I felt you suck the moisture through. I felt like I would come quickly again but I didn't want you to stop, I held you in place with my hands on your head as your tongue probed the edge of my knickers where my silky skin was oozing the juice you were thirsty for. Then you sat back and looked at the shape of me, trying to control your desire, weighing your options, I knew. I asked you what was wrong though, and you said you wanted to taste me. I urged you to do it, but you said if you took off my knickers that would be it. I said you didn't have to, then you tentatively pulled my knickers aside and you breathed closely. I trembled, watching you, urging you with my eyes.

  You hesitantly licked, slowly up and down, savouring the taste and texture, as I gasped. My clitoris was full and hard as you rubbed over it with your tongue, you were trembling as much as me! You lowered your tongue and I felt the heat and moisture inside me, and my head fell backwards. Our fingers embraced and we were locked in. I felt your nerves on your breath as you licked, fully charged, passionately French kissing around my clitoris, your lips and tongue revolving expertly. I saw a string of clear sap clinging to your tongue as you lapped up my juice. Your hand reached up to caress my breast. I knew I was building to a slow deep orgasm. I started to moan long and hard before it washed over me, and I whispered your name lightly before my breath failed me.

    I don't remember much else. I think I travelled to another dimension. I don't think I breathed for a whole minute, maybe two. It felt like I only came round once I'd exploded, or imploded, back into the present moment. You took me somewhere else. I was amongst the stars when you made me come. I'm sure that would be considered an out-of-body experience... it hadn't taken long for me to die in your arms before you brought me back to life. I'm sorry for crying afterwards, I felt overwhelmed when you came up and covered me with your body, I needed more than ever to feel your whole weight upon me. We lay together, shaking in silence. You wrapped me in blankets protectively. I wiped tears from your eyes. You said you were sorry for losing control. I said not to be sorry – it was amazing and felt right.

And afterwards, everything seemed a little different, I felt like I had grown up suddenly. We seemed to be new, adult, equal, I saw us as a couple for the first time. You treated me differently, with respect. You looked at me differently, like I wasn't a kid. Things were a bit edgy, but you let me stay the night, and we were closer than ever. You knew when I wanted to kiss, I knew when you wanted to be quiet. I knew when you were thinking, and what you were thinking about, and I knew when I should say something or not.

It was a big deal, I know that. More to you than me, in some ways, more to me than you, in ways you'll never understand. I love you so completely I'm afraid to tell you, that's why I write to you, like you taught me.

Nadia x

Unravel

Chapter Twenty-Eight

After reading this first entry, I sat sweltering in my Cheltenham office, wondering how much of it was true, and if so, which male had interrupted them. After a cool gin and tonic, I made plans to meet Nadia's father. The phone call I made to him, however, had brought to me the distinct feeling that he was a highly anxious man; I wanted him to be as comfortable as possible during our interview, so I arranged to meet him in his own home.

I enjoyed the countryside drive to Eastcombe, until I got in a pickle as my navigation device failed to lead me to the quiet, winding road where he lived. Once I parked outside the unkempt, depressed-looking property, my hope that my visit would be a pleasant one continued to descend.

Peter Sheridan looked exhausted when he came to the door to see me in. His body lacked sustenance, his muscles too lean. His face was etched with heavy lines around what I imagined used to be striking, almost handsome, piercing green eyes, though he rarely raised them up to meet mine. He looked older than forty-three, a little scruffy, but seemed otherwise intelligent, like any off-duty hospital worker.

'You'll have to excuse the mess, I've just finished a night shift, and Nadia isn't here,' he said, in rushed, crackling Irish. He spoke into the middle distance, somewhere just beyond my person, his lost gaze falling to the edges of my presence. He was shifting nervously as he showed me through to a room that seemed to be half kitchen, half squat, and his hands continued to fidget in and out of the back pockets of his loose, shabby jeans.

Without even offering me refreshment, Peter Sheridan rolled straight into a sob story regarding the circumstances of his isolation in the West Country. I found a seat in a grubby armchair next to his worn sofa, and I stared over the clutter of items surrounding him on the glass-topped coffee table, and the unclean carpet: a lighter; a rolling machine; an ashtray; a crumpled lottery ticket; an empty envelope, ripped violently at the edges. A few pen lids and some coins. Some empty packet of crisps or nuts, folded, and wedged into the space where the glass met the metal edge. Some dry flakes of tobacco on a folded, classified ads magazine: all associates of a miserable bachelor. I pulled out my notepad ready to catch the precious statements.

Perching against a chest in front of the windows, Mr Sheridan rolled a cigarette from his pouch without focusing on it at all, instead, he openly revealed that his wife left him for another man. The heartbreak sent him fleeing to England, however, after repeating himself with pitiful details, I learned that, technically, his wife hadn't left the marriage - *he* had – after catching her cheating. His expressions of pain, re-living that torturous period, accompanied dramatic gestures of stabbing motions towards his chest and gut that, whilst compelling me to keep watching, made me wonder if the man was always so theatrical, or if he was hamming it up for my benefit.

'I used to be a man, but that witch ripped out every last drop of goodness, of innocence,' Peter's jaw wrenched down with internalised agony. 'I used to be proud, but she ruined me... and I'm nothing now, and she's a whore!' he spat suddenly, 'and Nadia's just as bad, she's got her mother's cruel streak!' his voice lowered cruelly. 'She did something so sick, so impure; she brought shame on the whole family! And then she comes here!' He shouted, and winced at the unfairness of life. 'I never wanted her here!'

'What happened to Nadia in Dublin?' I asked. 'Why did she get sent here to you?'

He turned his bright eyes on me, they were washed out in colour, but still vibrant with intensity. 'I'll tell you what she did, and you can write it down!' he reared from the chest of drawers behind him, wobbling the dusty collection of magazines on top of it. 'That dirty little bitch got up to her elbows in sin, took up with the very daughter of that bastard who stole my wife!'

I should have held my poker face, but my shock was too immediate; it faded only as I processed what the man had actually said. I think it was safe to say, without need for further clarification, that Nadia had slept with her mother's boyfriend's daughter. That was why she had left Dublin – presumably, she had been kicked out of home - and consequently her father didn't want her either.

'Mr Sheridan, do you think Nadia is a lesbian? Perhaps she was crying out for attention?' I braved the question, half expecting the man to lose his rag altogether.

'Of course not!' he scoffed. 'She's just messed up! We all are! Sweet Jesus, between her mother and me, the girl's got no chance!'

I took this to mean that Peter Sheridan acknowledged he had some issues with his mental health. I wanted to seize the opportunity, whilst he had mentioned it, to ask a few delicate questions, but my timing was too sensitive; he continued his rant about his daughter.

'She's always been disruptive, ever since...' he rubbed his stubbly mouth and chin, his eyes burning into the dark-stained floorboards. 'She didn't cope with the divorce too well, I suppose,' he gestured with a hint of empathy I thought looked false on him. 'She went off the rails, my sister told me everything, dropping out of school she was, messing around with drugs, she ended up on the streets, but she couldn't hack it, she ain't that tough, she likes to think she can make it, but she's still a girl.'

I referred to my notes, wary of his anxiety rubbing off on me.

'Nadia was reported missing in Dublin,' I read, monotonic. 'Found by police, taken into care, social services contacted you, and you agreed to have her as long as she re-took her final year.'

'I never had a choice, let's make that clear, they dumped her on me and if it was up to me, she'd be out on her own, she's old enough to make her own decisions and if she wants to fuck her life up, well, she did that once, and look, she's done it again! I tell you, that girl is bad to the core.' Peter swept back his thinning hair. He was sweating, I noticed; his skin looked pale.

'Okay,' I pushed down a lump in my throat. The vague, uneasy presence of threatening violence hung in the air, not between us in particular, but around Peter Sheridan individually. There was something wrong about him, and I dreaded allowing my mind to start imagining up a shifty condition. He might have been an alcoholic. He had the drawn features and slightly bulging, glazed eyes of a junkie. I wasn't sure if I could diagnose him without asking deeply personal questions, which I didn't really want to do alone with him in his house. 'Can you tell me what you knew of Nadia's tuition?'

'Well, what do you want to know?' he shrugged as if the subject was unimportant. 'The school sent a letter saying she'd be receiving extra classes, I signed it, sent it back. They needn't have asked my permission for that! The more time she spends at school the better! As long as I didn't have to pay for it, I told them.'

'And you didn't ask any questions about who would be giving your daughter tuition?'

'I can't say I cared!' Peter exclaimed. 'As long as Nadia behaved herself and kept out of my way, I didn't give two shits who, or should I say *what* was teaching her, because I work all the hours God sends, I haven't got time to sit around thinking about stuff like that. The school said they'd take care of her - that was good enough for me, but they didn't, did they? They sent in a predator.'

His reasoning was aggressive, but fair, and I honestly felt trapped. I could see Mr Sheridan had neglected his daughter for the sake of familial pride, but he also had every right in entrusting Nadia's care to a reputable tutor.

'Mr Sheridan, could you recall for me the first time you met Nadia's tutor?'

The highly-strung father related to me how after working a double shift, he had finished early and walked home from the local bus stop, it was dusk, with no lights on the country road to his house, when he was nearly mown down by a sports car racing around the corners. The car stopped, the driver shouted at him, an argument ensued, which is when he realised Nadia was in the passenger seat.

'I begged her to get out, I was terrified that this crazy woman driving was going to have an accident the way she was going, I just wanted Nadia to be safe,' he whined.

I hid the twitch of my muscles at this subtle contradiction. Suddenly he cared.

'I mean, it was after dark, who was this *dyke* driving my daughter away? Where had they been? What had they been doing? That's what I want to know! I felt like my little girl was in danger - being taken away by this wreckless bitch that very nearly killed me! And her dog attacked me!'

Delving into my file again, I pulled loose the photo of Maria. 'Is this the woman you saw driving your daughter?' I asked, needing to ensure Nadia was only seeing the one "dyke".

'Yes,' Peter confirmed with an inflamed glare at the photo. 'That's her.'

'So you didn't know who she was at that point? She didn't introduce herself?'

Peter tapped his fingers against his chest, a rhythmic patting that reminded me of an autistic child. 'Actually, I remember now, she did, yeah, she did tell me she was Nadia's tutor, I forgot that part,' he smiled strangely, looking down to the floor again, still patting his chest.

Unravel

Memory is easily lost and recalled, whatever our state of mind at the time, or whatever influence we might be under, but it is usually retrievable with certain triggers. It crossed my mind that Peter only remembered what his condition permitted, and I naturally gauged he was on medication for something. Yes. That ticked a box. He had the vacancy of one prescribed.

'What upset you more, Peter?' I asked, feeling my power coming back. 'That Nadia was being escorted home by a dangerous driver, or the fact that the driver was a lesbian?'

Peter's eyes reared widely and his fingers ceased their tapping. 'What are you accusing me of?' he glared at me again; it ran a chill down my spine. 'Why are you attacking me? She's the one who fucked my daughter, not me! What does it matter what upset me more? The fact is I'm upset - full stop! And I have every right to be!'

'Mr Sheridan, please stay calm, I'm just trying to gauge when you first suspected Nadia was being intimate with her teacher,' I lied quickly to cover myself, my heart beating. I had heard Principal Woods mention something that I wanted to cross-reference with Peter's account. 'Was that the only time you met her?'

Peter Sheridan stood and went to a cabinet in the corner and swung open a small door. From inside he pulled out a bottle of alcohol, and a tumbler. He started to mutter as he poured himself a drink, something about coming face to face with the devil, before half turning to gesture the bottle towards me. I politely declined, (not that I wasn't gasping for a drink, but whiskey isn't my preferred tipple). Then, from behind the other cabinet door, Peter pulled out a small dark container with a screw top, spilled the small tablets onto the wooden counter, picked two and swiftly threw them to the back of his throat. He washed them down with all of his short drink, with his back to me, as if I wouldn't see.

Then he spun around, wiping his mouth, shaking his head.

'She'd been in my house, I don't know what she'd been doing, I don't even want to think about it, the dirty fucking bitch,' he snarled in his curling, cutting Irish. 'It was sometime late in the month of May, I opened my front door, and this bloody woman was coming out of my house, Nadia right behind her, saying: "Oh hi" - like there's nothing wrong!'

The account matched what Woods had said Peter told him. 'It was Maria?'

'I couldn't give a fuck what her name is, she's a filthy cunt!' he visibly spat and I saw it fly through the air in an arch toward me. 'She gave me this demented smile as if to say: "Guess who!" and saying Nadia had "given her a tour" - I bet she had! Her mouth was all red and used, like a whore's mouth!'

Unravel

I felt battered by his language, yet I had no problem imagining his disgust. I wanted to ask again if it was Maria's mouth that was red, or Nadia's, but I had the feeling that he was about to flip out if I made him specify. I wondered *who* had been kissing *where* if only one had red lips: it really did make a lot of difference.

'I knew right there and then that she was influencing my daughter! Leading her astray! Some teacher!' Peter rubbed his hand down the ravines of his face. 'Look, Nadia doesn't need any help finding out who she is, she's a feisty girl, but it's not right that some dyke should be allowed to tutor her. I didn't know what was happening, I should have been told!'

'Mr Sheridan, with all due respect, just because a teacher is a lesbian, doesn't mean she will try and seduce one's daughter,' I tried explaining. 'Ms Calver has an excellent track record as both a home and school tutor, and for all we know so far, Nadia is the one who instigated things.'

The father lowered his pinpricked eyes upon me, blazing with translucent emerald in the bright light of the hot morning. 'I have no doubt that little hussy led that woman into my house deliberately to hurt me, but that *woman*, that *teacher*, is twice her age and should know better!' he shouted, looking like the vein in his temple might pop.

'I knew what they were up to, I've seen that look before and they couldn't fool me with their smiles. As soon as Nadia was out of the house, I searched

Unravel

everywhere in that attic for some evidence that I wasn't just imagining things - and I came up trumps, didn't I? I found her dirty diary, didn't I? Christ, I've never read anything so disgusting in my whole life! "Maria" this, "Maria" that! *Maria* should be locked up with the other paedophiles!' he taunted, sounding childishly bitter.

'You write this down!' he went on, 'I've no faith in this country's justice system! They don't listen to long-suffering, hard-working men like me. That principal didn't believe me either, when I gave him the journal, he tried defending her, but I have ways of exerting my own methods of punishment to those who have offended me...' he tapped his fingers over his heart again. 'Personal retribution, that's the law of the land.'

Curious as to what punishment he intended, I asked what he meant.

His words came slurred, and I wondered if whatever he'd taken was having effect: 'Eye for an eye, you take what's mine and I'll take what's yours,' he smiled, creepily; he looked stoned with smugness.

My breath held in my lungs for a moment before I could summon words. 'Peter, I would seriously advise you not to take the law into your own hands.'

'I should think i'tis too late for all that,' he chuckled loosely, stroking his hands across his arms again.

I bit the bullet, now that he was sedated.

'Peter? May I ask what your medication is for?' I asked gently, then listened to his second, rambling bout of history, this time post-divorce, here in deepest, darkest Stroud.

The proud man he used to be in Dublin was a leading nurse, a specialist in head injuries, Peter told me, and finding work in England brought him to the hospital in Gloucester. However, alone and suffering in silence, he threw himself into work. He developed this habit, these routines: particular ways of doing things so he could maintain control of everything that had fallen away from his previous life. He said he didn't know who he was anymore, but when he felt anxious, the routines would make his brain hurt less. His thoughts became disturbing, he became paranoid of becoming lost like his patients, so he started turning to the very substances he issued to his patients in order to wake up and wind down between shifts.

After a year of managing by himself in this way, his bosses informed him they were concerned, sent him to a therapist, but he refused treatment. He lost his job, but was allowed to keep working in the same hospital, but only as a porter, and all his privileges were taken away. Except he still had access to the pharmaceuticals, since he still visited the patients he'd treated when they'd arrived, fresh with brains on the outside of their skulls.

These last eight months following his demotion had been spent in depression and using every hour of overtime to ignore his own trauma. Peter said he drank to ease the pain, and self-medicated with whatever drugs he could 'misplace'. This often caused his mood to spiral out of control, the very thing he was trying so desperately to grasp hold of again.

This is what Nadia was living with.

I had thought Peter Sheridan was tapped, but I wasn't expecting to pity him. The man had sunk down between his knees on the couch and was holding his head between his palms, pathetically. I wanted more than anything to advise him that he needed help, that therapy could benefit him in a multitude of ways, yet, ironically, he was more of a therapist than me. I was neither qualified in clinical psychology nor psychiatry and I felt out of my depth. Anyway, he had resisted help before and would resist it again. He was still proud, and a stubborn man. Part of him identified with pain, he lived with pain, inside work and out. He probably couldn't keep working if he wasn't thriving in some manner from his internal, eternal agony.

'Nadia doesn't know about this,' he wept weakly. 'I never told her about my problems... please don't tell her. She can't see me like this. I'd rather kill myself than have her look at me like I'm useless... like her mother did.'

I put my pad down and moved across to him tenderly, my hand shaking as it neared his hunched, shirted back.

'Peter, maybe Nadia needs you more than you know,' I held his thin, hot, trembling frame, and his shoulder felt moist and strange under my wrist.

Speaking softly again, I rubbed his back in a small circle that made me queasy, as if I were absorbing his anguish. 'Try to forgive her, she's your daughter... you can undo this cycle of pain and anger, she'll forgive you too.'

He glanced up so quickly he scared me. 'Why the fuck should I forgive her?' he shouted, turning on me. 'She's ruined everything! I've slogged my guts out my whole life to provide for her, and she destroyed our family. She's a stupid slut, just like her mother! Cycle of pain, what bullshit! And what does she have to forgive me for? I haven't done anything wrong! I'm not the one who goes around ruining other people's lives!' he stood up, the glass table shuddering. 'Why don't you get out?'

He walked out into the hall, still shouting, I heard him throw his fist into the wall. I jumped and grabbed my bag and notepad from the table. I heard him ranting about how we all thought we knew better than he did; opening his front door, slamming it back into the wall.

'I said get out, you stupid bitch!' he hollered from the front door.

I instinctively swiped a pill from his cabinet on my way out, and held myself tall and calm, though I almost anticipated a bash around the head from the volatile creature, but he turned me out into the morning sun unharmed. I slipped the pill into my handbag side pocket as I made my way to my car without looking back. I couldn't believe, seconds before, I had embraced him with empathy. As I pulled away in my Mazda, my overwhelming thought was of Nadia: there was no way she would ever, in her right mind, want to go back there.

Unravel

April 17th

Maria,

I know we promised we weren't going to do anything, and then we did, but since you swore we couldn't do anything like that again, it's been even harder to resist you. Just the fact that we broke our own rule has made things so much more intense, because we both know that we could, and it would feel amazing all over again, like we knew it would. In tuition, I couldn't concentrate until I'd kissed you. You said we couldn't in case someone came in, but I told you I only wanted to kiss your cheek, and it would only take a second. You smiled and I told you to trust me. My lips lingered on your cheek and I heard your breath suspend, so I moved my mouth to your ear and sucked the lobe. You twitched away and chuckled, I must have tickled you, but I wanted to do so much more.

  I came to yours after school separately, as we'd arranged, and on the bus I took off my bra because I wanted you to see my nipples poking under my school shirt and jumper when you opened the door. But you didn't notice. You were in a strange mood, hardly talking, working on your laptop and ignoring me fidgeting on your couch, where I was sighing and stretching my arms around in a bid to entice you over to me. Dinner was hardly romantic, just some pasta mixed in with soup, it felt as if you were trying to put me off. Then you said I had to go home, and we argued because I wanted to stay. You said I'd stayed enough this week and my dad would call the police. I could see why you were worried, so I agreed to go home.

    On the drive back, I put my hand in your lap, you flinched but I kept rubbing my hand against your thigh… you pretended to ignore it, but I knew you liked it. No one could see into your car in the dark.

    But when we came to pass our special place, I pulled on the steering wheel and you swore at me before driving in. I apologised as you drove us to our favourite spot on the beacon, explaining that I had to kiss you before I went home. We settled overlooking the city and I climbed over to straddle you. Something dug in my knees and my foot was twisted but I didn't care, I had to feel your body. You weren't smiling, you said we'd gone too far already, that we couldn't do anything else. I said nobody could see us, no one would ever know. I pulled off my jumper, zapping with static against my hair, it was getting hot quickly, and you must have only just realised I wasn't wearing a bra. I unbuttoned my white shirt but couldn't get it off so it stayed wrapped round my elbows, my nipples aching towards your hot mouth.

    I held your head in my hands and kissed your lips, but it was awkward until you rolled the seat back into a slight recline. I felt a craving shudder shoot up my thighs and I adjusted myself on top of you until I felt your hands against my hips. I rocked and dipped against your jeans, my eyes locked onto yours and my arms wrapped around your shoulders. When your hands lifted up to my waist I leaned back, arching up, knowing you were looking at me and wanting you to see me more than anything in the world. I held my hands over yours and wanted you to move in time with me. I couldn't feel you writhing under me but I saw your chest rising and your mouth open, panting. I taunted your lips with my nipples and you lurched, screwing your eyes up, helpless with desire. You held my butt cheeks tighter in your firm grip, tilting me forward until my breasts smothered your face and you groaned, sucking until my nipples filled your wet mouth.

 I was so turned on, I lowered my hand inside my leggings and began rubbing myself. I don't know if you even noticed as you seemed to be absorbed in my boobs. I was so wet, soaked, I wanted you to feel it. I asked you to put your fingers inside me, you looked out the windows either side and refused, said it wasn't safe. I laughed, asked what safe sex was, and said you wouldn't get me pregnant. You smiled and narrowed your eyes in that sexy way you do. I begged you to touch me just for a minute, just to see how wet you had made me.

You pushed your hand between us and down inside my knickers, twisting your palm up to glide your fingertips against me. You said I was softer than silk. I felt so hot and trembled, I felt your heart thumping under my breast. I pushed your elbow straighter, guiding you deeper. I wanted to sit on you, eat you whole. We whispered hot words into each other's mouths and I pleaded for you enter me. I lifted my body higher for you to get the angle right, and then I felt your solid fingers, stiff inside me, pushing up and forward, making me freeze in a taut buckle over you, only able to catch my breath in gasps between cries.

    Maybe you think I came, maybe I did in a way, but I wasn't finished. You swore, annoyed with me, or yourself, and withdrew your fingers but I wouldn't let you go. I kissed your mouth as deeply as I could, I didn't want you to stop but I couldn't speak. I rubbed your breasts through your shirt and kept writhing against you so you'd know to keep going, and you did. Your fingertips found my love button and you teased it expertly in the way you knew would get me there. I lifted my nipple to your mouth and you gripped it with your other hand, torturing me with your tongue. I released a cry louder than I have ever in my whole life. I wanted it to echo around the whole beacon, flood the skies above Gloucester, for everyone who we had to hide from to hear it.

Then I let you drive me home.

I slept well that night.

Nadia x

Chapter Twenty-Nine

The following day I awoke after a disturbed night of sleep. My dreams, whilst suitably faded by the time I'd showered and eaten breakfast, still left shadows of strangeness about me, and my head felt groggy from the sedative I'd resorted to at three o'clock in the morning.

I was due to meet Karen Lenholm, the head of games at GCH, however, after the debacle of visiting Mr Sheridan at his home, I arranged to meet Ms Lenholm in a mutual place for middle-aged ladies who lunch: a coffee house in Cheltenham town centre.

Just before leaving my house, I found myself gazing at the photo of Maria Calver, wondering what her smile was like. I considered Maria attractive, and wondered if Karen was attractive too. I thought it natural that Karen would have found Maria attractive, as a new, younger, lesbian colleague, and wondered - as I stared into my reflection at the cool shirt and beige, linen trousers I had adorned - if Karen would find me attractive. It mattered not, even with any attempts to get her on side, the wedding ring on my finger would let her know I wasn't interested in that way.

When I saw Karen, I relaxed. She was very smiley, held herself assertively, and made strong eye contact. She wore a pastel coloured gilet and trainers, and welcomed me to take a seat in the window of a comfortable booth of our chosen location. I ordered a cappuccino, but to my surprise Karen brought a slice of cake for me, against my humble protests, so I took out my notepad, to let her know we were there for business, however informal our greeting had been.

'I'd like to start with a brief character reference for Maria Calver,' I began. 'How did she fit in with the school staff? What did you think of her?'

Karen meshed her fingers together and propped them in front of her face, which twisted as she recalled. 'I thought she was nice,' she shrugged, though I could sense the underlying resentment. 'But, she kept herself to herself, everyone has always said she's elusive, because she never socialised with any of the staff... I tried to make her feel part of the team, I really did.'

'And tell me how you felt having another lesbian *on the team*, as you say, were you more inclined towards her than usual? Did you feel you had a connection with her?' I asked.

'Sorry?' Karen smiled tensely. 'I'm not sure what that's got to do with anything? I thought we were here to discuss Maria's relationship with Nadia Sheridan, not Maria and me! There never was a "Maria and me"! It was all fake, so she could keep me fooled while she played around with a girl half her age!'

I lowered my head, accepting my faulty questioning. I knew I shouldn't get off to a bad start with Karen: I wanted her to open up to me with some insider information on all the lesbian activity.

'I apologise, I didn't mean to offend you, I'm just trying to get an idea of how Maria's sexuality manifested at school... So, can you tell me when you first suspected Maria might be engaging with Nadia in ways you considered inappropriate?'

'That's okay, I want to help,' Karen refreshed herself with a sip of her coffee. 'Well, I guess the first thing that worried me was that Nadia seemed to be taking up so much of Maria's time,' Karen pressed her chin down into her neck, troubled by the memory. 'Maria confided to me that Nadia was having problems at home, and becoming very clingy, emotionally needy... Maria was feeling under extra pressure to help Nadia deal with more than just her academic programme.'

Having first-hand experience of what Nadia must have been going through at home, I sympathised now with her need for a supportive teacher's company.

Karen went on. 'I warned Maria about student crushes before, you know, that she could expect it, she's good-looking, right?' she faded slightly, then lifted her voice again. 'But, Nadia... she started skipping her other classes, that's when I really started to

Unravel

think she was an attention-seeker, those smart, calculating eyes... using Maria's tuition to supplement her real classes,' Karen shook her head.

Writing down as much as I could of Karen's revelations, between sips of coffee, I started to get a clearer picture of how Maria had conducted herself during those early autumn months. I found out that Maria had sought Karen's advice one day, but only to entrust her colleague with the fact that she had introduced Nadia to a nice boy she used to teach at the school, in the hope that he would provide extra-curricular activity and relieve pressure from herself in being Nadia's sole source of friendship. Karen said she supported Maria's decision.

'But what pisses me off is that,' Karen inhaled sharply, 'the only reason she told me that was to make it sound like she was bothered by Nadia's attention... now I know it was a sly, pre-meditated move to cover her tracks, and fool me into supporting her.'

I tried to look at Karen's logic objectively. 'Why do you feel Maria was lying to you? Surely if she was finding Nadia a boyfriend, it was for the girl's wellbeing, not for her own gain.'

'Look, you don't know Maria like I do, but you must know a woman's sneaky mind,' Karen raised her eyebrows. 'Imagine a woman who has her own agenda, and then add a clever teacher to the mix, and then appreciate that a lesbian is a smarter creature than most!'

I grimaced. 'What's your point?'

'My point is that Maria had ample opportunities to tell me the truth - if she *was* concerned by any lesbian feelings Nadia might be having and how that made her feel. I trusted that Maria wanted the best for Nadia, but she withheld critical information she knew would make me question her... like the fact that the boy was her dog-sitter, and that they regularly hung out at her house,' Karen gestured with a bony finger. 'I only learned that in Nadia's journal.'

Writing it all down, I stopped to sigh. There was no evidence that Nadia's journal wasn't pure fabrication - Nadia herself had even admitted that it was - and from what Principal Woods had told me, Karen had laughed at the journal on first reading, and had not taken it seriously until later on, when her own eyes failed to deceive her. I wanted to hear about that.

Resting my pen, I took up the fork and edged off a section of carrot cake. I could feel Karen's eyes watching me as I raised it to my mouth, I felt self-conscious, but the cake was moist enough for me not to care. I wasn't trying to seduce Karen with my oral motions and groaning, but it did cross my mind that it wouldn't take much to allow Karen to think what she liked. Maria was not at complete fault for misleading Karen: the woman was hungry for it.

'So, disregarding what you've read from Nadia's journal,' I asked, once I had swallowed, opening my folder for my case notes. 'Can you tell me your discoveries surrounding the events of Nadia's relationship with Samantha Burrows? Did you feel differently about her when she 'came out' at school?'

Taking the fork I had just used, Karen separated a chunk of carrot cake from the plate in front of me and shovelled it into her mouth while she contemplated her answer.

I was horrified, but hid my disgust as I watched her suck the crumbs from her pale lips, lacking any sign of self-consciousness.

'When I heard the rumours going around that Nadia and Sam were "an item", I was pleased,' she replied. 'It was very exciting to have a new couple to gossip about, and of course I felt proud that two of our year eleven girls were strong enough to make such a stand amongst their peers. In all honesty, we were anticipating a backlash, but I think everyone was too surprised by the fact that they were two pretty girls to have any objections.'

'Did you think Nadia was still seeking attention?' I felt I was justified asking that.

'Weelll...' Karen cringed at herself. 'I suppose I was a little biased, I wanted to believe they were genuine because otherwise why would you come out as gay? Who chooses to be ridiculed and alienated from one's peer group?' she shrugged. 'I thought they were very brave, I'd long suspected Sam was that way inclined and it made me think Nadia had some balls, some substance to her... it kind of helped me understand why she was troubled.'

'And how did Maria react to this news? She'd just found Nadia a boyfriend.'

Karen chuckled. 'No, she didn't believe it was real, she didn't even think Nadia was lesbian, I wound her up about that – that her own student couldn't come out to her because she was so...' Karen fell silent and the smile faded from her face. Something must have occurred to her, as her eyes clouded over and I couldn't read her.

'What is it?' I asked, probingly. 'Do you think Maria already knew that Nadia was gay but made out to you that she didn't? Do you think, in retrospect, that things were already occurring between them at this stage?'

'I don't know,' Karen sighed, shaking her grey head. 'Maria said she didn't know - that Nadia had never come out to her. I mean, if she was lying, I couldn't tell. She convinced me that seeing Nadia with Sam was the first she'd heard of it, and she seemed genuinely shocked. I guess I was blind... I was too excited and didn't care that it disturbed Maria... If I'd have thought about it, I might have questioned it deeper.'

I scribbled, thinking hard. Maria may or may not have been feigning surprise - all I had to go on was the un-impartial view of a pro-gay colleague who failed to notice anything untoward at all. I huffed, craving more carrot cake, repelled by the fork transgression.

'So, after that, how did you imagine Maria dealt with Nadia in tuition? Did she confide in any new stresses or difficulties with Nadia since she came out?'

'No, as far as we knew Nadia was seeing Sam so there wasn't reason to think she'd be interested in Maria, it seemed to me if Nadia wasn't so reliant on Maria it would vastly improve their tuition, even if the boyfriend had become somewhat redundant.'

'Didn't anyone question what a lesbian teacher was doing spending hours alone each evening with a lesbian student?' I marvelled.

'Listen, no one ever doubted Maria's professionalism!' Karen raised her voice with emphasis. 'She was always so serious, stern... she had problems with her own girlfriend, she was slightly depressive if anything, she wasn't the type to flirt or banter, she was a no-nonsense tutor and we never had reason to think she was being anything less than strict with Nadia...' Karen mused for a few moments, her frown pressing. 'Personally, knowing Nadia's mood-swings and demands, I suppose I thought that Maria was being a pushover - under pressure from Woods to pass a difficult student - but I never, *ever* thought Maria would stoop so low as to conduct a sexual relationship with Nadia. I *knew* they spent countless hours together, I *knew* Maria was escorting her home after tuition, but I thought Maria was too stiff, too aloof, to ever allow a student to sway her... I always thought she was straight down the line professional, a rock of a teacher... I had more than admiration for her.'

I was listening, but really all I could hear was how Karen kept contradicting herself. Even she seemed perturbed by her own defiant claims of Maria's solid character, since learning of Nadia's journal, everything she had thought she knew about her had been thrown into question. It was as if she felt hurt by the idea of Maria lying more than anything, but that struck the same chords of doubt within me that Principal Woods had. I needed more evidence, because so far Maria was sounding like a gem.

'Karen, after Mr Woods showed you Nadia's journal, you agreed to keep an eye on Maria, is that right? So you didn't consider it reason enough to question her – but why did you not show Maria straight away?' I asked. 'She could have cleared things up right there and then.'

Squirming in her seat a little, Karen shrugged. 'Because exams were in full swing and everyone had more important things to concentrate on.'

'More important than one of your teachers allegedly having a relationship with one of your students?' I smarted.

'Okay, I admit the journal wasn't taken that seriously!' Karen waved her hands. 'Woods told me that Nadia's father had mental problems and to placate him, that we should just say we're keeping an eye on things, which he asked me to do as Maria's closest colleague, so I did!'

I was hesitant to say so, but if Maria had meant to pull the wool over everyone's eyes, then events had conspired on her side to convince them of her innocence: Peter Sheridan was certainly capable of presenting his own insanity, irrespective of anything Maria may have initially planted in the principal's mind.

'Did you ever witness anything you could call intimate between Maria and Nadia?' I asked generically.

'Actually, there was one occasion, back in April, I walked into Maria's office, just to check up on her, see if she was okay, go for lunch, that kind of thing,' Karen sat forward and lowered her voice for a more private tone. 'I saw her sitting on her couch, crying.'

'Who, Maria?' I asked.

'Yeah, and Nadia was sat beside her with her arm around her. Of course, I asked what was going on, Nadia snatched her arm away and Maria looked really uncomfortable. It was tangibly awkward,' Karen paused to scratch her neck, her chin jutting out with all the ungainly pleasure of an animal. 'Eventually, Nadia said Maria's dog had been killed, run over by a car. Well, I felt awful for her and went over, but I wanted Nadia to leave so I told her I'd take care of Maria. Nadia gave this look, little madam. After she'd gone I hugged

Maria, she did seem genuinely upset, but I asked her if Nadia was getting to her, being inappropriate, you know. She said no...' Karen shrugged. 'See, that was another opportunity for her to tell me that Nadia was playing games with her emotions. But she didn't, and I had nothing else I could say.'

This was interesting. Maria's pet had died, she would have loved her dog, I could see that from the softness in her eyes, as motionless as they were in her photo. I wondered how Nadia, as her other beloved pet, would have shown Maria her support. A moment later and Karen could have witnessed an emotionally-fraught kiss... except, without Karen's actual visual, it was just a hunch, and I had a hunch that jealousy was playing a role here.

'Karen, were you upset that Maria didn't confide in you?' I asked suggestively. 'Regardless of the nature of the issues she was obviously having with Nadia, did you feel left out? I'm getting a sense from you that it almost didn't matter if she was engaging with Nadia emotionally, you were, perhaps, *envious* of the fact that Nadia was having a deeper kind of interaction with Maria than you were able to,' I held my pen to my mouth for protection.

To her credit, Karen Lenholm didn't jump across the booth and slap me around the face as anyone else might have been justified doing; I certainly would have refrained from asking Peter Sheridan that question if he were in Karen's unsightly, air-sprung trainers.

Instead, she pressed her lips with a burdened frown, and I was relieved that I had managed once again to dig successfully underneath someone's pretence.

'I can admit that it affected me that Maria was so unavailable,' Karen sniffed. 'I wanted to be friends but she was so withdrawn, I wanted her to be more personal, but... well, typical lesbian fool, I guess I fell for her in many ways. I felt like... she never really noticed me... she hardly even saw me as a friend, never mind anything more,' Karen's words faltered, her lips wobbled and I realised her lowered eyes were about to brim with tears.

Having a flashback of Mr Sheridan's weeping, I held firm and resisted reaching out.

'I should tell you,' Karen confided, 'during the last week of exams in June, after Woods had shown me the journal, I went to find Maria. I don't know if I was expecting to catch her with Nadia again, but I felt drawn to her. I told myself she needed me, I thought I could sense her distress, so I went to her office. She was there alone, she had her head in her hands, she looked so distant, I was really worried about her. I took her hands in mine, gave her a hug, she let me hold her and I felt something between us,' Karen's eyes spilled now, her chin wrinkling.

'I held her face close to mine, and she was not all there, her eyes were dark and really far away, so I kissed her, and she let me, she didn't push me away...

But Nadia appeared at the door, she saw us, and her face was a picture, she looked devastated, and just ran out. I was expecting Maria to go after her, but she didn't. I felt her heart beating, she just kept holding onto me. I've never felt her be so tender before, it was a really special feeling.'

Instinctively, I knew that Karen's feelings for Maria were not reciprocated. Whatever reason Maria had remained in her arms, it was not out of love for Karen. I guessed Karen knew that too, with hindsight. 'I think your feelings may have clouded your ability to see what was happening between Maria and Nadia,' I said, sensitively.

'I know that,' Karen collected the napkin from beside the fork and wiped her face. 'Even though the rumours about Maria and Nadia's close relationship had gotten around school, I was deluded. Don't you see? That's why it hurts so much - I hate that Maria was so secretive and deceptive when I was trying to give her my support. Those last few days of the end of term, I really thought we bonded, we spent more time together than we ever had, and though she didn't talk about Nadia, I could tell she was trying to distance herself from the girl.'

Happily free from delusional feelings of love, if I were Karen or a fellow teacher at the school, I would have thought it suspicious in itself that Maria and Nadia weren't interacting. My mind wandered slightly to what could have happened between the two of them; why

Maria was withdrawing from Nadia at a critical time during the girl's exams - it seemed to defeat the object of tuition. Then again, there would be no reason for them to have tuition anymore, now that Maria had successfully gotten Nadia to the point of sitting exams.

Karen was still whining. 'She was using me to distract from all the rumours. She even agreed to go with me to the prom... God, I feel stupid... she was obviously hiding how she felt about Nadia, she wanted someone younger than me... she made me feel old,' she blew her nose now, sobbing heartily.

Cringing at some attention we were attracting from the coffee drinkers at nearby tables, I made a terrible act of being casual regarding Karen's weeping, and picked at the carrot cake with my fingers, before I flinched away when Karen spotted me, and it ended up in my hair.

'Karen, can you tell me about the prom?' I asked, deflecting from the crumbs falling from my greying bush. 'Mr Woods explained you came to him in the staff room; that you finally blew the whistle on Maria. What did you see?'

Resting her face against her palm, Karen composed herself, exhaling heavily, and blinking the moistness from her lashes. 'I was so happy to be there beside her. I'd dressed up for her and everything, I mean, actually put on a dress, *me*! She'd picked me up in her car, it was like a date,' Karen smiled wistfully. 'We got there and everyone was remarking on us, happy that we looked like a couple, I mean Maria looked *incredible* in this dark suit and white silk shirt.'

'Karen, please get to the point,' I said flatly. I really didn't care what they were wearing.

'I'm telling the story!' she snapped, then continued at a deliberately slower pace. 'So, we had a few *drinks* and were in the *hall* because we had to mind the kids *dancing*, but then we noticed when Nadia and Sam came in together, fashionably late - everyone noticed them because they were arguing. Sam wore a baby-dyke suit and tie, actually, and it made me laugh that she was trying to replicate Maria's style, but Nadia was stumbling about in her dress and high heels. We realised she was drunk, and watched over them as Sam tried to get her on to the dance floor, but Nadia didn't want to go. She kept staring over at us – she'd seen Maria and I together and she had a face like thunder. Sam had to pull her back from coming over to us, and I was curious as to what she wanted to say.'

'What was Maria's response to this behaviour?' I queried, intrigued.

'I was hoping she'd want to show Nadia that we were an item by ignoring her again, by turning and talking to me, drinking with me, laughing with me, but Maria didn't seem to want to be affectionate. She'd said before that she didn't feel comfortable being physically intimate around others, especially in front of students, but I hoped she'd make this one important show of unity for my sake, so Nadia would get the hint and

Unravel

leave her alone. But, Maria couldn't take her eyes off Nadia and Sam arguing across the hall. It was like she expected something bad to happen... now I know she had every reason to panic.'

'Maria and Nadia were staring at each other - in what way? Did they look angry? Worried? Jealous?' I urged.

'Nadia looked hurt, I suppose, but Maria looked worried, she couldn't pull her eyes away from Nadia, she didn't seem to care that it was upsetting me. Yes, I felt jealous! I wanted to say something that would get her attention, so I mentioned Nadia's journal - that did it - she asked what I was talking about. I told her that Nadia's dad had brought it to Woods' office because he was suspicious of the way Maria was treating Nadia, escorting her home late and all that. Maria looked terrified, she asked if I'd read the journal, and I said yeah, it was filthy, that Nadia had put Maria in the centre of all her sexual fantasies and described lesbian acts so real that they had to be investigated. Well, Maria looked as if she might throw up, she started stuttering, looking back over at Nadia. I knew something was wrong then, I could see the way she was looking at Nadia that something *had* happened between them.'

'Go on...' I said, sitting forward, not writing, just listening.

'So, I asked her if Mr Sheridan had grounds to be worried: if she'd been letting Nadia stay with her late, alone, in the evenings; if she'd been letting Nadia spend time at her house; if she'd been making her dinner. I begged her to tell me it wasn't true, that it was inappropriate to let a student get so close to her, and why hadn't she told me that was happening? I asked if she'd let Nadia near her, I pleaded with her to tell me the truth, that Nadia hadn't touched her, that none of the fantasies in the journal were real. She just stood there, unable to answer me, I wanted to shake her. I shouted over the music, I said: "Tell me you haven't touched her! Tell me you haven't touched her!" I was jabbing her with my fingers, I couldn't believe every second that passed and she wasn't saying anything to deny it! She could have lied! But she was too shocked and it reeked of guilt!'

'She must have been overwhelmed, confused!' I reasoned. 'What if she didn't even know about the journal?'

'Why do you care what she felt?' Karen said defensively. 'I knew right there and then that everything I knew about Maria was lies, I could tell by the way she was looking at Nadia, and suddenly everything made sense. She had let Nadia get close to her because she enjoyed it! She'd allowed them to become physical and couldn't deal with the consequences once she'd been caught! I knew I had to go straight to the principal, she begged me not to go, but I had to!'

I didn't need to hear the rest, but took notes as Karen told me anyway: she'd pulled Xavier Woods away from his sherry, mortified at his journal recital to her colleagues, and dragged everyone out to hunt for Maria. She admitted she had punched Maria in the car park because she was holding Nadia too closely. She'd felt vindicated that she'd been the one to spot Maria's affair on the last day of term, and who knows how long it would have carried on for if she hadn't felt the jealousy that inspired her questioning of Maria's sidelong glances at Nadia.

The same question played on my mind long after the interview, and lights out in bed next to my dear old husband, Harry.

Indeed, how long would it have carried on for?

Unravel

April 23rd

Maria,

Last night was perfect. I'd managed to convince my dad I was studying with a friend, that we had to work on a science project, that I needed help and a classmate had suggested an all-nighter. I came to yours with my weekend bag.

You treated me like a princess. You made the most incredible dinner, things I had never tasted together before. You made the table look beautiful and you looked so utterly handsome in your black shirt. I fell in love with you all over again, and this time it was different, I felt grown up and it felt like you saw me for me, instead of some kid you were teaching. I still feel like a child sometimes, especially when you opened the ice-cream for dessert, it was pistachio flavour and I had to stop myself from wanting to rub it all over my face so you could lick it off. I couldn't stop blushing and I wondered if you were thinking about licking cream off me, too... off my breasts... letting it run down between my legs hoping you would catch my thighs open and lap it up. I had to sit upon twinge after twinge, getting creamy all by myself.

Afterwards, we moved to your lounge and you'd set up the coffee table with candles and wine, chocolates and a selection of movies to watch. I kicked off my shoes and sat amongst the cushions and blankets on the couch, it was so deep and comfy. You put on a movie and sat next to me, except you were too far away and I poked you with my toes.

You tickled my feet, then rested my legs over yours, you said you wanted to make me feel special, that I deserved better than sneaking around and doing stuff in secret, like in your car and your office. I said it was exciting, I didn't mind, but you said you didn't want to rush, that you needed to relax and to not be afraid of being caught. You said that came out wrong, but I understood. If we were caught, everything would be ruined. We had to keep this for ourselves. So I snuggled up beside you and we spent as long as we could together, relaxed and appreciating every moment.

    We drank some rose wine, and I felt a bit tearful as the movie was sad. You teased me for crying and I said it was the wine, but you kissed me and our lips just merged together perfectly. I wanted to pull your shirt open, but I did what you said and relaxed, just enjoyed kissing and felt my insides melting. The movie ended and you put on another, but I had no intentions of watching it. I kissed your neck as you skipped through the trailers, I could feel you smiling and sighing, but your body was kind of rigid still. I just wanted to absorb into you, get inside your clothes and breathe with you in your skin, I've never wanted to be that close to anyone. I ran my fingertips along every inch of your jaw, your neck and your chest, wishing you to look at me again with that soft gaze of love.

    Only when you put the control down did you rest your eyes upon me, with a smile and a stroke of my hair. I asked what movie we were watching and you said you'd forgotten, and we giggled and kissed again. You slid down with me towards the lamplight and cradled my head in your arm. You kissed my neck and stroked over my clothes.

    I curled my knees over your legs, and I felt our pelvises push together, we fit like a jigsaw. You held me into you, as close as possible, moving your hand up and over my hip to my waist, gripping and pulling me gently, before guiding me back and keeping me guessing. The way you worshipped my shape made me feel like a goddess, I felt like stardust moulded into the curviest earth woman by your hand. You ravished me. I wanted to touch you back but I could hardly co-ordinate my limbs, I was completely under your spell.

    I begged you to take off my tights, they were feeling so... tight. You hooked your thumb in the waistband and peeled them down over my hips, easing them down my thighs slowly, your nail, or maybe your ring, scratching me softly. I sucked the breath out of your mouth I wanted you so bad, and when I felt your hand against my bare skin, I actually quivered. You pulled the blanket over me, then lifted up my dress. I wriggled out of it, and felt nervous for a minute, but you snuggled the soft fur blanket around my back to keep me from shaking, and I remembered it was you holding me so tenderly, so protectively.

    You were trembling too. You eased my bra strap over my shoulder and kissed my breasts. I remember twisting the hair at the curve of your neck in my fingers. Your hand travelled slowly over my skin, unhooking my bra, stroking down to the small of my back, making me tingle. I looked into your eyes as you teased the edges of my knickers with your fingers, you smiled, knowing what you were doing to me, and I smiled too, knowing I would burst by the time you worked your way inside. When you reached the centre, your eyes widened at how wet I was, and through my knickers, I was dripping, I could feel it. I said you might as well take them off, but you said your blankets were brand new. I hit you softly, and kissed you, and then stopped as I felt your fingers curl around the crotch of my panties. You slid against my velvet pussy and over my clitoris, around and around only a few times before I felt my orgasm rising. My legs tightened over yours as I began to yelp and buckle. You clamped one hand over my mouth and sucked my nipple as your circles became smaller. I moaned long and loud into your hand as your other brought me off. Sensation shot back and forth from my clit, to my nipple in your mouth as you kept going until I'd calmed.

    I became slightly wild, I don't know what came over me, I was rampant. I wanted you more. I tried to pull you on top of me, wanting your weight on top of me again. I slid my leg under you as you held yourself above me but you wouldn't lay down. I said I wanted you to fuck me but you said you didn't have a dick. You smiled at my confusion, brought your knees up under my open thighs, and shifted me up over the arm of your couch. In that position, I could wrap my legs around you, and you could penetrate me any way you wanted. I propped myself on my elbows and watched you unbutton your shirt. Your arms were strong with muscles and I felt dizzy at how sexy you looked. You wore a really girly black, lacy bra and I had never imagined you would be such a lady underneath all your swagger. The chain around your neck swung towards me as you lifted me up to scoop my knickers over my backside. You leaned back and tugged them up my legs as I brought them together, feeling myself squish with moisture. You leaned over me again, and I held onto you, gazing into your eyes, as you placed your fingers at my entrance.

 I waited, dripping, begging for you to fill me up, but you watched me squirm. I prayed you weren't changing your mind and I pleaded, I swore I wanted you, needed you to take me. You rubbed against me, then eased your fingers inside, slowly, and deeply, you pulled out again, and slid in again, leaving me gasping. I rocked at your mercy, panting in time to your rhythm. I clutched my breasts, and saw you watching, so I did it more, for you. Then I had an overwhelming urge to touch you. I reached for your breasts, and tried to grab your shoulder to bring your head closer to mine, but you held my arms down. I tried to reach down to undo your jeans, I really wanted to, but you didn't let me touch you.

You paused for a minute, you said this was all for me, and I felt you nudge against my clitoris, and then you resumed your motion, pushing your fingers inside me, whilst your thumb twanged me like a guitar. It felt fucking amazing, I have no idea how you were doing it in the first place, let alone keeping it up, you must have had serious strength in your wrists, but I wasn't complaining. I held my hands over my eyes as I felt a gradual climax, it built so gently I could only ride along with it, with you, as it took me over. I had time to realise what was coming, and I asked, in a mumble, what you were doing to me, you half-smiled, the sexy sweat on your temple beading up.

Unravel

I just had a twinge now remembering how incredible it felt to have you working away at me, and when I opened my eyes you had closed yours, you were really feeling it too. I swore again and again, saying your name again and again. You held my hips and pushed yourself up against me, the pressure of your pelvis moving in time with your fingers, up and around, but your thumb never left me. I howled, feeling you were really fucking me. I covered my face with my hands, I couldn't stand the pleasure. I shut my eyes and bit the skin of my arm, feeling I was about to either pass out or catapult into the night sky. It felt like I came for ever. I swear I kept climaxing, in wave after wave, on different levels of consciousness. It was like an age had passed by the time I came around, and I felt like a mole, emerging from its hole, blinking in the bright light of the morning.

The movie had finished, got bored of waiting and started itself again. It was two-thirty a.m. We lit new candles, drank more wine, and picked at the chocolates. I asked if you were frustrated and you said you were fine, that you couldn't help coming when I did, just from rubbing against your jeans.

One day I'm going to get your jeans off, and I'm going you give you the world of pleasure you've given me. I'm not as experienced as you, but I'm learning from the best.

Nadia x

Chapter Thirty

I had a feeling on the phone that Samantha Burrows might be difficult to interview: the sixteen year old sounded reluctant and asked why she had to give a statement, as if spending an hour, or so, with me was an equivalent sentence to sitting in detention. The sulky girl made it clear to me that I was inconveniencing her social time, as if she were doing me a favour by meeting me. However, having grown up children at university, I am well versed in the ways and wiles of petulant young women, and was grateful I no longer had to tolerate teenagers in my own home.

Finding Samantha sitting near a bus stop in Gloucester town centre, I pulled up alongside the kerb, beeped, hoping it was her and not some other loitering youngster who would give an aggressive gesture in response to my hapless waving. As the streetwise, plump thing sloped off her ledge and skulked towards me, though, I guessed it must be her: swaggering with cocky, tomboyish confidence, her chunky calves as solid as her heavy, unlaced boots. Her sky-blue cheap market issue bomber jacket, edged with a fake fur trim, might have been deliberately too small, but it hardly fit over her large bosom; her shoulders rounded against the wind and her fists poised tightly inside the pockets as if she were clutching something, ready to stab anyone who looked at her in the wrong way. Her hair, once dyed black, I presumed, as it had faded to a wish-washy dull grey, was messy, and asymmetrical, and as she leaned down beside my window, her mouth slid into an easy pout whilst her eyes blinked into a bored roll.

'Where we going?' she asked, with no apparent need for civil introduction.

'Wherever you like,' I answered, slightly bewildered by her directness. She shrugged and crossed in front of the car to get in the passenger side and I was bemused by her willingness to get in without further communication: I could have been anyone. Luckily, for me, I only looked like a mother collecting her slightly wild-looking child and not like some pervert soliciting for business. It crossed my mind that Nadia must have gotten in and out of Maria's car and how that must have looked to their observers; I wondered if anything was wrong with that picture.

After I refused to take her to a pub, Samantha folded her arms and said she was hungry so I agreed to buy her lunch. We parked next to the children's play area on the central, sprawling patch of green in the city, and walked to the cafe serving hot food, except she

Unravel

wanted to sit outside so she could smoke. My cappuccino turned cold within five minutes and I was forced to tolerate the chilled wind that flapped the edges of my notepad while she devoured her burger and chips, seemingly oblivious to the unseasonal breeze.

'I don't know why you're asking me,' she shrugged. 'Nadia's my mate, I'm not going to slag her off. Ms Calver's the one you should be talking to, she's fucked up.'

'How much do you know about their relationship?' I exhaled my impatience, watching her push her chips into the pot of tomato ketchup.

'Relationship?' Sam baulked. 'I wouldn't call it that!' she shoved the chips into her mouth and continued speaking. 'I'd call it a head-fuck of epic proportions!'

I clenched my writing hand in my other to keep it warm as she talked.

'Wouldn't you say Nadia had genuine feelings towards Ms Calver?'

'No!' Sam asserted with a contorted expression. 'Nadia was messing around, she knew Ms Calver was a bit of a sucker, figured she could get better grades if she went along with it.'

'Went along with what?'

Sam huffed, resenting having to explain herself. 'With Ms Calver treating her like she was precious, obviously she had to have tuition to catch up, but all the "extras"...' Sam's fingers made quote marks in the air, 'that was a bit much - getting lifts home, texting her, calling her *Maria*!'

'Did Nadia express any concern that Ms Calver was treating her differently to you or the others?' I asked, though my question didn't sound right as it came out.

'I don't know, ask her!' Sam frowned. 'All I saw was Nadia getting more special treats than anyone else getting help with exams.'

'I'm trying to understand if Nadia didn't appreciate it... was embarrassed... in front of her peers,' I struggled, irritated by my sudden lack of vocabulary.

'Peers?' Sam sneered. 'Nah, she *was* different, she acted different, didn't really hang out with us lot, spent most days after school with *her*! We didn't really get a look in!'

I sighed, the wind kept blowing my hair in my face, and Sam was annoying me with her unwillingness to share information. I felt the meeting had begun out of my control and I had lost my power to a girl who made me feel like a bumbling idiot.

'Samantha, help me paint a picture here,' I lifted my hands in appeal to the youngster. 'I need to know events and times or general behaviours between them that might stick out in your mind as being unusual. So far, all I can say for my report is that Ms Calver and Nadia were fully committed to hours in tuition, and unless you can tell me anything you noticed that might prove they were engaging intimately, then I have no case to make at the hearing.'

'That's not my problem!' Sam remarked defiantly.

'Look, you might be the only witness who can make a stand against Ms Calver if she has abused her position of trust, so your statement is incredibly important,' I tried to bring the stroppy teen on side. 'You said Ms Calver was fucked up, why do you say that? What did she do with Nadia to make you believe that?'

Hearing me swear must have shocked her a little, at least it prompted her into spouting angrily that she just wanted to be friends with Nadia, who, in her words, had been stuck-up, acting like a geek for tuition, but then skipping classes. Sam admitted her usual trick of being mean failed to get Nadia's reaction, and then she found out Nadia got a boyfriend.

'Did you know this boy?' I asked, hoping she would confirm it was Maria's dog-sitter.

'Some twat called Christian Webb,' Sam nodded. 'He added her on *facecrack*, then, about a month later, after New Year, they announced they were "in a relationship". I wound her up about it, but it turned out she wasn't into him at all, she just felt like she had to, because Ms Calver introduced them and she didn't want to offend her. Nadia told me she actually liked girls, and we... messed around.'

My eyes narrowed. 'Wait, why did Nadia want Ms Calver to think she was interested in a boy?'

'She didn't want her to know she was into girls! She thought it might make tuition weird or something, but later on she came out, once she was proud to be with me,' Sam grinned, but then her face fell.

My pen hovered above my pad. 'What is it?'

Sam's mouth pursed to one corner, and she frowned. 'Nadia made me apologise to Ms Calver,' she sighed as she confessed she had given Maria a hard time in the past. 'But I only did it to please Nadia, I didn't question why she wanted me to. She said it would clear the air, like it mattered so much her to what Ms Calver thought of me... I think Ms Calver must have been dogging me up so Nadia wanted to prove I was all right, you know?'

Holding onto a train of thought, I asked Sam how Maria reacted, so I could interpret her manner, her behaviour. According to Sam, Maria accepted it graciously, acknowledged Nadia's need for support, and encouraged Sam to be a good friend to Nadia.

'Smug bitch!' Sam said before chewing a mouthful of burger.

'What can you tell me about how things changed?' I asked the girl. I felt hungry too, and desperately wanted a chip, but I couldn't possibly cross the professional boundary of sharing food with a teenager; it was worse than crossing the personal boundary of sharing a fork with a lesbian, and once

Unravel

again, I imagined what boundaries Maria had crossed in her shared activities with Nadia.

'I didn't really notice anything for ages, I was just happy that Nadia was my girlfriend, we all had exams to revise for...' Sam shook her head blankly.

'Come on, Sam, think back!' I pleaded. 'Nadia was your girlfriend! You must have noticed how she was behaving with Ms Calver, were they acting strangely? Any arguments? They must have been stressed. Aren't you supposed to have... *gaydar*?'

Grimacing, Sam gave me her palm. 'Don't ever say that again!' She vacuumed up the last chips, frowning with thought, leaving most of her burger on the plate. She rolled a cigarette as I waited.

'Okay, I'll tell you, but I don't want to get into trouble,' she licked the paper and lit it, exhaling smoke like an expert. 'Just before the mock exams, Nadia got really stressed out about her grades, she kept saying she was scared she was going to fail and I told her she couldn't fail because she had Ms Calver teaching her and she was the best, and all this shit...' Sam rolled her eyes and took a lengthy puff. 'I told Nadia that Ms Calver would do anything for her, she was practically in love with her! If she wanted to pass, she should keep Ms Calver sweet.'

I listened closely, my ear turned in from the wind. 'You thought Ms Calver loved Nadia?'

'Not like really... only in the way that Nadia made her look good, you know, she got paid more than anyone else in learning support... Nadia was more than her tuition student - she was like her protégé, her pet! I just thought Nadia could use that to her advantage and get out of it what she needed, so we joked that she could probably seduce Ms Calver if she wanted to...' Sam trailed off shyly, 'and then we made a bet.'

I felt something drop inside me. Somewhere between my breath and my gut, my spirit sank with a heavy wilt. On the evening of the prom, out in the car park, Principal Woods and Karen Lenholm had not heard wrong.

Sam proceeded to tell me that after their agreement, things became fun. She and Nadia enacted potential scenarios where Nadia could take the opportunity to seduce Maria. They ended up having sex, and Nadia would jokingly moan Maria's name. Sam said she wasn't worried, she regarded their teacher as being a bit lonely, sad sometimes, moody often; she understood Maria was vulnerable, but wasn't expecting her to take the bait.

'Nadia told me she was playing subtle games with Ms Calver, but I couldn't see anything between them, they didn't act any differently. I tried sitting in with their tuition, but I wasn't allowed...' Sam sniffed. 'In assembly though, I watched them a lot, but they weren't sitting there making eyes at each other, if anything, they didn't look at each other at all, it was boring! The times they did look at each other, they didn't really smile. I asked after a while and Nadia said nothing was happening, Ms Calver wasn't going for it, and I believed her... so we just got on with normal stuff.'

'Didn't you feel like stirring up the action, Sam? For entertainment? Did you imagine you could do any better? Perhaps you could up your grades too if you seduced Ms Calver...?'

'Don't get me wrong, Ms Calver's hot, but I didn't fancy her, we're too similar I think,' Sam exhaled and scowled, 'and I always got the feeling she hated me anyway.'

'But you must have been impatient,' I suggested, 'wanting all the dirty details? What about Nadia's journal?'

'I never saw Nadia's journal,' Sam said matter-of-factly. 'Well, she showed me it once and told me that Ms Calver gave it to her as a birthday present – another reason I thought she was soft on Nadia – but I never saw it after that. She never brought it to school and I never saw her writing in it. I'd forgotten it existed and presumed she had until the night of the prom – it sounded like that was the first time Ms Calver found out about it, too.'

When Sam mentioned the prom, my senses shivered. It seemed to be the one night when Maria and Nadia lost any smooth composure with each other, I wasn't sure about the psychic abilities of lesbians, but it looked as if they'd silently pre-arranged to pretend

Unravel

nothing was wrong. I wondered what had really happened in the interim.

'Was there anything else you can think of, during that time, those months between April and June?' I yearned for something more. 'You're a smart girl, Sam, you're not blind – you must have noticed something about their behaviour that you found strange, or different than before?'

'No, I never thought anything was happening – I mean, Ms Calver got really miserable at one point, and to be honest I thought Nadia was overdoing it a bit, like, pretending to be upset as well, just because her dog died or something. I know she was my girlfriend but I thought she was a bit cruel for manipulating Ms Calver like that.'

'How do you mean "manipulating"?' I queried, honed in with curiosity.

'I mean, I came to like Ms Calver,' Sam seemed to soften. 'She'd helped us all with our exam stuff, she was a really good teacher, and obviously she was a bit stupid for Nadia, but I knew Nadia was saying stuff to let her think she liked her, and it was kind of working... I guess I felt sorry for Ms Calver. I knew she'd be hurt if she found out Nadia was playing games with her. I wasn't going to tell her though!'

'Did anyone else know about your bet?' I asked, seriously.

'No, don't think so,' Sam pouted and stubbed out her roll-up. 'Although the rumours started going round school about Nadia lezzing off with Ms Calver, I tried setting them straight but you know what happens on *facejoke* - you can't stop it! And then the girls in our year started taking the piss out of me because they thought I was a mug, but I laughed it off - I knew what Nadia was doing with Ms Calver, and it was just to get grades, it's not like they were *actually* lezzing off together!'

'Are you sure about that?' I raised my eyebrow.

Sam's face flashed with anger. 'Look, I might have been jealous that Nadia was getting treated like a princess, but she is *my* girlfriend and she wouldn't have cheated on me - not with her teacher, anyway, that's gross! Nadia was just having a laugh, taking advantage - yeah Ms Calver fell for it, but it's not like they were fucking instead of studying!'

I stared at Sam. She was completely convinced that nothing had occurred between her Sappho associates; I wondered why she couldn't convince me. I wondered if she'd say differently if she'd seen Nadia's journal as I had. It didn't seem to matter: she was yet another witness who determined that Nadia was the instigator and Maria was a victim. No one saw anything or had any proof the women had actually broken any physical boundaries.

'Tell me about prom night then,' I asked. 'What was your experience?'

'Oh, that was a fuck-up from start to finish,' Sam said resignedly. 'Nadia had a really bad argument with her dad about something, he said she couldn't go to the prom for whatever reason, so she came to mine crying that she couldn't go back there. I tried to cheer her up but she was drinking loads, we got ready for the prom but she kept running her makeup 'cause she was bloody crying, I didn't know what was wrong with her, she didn't want to talk about it. Then, my brother's mate came round and gave us some pills, we had one each, I thought it would get her in the mood, but I think she was too upset to enjoy it.'

'A pill of what?' I frowned. 'Ecstasy?'

'Yeah, but, listen, I'm not going to get done for that, am I? I didn't buy it, I was given it!'

'Just tell me what happened,' I said, tersely.

Sam sucked her teeth and stared out across the park. 'We got there in a taxi, we were late, and everyone was in the hall dancing. Nadia was spinning out, I just wanted her to chill out and be cool, but she was swearing at me to leave her alone, she didn't want to hang out with our mates. I had a go at her because she spotted Ms Calver with Ms Lenholm and she was upset. I told her to let it go, we'd finished the exams now, she could drop the act with Ms Calver, but she wanted to go and speak to her. I pulled her back 'cause she was high and I didn't want her making a scene.'

'Were you both aware that Ms Calver and Ms Lenholm were seeing each other?'

'Yeah, Nadia told me she'd seen them kissing, she was unhappy about it, she said Ms Lenholm was too old, she didn't know what Ms Calver was thinking,' Sam shrugged. 'I didn't see why Nadia had such a problem with it, but she just said Ms Lenholm wasn't right for *Maria*.'

'So at the prom, you were worried Nadia was going to say something to that effect?'

'Yeah, she was going to embarrass herself *and me*, so I tried to get her to calm down, but Ms Calver had noticed and was watching us, I think she was worried too,' Sam began rolling another cigarette. 'There was definitely something going on between them that Nadia hadn't told me, I think there was more to the story than Nadia had let on, and I was upset that she wasn't telling me.'

'Did Ms Lenholm see all this?' I questioned. 'She must have noticed them.'

'I think she did, because I saw her poking Ms Calver, she looked mad about something, maybe she was telling her to stop staring at Nadia, it wasn't right... then she marched off and Ms Calver looked really shocked,' Sam lit her smoke and took a drag. 'Ms Calver came right over to us, grabbed Nadia under her arm and pulled her away from me, she was livid. I was scared, man, I didn't know what she'd just found out, but when I tried to intervene, she elbowed me in the tit and told me to mind my own business. It wasn't nice, she was angry! She dragged Nadia through the crowd and Nadia just stumbled along, everyone was looking.

They went out the back fire escape and the door slammed. I didn't know what to do.'

I marvelled at this news, and was fascinated to have a different view of this poignant event that matched Karen's account. I needed to hear about the car park, however, as I understood that Sam was present for the final showdown. 'What happened after that?'

Exhaling with a sigh, Sam recalled waiting half a minute, realising she was standing alone in the music-flooded hall, stressed out by all her year-mates dancing around her, and with the drugs charging her system, she impatiently went after them.

'I found them under the fire escape stairs, Ms Calver had Nadia against the wall,' Sam sounded confused. 'Ms Calver was blazing, asking about this journal, what Nadia had written in it, that everyone had found out, that it was going to ruin everything... Nadia was crying, saying that her dad had found it, that he had gone crazy...' Sam puffed, shaking her head. 'I shouted at Ms Calver to leave Nadia alone, stop hassling her, Nadia was well upset and she was making her cry even more. But Ms Calver told me to fuck off, and pulled Nadia around the corner, they disappeared into the dark, I couldn't see where they went... the stairs were doing weird things, and my head was spinning!'

Sam told me that she tried to look for them in the dark, she said her heart was beating really hard, feeling something bad was going to happen to Nadia. There were many creepy corners around the school grounds she'd never seen before in the dark and Sam admitted she was high and terrified, her mind playing tricks, imagining finding an incensed Ms Calver stabbing Nadia passionately in the bush.

'I heard some commotion from the car park, so I ran around and saw some mad Australian woman with a hockey stick beating the crap out of Ms Calver's car. She was yelling at her, saying she knew Ms Calver had been fucking someone else, but she never thought it would be her...' Sam took a long drag on her fag. 'I didn't realise she was talking about Nadia until I reached them. I tried to help Nadia, who was just standing there, freaking out. I figured this woman was Ms Calver's girlfriend, she was mental! She cracked Ms Calver one with the stick and we all heard her arm snap. She started shouting at me, asking who I was, if I knew what was going on, and who else knew.'

I couldn't write fast enough. This was all the crucial stuff I needed for the case. Sam was casual in her reportage, however, as if she was unwilling to comprehend what she had seen.

'The Aussie woman started yelling at Nadia, she slapped her face! She kept demanding to know what she'd said, what she'd done with Ms Calver... I just yelled at her to back off but then Ms Calver came in between them. She was trying to guard Nadia from this *crazy* woman, but Nadia was just in shock, holding her head and crying.'

Sam took a last toke, and stubbed out the butt in the ashtray. 'That's when Ms Lenholm arrived with Mr Woods, she must have thought Ms Calver was hurting Nadia and punched her, it was one hell of a smack, Ms Calver dropped like a stone... I held Nadia as Mr Woods started asking questions but Ms Calver couldn't speak, her nose was gushing blood, and the Aussie was shouting at them now. All the other teachers had come out and were all gawking, I felt really high, and sick, I was totally tripping.'

Letting Sam run herself dry, I needn't ask her how it all ended.

'Then Nadia comes out with it,' Sam continued. 'She said: "None of this is real!" She told everyone it had all been a game – that she and I had made a bet that she could seduce Ms Calver, that it had worked, and she had won. I was so pissed off, she made me look like a right twat!'

'Why do you think Nadia said that?' I asked.

'Because she was off her tits!' Sam scoffed. 'She said it really straight though, it sounded really harsh. Ms Calver couldn't believe it - she just stared at her. Everyone was staring at Nadia, I guess it was obvious she had totally manipulated Ms Calver, like she was playing her all along, but it wasn't like that... Nadia did like Ms Calver, a lot – I know she didn't mean to hurt her feelings. I think she said it so coldly because the principal was calling the police to have Ms Calver arrested, and Nadia knew she had to come clean. Ms

Lenholm asked about the journal, and Nadia just shrugged and said it was all made up, it was all lies, everything was, just to get her grades up.'

'And Ms Calver was subsequently arrested,' I said. 'Was anything else said between her and Nadia?'

'No, Ms Calver looked really hurt, I think she might have been crying, but she didn't say a word and got into the cop car with her... what's the word?' Sam searched the air, clicking her fingers. 'Dignity.'

My head was reeling. I asked where Nadia was now, and Sam told me she was staying with her for a while, since she couldn't go back to her dad's house, and she had no reason to now that she had finished school, so she was looking for a job, and was hoping to find someone to live with near Gloucester. I asked Nadia's contact details, for when I needed to speak to her, and Sam begrudgingly gave it to me.

'Don't tell her everything I told you!' Sam scowled. 'I'm supposed to be on her side.'

Assuring her she had my complete confidentiality I thanked Samantha for meeting me and promised she wouldn't get in trouble for her part in planning the seduction of a teacher. As we went our separate ways, I realised how clever Nadia was for allowing Sam to believe she was the one who had come up with the scheme in the first place.

Unravel

April 30th

Maria,

We can't stop. We're getting worse. This is out of control now... and I love it.

    Yesterday I came for tuition after school, and I sat at your desk with you, my legs naked, it was hot again and I wondered if you would catch my scent as I let my knees fall open a few times to release the sticky clutch of my thighs. I had taken my knickers off in the girl's toilet and masturbated myself thinking of you. I'd even dabbed some of my juice under my ear, right on the part of my neck where my artery pulses, in the hope it would waft the sumptuous temptation of my pussy right under your nose.

    It worked, I think. At least, you were distracted by my legs swinging, pivoting on tiptoes propped against my chair. Out of the corner of my eye, I saw you look down at my lap, and up again at my loosened tie, you must have noticed my flushed cheek and my attempt at trying not to smile. I glanced at you and you beheld me with a daring stare. You breathed in and out gently, your lips pursed shut, your nostrils pressing ever so slightly. Maybe you recognised me... you certainly were elsewhere for a moment.

    I kicked my foot around the leg of your chair and turned myself towards you, closing my knees in your direction. You grit your jaw and exhaled heavily, I wasn't sure if you were annoyed or what, it's hard to tell with you. I didn't want to upset you, you had refused me in school before, so I put my elbows on your desk and pretended to read the textbook to keep up appearances, whilst my ankle hooked around yours and swung there, tapping you. You rubbed your temple with one hand, maybe your temperature was rising, but your other hand slipped down off the desk, and discreetly cupped around the inside of my thigh. You squeezed softly, harder and softer again, but you wouldn't rise any higher, not until we resumed our discussion on exothermic and endothermic reactions.

Unravel

I understood you weren't able to display any expression in your face or body language, you sat rigidly forward as we continued our revision, but your hand relaxed in my lap and with my fingers I hitched my hem higher and inched closer to you so it would be easier for you to reach under my skirt. It was totally arousing when your fingers pressed against my naked lips and I felt a tremor of hesitance in your hand. We stopped talking for a moment as our breaths held in our mouths. You probed again and curled upwards, parting my slit with a slither of moisture from below.

You were always so nervous in school but I saw a look in your eye that flashed with lust. That same element of risk charged me and I reached down, held your arm, daring you closer. I felt my pussy lurch and I had to have you inside me. Your shirt sleeves were rolled up, your forearm was strong and I gripped it, pleading you to do it. You shifted uncomfortably but rose to my challenge, and pressed your fingers upwards and slunk deep within. I struggled not to groan so I folded my arms on the desk again and buried my head, biting my lip and huffing quietly whilst you worked slowly away at me. I opened my legs wider and you introduced another finger, your wrist gyrating hard whilst your shoulder remained as still as possible, just in case someone walked in.

    Just as I came all over your hand, I felt this release, this flood came out of me. I have only been able to do that a few times, but you seem to bring it out of me so easily. I hadn't even lifted my head up when you pushed back your chair, fell to your knees between my legs and began licking thirstily, everywhere I had soaked. I looked down at you through my arms, marvelling at your wild abandon as you lapped and sucked every trace of the juice you'd caused to spill. You're so tidy.

    Suddenly there was a knock on your door, and one of your colleagues put her head around it, ready to apologise, but then asked where you were. You had frozen behind the desk, my legs clamped helplessly either side of your ears. I looked up from my arms and knew my face was hot and flushed. She asked if I was alright. I quickly imitated the tears of frustration, said you had gone to the toilet to get me tissues. She soothed, said not to worry, that I'll get through the exams, and to tell you not to go so hard on me. I said I would. She said to tell you she was staying late tonight so not to lock up. She closed the door again and left us in silence.

    Sweet baby Jesus, Maria, I felt like laughing afterwards I was so scared. I thought you were going to have a panic attack the way you held your chest, sitting there on the floor. It took us a few minutes to compose ourselves before we could move and think about how close we had come to complete devastation. Just for a moment of passion, it felt totally reckless and not really worth it. But it was horny as hell, and it changed us. It made breaking the rules possible. You were being bad and it was awesome.

    Nadia x

Chapter Thirty-One

Obviously, the next essential person I had to speak to was the Australian woman whom Sam had met in the car park with Maria and Nadia. If she was Maria's girlfriend then I had to track her down, and after a few phone calls, I found out her name was Lois Vaughan and located her at a graphic design office where she was working in London.

When an attractively attired young woman stalked towards me on brightly coloured heels, I think both of our expressions twisted with curiosity. Obviously, she wondered who her unexpected visitor was, but when she saw my formal shirt and ID badge, she must have assumed I was a detective; she wouldn't have been half-wrong. She looked concerned, and immediately asked, in leaping Aussie, if it was about Maria.

I wish I could have reassured her it wasn't, as when I informed her that I needed to ask her questions regarding her knowledge of Maria's involvement with her student, her face twitched with irritation. She hurried me along a glass walled corridor, past offices of similarly shrewd-eyed colleagues, and ushered me into a sparsely furnished adjacent room. Not that it was clear from the logo, but 'Red Light' Ltd. was a high-profile marketing suite, where Ms Vaughan had been appointed a prestigious position as a chief consultant. My sources revealed she'd recently earned a huge commission, and she looked successful: her blonde, coiled hair, swept back into a French plait, along with her pointy edged glasses made her look both savvy and severe.

Still very much in business mode, Lois sat and began to tell me about her history with Maria, how long they had been together, how living together had nearly ruined their relationship, emphasising that she had rescued it by moving out; but I found her protestations overly conceited, and I wasn't interested in her.

'When did you first know about Nadia Sheridan?'

Lois adjusted her pert buttocks. Discomfort seemed to replace her visible annoyance, as if she hadn't prepared to talk about anything in Maria's world that didn't concern her. 'She was introduced to me as Christian's girlfriend... at Maria's house,' she said, reluctantly.

I nodded carefully. 'Maria didn't mention Nadia was her student?'

'No, not then,' Lois appeared thoughtful. 'She did tell me, about a month before that, that she had a new student... she'd been assigned a transfer, from Wales, she said.'

'Wales?' I exclaimed a little loudly. I doubted that Maria would have mistaken Nadia's Irish accent for a Welsh one, and wondered if it had been a deliberate plot to misguide Lois, or a genuine, perhaps absent-minded error, followed, unwittingly, by a failure to correct.

Lois wouldn't hear of it, however; she expressed outright denial that Maria would have misled her. She had no reason to be suspicious of Maria at that stage, and she thought nothing of her geographical gaffe.

'Were you aware that Maria was providing lifts home to Nadia after tuition?' I asked. 'As well as letting Nadia visit her house?'

Lois pulled a disagreeing face and waved her hand in a regal dismissal. 'Look, at the time, I wouldn't have thought there was anything wrong with taking a student home even if I had known it was Nadia.' I think Lois noted my doubt because she gestured a new appeal. 'The fact is I only found out Nadia was her student after she came to my exhibition party at Maria's house, and then I freaked out!'

'Sorry?' I struggled. 'Nadia was at a party at Maria's house? When was this?'

With a roll of her eyes, Lois drawled her explanation: how she needed a gallery space; her studio was too small to entertain guests and with *vee-eye-pee's* coming, Maria agreed to host it at hers as long as it was a joint, post-Christmas party. However, 'Christian just happened to invite Nadia,' Lois sighed. 'It wasn't like Maria wanted her there.'

Thinking about why Maria would not want Nadia to attend her social event, I wondered why Lois hadn't asked her reasons. I realised that Maria could not refuse without revealing Nadia was her student, and weighing that against Nadia's non-attendance - Maria evidently preferred to keep quiet, again. I wondered why Lois was so willingly defending Maria's apparent mistruths.

'So, your exhibition,' I rested my hands over my notepad. 'How many people were there? I imagine you were busy playing host. Did you notice Maria talking to Nadia at all?'

'You know what?' Lois smiled, her tone a little bittersweet. She leaned back. 'I remember thinking Nadia was really cool, she was young but confident, she was able to talk to my friends, and they're all in their late-twenties... but, no, I didn't see Maria talking to her.'

I wanted to ask if she thought that was strange, but as Lois had no idea of Nadia's real identity at that point, I felt it was useless enquiring about Maria's dynamic with the girl.

'And when were you finally made aware of Nadia's relationship to Maria?'

Unravel

Lois gave a half-laugh and shook her head, probably at my audacity for using the word 'relationship'. She hesitated for a few moments longer than I thought was natural, before she shrugged widely. 'Nadia must have had too much to drink, she was feeling a bit poorly so my friends took her upstairs, they looked after her in the spare bedroom...' she rubbed her finger underneath her nose thoughtfully, 'but when Maria came up and saw Nadia on the bed, she totally lost it!'

I frowned. 'Was she sitting on the bed or in it?'

'She was on it,' Lois' electric blue eyes slid sideways, 'just laid down.'

Nodding, I copied down this interesting event, hoping Lois would continue while I wrote, and she did, except it was only to blame Nadia for putting herself in that position deliberately to get into Maria's spare bedroom, as if she had masterminded the whole thing to get Maria's attention.

'I mean, Maria was horrified!' Lois railed. 'She shouted that Nadia shouldn't be there. I couldn't believe Nadia was in her school, so we argued, and she kicked everyone out! Nadia ruined the night, and I want you to know that Maria was anything but turned on by it all, I've never seen her so pissed off!'

'So everyone left?' I asked. 'What happened to Nadia?'

Lois shrugged down at her yellow shoe, twitching at the end of her leg. 'I don't know, I didn't care at the time. I assumed she got a taxi or something...' Unfolding her arms, Lois slowly rubbed her naked arms, suddenly goose-bumped by the air conditioning in the office. 'I know what you're thinking,' she continued in her Aussie drawl, 'but I don't think anything happened that night, even if Nadia tried it on, Maria wouldn't have put up with any nonsense, she's not like that.'

'What? Gullible?' I asked, a tad sardonically. 'Isn't that your whole argument - that Maria was swept up by this young Lolita?'

'I'm Lo, not her!' she snapped, then clicked her tongue at her own jealously. 'Look, Dr Richmond-'

'Evelyn,' I smiled patiently.

'Evelyn,' Lois smiled tightly, pressing her closed hands towards me, suppressing anger. 'I *know* that Maria was seduced by her student, she cunningly wormed her way into Maria's life by playing a little-girl-lost act! I'm not saying Maria is completely innocent, but I saw the messages Nadia sent, and she said as much when she got caught at that stupid prom,' she withdrew her hands, her skin flushed enough now to combat her chills.

'Tell me about these messages,' I requested calmly, pursing my lips.

Lois helped put a few things in perspective first: she'd been away for a few weeks at the beginning of the year, having gone back home to see her family, and when she got back, she noticed that Maria wasn't the same. She felt Maria was acting 'weird', quieter than usual, and secretive, but Maria assured her girlfriend that she was just stressed out with work.

'Anyway, something happened after I met this guy on the plane back from Melbourne, he was interested in my work, and I wanted a commission so I went for dinner with him, but Maria wasn't even bothered when I told her! So I met this guy sometime in February, we went for dinner, he got me fucking drunk! He was making it obvious he wanted me, but he said he genuinely thought my art had potential for his company, that I was exactly what he was looking for.'

Lois glanced across at the windows to check her colleagues were out of listening distance, then sighed wearily. 'Look, I know it was wrong, but sometimes you have to do things to get ahead, and I really needed this break. Plus, Maria didn't even flinch at me seeing this guy and... I might have wanted her to be jealous, I know she doesn't appreciate what I'm trying to do with my career, but it would be nice to have her attention. Well, then she goes and forgets my birthday, and I just lost it... I had such a go at her!'

Lois told me about the dinner she requested from Maria to make up for missing her birthday, as well as celebrating the signing of her contract. After champagne and lobster, Lois intended to start her new job with a clear conscience, so told Maria of her drunken evening with the man she met on the plane, but ended up arguing that her infidelity was justified for the

Unravel

progression of her ambition, not that Maria would understand.

'Maria just got up and left the fucking restaurant! I didn't know what was happening, if she was breaking up with me or not!' Lois sounded still shocked. 'Well, we didn't speak for over a week after that, and the next thing I hear is that her dog, Leon, has been run over by a car and killed, so I knew she'd need my support.'

I quickly flipped back to my notes from Sam and squeezed a number in the margin to cross-reference mention of the animal's name.

'So I travelled all the way to see her at her school and she was totally surprised to see me - but in a dodgy way, you know?' Lois asked rhetorically.

'Right?' I answered encouragingly.

'Anyway, she stopped to get petrol on the drive home and I found these texts on her phone, from someone called "Ruby",' Lois explained.

I gladly leaned forward to hear the details.

'They weren't explicit but there was a definite secretive element to them, this *Ruby* was being all sweet, making arrangements, wanting to see Maria, sending kisses... Maria had answered a few times, but never anything sexual, like she was being careful not to write anything in case anyone read them, *like me*, and they didn't match up in conversation, as if some of them had been deleted, you know?'

'When was this?' I asked absently, scribbling hard into my notepad.

'About April, I guess...' Lois' voice hardened. 'Now, you don't shag around just because your dog died, so I knew she was retaliating for what I did. It was obvious to me she was screwing some other teacher, I mean, with a name like *Ruby*, I imagined Maria had turned some *straight* chick, one of the bloody office girls... I had no idea it was Nadia!' Lois shook her head. 'I didn't even know Nadia was gay! I still thought she was dating Christian! So I phoned her cousin Ben to ask him if he knew what Maria was up to because she tells him everything - but he said it was nothing so I trusted him,' Lois rolled her eyes with hindsight. 'Seems even *he* didn't know.'

'Did you confront Maria about the messages?' I asked. 'What did she say?'

'Yeah, she went really quiet; I hoped she was freaked out, that me knowing had snapped her out of it, but she said nothing had happened, it was just flirting,' Lois recalled with a glint of sadness. 'I forgave her. I wanted us to work it out. I kind of blamed myself for driving her away, I know I slept with someone else, but it was meaningless, well, it had a purpose, but it meant nothing,' Lois shook her head rapidly, frustrated with herself. 'Okay I know I was a shit girlfriend! Had I been more loving she wouldn't have fallen under some kid's twisted spell... I even thought we could get married.'

Lois told me that, after this, Maria disappeared into an intensive exam period during the month of May, and Lois figured it was best not to add pressure to the rocky relationship.

'I called Christian to find out what was happening, if Maria was okay, and I suppose I wanted to know if he knew this teacher called Ruby,' Lois recalled. 'He said he hadn't seen Maria since Leon had died. He didn't know any teacher called Ruby but he did know that Nadia had been spending evenings at Maria's house, that she had broken up with him, and that she had an obsession with Maria.'

'Is that when you first suspected Nadia?' I asked.

'Yeah, it all made sense suddenly, the after-school meet-ups, the cute messages... I tried calling Maria but she wouldn't answer, I left voicemails but no response... I was going nuts! She had let me believe it was her colleague, someone I was calling Ruby because she had deliberately changed her name, I was fucking furious... I didn't want to believe it was Nadia, I didn't get it, I just wanted her to tell me herself, but she completely shut me out.'

I considered what Maria must have been going through during this time, undoubtedly under pressure with work, stress from Lois' infidelity, and sorrow from Leon's death. She might well have turned to her one constant companion, even if Nadia wasn't exactly loyal either.

Unravel

'I was devastated!' Lois went on dramatically. 'I was so disturbed by all these paranoid thoughts that Maria had probably been cheating on me all along, with Christian's girlfriend - her fucking student! I was tormented by images of them sitting in tuition touching each other, I cried all night, every night! And Maria still didn't call me, so then I got fucking angry and I started to think about confronting them,' Lois nodded for emphasis, 'at their dumb-ass prom!'

I didn't need to hear Lois unveil her plot for revenge. I knew she went to the school grounds, probably ranting to herself all the way in trains and taxis. I guessed it wasn't her style to barge through the crowds of dancing youth, seeking Maria out, only to struggle and shout to be heard above the music. I figured it would have been much easier to locate Maria's sports car in the floodlit school car park, source a suitable weapon from the gym shed, and smash the crap out of the windows and dent that lovely curvaceous bonnet I'd seen in the evidence photos, well out of shape.

Lois confirmed for me that she had been verbally abusive, unashamedly, in the car park that night, screaming that she knew Maria had been fucking her student because she had lied – the girl wasn't Welsh and her name wasn't Ruby, before turning on Nadia. She slapped the girl's stunned face, pulled her hair, called her a slut and a whore for sleeping with her teacher, shouting that she can't have Maria.

"Maria is mine!" I screamed at her, but Maria stood between us and pushed me away from Nadia like she was totally brainwashed!'

I took a moment to explain to Ms Vaughan that, having interviewed others present, I was aware of the outcome with the police, but I asked what she made of Nadia's confession.

'I guess when she said, "None of this is real" I thought she was just high - maybe she was - but she went on and came out with this plan, reeled it off as if it was practiced, you know?' Lois grimaced. 'And then it started to sink in how calculating this girl must have been to spend nearly a whole year doing that to Maria, I mean, think about it: that takes day-in, day-out deception, who is that sick? I thought she was obviously mental, and Maria must have been a fool to get sucked in.'

'You believed that Nadia would do such a thing?' I asked.

'Of course she would, I saw the way she acted around Maria, all shy and pretending like she was cool. She's got these pretty eyes and I just bet she knows she can get what she wants with them,' Lois drawled with contempt.

'And you don't know anything of this journal, I suppose?'

'No, I never heard of it until the teachers mentioned it... I don't know what's in it, but Nadia admitted it was all made up anyway, what does it even matter anymore?' Lois shrugged. 'In fact, why this whole investigation? It's pretty cut and dried in my head. Nadia manipulated Maria for better grades and if Maria did anything wrong, it was that she stupidly fell for it!'

'I'm trying to determine if Maria had sexual relations with Nadia, which is a serious breach of her position,' I replied.

'Look, I don't know about that... all I know is I've lost Maria and I miss her. I'm sorry I smashed her car up, I'll buy her a new one, I just want her to take me back! I genuinely want the best for her, I don't want her to go to prison!' Lois gulped with the first real sign of emotion. 'She is a great girlfriend and I took her for granted, I know that now! And I can tell you that since a long time before this Nadia creature came along, Maria has been, and will continue to be, a great teacher! If she had one moment of weakness, or madness, or whatever, she shouldn't be blamed when it was this girl's plot to seduce her. Nadia is conniving, *she* should be put away!'

As Lois snatched off her glasses and tightly blinked tears away, I had a fleeting impression of her masculinity and reassessed the dynamic in the relationship she must have had with Maria. In comparison, Maria sounded soft, malleable, if a little melancholic, and I had a little pang of anticipation thinking of meeting her soon.

Unravel

Before then, however, I had to find Maria's cousin, Ben. I didn't know he had been involved, and felt in my heart that he might know more than he had let on to Lois. It was up to me to find out what.

Unravel

May 8th

Maria,

Yesterday you took me on a road trip. It was beautiful riding along in the sunshine. You said you didn't know where you were going but kept driving until you felt it was far enough that no one could know us. We ended up in a pretty village somewhere near Bristol. The roads rolled between farms and we awed at tiny houses, local shops and a post-office built with lovely old stone. We found a luscious blossom tree with a footpath beyond that led across a stream. You parked and we took our picnic things. We followed the stream until we found an isolated corner of a field, high with long, wild grass, and far away from the footpath. You caught a mischief, threw me to the ground and rolled on top of me, squashing the grass underneath us. We laughed and rolled over and over, back and forth, then just as our hair was full with sprigs and hay, we got up and lay the blanket down. It was sunny but we had shade. We picked at food from the hamper, the olives, sun-dried tomatoes, and halloumi were so fresh and tasty.

And you fed me strawberries and cream, and kissed me. I slid my straps off my shoulders and you massaged sun lotion into my skin in case I burned. You kissed my neck and I leaned back on you, you rubbed over my breasts and I lowered your hand under my dress. You smiled into my mouth as I asked you to go down on me right there and then. You looked around, the sky was bright and the field was empty. You nodded okay and moved the hamper so I could lay back. I shifted my legs either side of you, feeling that shaking of excitement that arouses me so much. I felt myself twinge hard as soon as you lay down between my thighs and graze your hands against my bare skin. You eased my summer dress higher and hooked your thumb around my g-string, pulling it aside, and I felt the light coolness of the fresh air caress my exposed vulva. I think you sensed my exhilaration because you blew on me for extra sensation. I shuddered, then felt your hot mouth clamp down on me, sending my insides melting down into that concentrated pool of swirling sensuality. I love the way you lick my pussy - with all of you. Your shoulders move with your rhythm, your hands twitch against my hips and grip my buttocks. Your head twists and your jaw grinds and I feel the vibration of your voice through my clitoris whenever you groan with lust. You know the exact right moment to push your two middle fingers inside me, when I'm just starting to climb and it sends me reeling. They tuck up inside, pressing the right spot, and circling round, not withdrawing too much, you know how I like it now. Your other fingers massage either side, creating an inescapable flow of stimulation, tipping me helplessly towards the fall. I exploded into your mouth, over your fingers and cried out into the open air above me. I held your head, gripping your black hair, and you didn't stop until I came again, quickly, harder; I reached out to hold onto the grass beside me and pulled it out of the earth by its roots with passionate force.

Unravel

Afterwards you ravished me with kisses and told me I was the sexiest girl in the world. You laughed at the long knots of grass I picked from my fingers and said you were glad I didn't confuse my hands and rip out your hair in the heat of the moment.

Then we walked back to your car, springy and frisky. We talked about spending the evening together and you agreed we could go out again later if it was a warm night.

And last night, it was, and we snuck out and walked to the park after a few drinks. The park was moonlit and quiet, we ran to a shadowed tree and you pressed me against it, pulling my dress down over my breasts with your firm hands. You leaned me back against a dividing branch and sucked my nipples in the close air of the hidden tree. I really felt like the sexiest girl in the world, with you. I felt naughty. I lifted my leg around you and kissed your mouth hard, biting your lip. You pulled my hair back and kissed my neck with deep, wet sucks. Your fingers found my entrance, and as I gasped you thrust your hand upwards, roughly penetrating me with more than I was used to. I yelped but clung to you, opening my thigh wider, sucking you in. The weight of our bodies made it awkward and it hurt slightly but I loved it. It really felt like you were fucking me. After a few minutes and I told you to stop as my leg was starting to cramp. We kissed as you withdrew, you asked if you hurt me, I said you could kiss it better. You crouched down in front of me and lifted my dress as I stood there. I'd never done it standing up before, I felt my heart pumping so hard, it was glorious to have your soft tongue to soothe and lick me. I stroked your hair and closed my eyes, wanting to sink down too, but I felt a new kind of orgasm growing in my muscles. As they held me up, my legs trembled and throbbed with blood surging through them. When I came, it was a deep shooting all down my nerves, veins and muscles. I felt it in my feet! I couldn't believe it. When you looked up I had to lean on you, I thought I would fall over. You laughed and helped me over to the grass, where we both lay down and heaved our breaths back. We held hands laying there. It was so peaceful looking up at the stars. You said you hadn't had so much fun in years. I couldn't believe we had to go back to school and pretend we weren't completely in love.

    How could we possibly hide this?

    Nadia x

Chapter Thirty-Two

After finding out from Lois that Maria's cousin Benicio ran a hair salon in London, and as I was in the vicinity, I phoned up in the guise of a new client. To the receptionist, Issy, I enquired if the manager would be on site, and when she said he was fully booked up, I requested ten minutes for a consultation. She said to pop along before lunch and he might be able to squeeze me in.

After a night in a pleasant hotel, I drove over to the salon, and found 'Comb' in Covent Garden in good time. I had spent a few summers visiting my husband in London back in the nineties, while we were still courting, and we had sought out the opera and fine wines around the cleaner corners from Soho, though we returned there afterwards for late-night theatre shows and dancing. Still, it wasn't exciting to be back here, not under these circumstances.

When I came face to face with the handsome Sicilian cousin of my case subject, he was justifiably unimpressed with my trick to book his time. His stubbly mouth gave a sideways twitch into a pout and he looked me down, then up again, and lingered, most unbearably, at my thinning, Caucasian tresses.

'I was expecting to hear *of* you, not *from* you,' Ben said, returning his deep brown eyes to mine. His accent was delicious. He turned to Issy, to whom I had spoken on the phone, and asked her to ensure we were not disturbed, then he led me downstairs to the quieter salon floor. There he spoke to a junior stylist, poised in front of the only client sitting down there, reassured him that he could take his lunch break, and took over tending to the striking Black woman perusing through a magazine, her hair coated in a thick crème, waiting patiently for the treatment to work.

I sat beside them as he took out his silver comb and examined a strand of her hair.

'Do you mind if I record our interview?' I asked, holding up a slender Dictaphone.

Ben glowered at his client. 'Grace, I just need to set this lady straight, do you mind?'

'Don't mind me, love,' the woman flipped her eyebrows along with her magazine.

I pressed the record button and held it in my lap. He wasn't to know that after Lois' ramblings, I had grown unconfident in my abilities to take such hurried notes: I wanted to catch every little detail from Ben and the changeover from pen and paper to audiotape was more of a relief than my techno-fear had allowed me to previously embrace.

'Aren't you supposed to be interviewing Maria?' Ben asked a little sharply as he lifted the ledge in front of Grace, leaned it back and secured it against the mirror, revealing a sink underneath it. He spun the chair around and tipped it back, scooping her hair into the bowl as she settled her neck against the wash basin.

'I wanted to interview everyone else first, before I speak to her, just so I know what everyone else knows,' I answered, willingly honest.

'Well, I don't know a thing,' Ben responded, his voice a soft grumble. 'Maria didn't tell me what was happening so, to me, that means nothing happened.'

'You must be very close,' I smiled, watching him rinse Grace's hair. 'You must tell each other everything for you to be so sure that she would tell you about this student.'

'Yeah, we are, I am closer to her than her own brothers, I was the one she called from the hospital, I was the one she asked to pick her up, I was the one who saw her injuries,' Ben's eyes narrowed, 'and I want to know if the people who put her there are going to be charged!'

I looked up at him. 'Who, exactly?'

Ben cut a knowing expression. 'Lois, mainly... she damaged Maria's car, too.'

I asked Ben if he knew why Lois had attacked Maria, and with a long exhale from his proud nostrils that must have reached Grace's forehead, he revealed that Lois believed Maria was cheating on her. Apparently, Lois even phoned Ben to inform him of his cousin's affair. 'In case I didn't already know... then asked me if I knew!' Ben shook his head. 'She got the wrong end of the stick. Lois saw texts on Maria's phone from someone called Ruby and she interpreted that with her usual paranoia!'

Ben massaged conditioner into Grace's hair. 'You know what? For years I heard about Lois doing this and that, saying shit and upsetting my cousin, and after a while I knew Maria would be happier if she was alone - but she didn't want to be, she says she's lonely enough, but I told her that's no reason to stay with someone who's bad for you. I told her she's lost sight of how good things can be, when it's right... and one day she will find someone who's sweet to her and loving, but I never meant for her to look in the wrong place.'

I contemplated the fears, lies, and denials that must have rocked these young women's lives. I imagined Maria hiding the texts messages, changing the name in case Lois found them, knowing they were incriminating. I longed to know what they had revealed before they were destroyed.

'Did you suspect these texts from Ruby were really from Nadia?' I asked. 'It isn't very hard to make that leap if you've seen her hair colour, I'm surprised Lois didn't realise.'

'I never saw text messages. I live in the city, Maria lives in the country. The times I did see her, she never told me about or showed me any messages.'

'But once Lois told you, did she expect you to do something?'

When Ben admitted that he had gone round to Maria's house one warm, early April evening, flickers of recognition opened my eyes. I listened to him explain that he didn't think Lois had any reason to be worried, but he wanted to make sure, so whilst feeling no loyalty towards Lois, Ben made a spontaneous journey to Cheltenham and turned up on Maria's doorstep. However, when she answered her door, Ben said he pushed his way past his shocked cousin, and saw Nadia there.

'She was just sitting in the kitchen reading her books, Maria was in the middle of making dinner - there was nothing suspicious about it - I trusted they were doing nothing wrong.' Ben went on to add that Maria was only defensive at his insinuation, troubled that he had taken Lois' delusion seriously enough to try and catch her in the act. Ultimately, once Maria invited him to stay for dinner, Ben declined and returned home, feeling foolish, but pacified.

Wrapping her in a turban, Ben spun Grace around in her chair, closing the lid on the basin, which had acted as a genius splash-guard, and not one drop stained the generous, flattering mirror in front of her.

'So, you'd seen Nadia before then?' I asked calmly. He would have had to in order to make the association between Lois' accusations and Maria's young friend. Even if Maria had confided in her cousin, I doubted Maria would have described the colour of her student's hair, and it was even more unlikely that a male would remember a detail like that unless he'd seen her in the flesh. I deduced that there must have been some previous occasion that had brought Ben and Nadia together in the same vicinity. 'There was a party around Christmas?'

Ben began to spray some products through Grace's hair, but I didn't miss the roll of his eyes at my leading question.

'I admit I was surprised to see her there, as Maria had so far only complained that her new girl was too needy,' Ben huffed resignedly. 'But she told me Nadia was there with Christian, the boy she'd introduced her to, who was kind of my suggestion in the first place, so I wasn't worried, everything seemed to be under control.'

My fascination piqued. This was exactly the kind of interaction of which I needed evidence. 'How did they behave around each other?' I asked. 'Did you notice anything? You must have been able to tell if Nadia had eyes for your cousin - and vice versa of course.'

'I never saw them together,' Ben tilted his head, seeming to acknowledge the need for doubt. 'Maria only pointed her out, I was never introduced, and Nadia kept her distance. I guess it wasn't cool for a student to be at her teacher's party, so it's not like they could be seen drinking or laughing.'

'Ben, I think you must have been one of only a few people who knew Nadia was Maria's student,' I raised my eyebrows. 'Lois wasn't aware - why do you think Maria didn't tell her?'

'Hey, Lois is crazy,' Ben said scathingly. 'There's never a right time with her... a lot of the time Maria was scared to upset her,' he gesticulated with his sturdy silver comb. 'But Lois was on drugs that night at her exhibition, her friends were doing it upstairs and they were trying to give it to Nadia, that's why Maria freaked out.'

My ears pricked. 'What drugs?' I guessed cocaine having met Lois. 'Did Nadia do any?'

'I don't know,' Ben shrugged, tugging gently at a knotted end. 'I was with my wife and child downstairs. The next thing we knew Lois was tearing her prints off the walls screaming that the party was over. Maria told me what she'd seen and she was glad Lois had left, except everyone else left too. I helped her put the food away but she was tired and said I should head home.'

I nodded. 'Do you know how Nadia got home that night?'

'I don't know about that...' Ben shaded his expression by turning away, but his frustration was tangible, in the air as well as reflected in the mirror. 'I feel like you're not hearing me,' he turned back, his shapely nose and cheekbones highlighted under the lamps hanging from the ceiling. 'Lois is the one you need to be questioning, she is paranoid, fucked up... she was cruel to Maria, causing great unhappiness in their relationship.'

'Unhappy enough to find the attentions of a sixteen year old attractive?' I asked, ignoring his pleas.

Reaching over for the hairdryer, Ben set it onto a slow, hot heat, his mouth pursed with anger. At this, I winced a little: I hadn't accounted for the noise of a blow-dry impeding the audio recording of my interview with Ben, however, the low whirring was gentle as he rolled Grace's black hair around a wide brush and toasted it straight.

'I don't think Maria thought Nadia was even lesbian,' Ben spoke louder for my benefit. 'If she questioned the girl's attention, she would have questioned herself first because she is a decent person and a good teacher, an excellent teacher, a professional! I have full faith Maria never laid a finger on that girl, even if she thought about it!'

I wasn't so sure. Benicio seemed to know his cousin well, but, having met blonde, blue-eyed Lois, I wondered if he considered that Nadia's green-eyed, flame-haired kind of beauty might have been too tempting to resist.

Ben enthusiastically responded with a rehearsed sort of statement about Maria being Sicilian, strength and sexuality running through the blood – of course she would have considered the young temptress, but never acted on it – pride and honour also played heavily on their family traits. 'Maria's morals are solid, intact,' Ben asserted. 'She keeps her word.'

'But it worried you enough that she had to reassure you nothing was going on.'

'And I believed her!' Ben yanked Grace's head back with the force of his brush. 'Yes, Maria had a period of doubt, but it passed, she sorted it out.'

I exhaled, feeling that Ben was holding back. I understood he wanted to protect his cousin but I wanted him to know I was not out for Maria's blood: the truth could help her case. 'This period of doubt - how did that manifest in your eyes? How was she different?'

Shrugging, Ben acted blasé. 'She said she felt under pressure at school, she was breaking up with Lois. She didn't have enough time for herself, no time to see friends, I mean, she's not particularly social anyway, but it's when you can't that you want to the most... you know. She just threw herself into work. She was trying to balance her job with the extra work and trouble Nadia seemed to bring with her. I could tell she was drinking... she'd start crying...'

'Did she discuss Nadia, specifically, as a source of her stress?' I asked, but then felt exasperated, of course Maria hadn't. I pressed on for a better question.

Unravel

'I mean, beyond academic pressure, did you feel Nadia was causing a more personal crisis?'

Closing in on a section of hair, Ben brushed it tightly and focused hard on heating it through, his eyes locked and unavailable. 'I had the feeling she was,' he confirmed quietly after a while. 'I thought Maria was getting confused, this pretty girl with her almost every day and night, Lois treating her like shit, taking her for granted - and if the pretty girl has a scheme of her own, that's enough to send anyone under.'

'Would you say Maria has ongoing mental health issues?' I asked, not believing she did, but I had to ask, just in case.

'No.' Ben replied, shaking his head. 'This was a one off, a spell, you could say... yeah, she was definitely under a spell. It was a combination of events, you know, life circumstances, that led to a... little crisis... but Maria dealt with it! She didn't need to tell me the exact details of this dilemma - I knew that she would get through it. She has a good career - she wouldn't destroy that by being reckless... I knew she made a decision and I trusted she did the right thing.'

I processed what Ben was saying to me and realised he would have known nothing else between Maria reassuring him she would 'deal with it', and hearing from her after that disastrous night at the prom.

'So when you collected Maria from the hospital, what did she say then?'

'She was hurt, emotionally and physically,' Ben sighed. 'She said Nadia had fucked her over, been playing mind games to get favourable grades.'

'What did you think that meant?' I shook my head. 'How can you still believe nothing happened?'

Ben inhaled sharply, taking offence, and his voice rose passionately. 'It meant that Nadia had been trying her best to work her way into Maria's life: gain her trust; earn her respect; be the dedicated student she knew would impress her; give her the troubled history so Maria felt she was needed. She let her believe she was interested in her dog, in her neighbour, so she could get close to Maria; hang out with her, spend time at her house, make her miss her when she's not there; be a friend, and more, when Maria's going through a hard time. All these things...' Ben's face clouded with anger, 'all to make her fall in love.'

'You think Maria fell in love?' I asked.

'I think she did, yes,' Ben scorned, 'but it wasn't real, was it?'

'You believe Nadia would be that manipulative?'

Ben turned off the hair dryer and let his gaze fall directly, fully on mine. 'I don't know Nadia, I can't blame her... I don't know what happened or why she did what she did,' he smoothed Grace's hair down with the brush. 'All I know is she's a bit messed up in the head, you know, Maria was probably the best thing to happen to her but she screwed it up. I hope she realises what she's done and grows up before she breaks anyone else's heart.'

I admired Grace's flattened bob, but aimed my question at the skilled stylist. 'Whether or not this affair turned physical or remained emotional, it is still an affair, and Maria's teaching career is most likely in jeopardy, what do you think she'll do?'

'That's up to you, isn't it?' Ben sprayed something that smelled fruity, and tweaked the ends of the woman's hair. 'Maria has learned her lesson, and she has lost enough. She has lost Lois, she has lost her dog, and she will probably never see Nadia again. Well, she won't lose me, I am her cousin!'

'You don't believe she's susceptible to the wiles of young women?' I suggested.

'It won't happen again,' Ben said, glaring at me. He tugged at the Velcro at the back of Grace's neck, releasing her from the gown.

Just then, Issy crouched at the top of the stairs, her head dipping below the ceiling of the basement, and mouthed something down to Ben. He turned to whisper some salon-talk, and he gestured for her to escort Grace up the stairs. He gave his client a kiss on the cheek and held her hand closely as they said goodbye.

Ben's smile dropped as he turned back to me. 'My next client has arrived.'

I took the hint: we were done. 'I appreciate you seeing me,' I said, switching off the Dictaphone.

Ben stood squarely in front of me, his shoulders loose and muscular. He said softly. 'I know you'll give Maria the justice she deserves.'

I held his gaze. 'I'll do what is right.' I blinked at the futility of my position.

Ben grit his jaw and nodded, leading me up the stairs, and holding the door open for me at the top, like a gentleman.

I liked Benicio. I had a feeling, driving back to Gloucestershire, that I would like Maria, too. I had another twang of adrenalin about finally meeting this woman.

Before then, however, I had to speak to Nadia Sheridan, and my mood returned with a sombre gravity. I thought about Leon, Maria's dog, and if his death was circumstantial; for a second my eyes pricked with empathy. One thing was for sure, I had to toughen up if I was to interview the two women involved in this scandal. Any softness would make me look sentimental, and as it seemed - that was entirely what had put Maria Calver in this sticky position.

Unravel

May 14th

Maria,

We are getting so good at this. You had agreed to meet me in the girls toilets after school, the ones at the end of the second floor that everyone forgets about because three out of four cubicles were deemed out of order once, ages ago, and students became used to directing their primal urges elsewhere. Since then I have found them a wicked escape from classes. It was a thrill to lock the last cubicle door behind you and have you silently kiss me. The scent of your body overwhelmed me, your heat mixed with faded traces of perfume, emanating from your neck, the dip between your breasts and your strong arms around me. You turned me away from you to the small, mottled window above the cistern and I held onto the walls as you frisked me deliciously all over. You unbuttoned my shirt and rubbed my neck and chest, licking from my ear to my chin, and sucking my mouth into yours. You rubbed down my front from my breasts to my thighs, where you slid up again, under my skirt, pressing firmly at the centre of my tights, just once so I buckled. Then, you found the edge of my tights and pulled them down over my hips, over my buttocks, with desperate snatches. You pulled my knickers down and I bent over further, leaning against the ledge, tilting my pelvis up, wanting you so badly, I felt like a horny cat. You scooped up my juice with your fingertips before plunging into me, you eased your way around in firm strokes and held my hip close to you so you could feel my body seize under your discipline. The surge of immediate pleasure brought a flush to my cheeks and my breath struggled in bursts between agonizing seconds of rigid silence.

    Then we heard the door... Neither of us could believe when my friend's voice echoed around us, we froze in our incriminating positions, knowing to hush beyond any rustle of a flinch or even a slither of a finger. She called out to me, and I was helpless but to answer. I made my voice cool, and she asked me what I was doing, that she'd been waiting for me outside the gates but I hadn't left yet, and she was wondering if I was okay. I said I had menstrual cramps and was waiting for my painkillers to kick in. She asked why I was in these toilets and not the main ones, and I replied that I'd wanted a little privacy. She sounded like she was smiling as she apologized and we heard the door close again.

    You and I silently eased apart, turning to each other with wide eyes and fear making our hands tremble as we read each other's thoughts. You pulled some toilet paper and wiped your fingers. I hitched up my tights, wincing as the elastic slapped my skin, but when the noise of the flush covered us, we stole a brief kiss. We would have to leave separately, I would text you when the coast was clear.

    As I unlocked the cubicle door, I wasn't expecting her to be standing there still. She was grinning and leaning against the sink. I stopped dead and said her name out loud in surprise so you'd know not to follow me out. She wore a sloppy, smug smile, she thought she'd been clever, pretending to have left, but she hadn't seen you, there was no space under the cubicle door... unless she had followed you. I washed my hands, avoiding her eye contact, asking why she was still waiting. She said she was worried about me and grinned again, she put her arms around me but I batted her away, suddenly disgusted by her, and concerned what you would think if I let her touch me, but mostly because I didn't want her to catch your scent on me. She asked about you then, asking how you were, and I couldn't tell if she knew or not, so I brushed it off and walked out, praying she would follow me out and not check in the cubicle where you were probably holding in a heart attack.

    She did come after me, I still don't know if she suspected but I figured she couldn't have seen you or she would have accused me of keeping secrets. She thinks she knows about us you see, I never told you this and I can't, but I don't care about pretending with her. I only care about pretending with you, and we are good at it, aren't we?   Nadia x

Chapter Thirty-Three

I wasn't surprised that whilst Nadia was staying at her parent's house on the outskirts of Gloucester, Sam Burrows was screening her friend's phone calls. Obviously, she didn't want Nadia speaking to *certain people*, but I doubted that *certain people* would be phoning Sam's household anyway.

When I finally got through to the soft Irish voice, I requested Miss Sheridan's attendance to a formal meeting at the same office in which I had met the principal, in the Gloucester Council's building. I wanted her to regard our appointment as official; to be somewhat intimidated by the authority. I informed her that she was entitled to bring a witness, for support or legalities, but Nadia said she had no one and was fine to come by herself. I admit I was taken off guard by her cool acceptance, and felt small sprouts of excitement in combat with niggling doubts in my stomach.

When I saw Nadia Sheridan for the first time, she clutched her arms around her widely striped long sleeved t-shirt, before reluctantly extending her hand.

Unravel

She looked different to how I had imagined, not exactly prettier, but her face held expressive qualities I hadn't seen on a teenager before and I suppose my stare lingered. The seventeen year old was uniquely attractive; her red hair in a loose side plait, her fringe as scruffy as a horse's forelock. She looked to me expectantly, and I understood how Maria must have felt, having those stunning green eyes turned upon her, focusing sharply, radiating with energy now.

I smiled graciously. 'Have a seat,' I gestured towards the hard chair opposite me at the table. 'I'm going to record our interview, that's unless you have any objections, in which case I'll have to use pen and paper,' I eyeballed her, 'but I'd rather look at you than my notepad.'

Nadia shrugged as she settled in the chair. 'Have you spoken to Maria yet?' Her voice was a pleasant, Irish crackle.

I hurried to press record. 'No, have you?'

'No,' Nadia held me in steely regard. 'I'm not allowed.'

'I suppose Samantha is keeping ears and eyes open for you?' I suggested.

'*For* me?' Nadia grimaced. '*Against* me more like, she won't let me go out by myself.'

'If she's your friend then she's probably only trying to protect you from people she regards as a threat to your wellbeing,' I reasoned. 'It must be hard for her, all this coming out about you and your teacher.'

Unravel

'It is not!' Nadia scowled. 'It was her idea in the first place! She was the one who suggested I keep Maria sweet because I *had* to pass my exams... I never meant it to go this far, I never meant to hurt anyone, especially not Maria.'

Seizing on Nadia's sudden confession, I disregarded my plan to draw her story from the beginning and encouraged her to tell me about their profitless wager.

'Sam already told you, we made a stupid bet that I could seduce Maria, and it was easy!' Nadia said, frowning with defence. She must have noticed the harshness in her tone, however, and softened it, lowering her gaze to talk about Maria. 'I mean, she was lonely, she had this vulnerable side, but she was trying to be cool and I knew I could provoke a reaction out of her... I knew how to make her nervous and make her laugh, and I knew she would fall for it.'

'And it worked?' I asked. 'You made her fall for you?'

Nadia blinked up at the windows, her eyes squinting against the sun. 'I guess so... She was kind to me, she drove me home when I missed my bus... she made me dinner when I told her my dad wasn't around,' Nadia returned her gaze to meet mine, but she shrugged carelessly. 'She let me hang out at her house, I met her dog and her neighbour... I think she liked the company - her girlfriend, Lois, was just awful to her.'

'When you say 'neighbour', are you referring to Christian Webb, who was also her dog-sitter?' I asked. 'You began dating him, is that correct?'

'Yeah, but that was...' Nadia frowned. 'I thought that's what Maria wanted, Chris was nice, but to be honest, I only wanted to spend time with her dog, Leon...' At this, Nadia's mouth pressed down and her eyes brimmed rapidly and fully with tears.

'Why are you crying?' I had to ask, though it was obvious she had bonded with the dog.

Yet, the girl shook her head and froze her expression. 'I don't like being in trouble.'

'Who are you scared of?' I probed, slightly confused. 'Your father?'

Nadia turned moist eyes upon me, and I saw the flash of sincere pain within her. 'He went mental when he found my journal, can you please tell him none of it was true? I don't want him to think Maria did any of those things, if anything happens to her, it's my fault!'

I quickly moved with the topic. 'Why would you fabricate a journal?'

'God!' Raising her sleeves to wipe away the mascara prints she had blinked onto the skin around her eyes, Nadia sniffed. 'It was in case Sam ever found it - she would think it was real! You know, I wanted to win the bet, but there was nothing happening with Maria to prove it so I made up this shit, intending for Sam to find it and it would convince her I had won!'

I sat back, amazed. These girls were so competitive. 'Nothing happened?'

'No, I never did any of those things with Maria!' Nadia insisted. 'She never made a pass at me, we never got physical, or sexual, or intimate, whatever you want to call it... I mean, we kissed a few times but that was just to keep playing the game, it was nothing, it meant nothing!'

I almost believed her. 'So Maria never acted indecently towards you?'

Leaning her elbows across the desk for emphasis, Nadia appealed. 'Maria Calver was honourable from the start to the end of my time with her, she never behaved inappropriately... she is a great teacher and she deserves to be let off whatever charges the school and my dad have her up for,' Nadia took a shaky breath. 'Maria is innocent.'

'It's good to know you still feel so passionately about Maria,' I stated calmly. 'How do you think she feels about you?'

'She probably hates me...' Nadia replied, slumping back into her chair again. 'All the times I promised her that my feelings were genuine, and now she knows I lied... even when we agreed to run off together at the end of school.'

I smiled to acknowledge her casual drop of such vital information, but I would come back to that. 'So, when did you first come out to Maria?'

'I never discussed it with her,' Nadia answered, her eyes skimming over the table. 'It wasn't an issue, we carried on with tuition... I don't know if she even knew I was.'

Irritated by her evasiveness, I rounded on the girl. 'Nadia, you said that Maria was always professional, that you worked well together, that she was kind to you - why would you agree to a devious plan hatched up by a jealous, foolish friend to seduce a teacher who would have made sure you succeeded every one of your exams naturally, without need for manipulations? Didn't you want to know you could do it regardless? You're an intelligent girl, surely you knew it was pointless and destructive!'

'It was just a bit of fun,' Nadia shrugged pathetically, 'and then I couldn't stop it.'

I sighed. Nadia was falling far under my expectations with this girlish act.

'Then how did it come about?' I pushed. 'Huh? If she didn't even think you were a lesbian, how did you manage to twist your teacher around your little finger?'

Nadia gulped, and sat uncomfortably on her ankle. 'I kissed her... Maria was...' She hesitated, thinking with a frown. 'She didn't push me away... and from then, we just felt close, and tuition was... nice,' Nadia slid her eyes back in my direction, they looked dark the way she had them narrowed. 'I didn't enjoy misleading Maria, but it made her smile, and if she was happier, then I'm not so evil, am I?' Nadia lowered her gaze to pick at her nails; she tried another tack. 'For a while I thought Maria was playing a game too, it felt like she was waiting for me, to see what I did, as if she was teasing me. I thought maybe she knew I was playing around, and we were playing against each other, for a laugh.'

'You were both playing a game? Hmm...' I drawled derisively. 'So when did you first discuss your feelings? You mentioned running off together after school.'

Nadia rubbed one hand against her knee making me wonder if her palms were sweaty.

'We joked about it,' Nadia shifted, the fingers of her other hand flipped her plait dismissively, 'but Maria refused to be physical... whenever I tried to kiss her, she said we'd have to wait.'

'Did you want to have sex with Maria or were you just pretending?'

Nadia averted her eyes to the window, biting her lusciously full lower lip, the lip I imagine Maria yearned to bite time, and time again, in tuition. 'Maybe after a while I did want to,' Nadia said finally. 'I mean, she was a good kisser, so I figured.'

I watched the tension grow in Nadia's profile, and I wondered if delving into her memories again would spring up more tears for me. 'So all those journal entries were pure fantasy?'

Unravel

'Yep.' Nadia's chin remained firm as she pushed her thoughts down into her throat.

Uncaring of whether Nadia could see out of the corner of her eye, I took the moment to curl my lip. I sensed the girl was lying, having said the journal was to fool Sam, but now they were authentic fantasies. She would never have let Sam see them.

'Let's go back to when you first realised Maria was gay...' I said, exhaling deeply. 'As your personal tutor, were you not worried? You must have found her attractive?'

Nadia tightened her arms around her body and seemed to shrink. 'I knew she was, of course I knew, but like I said, we got on with tuition, we had so much work to do, I tried not to think about it too much.'

'But this was at the start of your tuition with Maria?' I clarified. 'Around October?' I carefully sewed around the edges of Nadia's story, drawing in tighter with every stitch. 'And Maria introduced you to Christian around when... November?'

'Yeah, she thought I'd like a boyfriend.' Nadia held my eye contact, wanting me to appreciate how generous and understanding Maria was to set her up.

I felt it was of great interest that Maria had made this move. By uniting her student with her neighbour and dog-sitter, Maria had effectively invited Nadia into her house, and I doubted it was ignorance that led her to permit an event that was anything but innocent. Nadia couldn't have brought this about herself; it couldn't have been part of her plan, that didn't come until later, apparently.

'So, explain this period of time for me,' I requested. 'You began seeing Christian, you spent time at Maria's house, you enjoyed her dog, Leon... were you ever alone with Maria?'

'No,' Nadia said breathlessly. 'That was before.'

'Before your bet with Sam?' I over-raised my eyebrows knowingly.

'Yeah,' Nadia nodded then shook her head. 'I wasn't with Sam then, I hadn't come out to anyone yet.'

'So tell me about this party during the Christmas holidays,' I changed suddenly, enjoying seeing Nadia's pretty features quaver with confusion. 'I've heard so much about it, I know you were there with Christian, but several people have told me that you didn't speak to Maria all night - that's strange, almost like you didn't want anyone to know you knew each other so personally,' I smiled, aware I was roasting the girl.

Nadia looked nervous and stared at me with trembling eyes. 'Christian asked me to that party, it was Lois' exhibition and she wanted people there, Maria didn't think I should go but she didn't want to upset Lois, so that's why she didn't say who I was and that's why I didn't talk to Maria at the party, because she didn't want me there!

'And what on earth were you doing upstairs with Lois and her friends? I'm dying to know!'

Nadia frowned resentfully at my interrogation. 'I was bored! I had some drinks upstairs with Lois' friends and actually enjoyed myself, but Maria came in and shouted at me, she embarrassed me in front of everyone, and that's when Lois found out I wasn't just Christian's girlfriend.'

'Okay, so having been deceived by her partner, and caught giving substances to a minor, Lois rightfully walked out...' I nodded, ready for Nadia's objection. 'And then what happened? Everyone left? Where did you sleep?'

'Maria set up the spare room for me...'

'That's not what I asked,' I smiled.

'Nothing happened! I promise!' Nadia exclaimed. 'Christian was asleep on the sofa.'

'When did things start happening, Nadia?' I urged, wanting to put heat on the girl. 'There must have been a point when you both knew the other was gay, that you had come out at school, that must have made things awkward in tuition; all that sexual tension must have been exciting, huh?'

'You don't get it!' Nadia blurted. 'I denied that I liked her at first because I wanted Maria to keep teaching me, I didn't want it to ruin our friendship!'

'Friendship?' I scorned. 'You're contradicting yourself, Nadia, you're supposed to be manipulating Maria, your friendship wasn't real, remember?'

Nadia retreated into her chair, hunching her shoulders, her mouth zipped shut. She looked out to the

Unravel

windows, her hair hiding her face, but I knew she was still listening, and thinking of her next excuse.

'I think I'm onto something, aren't I?' I taunted. 'I can see it clearly, Nadia, I'm trained in this stuff and you can't fool me. I think Maria knew you liked her from the start, even though you denied it... you're a pretty girl, she would have thought about it, thought about you... you knew she liked you, only two people can know these things. So, you made a pass at her, and she didn't mind it, and here's what I think...' I folded my arms and exhaled. 'I think you started going out with Sam as a decoy... that way, everyone, including Sam, is so busy fussing over the young new couple that they completely miss that you are really in love with your teacher.'

Nadia's mouth panted and gulped closed again. Her nostrils flared a little, and from behind her veil of hair, I could see her eyebrows twisting up with anxiety.

'Would you mind looking at me?' I asked flatly, and she turned her neck awkwardly.

'Your smartest move was getting Sam to believe she thought of seducing your teacher, that was genius!' I revelled. 'Because you were seducing Maria a long time before Sam was involved, and it had nothing to do whatsoever with improving your grades, isn't that right?'

Nadia stared hatefully at me, the corner of her eye glistened with a dwelling teardrop.

'Just like the journal - very clever - it reads like fiction, but you're skilled enough to have done that deliberately, creative writing is your best subject, is it not?' I laughed my relief at having caught Nadia out. 'And it wasn't just in case Sam found it – you never took it to school!'

'You don't know shit about me!' Nadia's heavily Irish outburst was followed by reddening cheeks; her hands flew to her face and she leaned on the table, covering her eyes.

'So tell me - did you keep your agreement?' I shrugged. 'Did you wait until the end of school like you promised? Because your journal entries describing how Maria masturbated you on several occasions in her office, and in her car, are criminal acts if judged to be factual – or did you not think of that when you were "fabricating" these stories?'

'I made them up!' Nadia slammed her hands onto the table, her eyes blazing. 'I was fantasising, I told you! It doesn't matter if my feelings were real or not! It doesn't matter if I went out with Sam as a distraction or not, because *those things* I wrote were just my imagination! I spent a lot of time in Maria's office and in her car, and I was just entertaining myself! We never did any of that!'

'Then tell me what you were doing all those evenings in Maria's house?' I demanded. 'After you finished studying... after dinner when you're both relaxed...? Christian must have been quite jealous that you had dumped him in favour of the person who had set you up!'

Looking more shocked than I could have hoped for, Nadia shook her head and refused to talk about Christian. She was quiet for a minute and slid back down into her chair slowly, as I pressed her for the truth, believing she must have been spending many evenings at Maria's for Christian to suspect enough to tell Lois of their social engagements.

'Let's talk about end of term... prom night,' I clasped my fingers over my knee, the sun was relenting, thank goodness; it was more apt for my serious topic. 'My sources so far have told me that you were upset about something, what was that? And how much of that was due to being under the influence of illegal drugs?'

Wiping her fringe away from her brow, I only saw now that Nadia was sweating under her long-sleeved top, her face was flushed and she rubbed her sleeve against her temple. Nadia spoke quietly, her mouth trembling. 'Yes, I'd taken a pill because I needed something, anything, to escape from my head... my dad had chucked me out, he said he was going to put me in a homeless hostel if I went to the prom. He told me he'd found my journal and he thought I was going to see Maria.'

'He had reason to be worried, Nadia, the only reason you were going to the prom was to see her, wasn't it?' I said coolly. 'Without tuition you must have been missing her.'

Unravel

'Of course I missed her! But I just wanted to talk to her, we hadn't spoken in ages...' Nadia's eyes spilled again now. 'I didn't understand why she was seeing Miss Lenholm, but they were there together... I was wasted.'

'As was Sam,' I frowned, 'and you two argued, she recalls, about Maria, because you wouldn't stop staring over at her with Ms Lenholm, and then you fought, and guess who broke it up? And took you outside,' I stated. 'What did Maria say to you?'

Pushing her hair behind her ear, Nadia sniffed back her congestion. 'She wanted to know what I'd written in my journal because Miss Lenholm was going to tell Principal Woods.'

'Maria didn't know anything about the journal?'

'No!' Nadia revolted. 'Why would I tell her what I wrote in it?'

'And when you told her?' I smiled. 'It must have been an arousing moment, you're high and upset, she's passionate and scared, you're alone outside, away from everyone, knowing that you've gotten that close and you're about to be caught, you must have kissed passionately!'

'We did not!' Nadia baulked. 'I was crying! Maria's not like that! She was angry!'

'Then explain why you ran away with Maria when Sam came looking for you?' I asked, my stomach jabbing with excitement. 'Why did you run to Maria's car? Was this the romantic end of school eloping you'd joked about?'

'I don't know! We just had to talk in private...'

'That's not good enough, Nadia!' I bellowed. 'I thought none of it was real – your words! When were you planning on telling Maria you weren't going to run away with her after all?'

'I was going to tell her that night, but I was too high... it all got confusing!' Nadia whined. 'I didn't want it to end the way it did, but everyone was there, shouting, so I had to say it in front of everyone.'

'And how do you think she would have taken it?' I pushed. 'Would it have been any less painful in private than it was for her being humiliated in front of her colleagues? Do you think she would have laughed at herself for falling for your game? Or did you want to see the moment you made her heart break? What did you plan to get from this? That's what I don't understand. How could you hurt the one person who looked out for you, looked after you? You would have got good grades anyway... It just doesn't seem to me like any student could be that cruel and manipulative to do that to her teacher,' I sighed. 'This makes you look like a terrible person, you know that? Even if you're telling the truth and you never slept with Maria or had any physical intimacy with her, you've still destroyed a gentle woman's heart and career.'

Nadia folded her hands over her eyes and wept into her sleeves, sobbing heartily, now that I had successfully broken her down.

I watched with no small amount of pleasure.

'Listen, I think I've heard enough. The hearing is next week, but I have to talk to Maria,' I stood up and paused. 'Is there anything you'd like me to say to her on your behalf?'

Lifting her face up, Nadia's shimmering eyes poured weary tears. 'Tell her I'm sorry!'

I nodded, pressing the stop button on my Dictaphone. 'Of course I will.' I adjusted myself to leave, and after a moment's instinctual maternal hesitation, I walked away from the solitary, sobbing girl in the council's office room.

Unravel

May 22nd

Maria,

Last night was incredible. I don't think either of us could wait to get out of school, the exams were heavy going for both of us and I sensed we both needed to let off some steam. My 'friend' had taken to waiting for me after my tuition with you so I told her you were taking me straight home and I wouldn't be able to walk with her to the bus station... I didn't tell her you were taking me to your home not mine...

Once safe inside, I ran a bath and made it extra sudsy. It felt good not only to wash the day's stress away, but to feel properly relaxed in your house. I was smooth and spanking clean when I emerged in your dressing gown. You had made your bedroom into a luxurious den, lighted candles either side of your deep-filled bed, gentle music and some wine on the side table. You kissed me on the nose and told me to get comfy, that you were going to shower so you smelled as good as me.

Unravel

While I imagined you in the shower, I drank some wine and led on your bed, touching myself and wanting you to come through and see me and be unable to stop yourself from licking my nakedness head to toe. But I suddenly felt nervous about being naked, and opened your wardrobe for something to wear. I touched your clothes, many of them I knew well from tuition, your shirts and waistcoats, but some I could not believe you had. Dresses! I pulled out a few I liked the look of and gazed at myself in your full length mirror, knowing you'd look amazing in them, and praying they weren't your ex's. I couldn't help it and tried one on that looked like it might fit me, it was a rich purple halter-neck with a flared swing in the hem, silk or satin maybe. It did fit, and looked divine so I had to try on some high heels, which looked like they matched, though they were a bit too big. Anyway, I was four inches taller and looked skinny and elegant, then I knew my hair would look better up in a twist. I fixed it quickly before putting on some lipstick and a slick of mascara.

Unravel

    I had some more wine just as you came through, looking so sexy in just a towel. You stared at me, frozen, and I panicked that it was your ex's dress and you didn't want me in it. But your eyes narrowed and your breath panted, you padded toward me and took my wine glass out of my hand, placing it down on the table. You said I looked beautiful like a real classy lady. I laughed that we were the same height, you pulled me in by my waist and kissed me. Your wet hair dripped over our lips but we smiled and licked the moisture in.

    I stroked your tattoo then gazed at your muscles as you dried your hair, I sat and drank more wine, but I had an idea — I wanted you to dress up too. I suggested one of the dresses I'd seen, sure that you would look stunning. But you shook your head with a loose smile and pulled out a white shirt. You slipped it on and looked soooo handsome, but then you pulled out a dark grey suit jacket with matching trousers. My jaw dropped with delight, mostly because I saw braces attached. As you started unhooking it all from the hanger you told me to find some smart shoes in the boxes at the bottom of your wardrobe. I knelt down and opened a box but it wasn't a shoebox.

When I saw what was inside, I held onto my gasp, and just reached in to touch. I pulled out a leather harness with a black dildo hanging from it, shapely and firm. I held it aloft and asked you if that only got an airing on special occasions too. You stopped, your smile growing slowly. I looked back at it, then back at you, and held it out to you, telling you to put it on. You hesitated, then took it, stepping into it and tightening the straps around your hips. I giggled as it swung mid-air in front of you, and you giggled too as you tried to stuff it into your trousers. I found your shoes as you slipped on the jacket, your collar unbuttoned low and your braces pressing either side of your braless bosom. I fastened the laces for you as you drank some wine and dabbed some perfume. You took my breath away you were so sexy. I stood beside you and felt so feminine. I kissed you, holding my hips against yours and felt your phallus pressing against my silky thighs. My insides squeezed with desire, I wanted you so much. I held onto you as we kissed and we kept turning around to look at ourselves in your mirror, disbelieving we looked like such a proper couple. Before we knew it we were dancing, swaying in time with the music, our bodies moving against each others, our lips locking. You stroked the back of my neck, loving my hair up. I enjoyed being cheek-to-cheek without getting neck ache. You gazed at me as an equal, a mix of pleasant surprise and wonder, with a softness about your dark lashes that I knew was your look of love.

  I felt in love too being so close and connected with you, and each moment was perfect. The deep red of your room, the scent of your perfume, the naughty thrill knowing what was under your suit. I wanted you and my legs were starting to tremble with the anticipation. We sat on your bed and drank more wine, I started to feel tipsy and took my shoes off, I didn't know what else to do. You took your jacket off. We kissed passionately and I touched it with my

Unravel

hand but I felt silly and pulled away. You told me to relax, it was still you, and you lay me back, kissing my neck, and I felt your whole body heating next to mine. I couldn't help lifting my leg over yours, wanting to feel the hardness of it through your trousers, it was you after all – it was yours and it might as well be your fingers. You slid your hands up my thighs and over my naked hips, guiding me towards you and easing your pelvis back and forth. My hair came unpinned as I rolled under your grasp, your fingers slid over and around my labia, warming me up, making me wet. You propped yourself up on your elbow, your hand cupping my head, your tongue flicking my lips as I pouted, my back arching, waiting as you fumbled with your fly.

    When I felt it press against my entrance, I clenched tightly, but you worked it against my vulva for a while so I got used to the feel of it and started to dribble with longing for it. You pushed it slowly up and down, I could feel your hand guiding it, and it twanged over my swelling clitoris. I was

Unravel

hungry for it and I pushed my leg under your body so you could lay on top of me. You smiled and asked if I was ready, I panted yes and wrapped my legs high around you. I saw your cheeks and neck flushed with arousal, and you lifted your hips at the right angle. I felt it press but it wouldn't go in. You told me to relax but I told you to push harder, then you shook your head and said you couldn't, it wasn't right. You sat back and rolled away, I was gutted. I felt ready to kick you for giving up. But you told me to wait a second and you reached for something in your drawer. You sat on the side of your bed doing something I couldn't see, and when I sat up I saw you were rubbing some lube onto it.   You looked at me, your eyes so dark with lust, and I just wanted to devour you. I pushed you back on your elbows and straddled you. I placed myself over the tip of your strap-on and felt its silky film meet with my fresh ooze. My lips opened around it and I sank down on it easily, halfway, before I adjusted my knees beside you and began to rock. You gripped my hips as my breath exhaled in shakes and my hair fell in my face, and as I held myself over you. I finally pushed myself up to the hilt I sighed with relief and fulfilment. I moaned and panted, holding the back of your head, and stroked your breast, huffing into your mouth as we kissed. You watched me as I sat up and leaned into your pelvis, swallowing you completely. I wished you could feel it like I did. I really wish you could fuck me for real like that. I think you had the same thought as you rolled me over and did me properly like you should have the first time. You gripped me around the waist and ground it into me as one might squeeze and turn an orange over a juicer, careful not to spill any precious nectar.

    As it happens, a lot of nectar got spilled, mostly mine, but after you took off your trousers and I went on top again, I reached back and felt between your legs. I touched your wetness and you were soaked, and so soft, but you sat up, shocked, and pulled my arm away. I lifted my fingers to my lips and tasted you for the first time, and your eyes widened, disbelieving I had done it. I smiled and licked my lips, you tasted amazing. I said now I'd tasted you I may as well go down on you, but you shook your head. Instead, you reached around me to touch yourself as I sat over your thighs, your dildo pressing up against my g-spot, and I followed your lead and masturbated too. We stared into each other's eyes and hardly moved, absorbed with close, intense friction. Seeing me come made you come, or maybe it was the other way round. Your eyes screwed up as my mouth opened and we both held our breaths before releasing long, throaty groans.

Quite simply, Maria, you are all the woman, and man, I will ever need.

I really fucking love you... and I really love fucking you!

Nadia x

Chapter Thirty-Four

My practice in Cheltenham is in the ground floor of a townhouse overlooking the flower-filled gardens next to the town hall, from where my large windows allow a lovely view and much sunlight. The front room contains an exquisitely comfortable Chesterfield sofa on one side, and my armchair on the other, with a short table for water and tissues, and a thick Persian rug between my client's feet and mine. There are no mirrors in the room, but paintings of inspiring landscapes and pre-Raphaelite era portraits adorn the walls, and greenery; tall potted plants, in the corners.

Though it presents as a therapist's lounge might, I hold only few interviews here, preferring to travel out to visit witnesses in comfortable or appropriate surroundings. This room isn't supposed to be comfortable: I want to keep it austere, so it remains unoccupied as a space to be used only for making confidential assessments. I work and write in the office next door where my desk sits, and files are kept in locked cabinets. My assistant works part-time hours, so, in the absence of any support, there is a panic button attached to my armchair, yet, unbelievably, no one has ever become violent in my presence.

    I felt nervous anticipating Maria's arrival. It had turned into a steaming hot day in August and there was hardly a breeze accessing the open windows; I sweated simply lifting the fan through from the office room, and plugging it in made my white shirt cling offensively to my rolling stomach. I stood in front of it to dry, and then I heard the door.

    When Maria Calver sauntered through, checking out the set-up, I was struck by her dark attire. Clad in tight black jeans and shirt stretching across her angular frame, she stood hands on hips as if she were one of the Avengers, all stance, and flashing eyes. All, that is, except for a clean, cream plaster cast that embraced her left forearm. Tall and lean, her shoulders rounded with muscle made me distinctly aware of her lesbianism, and the dusky shades of tan against the slick carvings of her eyes, brows and wavy hair left me doubtless of her Mediterranean origin and relation to her cousin, Benicio. Maria didn't smile or shake my hand, but paced in front of my sunny windows as if they were her best option for a hasty retreat.

    I introduced myself, encouraged her to call me by my first name, and watched as she slowly swaggered towards the low Chesterfield, attractively contrasted against the antique, deep green leather. She blinked widely, frowning slightly, suppressing the resentful pout that Benicio, had less graciously provided me. I let the air between us settle, observing how Maria squirmed under this opposing role dynamic: in my place, sitting taller, should be she, the teacher, authoritative; in her place, under a superior eye, should be Nadia: a shining new toy to play with. I could tell immediately Maria was used to being in control, but here I do not let my subjects hold sway over me. They speak when I press their buttons, and I was not about to let Ms Calver throw her weight around in my court.

I continued, after the indifferent glare returned with no comment, by stating, for Maria's information, of what she stood accused. Apologising for the delay in speaking with her, I explained that I had spent over a week acquiring statements from the witnesses who had most direct involvement, in the school, as well as in hers and Nadia's respective lives. It had been nineteen days since her arrest and with the disciplinary hearing imminent; it was time to make her assessment.

Maria exhaled moodily through her nose, and sat back, the leather squeaked against her shoulders as she folded arms, the good one cradling the injured.

'So let me recap where we stand at the moment...' I said, turning to pour us both some fresh water from the pitcher on the side table. 'Nadia Sheridan has made a formal statement confirming her previous, informal remarks, made on the night of your arrest, that any suspected affair between you and she was not real. Furthermore, Nadia has taken responsibility for the whole thing by asserting she had pretended to have feelings for you, for her own entertainment, and also as part of a bet with her friend, Samantha Burrows, who had suggested she could gain higher grades for her exams, by seducing you,' I reached to hand Maria the glass of water. 'I'd like to know how that makes you feel.'

Maria leaned forward to take it, and shrugged. 'Nadia's a clever girl,' she spoke with all the rich, husky tones of a morning cup of coffee, 'she would have done well anyway, there was no reason to bet on it.'

I agreed, and I had said as much to Nadia. 'But that's not what I asked.'

The way Maria locked her defined hazel eyes upon me was like halting mid-chew on a rotating knot of gum: a hesitant, breathless pause of surprised understanding. 'How do you think I should feel?' she growled, a hint of sarcasm on her lips.

'Well...' I tilted my head, thinking. 'If my student deceived me and taunted my emotions, I'd be angry and upset.'

Maria gave a wincing smile, and sat back again with the glass of water on her thigh. 'But I wasn't angry and I'm not upset.' Lifting the glass, Maria took a long drink of water, very coolly, not one quiver of her hand even as she wiped her mouth with the back of it. 'Nadia did what she felt she had to do, and if it helped her to amuse herself while she worked - then that's her choice - she still worked hard.'

I was curious. 'So you knew that Nadia was playing a game with you?'

'Of course I did,' Maria said. 'I'm not stupid, I know when a student has a crush on me.'

'And you played along with it?' I asked, hiding my disbelief.

Maria answered yes. She played Nadia at her own game. Far from being manipulated by Nadia, she let her believe they were in love so that she would study harder. 'And it worked,' Maria calmly insisted, 'I did my job, just as the principal asked: I got Nadia through her exams.'

If I was shocked to hear this, it was because I had already built preconceptions about Ms Calver as a victim, but I only let it disarm me for a few moments. 'It sounds like you're being defensive by pretending Nadia didn't hurt your feelings,' I countered. 'Your cousin Ben said you were hurt emotionally as well as physically when he met you at the hospital.'

Maria flatly denied her distress. 'I was tired from answering police questions all night, and my arm was broken,' she raised it an inch for my benefit, 'I was in shock, that's all.'

I sensed Maria was lying, and had to challenge her. 'I think you're too proud to accept or admit that Nadia played you, so you're claiming that you were the one who was playing.'

Unravel

She shrugged as easily as she could with heavy shoulders and a dead weight on the end of one arm. 'I have no hard feelings towards Nadia, just glad she finished her final year.'

Swapping my legs over to sit on my other cheek, I literally had to switch things around in my head. If Maria had manipulated Nadia's feelings - that made her even worse than Nadia. 'What kind of teacher would do that?' I asked, incredulous.

Maria swayed her head with nonchalance. 'One who has a glittering grade pass average and wasn't about to let a teenage drama queen ruin it.'

'That's a bit harsh,' I sighed and took a gulp of my water. If Maria was genuinely going to hold up this argument then I needed to find a hole in it. 'But, at the beginning, she must have told you about her difficult home life, her father? Didn't you feel sorry for her?'

Rolling her eyes towards the windows, Maria said she had heard Nadia's sob stories, all about her hostile and neglectful parent, but just like a nurse with a patient, she couldn't afford to care that much. Maria was a solid rock and Nadia blossomed under her wing. 'Letting the girl be close to me seemed to help... Nadia responded best that way.'

I knew it would be futile asking Maria why she gave Nadia her mobile number let alone challenging her on the manner of the text messages they exchanged. Silly, even, to ask something as simple as why she let Nadia call her by her first name: she would give the same smart answers, as if she had gone the extra mile for her superiors and they should be grateful, so I went straight for the jugular. 'Is that why you introduced her to Christian, and Leon?'

Maria seized up slightly at hearing both those names. She moved her glass to the floor between her smart shoes, and sat staring down, her elbows hooked over her knees. After a moment, her contemplation seemed to pass. Casually, she once again lifted her gaze to mine. 'I wanted... it was my intention to make Nadia relax so that she could focus on work,' Maria tried to sound more reasonable. 'She didn't have any friends and she was relying too much on me.'

'But why didn't you tell anyone at school what you were doing?' I queried. 'Why not the principal? Or Karen? Shouldn't you have covered your own back by telling them your plans?'

Maria huffed a half-laugh. 'There was nothing to tell! Listen, I did exactly what the principal asked me to do, and he never had a problem with me being close to Nadia as long as I made his school look good. But now he's turned on me because he's scared for his fucking reputation!'

'That's fair enough, isn't it?' I retorted. 'I'm fairly sure he never gave you permission to mess around with his students no matter how good their exam results might be!'

'I never intended to bring shame on anyone!' Maria responded passionately. 'I never meant to lie or deceive - my aim was to see a troubled student through her exams, my methods might have been unorthodox, but she succeeded... yet no one's giving me credit for that!'

'So you keep saying, Ms Calver, but I'm interested in how you executed this false affair,' I said in an elevated voice, eyeballing my Dictaphone to ensure it was definitely recording all this. 'What did you have to do to convince Nadia her feelings were reciprocated and genuine? Was it all words and promises, or did you have to prove your love physically?'

Maria shook her head. 'What does it matter if it was all an act?'

'Oh, it matters greatly, Nadia has already admitted you kissed, but see, I just can't believe that you weren't stimulated by this girl's attentions!' I exclaimed. 'I don't believe for a second that you didn't enjoy having Nadia so close to you, that when you kissed this pretty girl you felt nothing!'

However, Maria simply released a loose smile. 'Listen, I was manipulating Nadia who was manipulating me, so what difference does it make it we enjoyed each other's company along the way?'

I found her infuriating. She was too relaxed, too smug, not sorry enough for my liking. I had envisioned a tearful teacher, pleading for mercy, but here she sat, scratching the sweat from her beautiful, tanned neck, her knees wide and bouncing impatiently. I imagined her being a girlfriend to Lois, a cousin to Ben, a colleague to Karen, and found it hard to imagine the same person sitting in front of me being all those things and a lover to Nadia.

'Tell me about the journal,' I requested after she had stopped twitching. 'Why would you give that to Nadia if it wasn't for the intention of her writing your *secrets* in there?'

'Evelyn, you can give me a polygraph,' Maria looked me dead in the eye, 'I never knew what she wrote in that journal. I was mortified when I found out - of course I'm angry about it, that *work of fiction* has got me in this situation... but if that wasn't discovered, no-one would have any reason to be suspicious - there's no actual proof we did anything, is there?'

At that, I mentioned Nadia's father was a witness to two events that caused him concern: Maria nearly running him over with her car, and her coming out of his house. I asked her to explain why she had emerged with a reddened mouth, and Nadia hadn't.

Maria's face fell into a seething stiffness, her eyes fixed ahead of her, remembering. 'That man is insane, you have no idea what he's capable of... yes, I dropped Nadia home many times, but I only went in once or twice, *for a cup of tea*, and I may have had an allergy to the dust in his house... I didn't care what he thought of me, he'd hurt Nadia and he'd hurt me.'

'What do you mean hurt you?'

'Nothing, forget it,' she shook her head.

I felt as if I were hitting a brick wall, I didn't like the audacity at dismissing a father's natural concern, no matter if he was mentally unwell. 'I don't feel you appreciate the gravity of these accusations, Ms Calver,' I stated seriously. 'Your career is at stake here, regardless of your intentions, you are suspected of having physical relations with your student,' I leaned forward and lowered my voice conspiratorially. 'Wouldn't you rather come clean? Admit you had feelings for Nadia.'

'I did not have sexual feelings for Nadia Sheridan and we never had physical relations...' she spoke slowly and firmly. 'It doesn't matter how twisted our mind-games with each other seem to you, they weren't real. You can assess me all you want, but Nadia made up that journal - she said so herself. So, if there's no evidence of the charges against me, you have no case, do you?'

Sitting up, disturbed by her cool self-conviction, I tried to remain steady voiced, yet I felt my anger rising. 'I don't give up that easily. Now tell me why you really introduced Nadia to Christian? If you were *pretending* to seduce Nadia, why set her up with a boy?'

Without flinching, Maria gave her reason more humbly, looking at her arm. 'I knew Nadia would like my dog, that boy was a decoy.'

Finally standing up, I may have been improperly scornful. 'God, the way you use people, so fickle!' I paced lingeringly to the windows, turning my back on her. 'I just don't understand how two people could continue, when you both must have known the other was being insincere!' I cried out in disbelief. 'And it would have become redundant after a while - you would have dropped the act, surely!'

Maria seemed to mock my gradual, thoughtful steps, I could hear it in her voice from behind me. 'Lesbians can *tiptoe* round in circles for years and not admit the truth, and anyway, I knew she was playing with me but Nadia just wasn't as smart as she tried to be.'

I turned and rested against the window frame, catching the breeze from the fan as it alternated back and forth, but the sun still heated my back. The teacher was determined to place her one-up-man-ship over both Nadia's and my better judgement, and I felt in my sinking heart that put Maria's deluded beliefs in a different class. Possibly Peter Sheridan's.

'What about Lois?' I changed tack. 'Why wasn't she in on this? She wouldn't be jealous of a *silly* school-girl if you were honest with her.'

Stretching her long legs out, Maria squeaked against the hot sofa again as she told me that Lois was so self-involved that she wouldn't have cared even if Maria had told her. Lois, apparently, didn't give a damn about Maria's career and that's why she didn't tell her who Nadia was. Maria then admitted she liked keeping her business from Lois, who would only have ruined it by discrediting her, and that's why she changed Nadia's name in her phone.

I flipped my hands. 'Jesus! You were using Nadia to amuse yourself against Lois, too?' I was genuinely appalled at this type of disregard for the feelings of others, but I tried to understand. 'I suppose it must have been exciting to have Nadia at your house party when Lois had no idea?' I watched Maria cringe despite her pretences. I smiled. 'It backfired though, didn't it? When Lois found out.'

Maria was quick to recover, however, and she snorted with a little shuffle of her limbs back into an upright position. 'Let's just say it certainly spiced things up with Lois.' She tilted her head at me with a smile so I'd get her meaning, before drinking a gulp of water.

I wasn't about to let Maria alienate me by referring to lesbian acts of which she presumed I had no idea; the only act I find disturbing is when someone has the gall to lie to my face. 'If everything was so great and entertaining,' I asked, 'then what was that "dark period" Ben told me about? When you told your cousin that nothing was wrong, even though he felt you were upset – and he believes he knows you well enough.'

She obviously didn't want to talk about Ben; Maria's jaw clenched. I could sense I had touched that nerve, even from where I stood. 'That was work-related stress,' she said.

Catching her straight away, I jumped back towards her, wanting her eyes to meet mine. 'It wasn't because things were getting a little out of hand, or should I say, *in hand*, with Nadia?' I suggested, creeping back to my armchair. 'Other sources have said you were suffering a few heated rumours around school... the pressure must have mounted between you and Nadia - both of you pretending to have affections and simultaneously studying hard - tell me you didn't *accidentally* let a finger slip here, or a tongue slip there?'

'No,' Maria said firmly. 'We made a deal not to do anything until she finished school.'

My hands clasped in my lap sarcastically as I smiled. 'Oh yes - the pact to wait - how romantic! The desire to do so much must have been overwhelming, especially as you had *discussed* it, and *decided* mutually to do the *right thing*. That's very adult of you both...' I nodded with approval for her restraint. 'And of course, there's nothing that makes you want to fuck each other's brains out more than knowing you mustn't! Forbidden fruit - how delicious!'

Maria glared at me seriously now. 'I didn't bite.'

'Course not!' I shook my hair rapidly. 'You licked and sucked and did everything but - just so you could say you never *technically* had sex with Nadia! After all, what is lesbian sex? I mean you can play with dildos, but surely you only penetrate each other

Unravel

emotionally!' I felt my skin flush with a provocative sweat. 'You both say you only kissed, but what's in a kiss? How did you kiss Nadia? Show me! Kiss me!'

'You want me to kiss you?' Maria asked, grimacing. 'Is that professional?'

'Ha! Says she!' I laughed, then composed my humour and waved a dismissal. 'Yes, I'd love you to kiss me, but I wouldn't want you to be unfaithful!' I observed a hateful heat rise from Maria towards me for outwardly mocking her, so I grabbed it and ran with it. 'Nadia said you were a good kisser - it must have been one hell of a sensation, you both pretending to yourselves it meant nothing, yet trying to convince each other it was meaningful! I'm sensing a deep kiss, a passionate kiss that you can't reconstruct for purposes of research or evidence, the inappropriate kind of kiss you couldn't give to a member of your family, or even a friend...'

'Unless kissing is equal to having sex then I haven't committed a crime!' Maria interrupted, her voice booming defensively.

'Oh but you have!' I turned on her, raising my own reprimanding voice. 'I think you'll find you have breached your position of trust! The moment you allowed Nadia to a party with alcohol and drugs on the premises! The moment you let Nadia sleep in your house without her father's permission! The moment you kissed Nadia's mouth and let her believe you were in love with her, regardless of her reasons for doing so!'

Maria shut up. I had actually stunned her into silence. I had her now.

'I want to know where you kissed...' I quietly demanded. 'When and how often?'

Her dilated eyes blinked fully under a worried brow, Maria looked confused. 'What?'

'Come on, I want to know!' I reiterated. 'Did you kiss in your office? Was it before tuition to get her in the mood to revise? Or afterwards, as a reward for working hard? Was it a late night treat after dinner, cuddled up on the couch, watching a movie? Or was it in your car, round the corner from her father's house, before she had to go home? Was it all of these times? If kissing was the only act you performed, how often were you doing it?'

Evidently, my interrogations were too much for my poor martyr and Maria leaped up from my leather sofa. She stood over me, the cast of her left arm hitched beside her jeans, the other hand waving defiantly in the air between us.

'It wasn't any of that! It wasn't romantic, okay? It wasn't sexy! How many times do I have to tell you? I didn't enjoy it! You make it sound like we sat around *snogging*! We didn't, I'm a professional!' Maria broke away and paced to the windows. 'Kissing was brief, an incentive to work harder, fuck! It was mild flirting, so what? There was no stimulation! No breathlessness!'

I stood up too, determined not to be overpowered, ensuring my calmness made her temper

Unravel

look recklessly animalistic by comparison. 'So you kissed in your office?'

Rubbing her brow, Maria sighed heavily with annoyance, but relented and agreed they kissed there. I wanted her to understand that it was easier for her to submit to my questioning than trying to skirt around answering. I would go easier on her if she just confessed.

'It worked then? Nadia studied harder and improved her grades?' I asked. 'But tell me, were you aware of giving Nadia good grades because she had earned it or because you knew that's what she was playing for? After all, it would have spoiled the game if you had marked her down.'

Leaning against the window frame, Maria pursed her lips, her eyes were shadowed with tiredness, but she still put on that cool, tough front. She shrugged. 'Nadia worked hard... and played hard.'

'Karen saw Nadia consoling you after your dog, Leon, was run over... I'm wondering if losing one pet prompted you to turn towards your other one?'

Maria's heavy-lidded glower trembled with a dark shimmer. 'Leon didn't get run over - Peter Sheridan kicked him to death!' Her face went pale, her eyes blurry with sudden tears. 'Leon was trying to defend me, Peter was hurting Nadia so I stepped in and he pushed me... I couldn't get to him quick enough, Leon died in the car on the way to the animal hospital...

and no, mourning doesn't exactly turn me on, Nadia was just showing her support.'

This was, obviously, a shock to me, an awful, hideous end for her poor little dog. She must have been furious with Nadia's father, but perhaps too scared of the ramifications as well as his 'personal retribution' to dare to speak out. I suddenly reassessed her coming out of his house to face him as brave, and highly controlled of temper; maybe she felt smug knowing she had taken his daughter in much more satisfying ways than he had taken her dog. I allowed Maria a minute to compose herself back on the couch before I spoke again.

'Why didn't you share your grief with anyone, Ben or Lois?' I asked, sympathetically. 'Maybe you knew it would raise too many questions.'

Maria nodded a little rapidly, as if building up resentment. 'Maybe I realised I should have kept my home and work life separate.'

'And tell me what happened to Christian, as your dog-sitter, he must have wanted to share his grief with you, at least support you, but he was now Nadia's ex-boyfriend, he must have been forgotten, cast-out. He certainly noticed how often Nadia was staying at yours. He must have been jealous.'

'He was fucking stalking us!' Maria blurted. 'In all the chaos I forgot he still had my house keys.'

I jumped on this. 'He let himself into your house... and he saw something,' I stated, matter-of-factly, as if I already knew, but it was guesswork.

Unravel

Maria swallowed a thick gulp and she reached for her water, seemingly keen to shake her head clear. 'I had just come out of the shower, and I was undressed...' she revealed, and with a flippant shrug, she added that Nadia was just chilling in her room, listening to music. 'Whatever Christian thinks he saw, it was just his perverted imagination, what he wanted to see.'

Nodding casually, agreeing with her for thinking I had already spoken to Christian. I had to tread carefully, I couldn't make any specific assumptions without her realising I knew nothing. 'And what did you do?'

'I kicked him out! He had no right to be there, it was disgusting.'

'Nadia didn't mention this occasion to me.'

'Why would she? She was embarrassed.'

'But if nothing happened...'

'We were worried he would say something...'

'To who? The school? Lois?'

'Whoever! I didn't want him spreading shit around, he was obviously seeking revenge.'

'According to my sources there were already rumours going round the school about Nadia's 'crush' on you, you must have been afraid to have a witnesses testimony circulate?'

Scratching the back of her hair, Maria mumbled. 'I thought it would be better to back off for a while, cool it with Nadia, I didn't want things to get out of control.'

Out of control, I smiled to myself, and felt my brain whizzing with thoughts. I sighed. 'I'm thinking this event may have prompted your inclination towards Karen? She thought there was nothing to the rumours, she was still loyal to you, and you knew she would back you up, no matter what anyone else suggested.'

'You're right,' Maria gradually acknowledged. 'I needed a friend, I knew I could trust Karen - she wasn't involved - she was the only one who didn't confuse me.'

'But you didn't care if you confused her,' I winced. 'She trusted you, even when she had read Nadia's journal and was asked to keep an eye on you, you let her believe Nadia had an unwelcome obsession.'

'I couldn't tell her what was happening! It had gone too far and I just hoped I could get to the end of term without it getting worse,' Maria claimed.

'But hang on...' I held my hand up, thinking about the events that turned in that final week. 'I can appreciate why you didn't tell Karen so close to the end, but when were you planning on breaking the news to Nadia that you were playing her too? Prom night?'

I saw Maria's eyes narrow with a flinch that betrayed her prang of nerves. 'Huh?'

'Come on, you remember,' I encouraged, sitting back in my chair. 'I've heard all about it! Were you going to tell Nadia? Or were you hoping to ride off into the sunset with her? If Lois hadn't stopped you by smashing your car - where were you taking Nadia that night? Some place private you could have one last *non-sexual* kiss? Perhaps that was your opportunity to make sweet love for the first time, now that you'd kept your promise and finished school?'

Her mouth went to say something, but just dropped. Maria stared. She knew I knew.

I had her against the ropes, and I couldn't stop now. 'In fact, Nadia's revelation saved you the job of saying it all first – that must have been a relief, huh?' I mocked, but then, I narrowed my eyes and set my teeth on edge. 'Or did you secretly hope that Nadia really was in love with you? Maybe, just maybe, she would have come with you in the escape you'd dreamed of? It wasn't a joke for you, was it, Maria?' I waited, my heart thumping fast in my breast. I asked again if Maria was hurt by Nadia's claim that none of it was real, and searched her eyes for any truthful reflection.

'Earlier you said you weren't angry then and you're not upset now - that was very clever - because at the time you *were* upset... and *now* you are angry enough to keep up this pretence with me, when I can see right through you, Ms Calver! I think you were involved romantically with Nadia, and it just won't do your case any good to lie to a psychologist... you're denying the one thing that could save you earning the label of a sociopath - being in love!'

Her mouth tightened, and when she looked up, Maria's eyes had welled with tears.

'Aren't you tired of pretending?' I appealed. 'Or are you so accustomed to deceiving people that you've forgotten how to be true to yourself? You managed to convince everyone around you, but I have seen it from all sides now, Maria, and I get it! You're in love with Nadia, how could you not be? The girl is striking... and Lois, though she wants you back, is plain wrong for you. Long before she cheated on you, you must have craved a loyal girlfriend.'

Maria flooded with tense, helpless weeping and tried shaking her head, but the teacher sat rigidly, droplets of fear running down her face.

Sighing loudly for effect, internally I felt quite sick at my cruel show of disapproval. I remembered I was still recording and I needed to finish this interview but I couldn't expect Maria come clean: she wasn't the type to make a scene of pleading forgiveness no matter how much her shocked sobbing was giving her away. 'Well, unless you've got anything to say, then it's useless me sitting here, berating you when you'll will hear it all at the disciplinary.'

'I tried to do the right thing for Nadia!' cried Maria suddenly. 'I fucked up...'

Acknowledging her final statement, I nodded and looked down at the Dictaphone to switch it off. 'I'll see that justice is done,' I replied.

I thanked her for her time and said I had to prepare her assessment for the hearing. I ignored her nervous shivers, though my insides flipped at having

Unravel

reduced her to a shaking wretch. 'You're okay to get home, aren't you? Take the time to think about what you're going to do... maybe take up a different career, in a different country?' I suggested.

I saw her to the door. 'Oh, Nadia wanted you to know she was sorry...'

Maria tried to hide her face from me seeing her collapsing emotions as she walked out.

I continued: 'I'd like to tell her you're sorry, too... but never-mind.'

I closed the door behind her, firmly, cruelly, feeling strangely elated that I had left both Nadia and Maria alone and crying with guilt and self-pity.

My husband doesn't call me *The Terrier* for nothing.

Unravel

May 27th

Maria,

You have made my dreams come true. It started when you turned up at my dad's house, it was mid-morning on a Saturday and he had gone to work. Seeing you leaning against the porch in the bright sunshine made my heart flutter, and you bit your lip with that devilish daring in your eyes. I pulled you in and lead you to my room. It was exciting to have you there, where you weren't supposed to be, after so many times being in your bedroom where I wasn't supposed to be. I wondered if you felt as naughty as I did, or just nervous.

My room was just how I wished it could be, warm and pretty, long drapes hanging either side of a few, soft carpeted steps leading up to a mezzanine with my mattress positioned in the middle. I had just woken up and was naked underneath my nightie, but I put some music on and opened the windows. The fresh breeze lapped at my skin as you turned me around and kissed me. We turned and kissed, turning and kissing in a kind of stepping dance, ending up on the stairs.

    I sat and pulled you in front of me. You nudged me upwards and I shifted higher. You pressed my knees apart and I leaned back. You kissed my thighs and I closed my eyes. With my head resting back on the carpeted floor of my elevated boudoir, I felt you lift my nightie and close in with your mouth, your shoulders pressing under my legs. Your lips moved softly left and right, nuzzling your way in, making me twinge and gasp. You licked up and down the left side of my labia, then up and down the right side, flicking firmly but gently around my clitoris, teasing me. You sucked the inside of my thigh and pulled away, making me lift my head and wonder.

    You nodded to move up onto my bed, so I switched to my knees and crawled up in front of you, like a lazy lioness, waving my tail at you, until I reached the crumpled white bedding. I pawed my way across the deep mattress as you peeled off your summer shirt. You kneeled behind me and guided me back against you, and gathering my arms between us, you wrapped your shirt carefully around my wrists, binding them together. I swayed with a flush of anticipation, sitting on my heels, as you reached around to touch me. I felt your presence close and strong as you took my breasts in your hands, massaging them fully, making them swell and pucker. You tilted my head back and placed your mouth over mine, cupping my chin and neck. I loved feeling your hands travelling all over my body as we kissed. You slid my nightie up and over my head, tucking it behind my neck, making me feel even more bound. You flicked my erect nipples, then reached down to my thighs and stroked to the middle, dabbing your finger in my moisture before gliding it upwards to my clitoris. You lifted your wet finger to our mouths and we both licked my juice from it. Slowly, you bent me over and pushed me face down into my bed. My hands tied behind my back, my ass high in the air, I was helpless to resist it and I loved it.

Unravel

You slid your hand underneath and played with me, twanging and tweaking me, curling your fingers over my clitoris and tapping me like Morse code. I moaned into my duvet. I wanted to come but you kept stopping. You pushed your fingers inside me and pummelled me for a minute while I drooled into my clean sheets. Lowering your head, you pushed a strong tongue around my opening, then rolled a bank of moisture upwards, placing a tender lick over my ass hole, making me tense, then loosen with gorgeous stimulation as you worked the tip of your tongue inside, playing with my clit simultaneously. You panted along with my delirium, and then stopped again, just as I built up to a new climax.

You ruthless tease, you crawled underneath me then guided me down to sit on your face, eating me out from below. You went all out then, sucking me off with your whole body engaged with mine, your arms flexing, wrapped around the top of my legs. I felt that deep muscular orgasm rippling throughout my pelvis, burning its way down my stomach to the inner tension of my thighs. I found sudden strength to pull myself upwards, to sit back on your chest and smother your face with my cunt. I wanted to look down and see your beautiful eyes gazing up at me as I came. I loved the way your nose and cheeks moved as you closed your mouth around my clit again and again. I felt my breath panting hard, my hair fell over my face, but I could see you, and it was the image of you below me, between my breasts, over my pot belly, blinking at me with such love, acceptance, passion and knowing that tilted me over the edge into infinity. I fell back into the most luxurious orgasm I've had yet, I felt like the ceiling had opened up and the sky was pouring into me. Every inch of my body felt propelled as you licked me up into heaven.

    When I came around I had leaned back so far you'd caught me with your knees, and my head lolled against them, only then realising my hands were still tied behind me, clutching at your shirt. You helped me up, my shuddering body was almost limp, and I didn't mean to dive head first into my duvet again, but I was sort of dazed. You laughed and rolled me over, untied me, put your shirt back on and said you had to go. I couldn't believe you were leaving, but it added to the air of risk if we were caught doing it at my dad's.

When you left your mouth was red, still fresh from your divine assault on my vagina. It would have been impossible to have explained that away to anyone who saw us at that moment, but you did it with grace and style. I could only watch you drive off into the distance, wondering how long we could get away with this.

Nadia x

Chapter Thirty-Five

It wasn't hard to locate Maria Calver's neighbour and former student, Christian Webb, though actually getting hold of him was another matter. After leaving several voice mails on his parent's answer machine with no response over the weekend, I became increasingly desperate as every hour my interviews remained incomplete was less time I had to work out my closing arguments for Maria's disciplinary hearing. I had the feeling Christian's statement would be crucial – my instincts were screaming with curiosity for his interpretation of what he had seen that night in Maria's house. I decided, with nothing better to do, and no chance of enjoying my evening with my husband with this playing on my mind, to ring Christian's abode, incessantly, until someone picked up.

Eventually his mother, Clarissa, answered, and apologised for not responding sooner.

'I was going to call you yesterday, but Anthony had a works do, someone's leaving drinks I believe, and

Unravel

I had to go and collect him as he drank a bit too much, you know how boys are,' she chuckled low, her tone suggestive, 'and I had to go shopping earlier, sorry!'

'Mrs Webb, is your son home?' I asked directly down the phone. 'It's rather urgent that I speak with him.'

'Well, I'm afraid that's why I was going to call you,' she replied, her voice smiling. 'He's here but he just won't come to the phone. I've told him not to be such a baby, you only want to help clarify things around Maria's case, don't you? But he's hiding in his room. He hasn't been himself since Nadia broke up with him, and then, well you must have heard about little Leon, he loved that dog dearly, he's quite lost without him, he's sunk into something of a depression, but he'll come out of it, I'm sure.'

'Maybe you can help, Mrs Webb?' I sighed. 'Has he said anything to you regarding Maria or any events during the weeks leading up to her arrest?'

'Oh for goodness sake, I'm his mother, he won't talk to me!' she chuckled again down the line, then lowered, close and conspiratorially. 'He hasn't spoken to anyone, I don't think. But listen, I'm sure there's been a huge misunderstanding. You have to appreciate Maria Calver is a good friend and neighbour, she taught Christian privately and was never anything but completely pro-'

'-fessional,' I finished with her, rolling my eyes. 'Yes, I do appreciate that Mrs Webb, but I'm trying to discern how Maria behaved with Nadia and I think your son might be withholding some information.'

'Look, Dr Richmond!' Clarissa said, her voice turning clipped. 'I know Maria to be a great teacher, an upstanding member of our community and a warm-hearted person. Now if I know her at all, then I seriously doubt she did anything wrong... Nadia is evidently a clever girl who twists people around her little finger! Unfortunately, my son was smitten with her, and he is still hurting from the rejection, but surely it's not a far leap to realise Nadia has burned Maria in the same way, using her attentions and affections to get what she wanted,' Clarissa took a sharp breath to finish. 'I have no intention of allowing anyone to criticise Maria and I'll be damned if you try and rope my son into giving evidence against her.'

'Fair enough, Mrs Webb,' I drawled wearily. 'Thank you for your time.'

I certainly felt like I ruffled Mother Goose's feathers, but it didn't feel born out of defensiveness. Clarissa Webb, an upstanding member of the community herself, had known Maria a long time and would give a solid character reference, but she didn't seem to know her son so well. I needed his statement more than ever.

The next morning, I drove to the Webb's house, and staked out in my car until I saw a skinny young man leave through the front door. He looked down pensively at the pavement instead of observing his surroundings, so he didn't notice me approaching him until I called his name.

He reeled around, shocked. 'Who the fuck are you?' His pale eyes trembled under a floppy, brown hairstyle that looked like it needed a good trim.

'I'm Evelyn Richmond, I've been trying to speak with you for days,' I hurried, seeing his face change. 'I'm a psychologist, I need to know what you found out about Maria Calver and Nadia Sheridan so I can advise the board at her disciplinary hearing tomorrow.'

'You can't force me to make a statement!' he said, turning away to hide his distress.

'Christian, please!' I appealed. 'Tell me what you saw, it's of utmost importance.'

'I never saw anything!' he barked.

'Maria already told me what you saw,' I tried. 'I just need you to confirm it.'

That worked. Christian stopped and turned back to me, his bag slipping from his shoulder. 'She confessed?' his eyes reared. He seemed to catch himself; evidently, he was smartly sensitive. 'Look, it doesn't matter what I saw, I'm not coming forward as a witness. I can't have my parents and everyone find out the only reason I saw them was 'cause I was spying!'

'Christian, everyone knows that there was something going on between Maria and Nadia, you had reasons to be suspicious,' I appealed. 'You only did what anyone else would have done for proof, and I *have* to know what happened to make you want to keep it secret. Come on, talk to me?' I implored now, my hands pressed together pleadingly. 'I won't tell your parents, I promise.'

Stepping back into the hedgerow, Christian looked around him, back at his home, and let his bag slip all the way to the pavement. He hung his head as I closed in beside him.

'I *was* suspicious...' he sullenly confirmed. 'I felt angry since Leon died and Maria didn't call me. I couldn't help walking past her house to the park where I used to take Leon. I used to sit outside, and I saw Maria bringing Nadia home in her car all the time. Sometimes I'd go back later, like after eleven, and Maria's car was still in the drive, and the engine was cold, you know, like it hadn't run in a few hours. One time I rang the bell, just to see, and Maria took ages to open it. I saw Nadia's shoes in the hallway and I asked, but she said Nadia wasn't there, those were spares she said, but she sounded really nervous. I just knew Nadia was there, so I waited outside and then I saw shadows against the curtains, I knew it was Nadia, but I waited and she didn't leave all evening. I wanted to know what they were doing, 'cause I knew Nadia had a thing for Maria, so I let myself in 'cause I still had her keys...' Christian suddenly blushed hard and his story darted forward to the bitter end. 'Look, they were in her bedroom listening to music, and what I saw... I couldn't believe it... I wanted to record it... but I couldn't help...

I couldn't stop...' his words fell under his breath into a mutter.

'What?' I frowned. This was it. I struggled to reign in my imagination.

'I can't tell you!' he moaned, edging away.

'Please Christian! Tell me what you saw! I won't put it in my statement, it's just so I know the truth in my own mind,' I lied. 'Maria said she was undressed, is that true?'

Christian's eyes laid incredulously into mine. 'Yeah, but...'

'If that's not all, you have to tell me exactly what else happened!' I implored.

He pressed his hand against his head, wiping some sweat, looking pained at the recall.

'They were talking, almost arguing...' he spoke slowly. 'The door was just ajar so I could see through the gap in the hinges that Maria was holding her towel around her,' he sighed. 'Nadia was begging Maria to relax, to sit beside her on the bed, but Maria wouldn't. Nadia was pulling her down and kissing her, saying she wanted to give Maria pleasure too, but Maria got up again, saying it changed things if she "did it to her". Nadia was getting frustrated, saying Maria had double standards, and if Maria was serious about her then she should trust her, "otherwise what was the point of carrying on?" she said.'

I certainly felt frustrated by this, it wasn't clear what the subject was or if Christian had even seen anything besides a state of partial nudity. I encouraged the young man to go on.

'Nadia kept saying she wanted to show Maria how she felt, what she could do, and it pissed me off because she never wanted to do that with me, not after the one time she did let me when she said Maria's name!' Christian cast his hurt expression around the street to check we were alone.

'She said her name?' I exclaimed. 'What, during sex?'

'Fucking hell...' Christian swore with a grimace, then shouted, annoyed: 'Cunnilingus!' he sulked again. 'It was my fault for telling Maria that Nadia had said her name when I went down on her - that probably caused them to get together! I knew Nadia had a thing for Maria but I never thought Maria would do anything.'

'Was that before or after Christmas?' I asked quickly, thinking.

'Um... January...' Christian frowned.

I wondered if Nadia had said it deliberately, surely she would not be so foolish as to blurt out real feelings about someone else during such an act. Either way, I felt relieved that Maria wasn't aware of it when she let Nadia stay after the Christmas party. 'Okay, so go back to that night you heard them arguing?' I encouraged.

Christian sighed heavily and seemed to deflate with sadness. 'Maria gave in... sat on the edge of the

Unravel

bed... Nadia kneeled between her legs and... gave her oral sex.'

My jaw dropped open. It felt both sickening and wonderful to have this confirmation.

'Nadia gave *Maria* oral sex?' I gushed, trying to calm my breath.

'Yeah, and I was so... jealous... that I filmed it on my phone,' Christian gulped. 'I wanted to post it online, expose them... but I couldn't stop myself getting turned on... I thought they were lost in their... I thought I could use my other hand to...'

'You had a wank?' I finished for him, sensing his awkwardness. 'That's why you're so embarrassed? I'm pretty sure any young man would do the same.'

'But if I come out as a witness, it will go to court, and not just my parents, but my friends, my college, the press, the whole world will know I got busted jerking off over two lesbians,' he complained.

I didn't care about that. 'Do you still have the footage?' I prayed.

'No,' Christian lowered his head with a shameful shake. 'I made a noise... next thing I knew Maria flung the door open and caught me. She saw what I was doing and grabbed my phone out of my hand, she broke it half and threw it down the stairs, then she saw my dick and she pulled me up and punched me in the stomach. She threw me into the wall, she grabbed my balls and shouted in my face that if I told anyone she would come after me and cut it off.'

Unravel

'Maria *assaulted* you?' I asked, revelling in my shock. I knew now Maria had omitted the truth. She and Nadia had evidently been physical many times if this was the first time Nadia had reciprocated.

I swallowed my panting breath. 'People will understand, you should testify, she will get away with it otherwise,' I urged, shrugging my arms hopelessly for Christian's change of mind.

'No - she's been found out, hasn't she? It's over between them...' he responded. 'Look, I always liked Maria, I don't want her to go to jail, she's already lost Leon and she'll probably lose her job. I just want to put it behind me and try and forget Nadia.'

It was no use, I had to let him go. I faced a difficult evening writing the conclusion to Maria's assessment with the new information from Christian. My mind ached from going round in circles, and at every turn I felt that I had missed the one opportunity to see for myself and understand in my heart and soul what had physically and psychically occurred between these two suspects, by simply putting Maria and Nadia in the same room together.

♥

The school board had arranged to meet at the Gloucester city council offices, and on the day of the hearing, a small panel of officials convened for the shameful purpose of disciplining a formerly reputable employee. It was a stifled, serious affair: the panel consisted of a governor from the local education authority, a council trustee, and two members of the board, both community leaders and parents of past children at GCH. Principal Woods attended to represent the school as well as the accusing party. As the psychologist assigned to investigating this case, I brought my report in the form of analyses of transcripts, from which I had drawn excerpts of poignant quotations, and made copies for everyone. I brought with me Nadia's old social worker from Dublin; after Peter Sheridan had told me of his daughter's plight on the streets in her home town, I had contacted social services and they were able to provide me with Nadia's file. Gráinne O'Callaghan came in a raincoat, looking forlorn, gripping her handbag, and I hoped she would reveal some interesting facts in Nadia's absence.

Maria Calver came without a lawyer. If she had initially believed that show of confidence would convince them of her innocence, her paleness and thinness betrayed her intentions. Holding her plastered arm in front of her, she walked through the door of the drab, stuffy office looking like a handsome ghost; it seemed obvious she would be terrified, perhaps she was ready to accept her fate and the presence of a lawyer would be irrelevant. Then again, perhaps she was waiting to be formally charged with a crime before paying for legal support; Maria sat alone opposite the panel, remaining aloof in demeanour, her eyes unreadable under darkened hoods, her poorly arm hidden under the table.

'Thank you all for attending.' Governor Reeves addressed the table. 'This disciplinary hearing has been called in the case of Maria Calver, the advanced skills teacher at Gloucester City High school, who has been accused of having inappropriate relations with a year eleven student, Nadia Sheridan. At present, both parties are denying any physical relationship, therefore we are here to assess the findings of Dr Evelyn Richmond, a forensic psychologist who has interviewed those involved, in order to decide if the matter needs to be taken further...' he paused, then turned to Maria. 'Ms Calver, your success rates for helping students achieve top exam results are impressive, and your reputation until now has been sound. I understand that Nadia Sheridan herself has stated that you have been an excellent teacher, and though a close working relationship between you developed, she claims you never encouraged her or acted dishonourably. Miss Sheridan admitted she was the one who instigated inappropriate behaviours after making a bet with a friend to seduce you, and she also claims to have fabricated a sex diary...' he paused again. 'Is there anything you would like to say at this point?'

Maria lifted her eyes to the middle distance above the table. 'I never had sex with Nadia Sheridan.'

'Were you aware that Miss Sheridan had been making sexually explicit entries in a journal about you?' Mr Rowley, one of the board members, asked stiffly in his suit.

'No,' Maria replied, shaking her hair sincerely. 'I never saw anything Nadia wrote in that journal, and was definitely not aware of the nature of the content.'

'But you gave it to her,' Principal Woods frowned. 'Your inscription's in the front.'

'It was a birthday gift,' Maria shrugged.

'Some might call that grooming,' Woods minced his thin lips.

Governor Reeves raised his palm to the principal to hold back, and his eyebrow twitched as he looked to me: it was my turn to speak. I addressed the board members sensitively to provide my conclusion, and my assessment of Maria's sanity.

'Ladies and gents, after gathering all witness accounts, I have found no proof of a physical relationship between Ms Calver and Miss Sheridan, therefore there is simply not enough evidence to take this case to a criminal court,' I stated. 'With Miss Sheridan denying any sexual activity during the period of their engagement, we cannot presume beyond reasonable doubt that this diary of hers is not fabricated, as she insists it is. The fact is that Nadia has confessed to making a bet with her friend Samantha Burrows to seduce her teacher for better grades. This is backed up by Miss Burrows, whose account is contained in the documents in front of you.'

I watched as the faces of the trustee and board members turned to examine Maria's reaction, but of course, she remained poker-faced. I continued.

'I believe the only thing Ms Calver is guilty of is succumbing to her student's attention. Ms Calver's colleague, her cousin, and her ex-partner, as well as Sam Burrows, also believe Ms Calver fell for Miss Sheridan's trick. In other words, all witnesses view Nadia as the instigator and Ms Calver as the victim in all this...' I paused for emphasis. 'I could argue temporary insanity, however, I do not regard Ms Calver as mentally unstable or lacking capacity. She is human and she made a mistake. All statements concur that she was horrified to learn that she had been manipulated by Miss Sheridan. I would say it is highly unlikely Ms Calver would ever allow this to happen again, therefore I consider her fit to continue teaching.'

'I'm sorry, are we talking about falling for a trick, or falling in love?' Mrs Gibson, the other member of the school board asked me. She was a well-presented mother, but she looked just as uncomfortable in her suit as the others having to utter such words.

'Perhaps Ms Calver would like to answer that question...' the governor replied and lifted his eyes to Maria. 'In what way did you "fall" for Miss Sheridan?'

Looking painfully across the table, Maria bore her eyes into mine with a wide, worry-full blink of surrender. She then dragged them back to the table in front of her.

'I fell in love...' Maria's voice crackled finally. 'I believed Nadia was in love with me... but when we became emotionally close, I made her promise not to do anything physical until she was eighteen,' Maria spoke in a low monotone. 'Nadia agreed that if our feelings were real then... intimacy was... worth waiting for.'

The wind puffed out of my sails; I couldn't believe it. Maria had confessed her emotions in front of the panel. I felt slightly confused that she hadn't admitted them to me privately, and I wondered if my interrogation had made her think after all.

Mr Rowley and Mrs Gibson were speaking quietly and turned their heads to confer with the council trustee, Mrs Burgess. They nodded and flipped their hands.

The principal raised his voice in argument. 'Wait a minute, you must acknowledge that even if they weren't physical they have still broken professional boundaries!' He threw his fingers towards Maria. 'Driving Nadia around! Letting her spend time at her house! Giving her private numbers to contact her!'

Prompted to defend herself, Maria spoke up. 'Listen, I swear, introducing Nadia to my neighbour was merely to facilitate her social life and take pressure off myself because she was taking up so much of my time,' she glared at Woods. 'I told you this, and you ignored me whenever I tried to seek your advice... in fact, you bribed me with a pay-rise if I got Nadia to pass her exams – "Do whatever it takes", you said!'

Unravel

The panel turned on Xavier Woods.

'I understand Ms Calver had no choice but to tutor Miss Sheridan after school when her schedule was already full,' Governor Reeves raised his bushy brows at the principal.

'She didn't look that stressed!' Woods shifted irritably.

'Regardless of how she looked, Mr Woods, it seems you turned a blind eye to Ms Calver's call for support, in favour of exam results,' the council trustee, Mrs Burgess, piped up with dismay in her prim voice.

Woods shook his head at the table, his mouth making small gasps as he gathered his words. He looked angry, and decided to deflect with talk of Nadia's father. 'Peter Sheridan knows what he saw - his daughter with Maria! And he held Maria fully responsible!' Mr Woods said triumphantly. 'He was the one who brought that journal to me - he found it stashed in the attic amongst her things.'

Maria looked up sharply at Woods, but she quickly dropped her gaze to the table with a pensive frown. I wondered if she'd really been inside Nadia's father's house, and knew that her room was a camp bed in the attic, not the luxurious mezzanine she had described in her journal. Then I remembered Maria hadn't read the entries, and it made me curious.

I had to speak up, I felt Xavier Woods was making desperate reaches to dispel the flames of blame from his own back.

Unravel

'Actually, if you check the transcript, Peter Sheridan held his daughter responsible, calling her a "home-wrecker just like her mother"... ultimately, I found Mr Sheridan an unreliable witness,' I replied firmly. I went on to list the dreadful history of breakdowns and demotions, his access to pharmaceuticals, and detailed his vile attitude towards his only child. 'Included amongst your copies of my findings are the results of a laboratory test on some medication I secured from Mr Sheridan's personal items that I witnessed him using in my presence. The results showed the pill is an anti-psychotic drug, prescribed for depression, obsessive compulsive disorder, post-traumatic stress disorder and personality disorders. You might expect to hear he is in a hospital as a patient, not working as a porter.'

The bodies in the room shifted in their chairs, murmured, and scribbled some notes. As silence fell again, I introduced the woman to my right, Gráinne O'Callaghan, Nadia's old social worker, who had waited patiently, absorbing all the information.

Mrs O'Callaghan explained how Nadia had been brought to her attention - the girl was made homeless after her mother chose her boyfriend's side following a dispute involving Rene, his fifteen-year old daughter. Apparently, Nadia had dropped out of school after Rene announced Nadia's homosexuality to their schoolmates. The police picked her up on the street and social services were involved.

As I watched Maria's reaction, I could see that she was finally understanding that everything she had heard of Nadia's story was true.

'I tried to arrange for Nadia to live with her aunt nearby,' Mrs O'Callaghan explained, 'but there was too much scandal to repeat her final year at the same school in Dublin, so she was sent to live with her dad in the UK. Well, after some arranging, Gloucester City High school agreed to take her and I was reassured you would look after her,' she said to Principal Woods.

'After that, I had no contact with Nadia anymore. The school office only told me that she was in attendance, that she had extra help from a tutor, and was still living with her father... but I had no idea Nadia's father was unstable and wasn't welcoming, poor love.'

She sounded genuinely upset and I knew she felt responsible, but it wasn't her fault.

I nodded my gratitude to the social worker and sat forward again. 'Obviously, Nadia's mental state and emotional needs have been sorely neglected by the system supposed to be caring for young adolescents in this country. She was basically dumped in this town, in this school, as well as in her father's house, with no regard for what she had gone through.'

I was interrupted by the principal, still fighting to admonish himself of blame. 'We only knew she had a troubled background, had used drink and drugs and dropped out of her final year!' Woods defended himself with the royal *we*. 'We tried to contact her father but you can't force a parent to come in unless there's any problems, and Nadia was doing fine!'

'Thanks to that woman over there!' I gestured daintily in Maria's direction. 'In the absence of a school counsellor, all responsibility and pressure has solely been put on Maria - and it's amazing that she did such a good job. Nadia is, to all accounts, quite difficult and Maria did what she had to, in order to keep Nadia under her care.'

Maria looked at me with a mixture of relief and sadness, and I saw the light of hope in her eyes for the first time. I also saw the others were deep in thought.

The members of the board took a few minutes to flick through the documents on the table and then put their heads together for a brief whisper with the council trustee.

Mr Rowley spoke on their behalf. 'It seems that Nadia Sheridan has experienced some traumatic events which, combined with – perhaps - similar issues to her father, has led her to behave in this way. It is unfortunate she chose Ms Calver to manipulate, as it would be any teacher, and for whatever reasons she had are beyond our understanding. Of course, the girl should be disciplined, but she is only guilty of emotional blackmail, therefore it is not for the school to take action, also she's completed her education so our duty to her has ended.'

The ladies either side of him nodded solemnly. They assumed it was not worth trying to understand a teenage mind and were not going to bother with a girl who was leaving anyway.

'At this point, I think it's worth mentioning that I phoned through for Miss Sheridan's exam results,' the governor interjected, unfolding a note from his jacket lining. 'Nadia has passed all twelve G.C.S.E.s.' he stated dryly, though I could see a twitch of smugness in his lips. He had been sitting on that the whole meeting. He turned to address Maria. 'Congratulations, Miss Calver, you've earned yourself a pay rise.'

Principal Woods rubbed his brow then sat back, deflated, unsure whether he should be pleased or not with those powerful results.

Reeves went on. 'You have succeeded your student by going above and beyond the call of duty to help her, and for this we are grateful. You have said that you did not enter into a physical relationship with Miss Sheridan, but you have admitted to engaging in an emotional affair with her. Principal Woods may have failed to provide extra support, but he would not have ignored any suggestion that you were breaching your position of trust. We can't prove that any criminal act has taken place but for deviating from the recommended guidelines, you will have to be disciplined.'

I noticed my breath had been suspended and I felt slightly sick. The panel, the principal, the social worker, and I silently watched the muscles in Maria's jaw flexing with tension as Governor Reeves rolled off a lengthy monologue.

Her code of conduct had brought into question her suitability to work with children. A teacher should act, and be seen to act, in the child's best interests. Duty of care involved respectful and caring relationships, with adults demonstrating integrity, maturity and good judgement. Teachers are in a position of trust, power and influence, so it could never be a relationship between equals. An unequal balance of power should never be used for a teacher's personal advantage or gratification. Maria should have maintained appropriate professional boundaries, avoiding behaviour that might be misinterpreted by others. Maria should have reported and recorded any incidents with this potential. No child should be invited into the home of an adult unless agreed by parents. Children may develop infatuations, these should be discussed with the principal or parent at earliest opportunity. In any circumstances where children seek inappropriate physical contact with adults, it is the adult's responsibility to sensitively deter and help the child understand boundaries. Adults should not seek to have social contact with children, should not give out personal contact details, or give special attention, as this can be construed as grooming. Allowing a non-physical relationship to develop in ways which might lead to a sexual relationship is also a grave breach of trust.

With each sentence I felt myself buckling under the condemnation. Maria was in trouble. I knew she had committed all of these acts, and neglected to report them.

'Ms Calver, do you admit breaching these guidelines?' Governor Reeves asked.

Maria exhaled deeply, and nodded, her eyes glassy. 'Yes.'

After conferring for only thirty seconds or so, the panel nodded to Governor Reeves who raised his voice in a horribly authoritative way.

'Maria Calver, I'm afraid we have no choice but to end your employment. We appreciate everything you have done for the school and we do believe this case is unique and you would never engage with, or permit yourself to be taken in by another student in this manner, however we cannot be seen to allow that kind of inappropriate relationship to exist without sanction.'

'We are very sorry, you are an excellent teacher, we hope you will find suitable employment elsewhere,' Mrs Burgess said kindly, but received something of a scowl from Mr Rowley.

Maria accepted her fate with humility and grace. She stood up and thanked everyone, shaking hands, her plastered arm bowed gently behind her back. Principal Wood looked stunned and embarrassed as he nodded goodbye to her. Maria walked out alone, as she had walked in, but her head was held higher; her fate had been sealed. I watched her go and felt a swell of pride, she had told the truth - not all of it - but enough to leave with her dignity intact. She had lost so much more than her job, I thought about feeling sorry for her, but I didn't, Maria Calver had gotten away with it, after all.

Epilogue

Evelyn hurried out of the council offices and looked up and down the busy Gloucester street for Maria. She saw the dark, lean figure near the kerb in the near distance, the fingers of her plastered arm hooked in her left pocket, her right hand held aloft in the air, hailing down a taxi in the warm afternoon.

'Maria!' Evelyn called out. 'Wait!'

Maria turned with some alarm in her eyes, though they quickly shaded again as she lowered her hand. The taxi glinted past and Maria stared at the short, older woman warily.

'I thought I could give you a lift,' Evelyn said, fussing with her folder as she dug around in her handbag for her keys. 'I'm just parked around the corner,' she tilted her head in an assumptive motion for Maria to follow, and Maria hesitated before spinning on her heels, unsure whether she should, and could obey like a little dog. Maria felt a willing trust guide her along, a few yards behind Evelyn's path to her car.

Settling down in the passenger seat of the Mazda, Maria looked worriedly across at the psychologist, yet felt intrigued as to what the woman wanted now that her assessment had been made, and judgement passed.

'Hold onto that, would you?' Evelyn dumped her satchel on Maria's lap and threw her folder onto the back seat. Maria clutched it, the leather smelled like Evelyn's office, and that Chesterfield she had broken down on. She had ruined everything at that moment, and her defence had looked ridiculous. She had no alternative but to confess her idiotic mistake with Nadia. Now that she was clear of it, Maria could see how deluded she'd been, but it still hurt.

They drove in silence for a while, on the road towards Cheltenham, where they both lived, and Maria relaxed somewhat, perhaps it was an innocent lift and Evelyn was no longer interested in the case.

'I wanted to show you something,' Evelyn spoke suddenly, leaning closely into the steering wheel. 'I thought you should have it, it belongs to you really.'

Maria frowned inquisitively. 'What?'

'Open my bag, you'll recognise it, I'm sure,' Evelyn's voice was level, no hint either way towards it being a poisonous snake or a box of chocolates.

Prising open the flap of the satchel, Maria saw a leather bound journal with an opal gemstone in the centre. Her heartbeat lodged in her chest, she couldn't breathe as she lifted it out. It felt heavy, like a precious doctrine: it was Nadia's journal, the same one she had given her, but well-thumbed, the pages dog-eared. Maria's eyes darted across at Evelyn.

'Have a look, you'll be surprised,' Evelyn's profile almost smiled.

Maria opened it up, there was her inscription, and opposite, a photo of Maria taken covertly, sitting at her desk, staring at her computer screen, sucking the inside of her mouth as she did sometimes when she was concentrating. Nadia had caught that moment on her phone and printed it out. Maria blushed and flicked through the pages of handwriting beyond. It was filled with love hearts and doodles of female eyes and lips, even a full body sketch of an androgynous figure: a fitted black shirt cut down to the bosom, and boyish smart grey trousers, hands in pockets – it could have been Maria if the curly inked hair had not been obscuring the face. And there was a tattoo design, hers, Nadia had seen it on her body and printed it over and over throughout the diary. Surely, unless she had written about it, no-one would know it was Maria's, or whereabouts it marked her skin. Maria felt nauseous. Scanning through the entries, the words that jumped out at her were sexual, explicitly lesbian: kiss, fingers, hips, knickers, tongue, lick, clitoris... Maria. Her name was written everywhere.

Feeling herself flush with emotion, Maria didn't know what to think, what it meant. Was this real? It made her pine for the Nadia she had known and loved, but this was a product of lies, fakery, manipulation, cruelty. And why was Evelyn giving it to her? Why was she watching her instead of the road? Maria shook her head, she didn't want it.

'It's okay!' Evelyn said. 'I know!'

'What do you know?' Maria asked, her voice trembling.

Evelyn smiled. 'I spoke to Christian... he told me what he saw the night he spied on you and Nadia in your bedroom... you were lucky he didn't want to make a statement... because what he saw was genuine, tender love-making between two emotionally connected people. Nadia begged to reciprocate the love you had shown her, which you apparently had refused until that point out of respect for her. Even regarding what happened with Christian afterwards, I can understand that you were only ever behaving with that girl's best interests in mind. The love you felt for her was real, you wanted to protect her, and you and Nadia both did what you had to, to protect each other and your relationship.'

'Yes I wanted to protect what we had,' Maria burst out, shocked at Evelyn's presumption. 'But, Nadia never loved me, it was a game to her!

'Maria!' Evelyn pulled off the carriageway to take a back route. 'You can stop pretending now! Of course Nadia loved you, she has done nothing but protect you! She has lied to everyone *for* you, and apparently even *to* you! Think about it – she took full responsibility, pretended she had played you, to keep your ass out of jail!'

Creasing her eyes to squeeze out her confusion, Maria belligerently argued her point. 'But Nadia said she made a bet with Sam, and Sam admitted they did!'

Evelyn's eyes flashed across at Maria, wondering if Maria was seriously ignorant to all this or if she was still keeping up appearances. 'You know that Nadia's clever, she really did make a bet with Samantha but only to make out all her emotions and behaviours around you were deliberate, part of a plan, but they weren't, of course, they were real. If Nadia didn't tell you about this, then she really is smart! She played Sam, not you! She waved it right under her nose, just to throw Sam off track.'

Staring incredulously at Evelyn, Maria grimaced, recalling all the times Nadia had behaved oddly in Sam's presence, even that time Sam had wanted to sit in on their tuition, smiling slyly, and Nadia had tried to tell Maria something but she had been too hung-over to listen. Maria couldn't believe it, her own ignorance was concerning.

'But the journal...' Maria muttered. 'Nadia said she made it all up.'

Evelyn laughed. 'Read it! Those entries happened, didn't they?' Evelyn said as she slowed through a small village. 'Nadia's a talented author, she's written everything so descriptively: it could be taken as highly creative fiction. There are no real-life details, it's all fantasy-like, explosive, sexually-graphic, and shocking – you could interpret them as a compilation of stories, but they're not imagined, are they?'

As Maria read through some of the dated entries in more detail, her jaw fell open. She wasn't sure if the blood was draining from her face or rushing into it, but something was making her spin with disbelief. Nadia had written descriptively all right, graphic accounts of their evenings spent on the couch, in her car, in her office and in her bedroom. Maria didn't remember them like that, but then her perspective had been different, and some of the smaller intimacies rang with truth, like the *eargasm* she'd given Nadia just from licking inside her ear, and the goo that Nadia wrung from her knickers after Maria gave her a simple massage.

Unable to bear it anymore, Maria looked up at Evelyn, her eyes heavy with trepidation. 'Why are you doing this?'

Evelyn sighed and shook her head. 'I guess I'm a bit of a romantic... but let's say that I believe the universe fights to protect the real, natural things in life, and so, I too, want to fight on its behalf,' she indicated and swung her car under a furrow of trees, throwing dapples of sun on the windscreen.

When Maria realised where she was, she cringed with shame that Evelyn had read about this place from Nadia's journal. She hadn't been here in so long, and as the view opened onto the landscape of

Gloucester, Maria felt her eyes prickle with precious memories.

Evelyn's car crept down the drive and she parked up by the barrier in front of the steep drop into the valley below. 'I'm not supposed to do this, but I suppose it's okay to break the rules for love. You did because you had to... and I want to because you both deserve to be happy.'

Maria still wasn't sure what the strange, sentimental doctor was about to do, when she was distracted by movement beyond Evelyn's head, in the background of the hill. From out of the valley climbed an auburn-haired young woman, she stepped over the barrier in board shorts and trainers, and started walking towards the car, sauntering coolly in aviator shades.

'I told her to come here so I could tell her the outcome of the hearing, she wanted to know,' Evelyn gazed at Maria's trembling eyes. 'She's not expecting you either.'

'I promised Ben I wouldn't see her again,' Maria said pitifully, unable to take her eyes off the approaching girl.

'Maria, Ben will support you whatever you do,' Evelyn replied soothingly. 'So go to her, you're free now, you both are!' Evelyn waved to Nadia out the window. 'She loves you.'

Nadia stopped short suddenly, her hand on her chest. She was close enough to see Evelyn was not alone, and she would undoubtedly have recognised Maria's neckline anywhere.

Maria released her seat belt and opened the passenger door. She stood up, her black curls catching a warm breeze from the valley. Turning around, she saw Nadia frozen to the spot, but summoned her courage and moved around the car towards her.

Lifting her hands to her mouth, Nadia's shoulders shook with sudden tears of surprise and, Maria hoped, happiness.

Gesturing widely with Nadia's journal in the hand of her plastered arm, Maria held in her own tears as she stood a few feet in front of the girl. 'Look what I found...' Maria said lightly. 'It's nice...' she shrugged and couldn't help a nervous chuckle.

Nadia glanced across at Evelyn in the driver's seat, who returned with a thumbs up.

'It's okay,' Maria said gently, and gave Nadia the journal.

Gazing down at it, Nadia stroked the front, smearing her tears over the leather. She looked up into Maria's face. 'You like it?'

Maria smiled and took Nadia's shades from her eyes. She locked in to the beautiful green shimmers she had missed so much. 'I love it.'

Nadia collapsed into fresh tears as she raised her arms around Maria's shoulders and pulled her in tightly. Maria wrapped both arms around Nadia's waist and buried her face in Nadia's neck. They stood there, swaying slightly, Maria's back shuddering as she sobbed at long last.

Evelyn started her engine and pulled the car back, guessing she should leave them to it, now her work was done. She figured they would get a taxi wherever they wanted to go. She didn't want to interrupt them as she drove away, especially since their heart-breaking embrace had turned into passionate, desperate kisses. The journal was back in the author's hands.

Everything was in its right place.

Unravel

Acknowledgments

Thanks and love to everyone who has encouraged and supported me during the dreaming up of this book, the planning and the writing, the many drafts and years of editing: Mum and Dad, Lucy and Ash and all my family for your patience and acceptance. My friends Edita & Lucy, Deb, Luci Lou, Grace, and Leon, for your excitement and feedback on this story as it evolved. Special thanks to Brighton Dome for paying me to sit and write my filthy little story while I was sat on stage door. Love to my sweet dog Molly Biscuit who never left my side for eight years whilst I was selfishly writing instead of taking her out for a doubleyou-ay-ell-kay, you were the best girlfriend ever. Xena & Gabrielle, you were my inspiration for Maria and Nadia. Must credit Peter Greenaway's amazing film 'The Cook, the thief, his wife and her lover' for the bathroom scene which inspired one of Nadia's journal entries. Countless musical artists helped me write this, but mostly I'd like to thank Bjork for my title, Unravel.

Printed in Great Britain
by Amazon